Myth on the Modern Stage

Myth on the Modern Stage

HUGH DICKINSON

UNIVERSITY OF ILLINOIS PRESS

Urbana   Chicago   London

1969

To My Mother
ELLEN I. DICKINSON

and the Memory of My Father
CHARLES F. DICKINSON

CONTENTS

CHAPTER I

INTRODUCTION:
Myth and Drama

It will be observed by every one who attempts to render these legends malleable in his intellectual furnace, that they are marvellously independent of all temporary modes and circumstances. They remain essentially the same, after changes that would affect the identity of almost anything else. . . . No epoch of time can claim a copyright in these immortal fables. They seem never to have been made; and certainly, so long as man exists, they can never perish; but, by their indestructibility itself, they are legitimate subjects for every age to clothe with its own garniture of manners and sentiments, and to imbue with its own morality.

In the six decades of the present century, ten dramatists of note wrote plays based on classical myths of Greece and Rome. Three of them are American: Robinson Jeffers, Eugene O'Neill, and Tennessee Williams; one is English: T. S. Eliot; and six are French: André Gide, Jean Cocteau, Jean Giraudoux, Jean-Paul Sartre, Jean Anouilh, and Eugène Ionesco. Much of the time, the stage they wrote for was still dominated by modern realism, and nothing could seem more remote from that, in spirit or subject matter, than Olympian gods and ancient Greek heroes. Why, then, should these playwrights, as well as many others of lesser note, concern themselves with figures of a distant land-scape in a far-off time and with gods long since discredited?

Most of these writers were, when they flourished, conspicuous for their modernity, and one of the most conspicuous marks of that modernity has been a sundering of present from past. Yet in turning to classical myth, they continued a tradition in art that has never ceased since the Renaissance, least of all in France where by the middle of the nineteenth century Balzac and Flaubert represented the triumph of a literary realism that was reflected also in the drama, and where in its closing decades Zola's advocacy of scientific naturalism was to revolutionize the arts of the theatre. Yet, as the classicist Michael Grant points out of France alone: "Not that Greek mythology had been neglected in the nineteenth century: 582 French imitations, translations or adaptations of classical originals sprang from *le rêve hellénique* between 1840 and 1900." [1] Then what did the modernity of these ten consist of, that it set them off from earlier dreamers of the Hellenic dream?

It was partly a matter of looking at traditional material in a new way and for new reasons. Since it was a matter of form as well as of content, it raises the question: what dramaturgic problems confront a playwright when he uses myth on the modern stage, and how does he deal with them? As to why modern dramatists have concerned themselves with myth, I have taken as a working hypothesis this statement by Gilbert Highet and have given it a particular emphasis: "The central answer is that myths are permanent. They deal with the greatest of all problems, the problems which do not change, because men and women do not change. They deal with love; with war; with sin; with tyranny; with courage; with fate: *and all in some way or other deal with the relation of man to those divine powers which are sometimes felt to be irrational, sometimes to be cruel, and sometimes, alas, to be just.*" [2] If this is so, one may expect that these dramatists will, when they treat of myth, reveal in one way or another their beliefs about man's nature and destiny and the nature of the world he inhabits. And if they should seek to divorce classical myth from its religious origins and implications —that is, to "displace" the myth—what problems will they en-

[1] Michael Grant, *Myths of the Greeks and Romans* (Cleveland and New York: World, 1962), p. 232. The quotation at the head of the chapter is from Nathaniel Hawthorne's *A Wonder Book*; it was written 15 July 1851.
[2] Gilbert Highet, *The Classical Tradition: Greek and Roman Influences on Western Literature* (New York: Oxford University Press, Galaxy Books, 1957), p. 540. Emphasis added.

counter because of such displacement? In using old matter in an original manner, how do they transfer mythical plots and characters from epic and tragedy without succumbing to mere imitation? And how are they to make them acceptable and compelling to modern audiences? And how pertinent are the statements these plays make—psychological, ethical, metaphysical, or religious—to men and women today? The period in which they wrote coincided with the rise of theatricalism, one of the movements which, along with expressionism after World War I and the absurdist theatre after World War II, rose in revolt against realism. What, if anything, do theatricalism and its related styles contribute to the effective dramatization of classical myth?

These questions indicate the range of this inquiry, which I have organized by examining dramatic works by each writer in turn. The chapters follow a roughly chronological order. I have let each playwright's work reveal its own problems and emphases, and suggest particular kinds of treatment. Where comparisons and contrasts among the ten have seemed enlightening, I have drawn them; where the myth, as newly dramatized, has a famous forebear among the classic plays of Greece or later periods, I have tended to use that earlier work as a point of departure, while trying always to keep in mind that not only were the Greek dramatists supremely great writers, but they were also supremely fortunate in the age and audience for which they wrote, and that modern dramatists legitimately may have quite different aims and use quite different means, just as they assuredly write for a vastly altered world.

In general, I have concentrated on the *action* of a play, along with its dramatic method and theatrical style, rather than on language or imagery. For it seems to me that a play best makes its statement—and willy-nilly, every play makes a statement, although seldom discursively—through the nature and ordering of its action. But since plot may also be regarded as character-in-action, I have studied each playwright's creation of character, especially as it relates to the nonrealistic elements in a given myth. And I end by considering the picture of man which the playwright communicates through his dramatized myth, using it as a kind of mirror to draw some conclusions as to how characteristic of modern life and thought that picture may be.

Before turning to the background of my subject, I wish to

offer a common-sense, or working, definition of myth that will be adequate to my purpose. The modern literature of mythology as it relates to religion, psychology, anthropology, and literary criticism is vast and fascinating, but there is very little agreement among these disciplines, or even within a single discipline, as to the nature and importance of myth; so it is obviously impossible to offer, if such were needed, a scientifically derived definition that would meet with general acceptance. But where drama is concerned, the world of classical myth is still familiar enough to us as we know it through literature and art that we should hardly require scientific help to make sense of what we find. (If it were not so, these plays, and the very idea of art as well, would be invalidated.) Therefore, I consider myths simply as those stories, already immemorially old, received from the cultures of classical Greece and Rome which tell not only of man's relations with his kind, but also with his gods or the supernatural in whatever form it may be represented.

I.

It was in 1800 that Friedrich Schlegel, speaking for the poets of his time, complained, "We have no mythology." He was pointing to the one essential way in which, to his mind, the poetry of his age was inferior to ancient poetry.[3] Significantly foreshadowing the modern dramatists' stake in it, he coupled myth with poetry, regarding them as one and indivisible; myth was the bed or vessel for the eternal fountain of poetry. He used the latter term in the widest possible sense, as is sometimes done today; he saw poetry not only as verse but as art, beauty—even as love, the informing power of the universe, when its spirit is caught and expressed in the magical formulas of art. He doubted that art was worthy of the name if it could not imbue its forms with this spirit of love. The poets of his day, holding in common no living mythology, lacked a solid foundation and a shared tradition for their art: "They have nothing to hold to, no nourishing soil, sky or creative air." Therefore, since poets work subjectively, from within outward, from spirit to form, each had to

[3] Friedrich Schlegel, *Gespräch über die Poesie*, in his *Kritische Schriften* (Munich: Carl Hanser, 1956), pp. 283–339. I have paraphrased the section entitled "Rede über die Mythologie," pp. 306–13.

begin anew and follow his own path, and the strength of his enthusiasm wasted itself in isolated efforts.

Schlegel's *Conversation on Poetry* was partly an echo of Friedrich Schiller's poem *The Gods of Greece* (1788), but much more perhaps an answer to it. Schiller looked back with longing to a Greek golden age of faith that had charged the whole world with its spirit and thereby transfigured it; now he saw a world drained of divinity, consisting only of dead matter, because men had lost that animating spirit the Greeks possessed. He inveighed against materialism, against the scientific spirit that fostered and confirmed it, and, obliquely, against Christianity, which he said had a horror of death because it lacked a countervailing spirit of life.[4] Schlegel, by contrast, was enthusiastic and hopeful, with an optimism ironically born of that same Romantic movement to which Schiller made so great a contribution, and of the idealism which was its driving spirit. The troubled note in Schlegel's essay quickly yielded to enthusiasm. He looked to the future, not the past, to a new golden age, not an old one. In science, he found inspiration, not cause for despondency. He hoped that a new mythology might be consciously created by combining the great mythologies of the East and the West in a grand synthesis that would base itself on idealism and incorporate all the art of the past and the discoveries of science, particularly the "dynamic paradoxes" of modern physics.

Schlegel summoned the leading spirits of poetry to create a mythology that would not depend for its examples on the world of nature as ancient mythology had done. Rather, it should be formed from the profoundest depths of *human* nature, and hence be *entirely man-made*. They could not hope to do it by reason alone, for reason is inadequate where the highest values of life are concerned, but by the imagination and all that nourishes it, the "sacred dark of the imagination where the titans still live." This common venture should assimilate, of course, all the art of the ancients, for it constitutes a single, indivisible whole, and also great works like those of Shakespeare and Cervantes which seemed to Schlegel already a kind of mythology. Translators of genius should open to poets the treasure of Oriental mythology, especially India's, so that it might be as accessible to them as were the myths of the Western world; for

[4] See Highet, *The Classical Tradition*, pp. 576-77.

it was in the Orient that the highest romantic ideal should be sought and from thence that the new fountain of poetry would flow.

Classical myth, said Schlegel, had sprung from the childhood of the race, the "first flowering of childish fantasy," and so it was based in nature. Not nature but idealism, "the great phenomenon of our age," was to provide the new mythology with its secret source of unity, its universalizing base, and its invisible link between past and present, as well as between each future work of art and its fellows. Let the poet's fantasy invent the rich particulars of his art; so long as idealism provided their universal ground, the singular and the individual would be linked to what is primordial, universal, and eternal in the imagination.

There is an eternal longing and an eternal love. Unless these breathe in the work as its real soul, its reflection of the godhead in man, the spark of poetry will be dead. It is not enough to create characters, passions, and action, nor to devise artificial forms. "If you shuffle and reshuffle the old junk a million times, it still remains only the visible body of poetry," he said. It is the invisible that must be sought and found. "What else is true mythology but expressive hieroglyphics showing us surrounding nature through the transfiguring power of fantasy and love? *Mythology has one great advantage: that which perpetually eludes consciousness is here fixed and made visible.*"

Idealism, if adopted as a way of looking at life rather than as a philosophic system, would provide a fixed point in the world of the spirit from which man's creative power could spread in all directions with increasing intensity, yet be sure of returning safely to its source. Even classical myth, seen in its light, would spring to life again and assume new splendor. Yet idealism was only a stage in a perpetual revolution, part of the ultimate phenomenon, which was *man's struggle to find his own center.*

Schlegel's treatment of mythology is remarkable in several respects. His idea of synthesizing all the great mythologies and combining them with new scientific knowledge is more or less what modern anthropology and depth-psychology have since done in their effort to understand and assess myth, just as his vision of the "sacred dark of the imagination where the titans still live" anticipates many of their findings. And how representative of the Romantic afflatus is his desire for a mythology that shall be wholly man-centered and man-made, at the same time that he stresses man's struggle to find his own center. And finally, there is his conviction that myth is a kind of objective correlative, a way of rendering the unconscious visible.

His heady but troubled exhortation reduced itself to a problem of content and belief: what to believe? what to believe in? and how to find a faith that could be held in common? The artistic problem is at bottom a philosophic and religious one. For Schlegel, as for some of his fellow artists, it led to his embracing Roman Catholicism. Other Romantic poets took the way of Schiller. In England, for example, Shelley turned in *Prometheus Unbound* (1819) to classical myth partly in rebellion against Christianity in all its forms, the bourgeois evidences of which he, like others, regarded as hypocritical:

> To men like Shelley . . . myth became a new language in which the essential religious truths could be re-expressed. To the poets of England as to the symbolists of Germany, myth was the vehicle of religious utterance. It was no accident that when Blake and Shelley desired to give utterance to the yearning for a regeneration of mankind through love neither chose the figure of Christ for the sufferer and the redeemer; the one took the figure of Albion who should awake from his sleep, and the other the figure of Prometheus tortured upon his rock.[5]

It was a time, both in England and Germany, when many developments served to bring closer the poets and the mythologists [6] and to suggest that they plumb together a bottomless well: new knowledge about the age of the earth, Darwin's theory of biological evolution, the view of myth as a primitive account of natural phenomena, and equally the view that myth represented a poetic statement of early theosophical revelations, the increasing number of resemblances discovered among myths through comparative study, the emphasis upon fertility rituals and myths, and the symbolism—sexual or mystical or both—to be found in them.

In France popular theatre was putting classical myth to quite different use. Jacques Offenbach satirized the whole pantheon of Olympus in the operetta *Orpheus in the Underworld* (1858).[7]

[5] Edward B. Hungerford, *Shores of Darkness* (New York: Columbia University Press, 1941), pp. 12-13.
[6] *Ibid.*, p. 13.
[7] *Orpheus aux Enfers*, first performance October 21, 1858, Théâtre Bouffes-

But here myth became a vehicle, not for religious utterance or anti-religious criticism, but for political satire against the French emperor and his extremely corrupt court—a regime particularly susceptible to public opinion. Because of strict government censorship, myth served as a necessary disguise. In this version of the myth of Orpheus and Eurydice, husband and wife prove unfaithful to each other; Pluto rapes Eurydice; Orpheus, glad to be rid of her, begs for her return only at the insistence of Public Opinion (a substitute for the Chorus and a personification of social convention that insists upon preserving appearances); Jupiter resorts to trickery to force Orpheus to relinquish Eurydice and gulls Public Opinion in doing so. In all this, Offenbach and his collaborators were following a tradition of French literature that in the previous two hundred years "contained countless satires on antiquity," down to Honoré Daumier's mythological caricatures.[8] Yet the critic Jules Janin, forgetting or ignoring the traditional burlesque of the satyr play, protested in the *Journal des Débats* that they had profaned the gods and desecrated "holy and glorious antiquity" in a spirit of inexcusable irreverence. When Offenbach's *La Belle Hélène* provoked a similar scandal in 1864,[9] Léon Halévy came to its defense, remarking that the skeptic Voltaire would have been astonished to see present-day Christians so stoutly defending the pagan gods. If nothing else, this ironic state of affairs proved that classical myth is alluringly protean.

II.

Here we have our present age, the result of a Socratism bent on the extermination of myth. Man today, stripped of myth, stands famished among all his pasts and must dig frantically for roots, be it among the most remote antiquities. What does our great historical hunger signify, our clutching about us of countless other cultures, our consuming desire for knowledge, if not the loss of myth, of a mythic home, the mythic womb?[10]

Parisiens, Paris. Offenbach's collaborators were Ludovic Halévy and Hector Crémieux.

[8] Siegfried Kracauer, *Orpheus in Paris: Offenbach and the Paris of His Time*, trans. Gwenda David and Eric Mosbacher (New York: Knopf, 1938), p. 176. See Chaps. 5 and 9.

[9] *La Belle Hélène*, first performance December 17, 1864, Théâtre des Variétés, Paris. On this Offenbach collaborated with Ludovic Halévy and Henri Meilhac.

[10] Friedrich Nietzsche, *The Birth of Tragedy from the Spirit of Music*

These are not the words of Schlegel or Schiller, although they echo both; they are the words of another dreamer of the Hellenic dream, Friedrich Nietzsche, who, in the decline of Romanticism, published *The Birth of Tragedy* (1872). It is the ideas and influence of this philosopher, critic of culture, foe of Christianity, and religious prophet, that we are to consider next. Nietzsche is regarded as one of the seminal thinkers of modern times—a highly symptomatic, if hardly representative, figure of our age. Besides proposing a new view of Greek classic art and culture and ascribing an almost primary importance to myth, he anticipated depth-psychology in some respects and vividly stated the existentialist and absurdist dilemmas well before their time. He exerted direct and important influence on Gide, Jeffers, O'Neill, and Sartre, and pervasive if indirect influence on Giraudoux, Anouilh, Williams, and Ionesco.

I do not know it to be so, but the tragic figure of the hunchbacked thinker, the character Sokrates in Georg Kaiser's play *Alkibiades Saved* (1920), might well have been inspired by Nietzsche's life and thought.[11] If so, it would be ironic, for Nietzsche condemned the historical Socrates for having, as he says, so feared the implications of his disbelief in the gods that in panic he diverted the whole course of Western thought, turning it away from the tragic nature of reality (thereby destroying Greek culture and with it Greek tragedy), and introducing instead the scientific spirit and a preoccupation with morals—"the Socratic notion that knowledge alone makes men virtuous." [12]

Kaiser's fictional Sokrates suffers almost to madness from a thorn in his flesh, this being the literal symbol of his mind's incessant interrogation of all things, human and divine, that leads him to nihilism, to the abyss. And yet this Sokrates conceals to the end the nature of his wound and suffers its ceaseless torment in order to protect from humiliation the peerless Alkibiades. His sacrifice, however, is in vain. Despite himself, his questioning mind subverts and topples all the values of Athenian culture

---

(1872), with *The Genealogy of Morals* (1887), trans. Francis Golffing (Garden City, N.Y.: Doubleday Anchor Books, 1956), p. 137.

[11] Walter H. Sokel, ed., *Anthology of German Expressionist Drama: A Prelude to the Absurd* (Garden City, N.Y.: Doubleday Anchor Books, 1963), pp. 202-64. Sokrates and Alkibiades, the characters of the drama, are distinguished by spelling from their historical counterparts, Socrates and Alcibiades.

[12] Nietzsche, *Birth of Tragedy*, p. 79.

that Alkibiades both cherishes and exemplifies, so that Alkibiades, driven to frenzy by the darkening of his mind, overthrows and desecrates the sacred *hermae* of Athens. Whereupon the elders of the city-state hold Sokrates responsible for Alkibiades' crime and put him to death as the corruptor of youth.

As if suffering from the self-same thorn his life long, Nietzsche did not conceal it; he flourished it, gloried in it. In his adventure of the mind to nihilism and beyond, he is to one scholar "another of the Germans destroyed by their love for Greece"; to a second, he is the victim of a tension so great that the strain of maintaining his loyalty to the "joyous tragedy" of reality broke him, physically and spiritually.[13] But it was his pride and his boast to live always without illusions. He never withheld the truth as he saw it, either for the sake of a friend or to preserve Western culture. On the contrary, he insisted that reason in the service of truth required him to set about destroying the entire fabric of Christian society and all its diseased institutions, so as to make possible a transvaluation of all values, the existing ones having become hopelessly corrupt. Only this would insure the health of the cultures that should succeed it. To this end, he announced his famous dictum, "God is dead," and he proudly proclaimed himself His murderer.[14]

For Nietzsche, as for Ludwig Feuerbach, "man is the supreme being for man."[15] He had nothing but loathing for the God of Christianity: "Enough of such a God. It is better to have no God, to carve out one's own destiny, it is better to be mad, better to be gods ourselves."[16] He experienced a claustrophobic's sense of freedom in the open: "No god, no man longer *above* me! The instinct of the creator. . . . Give oneself the right to act."[17] For "*if* there were Gods, how could I endure it to be

[13] Highet, *The Classical Tradition*, p. 459; Otto Manthey-Zorn, *Dionysus: The Tragedy of Nietzsche* (Amherst, Mass.: Amherst College Press, 1956), p. 11.
[14] "The idea of death finally means a *willing!* This is where the originality of Nietzsche's atheism stands out. In the history of German thought up to 1881-2, Nietzsche is the first and only one to *will* that God should die." Paulos Lenz-Medoc, "The 'Death of God'" in Bruno de Jésus-Marie, ed., *Satan* (New York: Sheed & Ward, 1952), pp. 485-86.
[15] *Ibid.*, p. 483.
[16] Friedrich Nietzsche, *Thus Spake Zarathustra*, bk. iv, chap. 6.
[17] Quoted by George Allen Morgan, *What Nietzsche Means* (New York: Harper & Row, 1965), p. 27.

no God!—*Therefore* there are no Gods!" [18] Perhaps this is enough to suggest the personal ironies involved for Nietzsche in an atheistic humanism that tried to do without illusions, while having to accept the historical evidence that myth was of grave importance in the life of man. To widen the context, we may consider this view of Nietzsche's importance for the twentieth century:

He himself had no doubt where his chief significance lay: in his being the first atheist. The revolt against God is the mainspring of all his thought, as it is of the twentieth century's. If the twentieth century has not yet caught up with him, that is because it has not dared face the ultimate consequences of this revolt. It is still a timid century.

Nobody will blame it for that. It is a fearful thing to fall out of the hands of the living God—just how fearful, Nietzsche's destiny reveals: for he did face them.[19]

In some respects, he may deserve the description, "the most courageous but most tragic man" that ever lived.[20]

Nietzsche continued the German Protestant tradition of the Enlightenment which sought in myth profound philosophic or religious meanings. By then the problem of religious belief, which was at the bottom of Schlegel's quest for myth, had become acute in Western Europe. For Nietzsche, who also rejected philosophic idealism and any form of syncretism along with Christianity, it had become impossible. How then could so extreme a skeptic come to terms with myth, especially when he came to the conclusion that "without myth every culture forfeits its healthy, creative natural power: only a horizon encompassed by myths locks an entire movement of culture into a unity." [21] For the individual, moreover, myth directs and controls the vagrant forces of the imagination and of dream.

Nietzsche sought the meaning of myth specifically in the Greek classical experience of it: "What meaning did the tragic myth have for the Greeks during the period of their greatest power and courage?" At stake was not art, still less the Christian faith; it was a question of the worth of life itself: "The question was

[18] Quoted from *Thus Spake Zarathustra*, by F. A. Lea, *The Tragic Philosopher: A Study of Friedrich Nietzsche* (London: Methuen, 1957), p. 322.
[19] Lea, *The Tragic Philosopher*, pp. 332-33.
[20] Manthey-Zorn, *Dionysus*, p. 7.
[21] Quoted from *Birth of Tragedy*, by Morgan, *What Nietzsche Means*, p. 336.

one of value, the value placed on existence." [22] He hailed the culture of pre-Socratic Greece as the work of men who, moved by a Dionysiac spirit of the perpetual rebirth of life, could outface the Medusa of nothingness and joyously accept and affirm its tragic implications. He offered their Olympian gods and their art as proof that they had conquered despair.

Historians challenged Nietzsche's facts and interpretations, but he succeeded in advancing a new perspective of classical life and art that survived his colleagues' attacks and renewed the interest of later generations in Greek art and mythology. Nietzsche held, in brief, that the serene beauty of Greek art is the result, not the cause, of its nobility; that it was achieved at a terrible cost; that it represents a successful struggle with the darkest possible vision of life; and that it issues from the conscious fusion of the Dionysiac (the spirit of ecstasy) with the Apollonian (the spirit of dream). Nietzsche devoted the rest of his life and thought to elaborating this Dionysiac metaphor into a view of life and finally into a religious faith that possessed him totally. [23]

Attributing to the Greeks an "esthetic metaphysics," Nietzsche maintained that "existence could be justified only in esthetic terms," because "art, rather than ethics, constituted the essential metaphysical activity of man. . . ." For the Greeks (as for him) all process had "a purely esthetic meaning"; it resisted absolutely, said the great critic of European morals, "any moral interpretation of existence whatsoever." He spoke of the power of the universe as a "kind of divinity if you like, God as the supreme artist," but it is clear that he means this as a metaphor only. That power is amoral, indifferent, recklessly creative and destructive, infinitely doing and undoing to rid "himself" of "the strain of his internal contradictions." What he here personifies is simply necessity. The climax of this eternally apocalyptic esthetic is absolute illusion: "Thus the world was made to appear, at every instant . . . as an ever new vision projected by that grand sufferer for whom *illusion is the only possible mode of redemption.*" [24] Redemption from what?

[22] Nietzsche, *Birth of Tragedy*, p. 4.
[23] Manthey-Zorn, *Dionysus*, makes the Dionysiac spirit the central theme of Nietzsche's thought.
[24] Nietzsche, Preface (1886), *Birth of Tragedy*, pp. 1-15 *passim* (emphasis added).

The pre-Socratic Greek, Nietzsche suggested, had "a penchant of the mind for what is hard, terrible, evil, dubious in existence," and this penchant sprang not from sickness and disease, but rather from their exact opposites: "a plethora of health, plenitude of being." Faced with "the ghastly absurdity of existence," invaded by nausea, tempted to deny the will and retreat from life, the early Greek was "saved by art, and through art life reclaimed him." [25]

It would be a mistake to assume that Nietzsche here expounds estheticism and sets art over life.[26] It would also be a mistake to take at face value his strident insistence on the amorality of life; it is part of his determination at all costs to discredit Judeo-Christian standards of morality, the better to substitute his own ethic when it shall have been formulated. Art came to have less importance in his life than it had in his early, Romantic phase. As he elaborated his Dionysiac metaphor into a philosophic system, the creative artist yielded pride of place to the experimenter, who proceeded rationalistically and sought increasingly the sanction of "scientific spirit" and "scientific method"; eventually the artist was himself urged to work in a scientific spirit and to adopt scientific methods of observation and analysis in order to curb his egoism and direct the "indiscriminate vagrancy" of his imagination.[27] (The result would, presumably, have been Strindbergian naturalism, with which Nietzsche flirted.) But even at the outset he saw art as *functional*, as valuable because it helped man to accept and affirm existence. Similarly, he was careful not to confuse his exaltation of science with the indiscriminate pursuit of knowledge, that Socratic diversion prompted by fear. Nietzsche intended, by strict adherence to scientific procedures, to avoid entirely the temptation of metaphysical beliefs, misleading and full of false hope as they must have been in his eyes, because they dealt with things that could not be known by the light of reason.[28] Existence is good, or, because he would have disliked the moral connotations of the word "good," "life is at bottom indestructibly joyful and powerful." Therefore, man

---

[25] Nietzsche, *Birth of Tragedy*, pp. 51-52.
[26] See Morgan, *What Nietzsche Means*, p. 235.
[27] Quoted from *Birth of Tragedy*, by Morgan, *What Nietzsche Means*, p. 336. "Nietzsche seems finally not to claim to deduce his values *from* life, but to shape them so as to harmonize *with* life." *Ibid.*, p. 299.
[28] Manthey-Zorn, *Dionysus*, p. 46.

should exhibit those qualities that accord with the nature of reality—joy and power.

At first, sheer existence is enough: this is the ecstatic assertion of *The Birth of Tragedy*, where the value of existence as a creative process appears inherent and unquestioned. "Only as an esthetic product can the world be justified to all eternity," he says, implying that values have been implanted in it by the creator; even man is not the true originator of the realm of art, since he himself has been created by "the primal architect of the cosmos." [29] Man should see himself as the esthetic projection of "the veritable creator and derive such dignity" as he possesses from his status as an art work.[30] Strange words for an atheist. To be consistent, Nietzsche must banish this "primal architect," and he does. When Nietzsche discovers that he does not need him, we hear no more of him. There never was a "veritable creator" *because there never was a veritable creation:* existence has always been, will always be. This imposes on Nietzsche a thoroughgoing materialism in which space and matter are finite, but time is not.

As he worked out the implications of his atheistic humanism, he concentrated more and more on the creative spirit in the world of man rather than in the world of process. Culture, not nature, is his concern. He decided that value is not inherent in existence: value is what man confers upon existence through his own efforts to surpass himself.

It is not easy for Nietzsche to give up his tendency to deify the Dionysiac spirit in nature. He cannot shut his eyes to the tremendous spectacle of perpetual creation and destruction. He can, however, deify man, and if man cannot literally create himself, he can surpass himself—which is a form of creation. And just as he had transferred value from existence to man, so he shifted emphasis from the past (with its suggestion of a beginning, an original creation) to the future, projected that future into eternity through the idea of eternal recurrence, and linked it with man's creative urge to transcend self.

To achieve what?

If the fundamental will to power in all phenomena is life's desire to surpass itself, then that desire points to the possibility

[29] Nietzsche, *Birth of Tragedy*, p. 42.
[30] *Ibid.*, pp. 41-42.

of creating a race immeasurably superior to present man—the overmen. Nature will not make this race; Darwin's theory of biological evolution did not interest Nietzsche. Man will create it by his conscious efforts. Nietzsche reconciles in himself at last his two originally opposed views: man confers value upon existence because his will to power makes it possible for him to create the overmen, and existence has infinite value because it recurs an infinite number of times. "Man is the transfigurer of life if he knows how to transfigure himself," he wrote.[31] The overmen will be the apotheosis of man. *Ye shall be as gods.* What need will man have to imagine, to invent, gods as the Greeks did, when he can *make* them? "To create a being, higher than we ourselves are, is *our* being. *Create beyond ourselves!* That is the urge to procreation, that is the urge for the deed and the handiwork.—As all volition presupposes a goal, *so does man presuppose a being* which does not exist, but which serves as the goal of his existence." [32]

But this is to anticipate.

Let us return to the Greek experience and its value, in Nietzsche's eyes, for his own time. By means of their arts and their gods, the Greeks had affirmed existence. They had created their gods, just as they had created their tragedies—and for the same reasons. The Greeks used the Olympians as their mirror images: "in order to be able to live at all they had to place before them the shining fantasy of the Olympians." [33] Similarly, by recreating in their tragedies the *tragic myth* to which they were committed, that "image of all that is awful, evil, perplexing, destructive, ominous in human existence," [34] they provided for themselves a "metaphysical solace . . . that, despite every phenomenal change, life is at bottom indestructibly joyful and powerful. . . ." [35]

"The gods have returned to the bosoms of men," said Schiller. Nietzsche held that that is where they had always been and that the Greeks, out of their dreams, had created them in their own image, humanizing the gods and idealizing man in the proc-

---

[31] Quoted from Nietzsche's posthumous *The Will to Power*, by Manthey-Zorn, *Dionysus*, p. 201.
[32] Quoted by Morgan, *What Nietzsche Means*, p. 299.
[33] Nietzsche, *Birth of Tragedy*, pp. 29-30.
[34] *Ibid.*, p. 8.
[35] *Ibid.*, p. 50.

ess.[36] The importance of their pantheon was that it was a *human* creation, hence an esthetic object. While it may have been for the Greeks a veil of illusion which they drew across the abyss, it was also to Nietzsche proof that man could transcend the terror of the void by his own efforts—in this case, by artistic means. As Nietzsche saw it, the Greeks won their victory by accepting the Dionysiac nature of existence and by striving to overcome self. In this view, myth is not true or untrue. It is simply indispensable, like the Eleusinian mysteries: ". . . they held the world together from falling into chaos." [37]

How does myth work?

The action that unfolds in the great tragic dramas, for example, takes place on more than a human level, for it shows man in relation to the forces of the universe he inhabits. Moreover, when the tragic hero wills and suffers, he does so not merely as an exceptional man but also as the surrogate of the gods; by analogy all the gods are in their turn projections of the one suffering Dionysiac spirit that "appropriates the entire realm of myth for its own insights, which it expresses partly in the public rite of tragedy and partly in the secret celebrations of dramatic mysteries, but always under the old mythic veil." [38] Nietzsche says that what the playwright envisions, what the spectator sees, is not a set of gods in whom we must *believe*—belief is beside the question; what is envisioned and seen is an imitation of an action that expresses and affirms the tragic nature of existence itself. Hence, says Nietzsche, even a "profound Greek" like Aeschylus could freely treat his gods with skepticism because he had "an absolutely stable basis of metaphysical thought in his mystery cults." [39] One could wish that Nietzsche had said far more about the mystery cults, this source of metaphysical certainty and of an absolute stability in a world of flux! We must suppose, however, that Nietzsche did not regard the cults as constituting a religious faith or giving formal expression to a religious belief, since, to him, religion is a phenomenon that occurs only when the feeling for myth begins to wither. When myth decays, he said, "its place is taken by a religion claiming historical

[36] Morgan, *What Nietzsche Means*, p. 335.
[37] Thornton Wilder, *The Ides of March* (New York and London: Harper, 1948), p. 150. The character of Julius Caesar attributes the view to Pindar.
[38] Nietzsche, *Birth of Tragedy*, pp. 67-68.
[39] *Ibid.*, p. 62.

foundations." [40] And that, for Nietzsche, is an entirely different matter.

The great historical religions, unlike myth, not only claim historical foundations, but they also represent themselves as announcing and transmitting objective truth, divinely revealed— hence beyond the power of human reason to prove or disprove —about matters concerning man both in this life and in an afterlife "beyond the knowable world." They are uncompromisingly moral as well, treating and judging right and wrong in human motive and conduct. They are metaphysical and transcendental, relating morality to apocalyptic assertions about the nature and ultimate ends of existence.

It is all this that Nietzsche cannot abide; religion is to him no more than human error, seized upon by the weak to shield them from reality, then institutionalized and perpetuated by the treachery of clerics who seek not true self-transcendence but entrenched power. As such, it is quite opposed to the Dionysiac vision of life.

These distinctions once made, myth as Nietzsche first saw it may be defined as subjective expression of man's metaphysical longing for self-transcendence through the will to power. Myth provides no certitude for faith but rather an energizing—and culturally unifying—metaphor for the inexpressible. It also shapes and conserves man's efforts by limiting his horizons. It is a creation of autonomous man in an autonomous physical world. The myths of a culture animate, and then are embodied in, great works of art that provide man solace and refreshment by affirming the tragic nature of life. Myth and tragedy are analogical expressions of the ceaseless conflict at the heart of things, the internal contradiction that generates all phenomena. They are illusions mirroring man's life, the human means whereby man redeems himself. (Redemption from what, and why, we are never told. There is no sin, no forfeit, no loss in Nietzsche's world.) To heighten the contrast between myth and religion, we may say that he approved Greek myth because it was devoid of "moral elevation, sanctity, spirituality, loving-kindness," those religious virtues he despised, but abounding in "luxuriant, triumphant *existence*, which defies the good and bad indifferently." [41]

[40] *Ibid.*, p. 68.
[41] *Ibid.*, p. 29.

Nietzsche believed that he had examined classical myth both from the inside and the outside, had lifted it free of its historical context, and so shown the permanent nature and function of all myth as a continuing human necessity. For all his inconsistencies and inaccuracies, he enunciated a modern view of myth that in his eyes restored its importance for his own age, and he reached independently conclusions which anthropology and depth-psychology had only begun to draw. Developing a theory of "contradictory impulses," he made "perhaps the most original and influential analysis of the tragic energy." [42]

But his view of myth, like his view of religion, landed him in profound difficulties. To him "the demand for certainty" was "the inmost craving and deepest need—that which distinguishes the higher from the lower men." [43] How could he reconcile it with the relativity of truth, the conclusion to which his investigations of reality had led him? In a world where being was continually overwhelmed by becoming, in a world where that which is, *had already been—and would be again, times beyond number*, how could one hope to satisfy the human longing for absolutes that myth and religious revelation expressed and formalized in their different ways? The higher men should have to live by the certainty that there are no certainties, a skeptical conclusion; they have no recourse but to abandon the search for absolutes and accept eternal flux as the condition of existence as well as the opportunity for self-realization. Not for them the certitude of religion, nor even the mythic veil of illusion: they must be able to live without either, to subsist instead upon hypotheses, and the ability to do so was itself the sign of election.[44]

The affirmation of life, even in its most severe problems, the will to life, enjoying its own unexhaustibilities in the sacrifice of its highest types,—that is what I call the Dionysian, that is what I divined as a bridge to the psychology of the tragic poet. Not in order to get rid of terror and pity, not to purify from a dangerous passion by its vehe-

[42] Thomas Rice Henn, *The Harvest of Tragedy* (New York: Barnes & Noble, 1966), pp. 44, 60.
[43] Quoted from Nietzsche, *The Gay Science*, by Walter Kaufmann, *Nietzsche: Philosopher, Psychologist, Antichrist* (New York: Meridian Books, 1956), p. 199.
[44] "This is a religion for the elect only. The lower orders will be given religions appropriate to their stations," says Morgan, *What Nietzsche Means*, p. 366, fn. 67.

ment discharge; . . . but beyond terror and pity, to realize in fact
the eternal delight of becoming. . . .[45]

This meant not yielding to a spirit of nihilism, even though
society at large would eventually succumb to it in catastrophic
fashion, as a result of the "death of God." Beyond the wars and
revolutions that nihilism would produce, the higher men would
reconstitute society in new cultures. What should bind and unify
these cultures? Nietzsche was perfectly disposed to have the
higher men fob off the masses with lies or half-truths or "creative fictions" that would keep them happy and obedient in their
ignorance. For he never forgot that myth and religious faith are
great sources of human energy and therefore useful. Nietzsche
insisted that his view of life was fundamentally optimistic, by
which he meant purposeful; he gave life meaning by assigning
man a realizable goal in conformity with the nature of life.

His lifework could be described, quite without cynicism, as
an attempt to find a moral equivalent for God and to find a
moral justification and direction for sheer human power. He
undertook to forge a philosophy eventually based on four tenets.
The first two were: the autonomy of man's life and reason in an
autonomous universe, and self-transcendence as the highest human manifestation of the will to power. But when he added
eternal recurrence as his third tenet, his philosophy underwent
transvaluation into a religion. In all but words, eternal recurrence
is announced as a truth, as certitude, as religious revelation.

Appropriately, it did not come to him as an inescapable logical deduction, but as a vision, the result of a mystical experience
in August, 1881, by the rock of Surlej on the lake of Silvaplana,
"six thousand feet beyond man and time." [46] He had said once
in criticizing Kant's philosophy that no theory of knowledge is

[45] Quoted from Nietzsche, *The Twilight of the Idols*, by Henn, *The Harvest of Tragedy*, pp. 55-56.
[46] See Eric Bentley, *A Century of Hero-Worship* (Philadelphia and New York: Lippincott, 1944), pp. 99-100. Nietzsche seems to have had several such experiences. Bentley reports (p. 103) that a second ecstasy occurred in January, 1833, on Portofino Mountain, near Rapallo. Morgan refers to them as "the Dionysian experience"; see *What Nietzsche Means*, p. 303.

Bentley is one of the few writers on Nietzsche to give adequate weight
to the influence of Nietzsche's character, health, and experience on the nature and development on his thought. Another is Prosser Hall Frye, whose
early essay on Nietzsche in *Romance and Tragedy* (Boston: Marshall Jones,
1922), pp. 92-140, is still a welcome corrective to the uncritical esteem in
which Nietzsche is more and more held, especially by self-styled "Christian

disinterested, but rather is constructed to prove a conviction already held; he maintained, therefore, that the object of Kant's epistemology had been to strengthen faith in God. Similarly, Nietzsche's predetermined object clearly was to justify his atheism. As he saw it, reason originates in instinct, proceeds through insight, and issues in integrity. It was thus that he proceeded with eternal recurrence, for which he sought logical support *after* the idea of it came to him.[47] For this it was that would precipitate the crisis of nihilism, eliminate the weak, and resolve the convulsions of modern society in a longed-for transvaluation of all values. It came to him as an overwhelming conviction, and its importance to him cannot be exaggerated: ". . . it is possible that there has come to me *for the first time* the idea which will cleave the history of mankind into two halves. . . . *If it is true*, or rather: if it is believed true—then *everything* changes and revolves and *all* previous values are devalued." [48] What agonizing effort it must have been to resist the desire to proclaim the truth roundly, without qualification, instead of having to phrase it tentatively and to make it dependent on its being believed true! *If* true, it splits history in twain, devalues all previous values, changes everything. "It is possible . . . ." But how is one to induce belief? Can man be expected to act as if . . . ? But that was precisely what he said the "profound Greeks" had done, and what the higher men must be able to do. He was fatally unconcerned with how you move men to do it, how you instill or evoke the desire to do it. He must have thought—if he bothered to think about it—that this would come of itself. Would not other men be as enamored of this vision as he? How else account for his disillusionment with them?

If true, eternal recurrence would give Nietzsche's life unique importance in the history of the world; it would justify his lifetime of exhausting effort, of conscious self-sacrifice, of relentless

---

atheists." Unfortunately, the essay has been omitted from a reissue of Frye's book (Lincoln: University of Nebraska Press, 1961) on the ground that it is "intrusive."

[47] "It is evident that Nietzsche's belief was no mere doctrine of cyclical epochs but a superstitious obsession, an illusion, which in the manner of a paranoiac he built into a system." Bentley, *A Century of Hero-Worship*, p. 100.

[48] From Nietzsche's letter to Overbeck, *circa* Oct. 3, 1884, quoted by Morgan, *What Nietzsche Means*, p. 285.

self-overcoming that was also, paradoxically, to be his self-fulfill-ment. But to live as if a thing were true is extremely difficult, when it is of such great importance and when all justification de-pends on its being true. Men can accept the bitterest truths when they stare them in the face, but why should they joyously accept the mere possibility of an endlessly repeated existence?

For Nietzsche, it conferred upon each moment of life an in-finite value because the moment would recur an infinite number of times.[49] One could just as easily and reasonably confer an infinite value upon a moment of life because it occurs once and once only: then the event is unique. Also, a single event, even though repeated infinitely, does not add up to infinity; it is not a mere sum in addition. In eternal recurrence, if past repetitions cannot be remembered, then neither can future repetitions be proved certain. It is still the subjective sense of the unique mo-ment that makes for the highest intensity of awareness.

What are the implications for Nietzsche of this possibility? Is eternal recurrence his escape from a single, irreversible existence and the brute fact of death? Is it his answer to an unacknowl-edged need, his substitute for the Christian belief in eternal life? Appalled at the unending destructiveness of life, must he invent eternal recurrence in order to confer a kind of cyclical immor-tality on all that was of value in his works and days?[50] Is not infinite repetition immortality of a kind—without the stifling presence of God? I think the answer to each question is clearly yes.

It might also be said that by means of eternal recurrence Nietzsche substituted myth for history, reinstating the cyclical view of archaic societies that the linear, irreversible view of his-tory had replaced. In archaic societies events and actions gain their value from the fact that they are repetitions of an arche-type, which is the ideal or exemplary event or action that first manifested the sacred. In Nietzsche's vision each event and each life has its own archetype, to infinity; or, it would be more exact to say, each *is* its own archetype, which manifests only itself and does not depend upon the original action of a god or culture-hero. Yet there is a sense in which Nietzsche's life is rendered

---

[49] Morgan, *What Nietzsche Means*, pp. 365-66, calls eternal recurrence and the overman the "twin myths" of Nietzsche's Dionysian view.
[50] *Ibid.* Morgan says it "assures the immortality of realized values."

doubly archetypal, both because he is the conscious and willing exemplar—the initiator and therefore culture-hero—for those who shall unite to create the overman, and because the exemplary values of his life will become immortal through repetition.[51]

One can imagine, then, the increasing excitement with which he composed *Thus Spake Zarathustra* (1883-85), wherein both eternal recurrence and the coming of the overman are propounded. He felt inspired, both by the metaphor of Zarathustra, who speaks for him in the parable, and by the way in which the vision of the eternal return could yet leave room for the evolutionary or progressive idea of the overmen. Not only is the message presented as parable, a highly uncharacteristic mode for Nietzsche, but also the style is grand and biblical, as if it were a holy book. For Nietzsche, it was *the* holy book, and *he* had written it. The annunciation of the overman—the fourth and final tenet of his new religion—has the prophetic tone appropriate to an apocalyptic vision. I have said that Nietzsche speaks through Zarathustra; in an eerie way, Zarathustra also speaks through Nietzsche: "It is especially at times when barriers of personal repression are removed and images of 'cosmic' character are arising freely, that the fantasy figure may appear of some great prophet or hero, who tends to assume control of the personality."[52] This is how C. G. Jung describes the "Mana Personality" in a case-study. It reads as if he were recounting what happened to Nietzsche in the composition of his book. The ecstatic tone of the lawgiver bespeaks a revelation that will "command" new values. These will realize the aim of humanity by creating a "new perfection," nothing less than "the meaning of the earth": the overman.[53]

Existence alone, we found, was not enough; and man, we now find, is not quite the supreme being for man. But the *overman* will be; he will be the true apotheosis of human life and culture, so superior to present humanity as to be divine. ("Glory to Man in the highest," as Swinburne said.) He is to be our god, and Nietzsche is his prophet.

[51] I am indebted for this idea to Nicholas Moravcevich. The context is, of course, indebted to the ideas of Mircea Eliade; see his *Cosmos and History* (New York: Harper, 1959).
[52] Quoted from C. G. Jung, by Maud Bodkin, *Archetypal Patterns in Poetry: Psychological Studies of Imagination* (New York: Vintage Books, 1958), p. 17.
[53] Morgan, *What Nietzsche Means,* p. 301.

The philosopher had become the founder of a religion. By his own reckoning, he was the first to discover the true nature of reality, the true meaning of history, the true vision of the future, and the true mission of man. It is hard to suppress the suspicion of megalomania when one reads what he told his sister: "Speaking quite literally, I hold the future of mankind in my hand," [54] and impossible to suppress it when one reads in his autobiography, *Ecce Homo*: "I know my destiny. There will come a day when my name will recall the memory of something formidable —a crisis the like of which has never been known on earth, the memory of the most profound clash of consciences, and the passing of a sentence upon all that which theretofore had been believed, exacted, and hallowed. I am not a man, I am dynamite. . . ." [55]

One cannot examine Nietzsche critically for very long without being made aware of the astounding inadequacy of his concept of God, the God whom he felt he had to overthrow. It seems not to have developed much beyond what it was when he was ten years old and to have become, besides, badly confused with his ambivalent feelings for his mother, who was pietistic, puritanical, and censorious. One wishes he had heard and heeded Diderot's maxim: "Enlarge your idea of God." The same seems to me true of his understanding of Christ and the gospels, for all he insisted that "I know both sides because I am both sides." Here is Swinburne's "pale Galilean," turned into an Apollonian dreamer, and Nietzsche must transcend him too.

As for history, to account for the course of Western culture since the ancient Greeks, he had to develop a devil-theory that imputed blame first to Judaism, then to Christianity (as "corrupted" by St. Paul), then to Protestantism; suppression of the truth and subversion of the will to power were the result, ages long, of a conspiracy of priestcraft in general, exploiting the resentment of the weak in a permanent cabal against truly superior men.

In curious ways Nietzsche's repudiation of Christianity caused him to parody it, so that elements in his life and thought are like a shadow-religion. It is hard to know to what extent he was aware of it. He said Christianity rejected this life for an after-

[54] Quoted by Lea, *The Tragic Philosopher*, p. 247.
[55] Quoted from *Ecce Homo*, by Lea, *The Tragic Philosopher*, p. 314.

life impossible of proof; yet what did he do but end by rejecting the present as of no account, except in so far as it could be
made to create a future in which man shall have achieved divinity? Being is nothing, becoming, everything. He incorporated
into his own faith, as the future, the other-worldliness he despised. In Greece of the Golden Age, he exalted the past; he
scorned and reviled his own day; and he pictured the future as
containing another golden age, "the new perfection." Adam, the
archetype of perfect man, did not yet exist—he was to be the
overman. And to prepare for his coming, Nietzsche actually pros-
pected for a monastery to which he and a faithful few would
retire. He had become an "other-worlder."

After repudiating the ethical emphasis of Socrates and the
moral emphasis of Christianity in favor of an esthetic amorality,
he converted his entire philosophy into a moral program whose
terms are exigent indeed, as his own life best illustrates. What
is self-transcendence but the moral equivalent of the will to
power, the motive for harnessing all that was joyful, luxuriant,
triumphant in natural energy, and putting it to work? How per-
vasively moralistic in a utilitarian sense he becomes. Whatever
does not contribute to the creation of the overmen, he disdains.
How spurious are all his references to the presupposed playful-
ness and sportive joy of the supermen, qualities he nowhere exemplifies. And the laborious alchemy of transvaluation, which
is to change everything—how wearisome it finally becomes, until it seems little more than the resentments of the chronically
dissatisfied. And which is the more claustrophobic, his materialism or eternal recurrence? How much of humanity would have
to be thrown out, to accommodate his humanism?

If faith in God is a gift, and there is no learning it, as theo-
logians say, then for one in Nietzsche's position faith in man
ought to be the categorical imperative. But there is a flaw in his
philosophy of total humanism: while he was prepared to worship man, he could not like him. Actual man drove him frantic,
irritated him to the point of exasperation, cast him into black
moods that nearly broke his spirit, and brought out the least
admirable side of his nature: his arrogant contempt for the ma-
jority of mankind which he dismissed as blighted by a herd-
mind, a slave-mentality, and motivated by resentments that had
wrenched awry the course of history and, for the elect, perverted

life almost irremediably. He had imputed to man, however imperfect, all the values that man tended to impute to life itself and to God; man had endowed them with their beauty and sublimity—"man as poet, as thinker, as god, as love, as power. . . ." [56] But where does Nietzsche show an amused tolerance of human weaknesses or foibles, let alone anything so positive, so "yea-saying," as a genuine fondness for the breed? Considering how he felt about the real thing, is it any wonder he had recourse to an idealized image of man? Humanism is a curious faith for a misanthrope.

As a man, he longed for love and friendship, and suffered loneliness. As a teacher and philosopher, he longed for understanding and disciples. But few could understand him, and fewer still would listen to him, let alone follow him. His audience dwindled while his megalomania increased; to his loathing for God was added finally his loathing for man: "I utterly hate all men, myself included." [57] Where before he accepted destruction for the sake of creation, in his last year of sanity he seemed to delight in destruction for its own sake. He found perverse enjoyment in having read to him dispatches about the eruption of Krakatoa, where nearly 40,000 natives on Java and neighboring islands had died in a single night. "It's magnificent!" he exclaimed. "This is how humanity should come to its end—how one day it will end!" [58]

Yet his whole life had been a conscious work of self-sacrifice for humanity. Or so it would seem to have been. Nietzsche might despise altruism as hypocrisy, one of the Christian "virtues"; he might deny the possibility of disinterested action as contrary to the inherent nature of the will to power; but it is impossible to believe that all his work was solely motivated by egotism, by fantasies of self-aggrandizement in which, by work-

[56] Quoted by Morgan, *What Nietzsche Means*, p. 296.
[57] Quoted by Lea, *The Tragic Philosopher*, p. 292.
[58] *Ibid.*, p. 320. Lea's verdict is grave: "The cruelty of Nietzsche's final period is sublimated sadism—and not always sublimated. . . .

"Whichever way we approach the matter, this lust for destruction has to be pronounced a perversion; and, when Nietzsche invokes *Zarathustra* in defence of it, a perversion of his own doctrine. Create, and destruction will take care of itself: that is the gospel of *The Twilight of the Idols*. Destroy, and creation will take care of itself: that is the gospel of *Zarathustra*. By the use of the always-equivocal term 'Will to Power,' Nietzsche concealed the difference between them, yet it is the difference of life from death. . . ."

ing for the overman, he exalted himself. In his sufferings, did he never compare himself to Christ or consider that his motive might be love?

Like the hunchbacked Sokrates of Kaiser's play, Nietzsche failed. His mind had given him no rest, yet his efforts had been in vain. He had sought to overthrow idols, but no one worshipped the god he set up in their place or worked for his coming. All that his particular optimism had done was to increase the pessimism and nihilism of his age without providing against the future. His last months of sanity were desperate. He suffered frustration, disappointment, and the exhaustion of spirit brought on by a lifetime of unremitting struggle. Sane or mad, he was truly a pitiable figure. In the last ten days before his mind gave way, he signed his letters with the terms "Dionysus" and "The Crucified." Apparently, both impulses were still at war within him, and the issue was undecided. Yet from his earliest manhood, he had thought like Judas in Yeats's play, *Calvary*: "Whatever man betrays him will be free. . . ." And, "If a man betrays a God / He is the stronger of the two." He himself had said: *It is better to be mad, better to be gods ourselves.*

And so he had his way, or nearly so.

Nietzsche had gone from the analysis of myths to their creation in his two "myths of the future," his legacy to the elect. He decided that the higher men, however much they shall have learned to live without illusions or certitude, will have need of myth after all. These myths will provide the elect with "the hedge of a great and comprehensive hope," and they constitute "true" myths, for they accord with the basic assumptions of modern science, and men can realize them if only they will do so. Hence, the overman is neither a mirage nor a fiction but an attainable goal, and eternal recurrence is his immortality.[59]

If we look beyond its moral inspiration, we shall see that Nietzsche's is a maimed mythology; it has lost two-thirds of its vital organs and therefore has no organic shape. It has nothing to say about the past and the present, but only about the future. It is no more than apocalyptic, and there is something monstrous about man when he lives only in the future, even though it might

[59] Morgan, *What Nietzsche Means*, pp. 365-66.

be countered that past, present, and future are interchangeable in a world of eternal recurrence, because what is going to happen has in fact already happened.

Myth has here undergone a drastic change of meaning. Here it is synonymous with a goal or an aim, and with hope; scientism has won out with a vengeance over poetry. These myths and their optimistic purpose are the product of the conscious mind and rational reflection. They are abstract, where myth is concrete; static, where myth is active and dramatic. It is astonishing that a philosophy of dynamism or vitalism should yield so passive, vague, and colorless a figure as the overman. He is eugenic, antiseptic, industrious, humorless, and repetitious. Nietzsche the good European has created a Junker demigod and cannot understand why the world will not give its heart to him. His moral earnestness betrays him into offering us these "myths" on the ground that they are realizable, not that they are mysterious, alluring, troubling, frightening, protean, or fascinating to the vagrant imagination.

III.

With this examination of Nietzsche's view of myth as it relates to his thought and life, we have glanced quickly at many of the ideas and attitudes that we are to encounter, treated artistically, in the plays of our ten dramatists; we shall find that the scientism with which he concluded was itself one of the things that caused the poets to flee his vision and return to myth. At the same time, science, as distinct from scientism, was doing much to stimulate that return.

In the 1860's a general agreement was reached among scholars as to the similarity, although not the universality, that connected the known mythologies of the world; in 1890 Sir James Frazer published *The Golden Bough*, a huge synthesis of information on magic and religion that has been called "a milestone in the interpretation of man's cultural past" and "a profoundly significant contribution to the history of ideas." [60] Its immediate relevance can be seen in the further statement that "no other work in the field of anthropology has contributed so much to the

[60] Theodor H. Gaster, ed., Foreword, *The New Golden Bough* by Sir James G. Frazer (New York: Criterion Books, 1959), p. v.

mental and artistic climate of our times." [61] T. S. Eliot, for one, attested to its influence on his poetry and his adoption of a "mythic method." The researches of Sigmund Freud and Carl Jung brought psychology to bear on myths as projections of the unconscious mind. With these influences interworking, the enormous growth of interest in myth characteristic of our day began.

But the situation was quite different on the international stage: naturalism, led by André Antoine and Émile Zola, created a revolution in the theatre. Myth had all but vanished from the French stage as a subject for drama, except for the neoclassic dramas maintained in the national repertory of the Comédie-Française, or plays written in imitation of them, and the opera-bouffe of Offenbach (whose comic treatment of myth was to prove a fruitful influence). Exalting the "experimental and scientific spirit of the age" in his preface to *Thérèse Raquin*, Zola gave it as his profound conviction that only from that direction could come the regeneration of the stage. He called for "the abandonment of all legendary tales," because "the past, indeed, is dead. . . . The rotten framework of the drama of yesterday has brought about its own downfall. There must be a clean sweep." [62]

But even as he buried the past and its legendary tales, his literary and dramatic standards were still those of Greek epic and tragedy, and he was actually seeking their literary equivalent in naturalism. He simplified his characters deliberately, in order to give them epic stature, and by the device of "pantheification" he created in his novels (if not in his plays) fictional worlds as animistic as any ancient Greek could wish. [63] Zola had the *Iliad* in mind as he looked at the peasants and factory-hands of France for models: "With the lower classes . . . you have your feet on the ground, you find the human being just as he is, springing from his native soil, *you reach back to the cradle of the world.*" [64] He sought to "rediscover the breadth of the heroic ages," and in heredity and environment, particularly the

[61] *Ibid.*, p. xix.
[62] Émile Zola, Preface, *Thérèse Raquin*, trans. Kathleen Boutall, in Eric Bentley, ed., *From the Modern Repertoire*, Series Three (Bloomington: Indiana University Press, 1956), p. 516.
[63] F. W. J. Hemmings, *Émile Zola* (Oxford: Clarendon Press, 1953), p. 199.
[64] *Ibid.*, p. 201. Emphasis added.

former, to provide a scientific substitute for Greek fate. Zola was not a consistent materialist, but the idea of materialism as the scientific position of the nineteenth century fostered the impression that his plays and novels were actually scientific studies.[65] He touted naturalism in what looks like a disingenuous spirit: "I don't take the word *naturalism* any more seriously than you do," the brothers Goncourt quoted him as saying, "but all the same I shall go on repeating it, because things have to be baptized to make the public think they are new." [66] His works relied on symbolism to such an extent that one is tempted to see naturalism as not much more than a slogan in the press campaign he conducted to promote them.

Beyond his manifestoes for naturalism, Zola's importance for the stage lies not in his dramas themselves but in the fact that his campaign and plays paved the way for an actor-director of genius, André Antoine, who developed naturalism as a style of acting and of décor, to complement its use in playwriting. His method found in Parisian playgoers an answering fascination with the photographic imitation of life's minutiae. From this came the spread of realism—that is, diluted naturalism—as the dominant theatrical mode, with the result that an atmosphere was created in the theatre which was dedicated to the here, the now, and the literal and was inimical to the use of anything so "nonrealistic" as classical myth.

The artists of the time, increasingly on the defensive since the beginning of the nineteenth century, were forced to redefine their relation to society, and then either turn away from an uncomprehending or uninterested world or use their art as the jawbone of an ass with which to smite the philistine. The advance of industrialism made them look back nostalgically to earlier times, when man lived closer to nature and thought mythopoeically; their instinct told them that the artistic impulse was closer to the thought and culture of the myth-makers than it was to the institutionalized, commercialized materialism that was proliferating about them. Or their fears made them doubt the nature of their gift, as perhaps a way of knowing inferior to science.

[65] *Ibid.*, p. 29.
[66] Quoted from *Journal des Goncourts*, entry for Feb. 19, 1877, by Hemmings, *Émile Zola*, p. 120.

If the last is true, their confusion is understandable. Here, for example, is the philosopher, George Santayana, calling for an alliance between poetry and science and presenting a view of myth very similar to that held by Nietzsche in his last days: "A rational poet's vision would have the same moral functions which myth was asked to fulfil, and fulfilled so treacherously; it would employ the same ideal faculties which myth expressed in a confused and hasty fashion. . . . Such a poetry would be more deeply rooted in human experience than any casual fancy, and therefore more appealing to the heart." [67] Santayana supposed that poets wandered through their "half-mythical" world "for want of a rational education." The poets we shall be concerned with do not suffer from this want: they go back by choice to a world that is fully mythical, in full knowledge of what they are doing. They do so precisely because they believe their dramas will thereby be more deeply rooted in human experience and therefore more appealing to the heart.

[67] Quoted from Santayana, *Reason in Art*, p. 111, by Susanne K. Langer, *Feeling and Form* (New York: Charles Scribner's Sons, 1953), p. 386. Dr. Langer deals with the reasons for the confusion of art with science in Chap. 20, "Expressiveness."

CHAPTER II

ANDRÉ GIDE:
Prometheus as Puritan

My heredity and then my Protestant upbringing turned my mind almost exclusively toward moral problems. In those early years I had not yet grasped the fact that duties toward God and duties toward myself could be the same. At present I have a great tendency to confuse them, perhaps too completely. I am still exigent: much more toward myself than toward others, but have ceased to believe that there is anyone outside myself, any power superior to and independent of me, that does the exacting.

In France, well before World War I, André Gide began to use classical myth both in drama and narrative with influential results. He provided a clue and an example for the emerging writers of his own generation and the next. His interest in Greek mythology and its literary possibilities came to him primarily by way of the translations of Leconte de Lisle, the leader of the Parnassians and a disciple of the chemist and historian, Louis Ménard. Ménard's influential work, *Hellenic Polytheism*, taught that "the myths were not echoes of single events, but cryptic representations of profound philosophical truths." [1]

[1] Gilbert Highet, *The Classical Tradition: Greek and Roman Influences on Western Literature* (New York: Oxford University Press, 1949), p. 522 *et seq.* See also Justin O'Brien, *Portrait of André Gide: A Critical Biography* (New York: Knopf, 1953), p. 8. The quotation at the head of the chapter is from André Gide, *So Be It; or, The Chips Are Down*, trans. with Introduction by Justin O'Brien (New York: Knopf, 1959), p. 31.

Gide, like the Parnassians, adopted Ménard's view of the universality and profundity of myths. But it was characteristic of him that he took the great significance Ménard had conferred upon them and gave it his own emphasis—one more psychological than philosophical and not at all religious. The myths became important to him as revelations of the human psyche—his own, first of all, that made them a perennially interesting source of literary themes. Gide took independently in literature the direction Sigmund Freud and C. G. Jung followed in psychology: myth as a clue to the unconscious.

Gide had encountered the classical tradition in his education and in the neoclassic heroes and heroines in the plays of Corneille, Racine, and Molière which were basic to the repertory of the Comédie-Française. But now these figures of myth were invested with the enthusiasm of Romanticism, and it was evidently this, as well as the beauty of Leconte de Lisle's style, which struck him with such force in the translations: "Through them I contemplated Olympus, and man's suffering and the Gods' smiling severity; I learned mythology. I embraced beauty, hugging it to my eager heart." [2]

Out of this, Gide began to create a myth of his own, although it was anything but a new one, and one allied to the Romantic cult of nature. He reinvented a Golden Age of Greek paganism, paradisaical in its innocence and freedom; again following the lead of the Romantics, he set this earthly paradise in opposition to traditional Christianity. The resultant clash was to be for years the principal conflict of his life. As early as 1898, he was dramatizing themes from classical mythology. But his own myth was not expressed in its fullness until after 1912, the year when the following ambivalent entry appears in his journal:

Copernicus: The wonderful revolution effected by Christianity consists in having said: the kingdom of God is within you. *Happy paganism saw no enemy that was not outside man.*

The Augean stables, the hydras, the swamps to be cleaned up are *within us.* It is within us that Hercules must labor. Christianity = the inner operation.

Radiant morning of the world; man's powers undivided.[3]

[2] Quoted by O'Brien, *Portrait of André Gide*, p. 39.
[3] André Gide, *The Journals of André Gide*, trans. Justin O'Brien, 4 vols. (New York: Knopf, 1947-51), I, 326. Emphasis added, except for the phrase "within us."

His study of history and Greek drama might have been expected to make him skeptical of such a view; tragedy, the very
idea of which turns upon the agony of choice in divided man,
should have cast doubt upon the existence of this Tom Tiddler's
ground, free of all moral restraints and accumulated guilt, that
beckoned to him so seductively. Yet, so far as I know, he never
repudiated the reality of the pre-history he was inventing; perhaps because, true or not, the dream perfectly expressed his life's
wish, and, *mutatis mutandis*, it was to dominate him thereafter.
If it had not existed in the remote past, that scarcely mattered;
it should do so in future.

Gide was then in violent reaction from his mother's domination
and, more generally, from all that she represented: the extremely
puritanical and repressive version of Huguenot Protestantism
in which he had been reared. In the struggle to break away and
find his own identity, his beliefs underwent a radical change,
ultimately issuing as an extreme individualism that obligated
him to forge everything anew for himself. He selected and rejected doctrines along lines which, consciously or not, permitted
him at last to think and act exactly as he pleased. Reading his
interpretations of the New Testament is a little like hearing Lady
Brute, in Vanbrugh's *The Provok'd Wife*, contemplate adultery
to spite her husband. "But you know," says her niece, "we must
return Good for Evil." Lady Brute says flatly, "That may be a
mistake in the Translation—."

The result was titanism. He came to believe that every individual achievement, all human progress, had been throughout
the past—and therefore must be in future—obtained only as the
direct consequence of man's rebellion, whether against pagan
gods or the God of Jew and Christian. Nietzsche had pronounced
this idea in *The Birth of Tragedy.* "In fact, the myths of Philoctetes, Oedipus, and Theseus, as Gide utilizes them, all lead to
the exemplary figure of Prometheus who, in a sense, could be
said to subsume them in the writer's 'inner Olympus.' " [4] In the
private creed he forged for himself, the duty of rebellion bore
an ethical qualification: "Follow your own slope—upward." In
1898 he had put the same idea into the mouth of Philoctetes:
"Whatever we try beyond our strength, Neoptolemus, that is
what we call virtue." [5]

[4] O'Brien, *Portrait,* p. 242.
[5] *Philoctetes, or, The Treatise on Three Ethics,* in André Gide, *My Theatre:*

But at the outset, the "radiant morning of the world" had borne a somewhat different cast. Gide's formulation of a philosophy of "unrest," which directly reflected his own emotional disturbances and moral dilemma, was being attached to, or derived from, the heroes of mythology:

Journal 1896—MEDITATION II (outline)
The value of ill health. . . .
Ill health a source of unrest.
You can expect nothing from "satisfied people". . . .
The need of ill health that antiquity felt. . . .
The vast sickly unrest of ancient heroes: Prometheus, Orestes, Ajax, Phaedra, Pentheus, Oedipus.[6]

Here "ill health" is in part a guarded euphemism for Gide's homosexual passion, which had become overt in 1893-94.[7] He loved ancient Greece not only for the beauty of its art and literature but also for the sense of moral freedom it imparted, and specifically "for the homosexuality which was practiced there," although to a far lesser extent than Gide, again misreading history, imagined.[8] Rejecting the Christian teachings on sexual morality, he sought authority for sexual license in Greek paganism in order to legitimize his own propensities. Thus, he had found a culture sharply different from his own, one congenial to his own tendencies, with a literature full of the universal significance of myth.

Nearly thirty years after he began his literary career, Gide published in 1919 his "Thoughts on Greek Mythology," a fragment of what was to have been a much longer work.[9] It shows how closely his treatment of Greek myth accorded with his thought in general. His interpretation of the myth of Theseus was already what it would be nearly three decades later when he published his tale of *Theseus* (1946). That of Oedipus, which he was to dramatize in 1931, is already there, if only by implication.

Five Plays and an Essay, trans. Jackson Mathews (New York: Knopf, 1952), p. 157.
[6] Gide, *Journals,* I, 80.
[7] O'Brien, *Portrait,* pp. 99-100.
[8] Highet, *The Classical Tradition,* pp. 446, 457.
[9] "Thoughts on Greek Mythology," trans. Jeffrey J. Carre, in André Gide, *Pretexts: Reflections on Literature and Morality,* selected, edited, and introduced by Justin O'Brien (New York: Greenwich Editions, Meridian Books, 1959), pp. 227-33.

We associate myth with emotion, with intuition. But Gide, with ironic overstatement, took the opposite view: "It is to reason first and to reason alone that each myth appeals: you have understood nothing of the myth if you have not first accepted its reasonableness." In accepting myths, he opposed his reason to Voltaire's rationalism in rejecting them. Nonplussed before some elements of the Theseus myth, he maintains: "I know not why, but I do know that there is a reason for it. In the Greek fable there is always a reason." The answer, when found, will lie in the psychological paradoxes of a character; and so the miraculous or fantastic elements of a myth are to be reduced by psychological interpretations, for these latter are for him far more suggestive than solar myths and totems. Indeed, their source is inexhaustible, despite the fragmentary nature of Greek fable; the "shards of myth" that have survived invite the literary imagination to recreate the full story and divine the full meaning.

Pursuing the psychological, Gide deals with fate, submission, and morality—mostly by eliminating them. He would detach Greek myth from Greek religion, since for him pagan mysticism contained no mysteries beyond "a few great natural laws"; he regarded it as an error to interpret myths as "only the figurative representation of physical laws, and to see in all the rest only the workings of *fatality*." In fact, in order to explain the myth, chance must be eliminated and the role of fate reduced. Remove fate as a physical law, says Gide, and you reveal the psychological truth of the myth, which now has more to teach us and speaks with more compelling voice. The miracle of myth is not its miraculous events but its endless meanings for us.

The heroes of myth bear an "inner fatality"—a psychological fatality—which is by implication the thing that makes them heroes. This fatality is not the love of fate, *amor fati*, which Nietzsche admired; it is the thing in the hero's own make-up that "leads him, that drives him to his exploits." He is "unsubmissive"; he does not allow chance, or fate disguised as chance, to lead him. The Gidean hero *is* his fate, as, a generation later, the Sartrean hero *is* his freedom. And so Theseus, for example, left on his ship the black sail that caused his father's suicide, but he did so by unconscious choice, not by chance. But the same quality in two men can lead to different results. "I admire in

Theseus," says Gide, "an almost insolent rashness." For Theseus, that rashness leads at last to a worldly success story, very like Gide's own in its canny complacency; for Oedipus, it leads to blindness and exile.

Hercules, "of all the demigods, is the only *moral* hero of antiquity, the one who, before setting forth, finds himself momentarily hesitating between 'vice and virtue,' " says Gide; and therefore he is the only uncertain, the only melancholy hero. Why should this be true? Because, he says, Hercules was "the one child of Jupiter whose birth is not the result of a victory of instinct over modesty and propriety": Jupiter, to possess Alcmena, had to resort to deceit. "If, doubtless, the theory of the laws governing heredity is of more recent formulation than the myth, I admire all the more that the myth can offer us this exemplary interpretation," he adds in conclusion.

For Gide, therefore, myth is not miracle but motive. And if there is mystery in life, it inheres not so much in "a few great natural laws" but in the individual man's nature and its possibilities. Whatever the question, says Gide, the answer is Man.[10]

I. *Philoctetes*

In 1899 Gide published two works derived from classic myth—one, a *sotie* or satirical farce in narrative form, *Prometheus Mischained*; the other, *Philoctetes*, a reworking of that play by Sophocles which has been called "perhaps the most modern in feeling of all Sophocles' tragedies, as Sophocles is the most modern, the nearest to us, of the three Greek tragedians." [11] Gide's play is written in traditional five-act form with full stage directions, but according to critics, not meant for performance.[12] But it seems to me at least as viable as his other plays

[10] His approach to the Scriptures was essentially the same. In 1922 he wrote to François Mauriac: "I consider the Scriptures, just like Greek mythology (and even more so), inexhaustibly, infinitely resourceful and destined to enrich themselves with each interpretation suggested by a new intellectual orientation. In order not to cease interrogating them, I do not confine myself to their first reply." Quoted by O'Brien, *Portrait*, p. 167.

[11] David Grene, Introduction, *Philoctetes*, in David Grene and Richmond Lattimore, eds., *The Complete Greek Tragedies*, II (Chicago: University of Chicago Press, 1959), 396.

[12] It "belongs among the symbolist treatises [and] . . . it was never intended for the stage." O'Brien, *Portrait*, p. 145.

It was "not primarily written for the stage," says Wallace Fowlie, *Dio-*

obviously intended for performance, none of which (with the possible exception of *Oedipe*) has achieved "any significant success." [13] It is an earnest work, whereas the *sotie* was humorous, bizarre, full of unexpected events which modernization of the Promethean myth, transferred from the Caucasus to *fin de siècle* Paris, made more startling. Gide's narratives on classic themes struck a more modern tone of novelty, inventiveness, and offhand wit than did his plays and, therefore, had more influence on French drama than his own early efforts for the stage.

"I believe that to have a new drama will require a new ethic," he wrote that same year. "Do we have it? I think so. . . . Nietzsche has given us that ethic." [14] *Philoctetes* is his own version of it for the "new drama." It examines the ethics, rather than the psychology, involved in the myth of the hero whom the Greeks exiled because he suffered from an incurably offensive wound, but who nonetheless possessed a magic bow and arrows, the gift of Hercules, without which (so the gods predicted) his fellow Greeks could not hope to win the Trojan war. For all the emphasis placed on psychology in "Thoughts on Greek Mythology," Gide never abandoned ethical or philosophical considerations, and the play indicates how he began to use mythological themes to propound them.

He made two structural changes of far-reaching consequences. First, the gods' conditional prophecy is altered, so that the action does not require Philoctetes to accompany the Greeks to Troy —his bow and arrows are enough. This alone eliminates the whole purpose of the play Sophocles wrote. Second, the epiphany of the deified Hercules, Philoctetes' friend, which was necessary to accomplish the action, is now also rendered pointless. Accordingly, Gide replaces it with a final tableau representing not the epiphany of Hercules, but the apotheosis of Philoctetes. These changes and the meaning they effect are discussed below.

The chorus of sailors is abolished along with Hercules, for the drama now concerns the individual's loyalty to his own ethic,

---

nysus in Paris: A Guide to Contemporary Theater (New York: Meridian Books, 1960), p. 160.

[13] Fowlie, *Dionysus*, p. 159. Since World War II, both Jean Vilar and Jean-Louis Barrault have included *Oedipe* in their repertories and acted the title role.

[14] Quoted from "Lettre à Angèle," *NRF*, September, 1899, by O'Brien, *Portrait*, p. 163.

rather than his obligation to the group; the number of characters is reduced to three: Philoctetes, Neoptolemus, and Ulysses, who in a vague way suggest, respectively, mind, heart, and will. The action is set symbolically not on Lemnos, but on a mysterious island in Arctic seas where all life is frozen. It is inhabited only by Philoctetes and the birds that nest on the cliffs.

The result is a conversation piece on the question: What is virtue? To what should one dedicate his life? The ethics examined, however, are not those of means, but of ends. Indeed, the means are taken for granted: sincerity, straight-dealing, and persuasion are good; hypocrisy, guile, and force are bad. It is the ends that are in question. The ethics—the ends—of the three men are contrasted with each man, ironically, representing himself as disinterested and therefore able to judge objectively.[15]

Ulysses says: "And now it seems that on this distant island, *all passion put behind us,* our great destinies at last are to be resolved, and our hearts, here, more completely dedicated, are at last to achieve the most perfect virtue." "Teach me, wise son of Laertes," says the young and untried Neoptolemus, eager to launch into life and succeed on this, his first mission. Ulysses' commission from the Atreidae is (in this version) to obtain the magic bow and arrows from Philoctetes. He may use deceit or force to do so: if deceit fails, he can "force virtue" on his countryman to achieve his purpose. He acts in the name of country and religion, and for him this end justifies the means: "The gods' commands are cruel; they are the gods."

Neoptolemus, as innocent of guile as he is untested by life, wishes to die for his country and to show his respect for the gods: ". . . this seems like death already, here; every hour my mind has been growing so much colder, and purer, *all passion gone,* that now nothing is left but for the body to die." He is the son of Achilles, Philoctetes' friend, and ready for a hero's death. Because he is ambitious for glory, he regrets that his sacrifice will not be seen by his fellow Greeks. But he is not to die if Ulysses can help it: dying is too easy—and bad for Greece. Rather, he is to serve as a blind for Ulysses' trickery. This discovery revolts him, as do Ulysses' sophistries. Neoptolemus cannot bear to betray his dead father's friend. But, however much

[15] In the speeches quoted, I have italicized the phrases that indicate this.

he rebels inwardly, he keeps silent when they meet their exiled countryman, and he conceals their secret purpose.

Philoctetes, with his wound, is in some ways Gide himself: "It is interesting that André Gide should have begun with the wound rather than with the bow or the exile. For several years already he had shown a special concern for the individual, the exceptional. Physical and psychological abnormality had come to be equated in his mind with uniqueness." [16] Or rather, he is Gide, burdened with his own anomaly, externalizing in Philoctetes the various possibilities (which he sees as dangers) open to him. The exile, added to his catalogue of Greek heroes who suffer from a "vast sickly unrest," has reached a point where for him the world, too, is sick. Nature, he says, "seemed the image of my distress; it seemed that I was nature's voice and that the mute rocks were waiting for my voice to tell their illnesses; for I learned that everything around me is sick. . . ."

Only by living apart from men, he asserts, has he learned to understand virtue: "The man who lives among others is . . . incapable of a pure and really disinterested action." This is the nub of the matter; for Gide, it is this psychological reality that is the starting point for all considerations of ethics. Ironically, in my reading of the play the action proves Philoctetes to be as interested and self-deluded as the other two. On this strange island where the life of the mind is so intense, Philoctetes feels as if his acts and words were frozen in permanence about him: "And because I find them there every day, *all my passion is quieted*, and I feel the Truth always firmer—and I should wish my actions likewise always sounder and more beautiful. . . ."

His exile has become a solitary quest for virtue, a cold, "abstract" life of speculation that he both desires and fears. He learned, he says, to silence his suffering by accepting it and creating from it poetry that was its own solace. But away from men, he found that poetry, when it has no one to speak to, freezes and dies; and the flame that animates it gutters to its end like a wounded bird dying of its need to fly. (He recites some of it; but it turns out, anachronistically, to be from Aeschylus, as Ulysses recognizes.) He has ceased to hope, to feel elation, to do anything but think: "I could get nothing from others, it is true, but a great deal from myself; it was then that

[16] O'Brien, *Portrait*, p. 148.

I began to desire virtue; my spirit is now wholly occupied with that, and *I am at peace*, despite my pain." Neoptolemus' response to him is the same as it was to Ulysses: "Philoctetes! Teach me virtue. . . ."

Philoctetes begins to do so. But by chance he overhears Ulysses and Neoptolemus arguing about the scheme to trick him. (This use of happenstance, although dramatically weak, is Gide's way of throwing emphasis upon Philoctetes, whose inner struggle now parallels and dominates Neoptolemus'.) Unaware that Neoptolemus is proceeding unwillingly, the older man is horrified at his deception. All the longing for companionship, for homeland, which had come flooding back to him upon their arrival, is checked and turned to disillusionment, resentment, and rage. The shock is so great that he scarcely remembers what he had taught the youth who appeared so eager to learn virtue, except for this: "But the truth is . . . there is something above the gods." What is that something? "I don't know any longer. I don't know. . . . Ah! Ah, *oneself!*" [17]

He shows him virtue when Neoptolemus, himself also exhibiting it, confesses the trick they planned and gives him the phial with which they were to drug him. Philoctetes' action is to drink the contents, as if, now that deceit is impossible, he would deprive them also of the necessity of force. The appeals to religion and patriotism are, at one stroke, to be rendered pointless. Ironically, Philoctetes has forced virtue upon *them.*

The phial is Gide's substitute for the agonizing pains that overwhelm Philoctetes in Sophocles' play, where, before he sinks into a coma, he entrusts his bow to Neoptolemus and exacts a promise from him not to desert him. Again, Gide's device throws dramatic focus on Philoctetes instead of Neoptolemus and permits the playwright to transpose the order of events. Philoctetes' action, although somewhat melodramatic, is voluntary and therefore dramatic.

In the delirium which the drug brings on, Philoctetes rages against the Greeks, regretting that his act of devotion will serve his homeland. He longs for Ulysses to admire his action (again

[17] Emphasis added. In March, 1898, Gide wrote in a letter: "The fact is that of the three relationships taught by the catechism—with others, with God, and with oneself—the first seems to me reducible to the second, which seems to me reducible to the third. . . ." Quoted by O'Brien, *Portrait,* p. 168.

the touch of self-interest in all virtuous action), but also to understand that in performing it he was devoted to something beyond Greece. Delirious, he tries to cast the bow and arrows into the sea, but fails. He now recognizes his own bitter, sustaining pride, and the mixed motives of self-love, love for Neoptolemus, and desire to compel Ulysses' admiration so as to show himself superior to the man who wronged him—all the things that prompted his act. "Whatever we try beyond our strength, Neoptolemus, that is what we call virtue. Virtue—I don't believe in it any longer. . . . Neoptolemus, there is no virtue." But under the circumstances this cynical conclusion is suspect, and Gide will not let the play end on that note.

Ulysses bends over the drugged warrior, convinced now that he has seen virtue in him, and "it is so beautiful," he says, "that in your presence I no longer dare to act. To me, my duty seems crueler than yours, because it seems less dignified. Your bow— I can't, I no longer want to take it: you have given it.—Neoptolemus is a child: let him obey." And so, after all, he does dare to act—through the youth, whom he commands to take the weapons: "Isn't it enough to have betrayed me? Do you wish to betray your country as well? Look how he has devoted himself to his country."

On this ironic note, Neoptolemus obeys, and they depart. Ulysses wishes that Philoctetes could know how admirable he thinks he has been, and that, through Philoctetes' sacrifice, the Greeks will win at last. Here the Gidean ironies, turning into ambiguities, are almost self-defeating. But there is a fifth act which, depending on how one interprets it, resolves—or increases —them. The act can be quoted in full:

[*PHILOCTETES is alone, on a rock. The sun is rising in a perfectly clear sky. Over the sea, in the distance, a boat is moving away. PHILOCTETES looks at it, long.*]

PHILOCTETES [*murmuring, very calmly*]: They will never come back; they have no more bows to seek. . . . I am happy.

[*His voice has become extraordinarily mild and beautiful; around him flowers are showing through the snow, and birds from heaven come down to feed him.*]

END

The cold sterility has ended, the sun has broken through the gray clouds, life has returned to the island, and the birds feed

Philoctetes, who was left defenseless. It is his apotheosis and
the ratification of his virtuous act of self-transcendence.

The first questions that arise are these: why did Philoctetes remain on the island, and what does Gide wish to show by it?
They send us back to Sophocles and *his* version of the myth, to
see what Gide may have gained or lost by deviating from it.
There, the conditional prophecy of the gods is most explicit: not
merely his magic bow and arrows, but Philoctetes himself, must
go to Troy; if he does, not only will Troy be taken, but he will
recover from his wound, slay Paris, help to sack the city, and
win the fame and fortune that are his right as a victorious warrior. Not virtue, but quite specific rewards are held out to him;
yet despite their number and weight, despite the appeals to
patriotic and religious duty, they cannot outweigh Philoctetes'
proud resentment against the Atreidae. And in the Greek view
his angry pride is in every way justified.[18]

Even so, his stubborn will is overborne by the gods in the
person of his dead friend, the now deified Hercules: "Go with
this man to Troy." And the divine command makes it plain that
Neoptolemus is as necessary to Philoctetes as Philoctetes to him:

> Son of Achilles, I have the same words for you.
> You shall not have the strength to capture Troy
> without this man, nor he without you,
> But, like twin lions hunting together,
> He shall guard you, you him.[19]

The point is clear: no man may live for himself alone, because
his life is bound up with others', as theirs with his.

Philoctetes' final refusal is the refusal of a man so wounded as to be
unwilling to resume normal life itself because, with that life, will
come new and unpredictable suffering . . . [But] only at the cost
of suffering does life itself exist. As Philoctetes' final refusal is the
mark of the play's truth to humanity, so is his final acquiescence in
Heracles' order the mark of a truth to a universal principle, more imperative than humanity. . . . What follows is what might well happen
in the world as in the theater—the surrender of the individual life to
the universal demands of life itself.[20]

[18] As H. D. F. Kitto is at pains to show in *Form and Meaning in Drama:
A Study of Six Greek Plays and of "Hamlet"* (London: Methuen, 1956).
See Chap. 4, pp. 87-137.
[19] Grene and Lattimore, *The Complete Greek Tragedies*, II, 459.
[20] *Ibid.*, pp. 398-99.

Now it would seem that although Gide was not attempting to do or say the same things as Sophocles, this part of the ending of the older play would be just as valid, and perhaps more so, for his play. It says something that an audience would assent to because, however harsh, it is one of the facts of real life. And it would avoid the puzzling and possibly misleading ending he devised. If virtue consists not in speculation or living for one-self, but in action rendered for others (however mixed—because of the human condition—the motives involved may be), then Gide has only beclouded its meaning by altering the prophecy and requiring Philoctetes to win the struggle with his pride, yet stay on the island. There is an element of the perverse here, almost as if Philoctetes willed his own abandonment. If so, his virtuous action belies itself; for however transfigured, he con-tinues to lead the solitary life that Gide has examined and re-jected. If not, then the blame for abandoning him rests not only on Ulysses, but also upon Neoptolemus, his unwilling but obedi-ent accomplice. In that case, and even though Gide has omitted the promise exacted of Neoptolemus in the older play, what be-comes of the youth's schooling in virtue? His obedience cancels the virtue of his confession, and the treatise risks having been written for naught.

The world of Gide's play is very much his own world or the world of his desire; in it the gods are not to overrule human de-cisions. This is because "there is something beyond the gods— oneself!" Gide, thinking of Oedipus and the Sphinx as a figure of man's encounter with life, was to formulate his "new intellectual orientation" thus: whatever the questions, the answer is Man. So it is here. Virtue resides in man, to be created by him in serving his fellows. (We ignore Philoctetes' delirious denials of it, since the ending of the play obviously negates them.) Virtue is too grave a matter to be left to the caprice of the gods: only man is responsible enough to deal with it. Besides, in this play the gods do not exist; they are merely something that Ulysses and Neoptolemus speak of: the former to invoke them as a sanction for dirty deeds, the latter to identify them with his homeland. Philoctetes' virtuous action is achieved by obedience to his own conscience, not to the will of the gods.

In Sophocles' play Philoctetes' wound, mysteriously inflicted upon him for having trespassed in a sacred grove, will be as mysteriously cured if he goes to Troy. Gide cannot have it so, since from the outset he has dispensed with the magical and mysterious as much as possible; they are concepts he regards unsympathetically. The element of magic is a mere datum of the myth, something to use and forget about. But in a sense his treatment of fabulous materials automatically increases their importance: we look for the symbolic values conferred upon the weapons and the wound. But the meaning of their application is something that the play does not deal with. What is it that the Greeks need of the man they exiled, and what is the nature of his wound, that it cannot be cured? If we answer the second question naturalistically, by reference to Gide's homosexuality,[21] it only leads us back to the first. The magic bow and arrows can perhaps be interpreted as Gide's art, if one wishes to subscribe to the reductive view that art equals neurosis.[22] But the thing that makes the play a *pièce à clef* is that Gide, having assigned this secret meaning to the wound, is at pains not to dramatize it. And so the wound, like the bow but perhaps for a different reason, becomes only a datum in the initial situation, a constant but inoperative element.[23] It is as if Philoctetes, although the protagonist, acts upon motives that must ultimately be kept secret, whether because no acceptable analogue of action was found to deal with them, or because of some consideration extraneous to the play. Hence, the foreground must be devoted to a question of ethics that does not seem to come to grips with the real issue, which is the secret meaning. Or else, to state it the other way round, the secret meaning obtrudes upon and confuses the real issue, which is a question of ethics.

Within the supernatural framework of myth, Gide is working naturalistically; thus the elements of the play must be assigned values symbolic of something other than supernatural or religious values. He is also attempting to subject the ends of ethical action to a process of conversion entailing nothing less than a "new

[21] Justin O'Brien's *Portrait of André Gide* shows repeatedly that there are good grounds for doing so.
[22] Although his statement of it is not so flat-footed, this is essentially Edmund Wilson's position in *The Wound and the Bow* (Boston: Houghton Mifflin, 1941), Chap. 7. See especially pp. 287-88, 294-95. I believe Gide himself outgrew this view.
[23] Recall that he eliminated the agonizing pains and incapacity which the wound induces in Sophocles' hero. This is strange in an author fascinated by heroic "sickness."

intellectual orientation," one very similar to Nietzsche's revaluation of all values. But while presenting the self as higher than the gods, he dramatizes also the hazards of the introverted life —to thought, art, and the wellsprings of human feeling. These hazards are the temptations to religious and ethical egotism, intellectual sterility, and the folly of supposed self-sufficiency.[24] The conclusion we are given, however, with a transfigured Philoctetes miraculously fed by birds, appears to be intended as an apotheosis, the dramatic statement of Philoctetes' triumph through self-transcendence. Yet it is disquieting and unsatisfactory, because it is also an immolation; and his symbolic transfiguration then is seen not as part of the action, but rather as a piece of theatrical machinery that has little, if any, relevance to the theme as demonstrated in the action.

When the moral law inheres only in man, there can be no supernatural because there is no other referent. And when, further, the only referent is oneself, which of course is basic Gidean doctrine, we have introversion with a vengeance. Esthetically, this is reductive, because the world of the play is smaller than that prefigured by Sophocles' play. In the Greek dramatist's view man must submit, even when he is fully justified; and so the epiphany of Hercules has meaning in the structure of the action as well as in the world of the play. In Gide's play, Philoctetes' apotheosis after his abandonment has meaning only for the secret issue behind the action. It is emotional compensation, demanded by the author's self-pity: ". . . the psyche is forced to gratify itself symbolically, proceeding to identify the object of desire with itself, as if to say, I need nothing but myself; the subject is taken for the object. . . ."[25] What the ending of the play gives us is compensatory wish-fulfillment—which is, by definition, narcissism.

[24] Edmund Wilson takes completely at its face value the Gidean hero's account of his exile. And so he assumes that it has enabled Philoctetes to "perfect himself"; he sees him as a "moralist and an artist, whose genius becomes purer and deeper in ratio to his isolation and outlawry." Wilson, *The Wound and the Bow*, pp. 288-89.
[25] John Senior, *The Way Down and Out* (Ithaca, N.Y.: Cornell University Press, 1959), p. 5. I am quoting Senior out of context; in defining narcissism, he is not writing about Gide, but describing Freud's theory that "the development of the individual psyche corresponds" to "three evolutionary stages in the history of humanity—magical, religious, scientific . . . ." *Ibid.*

II. *King Candaules*

"The Evolution of the Theater," a lecture which Gide delivered in 1904 at the Société de la Libre Esthétique in Brussels, throws further light on his purpose in using classical myth. The importance for the artist of heroic, historical, or legendary figures is, he said, their remoteness: ". . . time, or any kind of distance, allows an image to reach us only after it has been stripped of everything episodic, bizarre, and transitory, leaving only its portion of profound truth to work on." [26]

For his second play, the image that reached him—presumably stripped of everything bizarre—was that of King Candaules, whose story he found presented as myth in Plato, where it involves a magic ring, and as history in Herodotus, where it is simply a curious tale with puzzling psychological implications.[27] With his treatment of the Philoctetes myth in mind, one might expect Gide to choose Herodotus only and work out naturalistically the situation of a king so proud of his wife's beauty that he must have his best friend gaze upon her nakedness. Instead, he added a large dose of magic to the myth: he combined parts of both his sources with the account, also found in Herodotus, of Polycrates of Samos. Polycrates, out of a superfluity of pleasure, threw into the sea a ring he cherished, only to find it again in the belly of a fish served him at table. In Gide's version it is a magic ring—engraved with the cryptic legend, "I hide Happiness"—that confers invisibility upon the wearer. And so it enables the king easily to gratify his strange desire to have his wife admired nude. Thus, the ring serves not as a symbol, but as a plot device out of folk-tale that permits King Candaules to indulge his excessive generosity ("to the point of vice," as Nietzsche said). Also, it permits Gide to go further than his predecessors and add to the plot the folk-tale device of the substitution, or "bed trick": Gyges, the King's friend, may not only look upon the queen, but he may also lie with her.

But for all this, the emphasis in the play is on Gide's concept of "psychological fatality"—that thing in a man's nature which makes him exceptional, which leads or drives him to his exploits.

[26] Reprinted in André Gide, *My Theater*, pp. 257-75.
[27] André Gide, *King Candaules: A Verse Play in Three Acts* (1900), printed in *My Theater*, pp. 161-235.

Nietzsche wrote: "It is a curious thing to note that excessive generosity does not go without loss of modesty." For Gide, who quotes it with approval, this statement evidently served as the index of Candaules' character. That the king's rash act brings about his death at the hands of Gyges is an ironic reversal that Gide fully appreciates; and when Gyges succeeds his victim, both as ruler of the land and the queen's husband, Gide even adds to it by having Gyges, as his first official act, order the queen to veil her face for good.

Yet Gide intends the central irony to be tragic, not sardonic; to him, the death of King Candaules represents "the defeat, almost the suicide, of an aristocracy whose too noble qualities first easily undo it and then keep it from defending itself. . . ." [28] He speaks of the king as "too great and too generous," as one forcing himself to the extreme, so that we are reminded of Philoctetes' touchstone: "Whatever we try beyond our strength . . . that is virtue." And when the idea occurs to Candaules to have Gyges look upon the queen, the king, restless and disturbed in thought, runs to meet it: "What is this you suggest, my unquiet fancy?" He does not struggle against it; on the contrary, he invites it, he solicits it. He fortifies himself with wine, not to give himself Dutch courage, but to free the impulse which the "base" part of him still opposes. Earlier he had said:

> Drunkenness can only manifest
> What we have within ourselves.
> Why should a man be afraid
> Who has but what is noble to be shown?
> Drunkenness does not deform, it exaggerates;
> Or rather it makes one surrender
> What often in excess of modesty he would hide. . . .

Temptation to evil is reversed in Gide's morality—or rendered meaningless.[29] The lure of fatality is an imperious command before which prudence must give way as cowardly, even though it represents the moral bent of a lifetime. King Candaules' is a self-conscious surrender, for he watches himself yielding:

[28] *Ibid.*, Preface, p. 167.
[29] "To obtain what I want I am tenacious, bold, even foolhardy, and without a thought for the obstacles, but to resist what puritans call 'temptation' I am no good. I don't even try. If I believed in the devil (I sometimes pretended to believe in him; it's so convenient!), I should say that I come to terms with him at once." Gide, *So Be It*, pp. 67-68.

> Louder, speak louder, my youngest thought!
> Where do you mean to lead me? Ah, strange Candaules!

And so he works upon the scandalized Gyges, shows him the power of the ring to render its wearer invisible, gives him it, persuades him to put it on, quenches the torches in the bedroom, and summons the queen. "Be strong!" he tells himself. "Bear up, my reeling thought!"

Plying himself with wine, he tells the queen of his great love for her and—with the invisible Gyges looking on—begins to disrobe her. There follows a prolonged striptease, with the queen quite unwitting of the fact that her husband is acting as pander. Gyges remains "hidden"—that is, offstage—during all but the last moments of the scene, as if Gide feared to exhibit *all* the dramatic reactions in this peculiar triangle that Candaules is creating. Yet, in having gone thus far, Gide has deprived himself of any esthetic justification for veiling Gyges' reactions—which are precisely the point of the scene—while unveiling the queen. The result is that the audience finds itself, uncomfortably, acting as Gyges' surrogate.

While she undresses, the queen exacts a promise which Candaules blindly agrees to, only to be brought up short when he learns what it is:

> That you will never again lift my veil
> Before other eyes than yours.
> [*CANDAULES, in anguish, reels*]

To divert her, he asks for more wine; and says to himself:

> Oh! Oh! Oh! What is this I dare to do?
> I can't go on.
> [*clenching his fists*]
>   Candaules, you are weakening!
> Who would ever do this if not you?
> Bear up!

He must strain every nerve to prevent the play he is staging from ending abruptly or defeating his purpose. Gyges, his cloak covering his face and trying not to look, appears and hurls to the floor the remaining torch. He is "completely maddened." The king, "exalted and drunk with what he is about to do," commands him "imperiously" to stay, and leaves, saying, "And now, all those about me, be happy."

Gyges lies with the queen—with what ironic results may be imagined. The "bed trick" has worked; Candaules, having cuckolded himself through his friend, discovers that he cannot complacently play the wittol: he has become jealous.

> You jealous, Candaules? Ah, no, fie!
> Evil passion, you will be quiet.
> [*He makes a gesture of self-control.*]

Later, having been present invisibly while the queen expressed to Candaules her raptures over the night she supposes she spent with her husband, Gyges reveals himself, confesses the trick, and gives her his dagger to kill him. Instead, her command to Gyges is: "Stab him." She overcomes his resistance, and Gyges, using the power of the ring, treacherously kills his friend—and the play ends as I have described previously. Candaules' dying words are:

> What! It's you, my own Gyges?
> Why did you strike me?
> I felt nothing in me but kindness.
> Nyssia! . . . Gyges, I gave you the knife too.
> Take off your ring—
> I want to see you again.

Gyges, "terrified and grieved, kneels to Candaules, leaning toward him," and says, "Candaules, my friend—"

The most credible thing in this incredible drama is, oddly enough, the magic ring. One accepts it as a conventional device for producing the situations that will reveal the stuff of drama: motives and reactions; and one accepts it all the more readily because Gide has handled it with admirable forthrightness: in providing "a cloak to go invisible in," he is as direct as any Elizabethan dramatist. It is not the plot premise of the ring, but the *psychological* premise of Candaules' motive, that defeats one's willingness to believe; yet it is this, rather than the ring device, which must impose itself authoritatively on the audience, if the play is to achieve conviction and sustain the drama it presents. And it fails to do so, as—according to the theatrical record of the play—it has consistently failed. Gide has already anticipated this objection: he justifies himself by saying: "Whatever falls outside the conventions, in the theater, seems false."

Before it can accept an exceptional character, he says, an audience must protest, because it dislikes being freed of its conventions. Conventional or not, audiences at this play have resisted having virtue forced upon them in new guises.[30]

Gide is deadly serious in all this, but he is not incompetent: his dramatic sense is at least alive to the ironies of the situation, so that the final scenes of the play, beginning with Gyges' disclosure, are the most dramatic he ever wrote. The recoil, which is all there in Herodotus, carries the plot to a powerfully shocking close—if one could believe its premise. Equally shocking is Gide's principal addition, Gyges' earlier killing of his wife, Trydo, for faithlessness. These scenes, it is true, are preceded by many undramatic ones—*longueurs* devoted to sybaritism—*fin de siècle* tushery like the airless sensualism of, for example, *The Picture of Dorian Gray*. The cast of characters includes a gaggle of parasites and toadies instinct with boredom. Actors could animate these roles, but I doubt that the roles could animate the actors. To give Gide his due, he designed the play to shock. In advancing his exceptional ethic, he intended to flout bourgeois morality—and wrote accordingly. He could hardly have been surprised that he enraged it further by confronting his objectors with the purity of Candaules' motive.[31]

Consider the premise. The king offers his wife—whom he says he loves more than himself—to the fisherman Gyges, out of promptings of deepest friendship. Candaules' rash altruism is the fundamental insight Gide wishes to bring to the play. That it contains its own fatality—that his rash act will cost him his life—detracts not a whit, in Gide's eyes, from the splendid audacity it reveals: "Miraculous ring. . . . Now protect the happiness of my friend Gyges, hide him!" There is a repetition of this idea in a journal entry Gide wrote later about a friend who was persisting in an *amour* that was doomed on the face of it to fail: "Where will all this lead him? Certainly not to happiness. He knows it, moreover. But what does that matter! Do we ever really seek happiness? No, rather the free development of

---

[30] Gide, *My Theater*, p. 167.

[31] Mario Praz finds in Gide's psychological ambiguity "the sadistic pleasure of the sensation of pride in one's own humiliation, and of violating and shocking the modesty of others. . . ." For more on this, see Praz, *The Romantic Agony*, trans. Angus Davidson, 2nd ed. (London: Oxford University Press, 1951), p. 366.

whatever is newest in us." [32] He could have been speaking of
Candaules, who, for following the promptings of his nature and
daring to make his own morality, belongs among his sick heroes
of myth. Candaules flouts tradition, whereas Gyges represents it:
"Master, what words are these . . . ? Of old men have discovered fair doctrine for our learning, whereof one lesson is this:
that each man look upon his own." [33] As the action proves, the
king's willfulness is a thundering error of judgment; but that,
to Gide, is neither here nor there. Now when a tragic hero makes
the error of judgment that fells him, an audience catches its
breath in horror, precisely because he did what he should not
have done. But when Candaules follows his slope upward to his
fall, it is as if Gide wishes his audience to gasp in admiration
as well. Unlike the hero of idealistic tragedy, King Candaules,
in his death, comes to no recognition of his error, because for
Gide there has been none. In Gide's vocabulary the word "error,"
as applied to an exceptional act, is meaningless. Instead, the
king reaffirms the rightness of his action: "I felt nothing in me
but kindness." And he forgives Gyges, even when he realizes
that his friend killed him at Nyssia's behest: "Take off your ring
—I want to see you again." He triumphs in his death; for his
act, however "suicidal," is a gesture of revolt whereby a new
morality is forged, and virtue, as we know, consists in transcending oneself by *whatever* means.[34]

But it was demonstrated in *Philoctetes* that the man who regards himself as disinterested is self-deluded. Not that that made
virtue impossible, but self-interest blinds a man to his real motive, or mixture of motives. Candaules' motive ought not to be
taken at his own valuation, nor, for that matter, at Gide's. It will
require fuller examination.

Gide, adept at having it both ways, contended in his *Journal*
(1928) that each of his works hid under its "apparent poison"
its own antidote, that "each one of them does not so much disturb as it warns." [35] But despite Gide's well-known ambiguity,

[32] Gide, *Journals*, I, 131 (May 16, 1905).
[33] Herodotus, *The Art of the Logos*, trans. J. A. K. Thomson (London:
Allen & Unwin, 1935), p. 88.
[34] Note, too, the recurrence of the word "whatever" in Gide's journal entry
quoted above, p. 50.
[35] Justin O'Brien says that Gide, "during the years immediately following
[*Les Nourritures terrestres*], made every effort to multiply the antidotes

the play is clearly intended to be not cautionary but exemplary.

It is on this ground that the play raises the question: does Gide himself, challenged to justify a perverse act by ascribing to it the most selfless motive, really understand its implications in the character of his own protagonist? Justin O'Brien, speaking of Candaules as "a true Superman," one "fully conscious of the originality and boldness of his deed," interprets the king's "extraordinary impulse" as that of a man "pathologically unable to enjoy anything in secret." [36] This seems to me an entirely accurate description, but it does not jibe with Gide's presentation of Candaules' motive. And if by "pathological" O'Brien means "unnatural," Gide has already anticipated this judgment. Candaules is "exceptional," not "unnatural"; the latter is for Gide a meaningless category; he is interested only in possibility. "All possible feelings exist in man, but there are certain ones that we exclusively call natural, instead of calling them simply more common. As if the common were more natural than the rare! . . . Everything Candaules does is natural." [37] Since Gide's psychological approach to myth invites the spectator to search for motives which the characters themselves do not recognize, we may legitimately apply the technique to this play with interesting results. In doing so, we assume that Gide *does* understand their motives, although his view of them may be different from ours.

Let us begin by questioning the nature of Candaules' affection for his wife, for this will reach its sharpest definition in his friendship for Gyges. He declines thanks at the banquet for sharing with his guests the beauty of his unveiled queen, explaining himself thus:

> Indeed, to be alone in the enjoyment of her
> Has made me suffer much.
> The greater my admiration of her,
> The more I felt how much I deprived you all.
> I seemed a greedy monopolizer
> Wrongfully withholding light [I, 3].

and make them ever more efficacious. The two plays *Le Roi Candaule* and *Saul*, and the novel *L'Immoraliste*, as well as the moral farce of *Le Prométhée mal enchaîné*, were all written as correctives to [it]." *Portrait*, p. 143. This is not, however, what Gide himself said, i.e., that each work contains its own antidote.

[36] O'Brien, *Portrait*, pp. 162-63.
[37] Gide, *My Theater*, p. 167.

It should be noted that in thus exposing her, he had to overcome the queen's vigorous objection, and that she further objects when he unconsciously echoes a guest in referring to her
as his "property": "Fie, my lord! You seem to forget that the
property you speak of is myself." When she is asked what she
thinks of "this sharing," she answers: "I think there are kinds
of happiness / One kills in trying to share them."

This king, devoted to pleasure, never seems to rule—merely
to command. We discover more than once that he has a view
of his kingdom quite at variance with facts: he has deluded himself into thinking that there are no wretched poor among his
subjects. "I thought my happiness was so great, so radiant, / That
nothing poor was possible around me." Drama is a shorthand
language, where a flaw of character in one respect suggests a
similar flaw in another—unless the dramatist specifically shows
the contrary. If the king can be mistaken about so considerable
a matter, one he could easily determine for himself if he emerged
from his self-absorption long enough to do so, he may well be
mistaken about so intangible a thing as his own motive. For all
his fine talk, it is his actions that speak in the theatre; and they
show him to be an egotist, a voluptuary, and—despite the queen's
love for him—a lonely man. Justin O'Brien's comment in this regard is revealing and significant: "That he treats her as a mere
object, the rarest of his many possessions, disposing of her as
he does of material things, is his unforgivable crime. *But Gide
makes little of this element in the tragedy,* leaving it rather to
Nyssia to avenge herself . . . in none of the other versions of
the story has she had equal cause to do so." [38] A relationship in
which one party treats the other as an object—as, despite his
denials, Candaules does the queen—is not worthy the name of
love.[39] Yet the king protests he loves her more than his life. That
Gide makes little of it nonetheless tells us, in the shorthand of

[38] O'Brien, *Portrait*, pp. 162-63 (emphasis added).
[39] Gide attempted precisely this in his personal life, thinking to separate
absolutely love and desire—in which case the person desired becomes
simply the *object* of desire. But he found, for once, that he could not
have it both ways; and so he betrayed his own ethic. He was dishonest
enough, moreover, to maintain thereafter that he had not done so; it was
his "major deception." See O'Brien, *Portrait*, p. 266; also Pierre Herbart,
"A Key to André Gide," in Cecil Hemley and Dwight Webb, eds., *Noonday 2* (New York: Noonday Press, 1959), pp. 4-33, especially the quoted
remark: "I have always on my part disassociated love from pleasure."

drama, something about *the king*: it tells us that his protestations of love for his queen are the unconscious hypocrisy of a
man who only thinks he loves. There are even indications that
the king does not desire the queen very much. She herself com-
plains of neglect. He prefers, to enjoying her favors in private,
suffering fools gladly in public, because they constitute a captive audience before which he can give command performances
with himself in the starring role. And so it is possible that the
ardor he shows the queen, as a means of debauching Gyges,
comes from the fact that Gyges is present and is watching *him*.

The king is restless, unquiet (inveterate traits of the Gidean
hero), and unhappy. To the queen, whom he angrily offended
before his guests, he says:

> Believe me, I had no wish to hurt you. . . .
> The truth is, on the contrary, that for me
> My happiness seems
> To draw its strength, its violence, from others.
> It seems to me sometimes that it exists
> Only in the knowledge others have of it,
> That I truly possess
> Only when others know that I possess [I, 3].

One is reminded of Philoctetes: "Child! Ah, if I could only
show you virtue. . . ." Or: "And you shall admire me, Ulysses;
I want to compel you to admire me. My virtue rises above yours
and you feel yourself diminished." Risk, Candaules says, is "the
rich man's happiness"; and the thought of jeopardizing what he
has, including the queen's love, causes him to exult. When Gyges
kills his wife for infidelity before the assembled guests, the
king is struck with admiration. Indeed, he so admires the man
for doing a bloody deed—possessive and directly contrary to his
own bent though it may be—that he offers him friendship on the
spot. He installs him in the palace, showers him with favors,
solicits his affection, and seeks to possess his life and emotions
in a most prying way. It is then that the fatal idea is born, and
the following exchange takes place:

KING CANDAULES: Gyges, do you know what first brought me
    to love you?
You alone realized the beauty of the Queen. . . .
Poor Gyges! Before you saw her,
You thought your wife was beautiful. . . .
But I saw you suddenly look at Nyssia,

And all at once Trydo seemed no longer beautiful.
Gyges, that is why you killed her, isn't it?

GYGES: O King! How can you think such a thing?

KING CANDAULES: Eh! Am I clever at finding you out?

GYGES: As true as I believe in God, that is not so.

KING CANDAULES: Do you believe in God?

GYGES: Certainly, yes.

KING CANDAULES: I don't, very much. You are simple,
You imagine only simple things,
But I—

The fatal idea grows stronger, and with it the debauchment of Gyges—in the name of friendship.

By this time, surely, the king's altruism must be regarded as suspect, and his friendship for Gyges a questionable motive. Two interpretations seem to me likely, and neither is pretty. Either Candaules' desire has palled (or was inadequate to begin with), and it is stimulated by his knowledge that his love-making is being watched (this is exhibitionism, or voyeurism in reverse); or else, although Candaules may desire the queen, he also desires Gyges homosexually, and this uranist love, since he may not be conscious of its nature, he interprets as the most selfless altruism. If, as I think, the latter case is the true one, then by rousing Gyges' lust for the queen and giving him the ring that makes it possible for Gyges to substitute for him, the king is, in his imagination, changing places *with his wife.* So, while he would seem to be playing pimp to her, she is, as it were, unwittingly playing bawd to her husband.

If this sounds absurd, one has only to compare it, *mutatis mutandis,* to Dostoevski's *The Eternal Husband,* which Frank O'Connor has studied as the first example in literature of what he calls "the unnatural triangle," by which he means "the eternal triangle of husband, wife, and lover, or husband, wife and mistress, *as it presents itself to the mind of the . . . adolescent and neurotic.*" [40] Neither the adolescent nor the neurotic has made the necessary emotional differentiations which maturity demands. And in the story, says O'Connor, the neurotic characters—the cuckolded husband and the lover—confuse the subject-object

---

[40] Frank O'Connor, *The Mirror in the Roadway: A Study of the Modern Novel* (New York: Knopf, 1956), pp. 206-10 *passim.*

relationship between them, "thereby confusing the emotions appropriate to it." He continues: "The woman involved seems to have nothing to do with the male characters, who merely use her as an excuse for their own performance. They seem to have no real subject-object relationship, and are treated almost as parts of one another . . . people who at an unconscious level are necessary to one another for the performance of a particular action, to such a degree that there exists between them a real homosexual attraction and that at certain moments they can exchange functions." [41]

Now in *King Candaules* this is not what actually happens— for Gyges does not reciprocate the king's homosexual love—but what the king would like to happen. Before Gide, incidentally, no other teller of the tale made it possible for Gyges to lie with the queen. And it is especially interesting to note the relevance of O'Connor's further comment on Dostoevski's novel: "This is the story to which Gide rightly attached so much importance, for it is a situation that occurs in his own work, particularly in *The Counterfeiters*. . . ." [42] If O'Connor's study had extended beyond the novel, he might well have cited Gide's play too.

In this reading King Candaules, for all his daring in transcending himself, does not and cannot come to a recognition of his error, that is, of his true motive, for his homosexuality is latent and unrecognized by him for what it is. And in this reading we find quite a different play from that with which we began. There seems to me little point in raising the question as to whether it is the play that Gide meant to write—and disguised—or whether (and this would make the dramatist resemble his character) it is the play that he unconsciously wrote. [43] It is reductive of art to assume that the artist does not know what he is doing. And

---

[41] *Ibid.* To point the similarity to Gide's plot, I have changed "women" to "woman," and substituted singular for plural pronouns accordingly. In Dostoevski's novel, this curious semi-homosexual relationship persists between husband and lover beyond the death of the first wife and into the husband's second marriage! Not so in Gide's play: Gyges—or rather Nyssia—sees to that.

[42] O'Connor cites similar situations in Proust's *Remembrance of Things Past*, James Joyce's *Exiles* and *Ulysses*, and D. H. Lawrence's *Sons and Lovers* and *Jimmy and the Desperate Woman*.

[43] Various elements of the situation were anything but foreign to Gide's own life. In 1893 in Biskra he shared with Jean-Paul Laurens the favors of a sixteen-year-old prostitute, Meriem, and later that winter discovered himself to be homosexual. See O'Brien, *Portrait*, pp. 97-102.

with Gide, devious and labyrinthine and quite deliberate as his mind and strategy and purpose are, it is especially necessary to avoid this error. Gide presents Candaules as "a man who is unable to feel the full immensity of his happiness unless he shares it with others," says his biographer, George D. Painter. "Or so he alleges in his preface; but he cannot have been unaware that the voluntary sharing of one's wife, whatever its metaphysical implications, is also a well-known form of sexual perversion." Painter adds that later Gide "was pleased to find himself anticipated by Dostoevsky (Myshkin's surrender of Nastasya to Rogozhin in *The Idiot*). . . ." [44] But if we accept the pathological interpretation, for which there are good grounds, we nonetheless encounter the Gidean doctrine which ultimately makes no distinction between natural and unnatural, holds individual desire to be the final tribunal, and sees in revolt as such the whole history of human progress. All the more reason, then, for assuming that Gide understands fully the implications of his protagonist's action.[45] And if that is so, then still more vainly do we look for the warning in the play, the antidote to the "apparent poison." Again, as in *Philoctetes*, we are dealing with the play Gide only seems to be writing, and not the one he is really writing. But to what end is all this elaborate secrecy in a play paradoxically concerned with exhibitionism? This time it is the warning or antidote (if it is such) that is plainly "apparent": Candaules' self-victimization and death; hence it is the "poison" which is now hidden beneath. One is therefore inclined to say (as Gide said in another connection) that now the problem is to find a cure for the remedy.

III. *Oedipus*

Sophocles' Oedipus blinds himself because he saw what he

[44] George D. Painter, *André Gide: A Critical and Biographical Study* (New York: Roy, 1951), p. 62. Gide's comparison of the incidents in the two works is made in his *Journal* entry of December 2, 1916.

[45] Gide himself was inclined to attribute frequent unconscious motivation to the works of Dostoevski and Oscar Wilde. This sort of approach, however, will not do, says Justin O'Brien: "But . . . Gide, except in his extreme youth, was always eminently lucid about himself. In relation to almost every aspect of his life and work, one must be suspicious of explaining anything with reference to the unintentional. Gide was conscious to the point of self-consciousness." *Portrait*, p. 275.

should not have seen; the Oedipus of André Gide blinds himself because he did not see what he should have seen. Sophocles' hero answers a question and reveals the will of the gods; Gide's hero poses questions and exalts the will of man by defying the will of the gods. Sophocles' play provided the Western world with perfect examples of a tragic hero and a type of Greek tragedy; Gide's play—what does it provide? [46]

Oedipus, which was to prove his last use of classical myth in drama, was written when he was sixty-two years old and at the height of his maturity. The seed of the play had been sown in his mind decades before; and the journal entries regarding it show not only that the Oedipus myth held a special importance for him, but also that once he had imagined the central action, it did not change. In 1911 he wrote: "It is worthy of consideration that the two most *solemn* dramas that antiquity has bequeathed to us, *Oedipus* and *Prometheus,* offer us, one the notion of good and evil, or rather of the permissible and the forbidden, in its most arbitrary terms, the other the sanction. . . ." [47] This characteristically ambiguous statement juxtaposes the Greek hero who suffered the most peculiarly horrible fate of all and the titan who successfully withstood Zeus. What if one were to transpose the heroes, while retaining the myths? A year earlier, formulating an esthetic of dramaturgy, he had wavered between the Shakespearean drama, where (he said) the character creates the event and reveals himself in its subsequent developments, and the Sophoclean and late Ibsenite drama, with Oedipus as prototype, where "the revealing event should already have taken place . . . and the drama should then furnish the progressive explanation of the event. . . ." When he finally came to write the play, he chose the latter form and had his hero advance, as he originally envisioned him doing, "from happiness in ignorance to unhappy knowledge." [48] When he was still working on *Oedipus* there occurs this entry: "How easy it is to

[46] André Gide, *Oedipe* (Paris: Gallimard, 1931). Quotations are from Gide's *Two Legends: Oedipus and Theseus,* trans. John Russell (New York: Vintage Books, 1958), pp. 3-43.

I omit consideration of *Persephone* (1933) because it is "An Opera in Three Scenes," and should therefore be judged by other than exclusively dramatic standards. In it Gide uses the myth of Persephone to stand for Communist concern for the downtrodden.

[47] Gide, *Journals,* I, 297-98 (detached pages, 1911).

[48] *Ibid.,* pp. 267-68.

work according to an esthetic and a morality already given! Writers who are submissive to a recognized religion advance with the confidence of a sure thing. I have to invent all. Sometimes it is an immense groping toward an almost imperceptible light. And sometimes I wonder: what for?" [49] Gide's self-pity is rather overdone, if one recalls that by then he had established his literary eminence, achieved an international hearing for his ideas, and—by sticking close to the myths—actually had to invent very little. Why the immense groping, when his attitudes and conclusions were by now as predictable as the ending of the Oedipus story itself? A spectator might be shocked by what he heard or saw at a performance of *Oedipus*. But he could scarcely be startled by new ideas, for there are none: it is the mixture as before, a synthesis and summation of Gide's thought for the previous forty years.

It is more likely that his difficulties arose from the fact that he was writing in a medium for which he had neither a natural flair nor, as a creator, a natural sympathy. He envied "the increased eloquence an artist owes to his faith, but also the increased receptivity on the part of the believing auditor or spectator when faced with a work of art of religious inspiration; it is the mystic communion between artist and public, which only that common belief allows." [50] Yet he had striven "deliberately to be banal, because he thinks heroics are false while banality is real"; [51] he chose to write entirely in the modern critical spirit which takes nothing for granted, to regard religion and the family as "the two worst enemies of progress"; [52] and concluded: "As for me, I want a work of art in which *nothing is granted* in advance, before which everyone remains free to protest." [53] But in the end he ceased to have respect for the theatre, in which he had repeatedly sought success but found little of it. In the last years of his life, when he was adapting *The Vatican Swindle* for the Comédie-Française, he wrote: "Decidedly, I do not like the theater; it involves too many concessions to the public, and the factitious always wins out over the authentic, adulation over

[49] Van Meter Ames, *André Gide* (Norfolk, Conn.: New Directions, 1947), p. 205.
[50] Gide, *Journals*, II, 399 (May 7, 1927).
[51] Highet, *The Classical Tradition*, p. 537.
[52] Quoted by O'Brien, *Portrait*, p. 324.
[53] Gide, *Journals*, II, 400.

sincere praise." [54] Where *Oedipus* was concerned he was entitled
to his sour grapes, for he made no concessions whatsoever.

In January, 1923, Gide attended *Antigone*, as adapted by Jean
Cocteau and performed by Charles Dullin's company at the
Vieux-Colombier. He said he "suffered unbearably from the
ultra-modern sauce in which was served up that wonderful play,
which remains beautiful more in spite of Cocteau than because
of him." Evidently he was as much, or more, put off by the
bizarre costuming and décor and the highly unusual staging as
by Cocteau's modernization of the text. And he was suspicious
of its success; for "those who applaud him are those who to begin with considered Sophocles as a great bore and who have
never drunk of 'the true, the blushful Hippocrene.'" Cocteau
had said that masterpieces had to be reworked in order to remove from them the patina of time, since it is this which hides
them from the view of later generations, so that they cannot
really see them. Gide disagreed acidly: "Patina is the reward of
masterpieces." [55]

One cannot doubt the genuineness of Gide's love of Greek
drama or his considerable feeling for it. But when he came to
use the myth of Oedipus for his own purposes, he stayed surprisingly close to the structure and incidents of Sophocles' work,
while attempting to say quite different things with it and to
quite different effect. He found also, as we shall see, that an
"ultra-modern sauce" was precisely the production style his play
required. *Oedipus* depends unwisely on one's familiarity with
the original, as it relies on one's knowledge of the myth; and
it is very difficult to imagine what its effect would be without
them. Georges Pitoëff staged the play with generalized Greek
costumes and décor and gave a performance of the title role
that Gide praised warmly: "You knew how to bring to light the
most secret feelings of a particularly complex soul. That required
so particular an understanding of my text, that I might have
despaired of finding it so soon." [56] But many spectators were
put off, as Gide confided to his journal, by the "more or less incongruous jokes," the deliberate anachronisms, and (one suspects) the difference of tone in a play that repeatedly reminded

[54] Gide, *So Be It*, p. 14.
[55] Gide, *Journals*, II, 321-22.
[56] Gide to Georges Pitoëff, December 22, 1931, quoted in the latter's *Notre
Théâtre* (Paris: Messages, 1949), p. 79 (my translation).

them of Sophocles' tragedy. Gide attributed the play's lack of success in great part to such "easy effects." [57]

But a curious thing happened when Gustave Hartung staged the play in Darmstadt. He juxtaposed columns of a Greek temple and a backdrop projection of Notre Dame de Paris, dressed the actors in "outrageously contemporary costume" over which they wore their "tragic finery," and underscored and motivated all the anachronisms of the play. The result, said Gide, was that the anachronisms "ceased to appear forced," the scenic illusion vanished, and the audience, thus prepared for the un-Greek and the nontragic, "was grateful to me for bringing them into collusion with me and understood that the interest of my play was elsewhere: in the clash of ideas, and that the drama took place on another plane from that of the ancient tragedy." [58] The "modern sauce" Gide had deplored in Cocteau's adaptation had in this instance saved the play which Gide nonetheless had repeatedly referred to as "tragic," and which did considerable violence to the patina that overlay *Oedipus Rex*.

The myth is all there, as in Sophocles; but everything has been changed—characters, tone, viewpoint, and meaning—and certain things irremediably lost—the stature of the characters, the poetry of the language, the excitement of the hunt, as well as the sense of communal crisis in a world where the divine and human intersect and explode. Sophocles condensed the fate of Oedipus into 1,530 lines of verse of extraordinary density; Gide packs his into forty pages of prose, divided into three acts. This modern version eliminates the old shepherd who exposed the infant Oedipus and who was in Laius' train when the king was killed, the other old shepherd who comes as messenger from Corinth to tell of King Polybus' death, and the messenger from the palace who narrates the suicide of Jocasta and Oedipus' self-mutilation. But it adds the king's sons, Eteocles and Polynices, invents scenes for them and their sisters, Antigone and Ismene, and includes frequent foreshadowings borrowed from *Antigone*, *The Phoenician Women*, and *Oedipus at Colonus*. Although the play is much busier than Sophocles', it seems to have less drive, and certainly less tension, than the Greek tragedy. In sum, it is far less dramatic.

[57] Gide, *Journals*, III, 234-35 (June, 1932).
[58] *Ibid.*

But if it is a play at all and not simply a *raisonnement* ("disquisition on abstract themes") or a "clash of ideas," it will have a central action; and it does. In formulating it, it will be instructive to continue the comparative method.

Francis Fergusson defined the central action of *Oedipus Rex* as "the quest for Laius' slayer," and the over-all aim of the play "to find the culprit in order to purify human life." [59] Gide's play has for its central action "the undermining of Oedipus' happiness"; the over-all aim of the play is "to destroy the happiness of Oedipus, in order that he may defy the gods by transcending himself." If this formulation is correct, it will be apparent at once that, although Gide's drama retains the Sophoclean framework, the two plays differ greatly in their basic action and their ultimate meaning. Gide's play lacks the seeking action, the excitement of the hunt—and does so to its detriment. Two-thirds of the play is given over to Tiresias' efforts to undermine the king's happiness in order to teach him the fear of God. To accomplish this, Tiresias, the priest (dressed as a friar, so that we shall not fail to realize that he represents organized religion), enlists the help of Creon and Jocasta, and even exploits the piety of Antigone by directing it against her father. Since the initiative belongs to Tiresias and since he is rendered even more important because Gide omits the two shepherds, whose stories dovetail and thus prove the fulfillment of the oracle, Oedipus is rendered relatively inactive—the more so in that he is ignorant, for much of the time, of the direction and purpose of events. He cannot be the highly volitional character his prototype is. Only when Tiresias, by shrewd questioning, induces Oedipus to point the finger of guilt at his own breast, is the king shaken enough to take the initiative and finish the hunt. When he discovers the trap the gods laid for him, he rebels and resolves to "invent some new form of unhappiness—some mad gesture to astonish you all, and astonish myself, and astonish the gods." The new form of unhappiness is self-mutilation—gouging out his eyes; thereby he succeeds in destroying what remains of his happiness. That he concurs in his own destruction is, of course, ironic— even doubly so. For he does it not in order to submit to the gods in penitence, but to defy them; and thus he not only defeats

[59] Francis Fergusson, *The Idea of a Theater* (Garden City, N.Y.: Doubleday Anchor Books, 1953), p. 48.

Tiresias' intent but also achieves renewal by transcending himself. Unlike *King Candaules*, this play has both *hamartia* and *anagnorisis*. Until Tiresias exposed him as his father's slayer, Oedipus was sunk in a twenty-year lethargy of his own happiness; despite his self-warnings, he inhabited a fool's paradise. His error lay in thinking that the sphinx, once slain, remains forever dead; whereas, it is not youth only, but all life, that is seen to be a perpetual encounter with the monster; and so the monster must be repeatedly worsted by continual reiteration of "Man" as the answer to all its questions. Tiresias' aim is to bring Oedipus to heel before the power of priestcraft (rather than to purify the communal life of Thebes)—sufficient indication that this "clash of ideas" takes place "on another plane from that of the ancient tragedy." And Oedipus' motive in blinding himself is to astonish the gods by his defiance (rather than to ratify their supremacy by punishing himself for what he has done). By rejecting happiness, Oedipus becomes the perfect exemplar of Gidean doctrine. And with this play, as well as *Philoctetes*, in mind, we can see the differences of purpose and direction between the two dramatists: away from life with others, to life for oneself; away from submission to the gods as the law of life, to assertion of the individual will as the only law that binds. The theme, differently formulated, is the same as that of *King Candaules*—and a disturbingly puritanical one it is. Happiness is a vicious trap which tricks man into false security, wastes his powers, and blinds him to his true destiny—that of a perpetual becoming through self-transcendence. Oedipus blinds himself for having failed to recognize this, not for what he has done. Gide has stood the Sophoclean version on its head.

Considered purely as plot, Sophocles' play is probably the most delicately balanced in Western dramatic literature—and Gide tampers with that balance at his peril. It is a "detective story" where the placing of clues and the order of successive revelations are vital to its equilibrium, in which the divine and the human coexist and meet. Even the removal of supposedly minor characters like the shepherds has had its effect, and much more so, the fact that this Oedipus is horrified at having slain his father but not at having married his mother and begotten children on her! This last, of course, goes beyond the intricacies of play-making: Oedipus, as a good *raisonneur*, is demonstrating

Gidean doctrine, not reacting humanly; his responses have been preconditioned. It cannot have been easy to imagine such a character. As Gilbert Highet says of Gide's treatment of the Ariadne myth: "Bad taste on Gide's level, like Nero's poetry or Gaudi's architecture, is as difficult to achieve as good taste, and is at least as rare." [60]

Gide retains the supernatural framework of Sophocles' play —the past, with its two identical prophecies that have already been fulfilled, and the plague with its oracle—and he succeeds, almost too well, as will be seen, in relegating the gods to the background. In *Oedipus Rex*, Apollo, the unseen antagonist, makes his presence felt more and more insistently, the harder the king struggles to escape his fate. Here, his place is taken and held by Tiresias, not an inspired seer but a venally human representative of priestcraft intent on maintaining his power by undermining the king's, so as to bring the latter to his knees in full submission. The supernatural diminishes as the importance of Tiresias increases. He exhibits the dishonest motives which Oedipus in the older play only imputed to him out of fear and anger. He claims to read people's thoughts at a distance, but his clairvoyance is realistically motivated as the ability to pick people's brains, read their characters, and make shrewd guesses. He has the ear of the people, in whom he instills the belief that their fate depends on that of Oedipus. "Besides," says the Chorus, "we can't help thinking that your happiness and our unhappiness are linked in some mystical way; at least, that is what Tiresias' teaching has allowed us to glimpse." Later, we hear him telling Creon: "I do not speak to you in my own name, but in the name of the God whom I represent . . . and in the name of the people, who live in terror, inferring from the scourge which now afflicts them that they are being punished for their king's incredulity. . . . You yourself, Creon, must see that it is in everyone's interest that a king should bow to a higher power to whom each and all may appeal—be it even against their king" (Act I). This interpretation discredits the gods as well as Tiresias and destroys the bond of community between king and people, making the latter a gullible herd of hypocrites motivated solely by self-interest. And so they prove to be, in one destructive strophe and antistrophe after another. Under such circumstances gran-

[60] Highet, *The Classical Tradition,* p. 537.

deur is impossible, only banality possible. For that matter, Oedipus himself is unaware of any such bond; like Candaules, he proves it by congratulating himself on his happiness, as if in complete ignorance of the plague devastating the city—and in complete unconcern: he has to be told by his children what is happening in his own kingdom.

The result is not unlike Voltaire's rationalistic version. (It will be recalled that Gide took issue with Voltaire in the matter of myth, opposing his "reason" to Voltaire's rationalism.) Francis Fergusson writes: "The critics of the Age of Reason tried to understand [the myth] as a fable of the enlightened moral will, in accordance with the philosophy of that time. Voltaire's version of the play . . . [presents] it as essentially a struggle between a strong and righteous Oedipus, and the malicious and very human gods, aided and abetted by the corrupt priest Tiresias; he makes it an antireligious tract, with an unmistakable moral to satisfy the needs of the discursive intellect." [61]

At the same time that he was seeking to diminish the force of the gods in the play, Gide blundered by introducing the idea of predestination: "This [he said] is one of the pivots of the play, but the fight of the individual against tradition, of the hero against religion, seems to me more important still and I think, more tragic. . . ." [62] The reviews of the play emphasized the opposition between free will and predestination, and Gide regretted the indiscreet emphasis he had put upon this theme. He wrote in his journal: "Perhaps if I had not raised that question at all—the hero's struggle against Tiresias, of individuality against religious ethics, might have been even more tragic; more apparent in any case. . . ." [63] But the spectre of determinism, while of no appreciable effect in the theatre (Oedipus and Thérèse Raquin seem as free beings as Sganarelle or Autolycus), threatened to diminish, if not destroy, the significance of the king's self-transcendence, as an independent action. The Oedipus who says to Tiresias, "For either your oracle was lying or I had no possible escape. I was caught," must work his way out of the corner with sarcasm: "And now am I still God's puppet? Has

[61] Fergusson, *Idea of a Theater*, p. 29. At one time, Gide planned to title his play *The Conversion of Oedipus*. See Gide, *Journals*, II, 402.
[62] Gide to Pitoëff (my translation). See above, note 56.
[63] Gide, *Journals*, III, 215-16.

the oracle foretold what I must do next? Must I still consult it? And find out, O Tiresias, what the birds have to say? . . . If only I could escape from the God who envelops me, escape from myself! Something heroic, something superhuman torments me. I should like to invent some new form of unhappiness—" (Act III). And so on.

In Sophocles' play the will of the gods is made manifest with crushing irony, the more so in that we have seen Jocasta denounce Apollo's oracle as false, immediately after praying to the god, and have seen Oedipus decide that he is the son of a god, the child of Fortune, after learning of Polybus' death. But in Gide's play Oedipus *begins* the action convinced that he is the child of Fortune; Jocasta, entirely subservient to Tiresias' wishes, does not seem very clear as to what is going on; or else she is being disingenuous. Consequently, we have much less sense of Oedipus' need to "escape from the God who envelops" him. And in eliminating the two old shepherds, whose corroborative accounts dovetail with such devastating effect, Gide has deprived us of the visible fulfillment of the gods' will. Nor has he found anything to put in its place that can begin to match the awful tension of that exchange:

SHEPHERD: Ah, I am on the brink of dreadful speech!

OEDIPUS: And I of dreadful hearing. Yet I must hear.[64]

Oedipus in Gide's version is the victim both of the gods and of men. Tiresias enlists against him his own wife and his brother-in-law Creon, and these two undergo strange transformations before Gide is done with them. Creon, not surprisingly, has become a middle-class pragmatist who thinks (like the eighteenth-century rationalists who subscribed to the theory of double-truth) that religion is all very well, good for the people, but rulers should interpret oracles to serve their own purposes. He is made the butt of the audience's ridicule so much that when he objects to the incestuous attentions which Oedipus' sons are paying to their sister Ismene, the audience is expected to find his protestations absurd. At the height of the final confrontation between Jocasta and Oedipus, he destroys the dramatic tension with his sputterings: "Well, upon my word! What's

[64] Dudley Fitts and Robert Fitzgerald, trans., *The Oedipus Rex of Sophocles* (New York: Harcourt, Brace, & World, 1949), ll. 1250-51.

that I hear? That would make my sister his mother! Oedipus, whom I thought so much of! I can't imagine anything more abominable! Not to know if he's my brother-in-law or my nephew!" (Act III). It is to him that Gide gives a much condensed version of the messenger's speech that tells of Jocasta's death and Oedipus' blinding. Risks taken in the theatre dazzle —when they come off. But it is hard to see what Gide hopes for in such "easy effects," as he calls them, although they are really uneasy mixtures of flippant satire, solemn preaching, and violence rendered incongruous by their proximity.

The treatment of Jocasta is even less credible and even more willful. *Immediately before* Oedipus' discovery of his true identity, we have this disastrously comic deflation which destroys all theatrical illusion:

OEDIPUS: If I was to have this throne, this bed, they had first to be made empty. Only the king's murder allowed me to have them. But you—you didn't know, then, that you were already free?

JOCASTA: *Dear, dear Oedipus, do not call attention to it. None of the historians has noticed yet.*

OEDIPUS: Now I see it all. You knew— The man who killed the king. . . .

JOCASTA: Stop!

OEDIPUS: The man who killed the king was I.

JOCASTA: *Not so loud!* (Act III)

Now the myth of Oedipus is not sacrosanct; neither is the tragedy of Sophocles. A satyr play on the subject might be very funny, and the tragedy would of course survive burlesquing. If Gide's method is serious, in the sense of purposeful, it is hard to see what the purpose can be, *except to degrade the attitudes and values implicit in the tragedy*, the better to further the Gidean views it is made to carry in this version. One is reminded of Voltaire's rationalist exclamation, when he examined the myth: "Why, then! this Oedipus is an ass!"

I suppose one should admire, perhaps even esteem, such calculated dissonance, such restless experimentation with both tragedy and parody of that tragedy in the same work, through the use of discontinuous effects that anticipate absurdist techniques. Yet, again it is Gide wishing to have it both ways; and it would look better coming from a dramatist who had learned to transfer a semblance of felt life to the stage and had succeeded in creating at least one living character. It is one thing to make your characters serve the art-work and quite another to make the art-work fit the Procrustean bed of a programmatic thesis. Once more, the play is better understood as a *piece à clef* than as an autonomous drama—as shown by the example of its determinism, "that obvious conflict which tormented me greatly in my youth, but which long ago ceased to disturb me. . . ." [65] Or it is shown by the fact that it was the extreme puritanism of his upbringing that led to his equally extreme revolt as an immoralist—neatly condensed here in the Gidean irony that it is not Oedipus, but the meddling Tiresias who precipitates the discovery of the king's identity by regarding his "untroubled happiness" as blasphemous and seeking to "start a little crack in that happiness." (This anticlerical twist is an original contribution to the myth; but the play leaves us wondering how much difference there is, in the end, between Tiresias, who holds that people should seek salvation, not happiness, and Gide-Oedipus, who longs to astonish the gods by achieving his own salvation through the invention of some "new form of unhappiness.")

It is also shown by the lengthy demonstrations of the effects of Gidean doctrine on his disciples (here represented as Eteocles and Polynices), who have, as Oedipus says in repudiating them, "picked out from my example merely what flatters them—authority and license—and let slip what is best and most difficult—self-discipline." These scenes, however distasteful, [66] *are* related to the play, although more so thematically than dramaturgically. They are discussed below.

Because Gide is maneuvering puppets instead of dramatizing life (he is always moralistically telling us what must be done to life, instead of showing us what life does), the characters are curiously numb or indifferent to normal human reactions; and none suffers from this more than Jocasta. She is revealed, finally,

---

[65] Gide, *Journals*, III, 215.

[66] "André Gide stands apart from all the others [the neo-Hellenic playwrights of France] as an inventor of repulsive new episodes and vicious motives. For more than two thousand years men have rehearsed the awful history of the Labdacids; but Gide was the first to suggest that the sons born of Oedipus' unknowing incest were deliberately (and not without success) trying to seduce their sisters." Highet, *The Classical Tradition*, p. 536.

as a woman with a past who has become a model of church-going respectability (a not incredible type). She took Oedipus as her husband before ever learning of Laius' death. (This is how Gide interprets lines 755-65 of Sophocles' play.) And she pleads faulty memory whenever he asks any touchy questions about that time. She is quite willing that Tiresias should force Oedipus to submit, yet she laments that Oedipus insisted upon knowing the truth and thus foiled her efforts to protect their happiness. Gide has cast a great deal of confusion over her knowledge and, consequently, over her motives. She is represented as having known a great deal—perhaps all—about the king's murder of Laius, and as so devious in other respects that one begins to suspect that she also knows Oedipus to be her son. Her sincerity is rendered so suspect that we begin to doubt it in everything but her love for Oedipus. And, for all her religiosity, she shows the same kind of moral numbness toward incest as does Oedipus himself. When the discovery is made, she is not horrified, but rather simply concerned to hide the truth:

JOCASTA: Why make public what may still be our own secret? Nobody would have guessed. It's not yet too late. People have forgotten the crime. So far from hindering your happiness, it has made it possible. Nothing has changed (Act III).

When Oedipus rushes into the palace, intent on astonishing the gods, Gide gives her an exit speech containing more of the same. Only at its very end does she strike a note of authentic grief. But it so jars against what has preceded that the already incredulous spectator must be the more confused:

JOCASTA: O unhappy Oedipus! Why did you have to know? I did what I could to stop you from tearing aside the veil that protected our happiness. Now that you have repulsed me, left me hideously exposed, how can I dare to reappear before you, before our children, before the people whom I hear approaching? . . . If only I could turn back and undo what was done—forget our shameful bed and face the dead who await me as the wife of Laius alone, whom I long to rejoin! . . . (Act III).

I propose that the key to the play lies in this idea: *the past regarded as incest*. Incest is the central circumstance of Oedipus' fate, as it is the central image of the play. That is why Gide thrusts to the fore the children, issue of an incestuous union for which Oedipus holds the gods responsible and why he shows the brothers attempting to seduce their sister. Yet Gide, while emphasizing it far beyond anything in Sophocles' play, deliberately tries to drain the literal fact of all its horrors and to project that horror upon other things. Thus, the source of shock and confusion which the play produces is traceable to the fact that Gide has subjected the *myth* to a transvaluation of all the ethical values found in *Sophocles' tragedy*. If this is kept in mind, Gide's play makes more sense or at least becomes clearer. But to do so, one must regard actual incest almost as morally indifferent; and instead, attach *to the past*, i.e, to tradition, religion, family, community, and happiness, all the physical and moral abhorrence normally attached to *incest*. (Gide permits us still to consider murder reprehensible.) In Sophocles it is the past erupting into the present that brings about the tragedy. In Gide, the past is the enemy, personified by all those about Oedipus who live by values and moral imperatives different from his and who wish to bind him to them. Man looks to the past to find out who he is, just as Oedipus sets out, after hearing the fortune-teller's prophecy, to question the oracle about his identity. But after he killed Laius he turned off, instead, and took the road to Thebes and the Sphinx. In Gide's play he wished to find out what there was in him that he did *not* owe to his forefathers, he wished to take after nobody but himself; and so he decided that "To know nothing of one's parents is a summons to excel." He tells his sons not to look to yesterday for approval and advice. He warns them mildly that they must respect their sisters, because "The conquest of what lies too close at hand can never be very profitable. To grow up, one must look far beyond oneself." Whatever the goal is, it lies ahead—in the future. Gide himself approves this assertion of independence, for it sunders the past at one stroke and leaves a man free of all fetters: "Ah, my whole soul longs for that 'nomadic state' in which man, without hearth or home, will no more localize his duty or his affection than his happiness on such creatures. . . . Endless broadening of the object of love as soon as the family is negated." [67] When Creon exclaims about the revelation of incest, Oedipus' answer is simply: "Why bother my head with such problems? If my sons are also my brothers, I shall love them the better for it." His children

[67] Gide, *Journals*, I, 78-79.

are not the past—but Jocasta is: "And for me, who congratulated myself on not knowing my parents! Thanks to which I married my mother—alas! alas!—and with her all my past. I see now why my valor slumbered. In vain did the future call to me. Jocasta drew me backward—Jocasta, who tried in her madness to suppress what had to be, whom I loved as a husband and, all unwittingly, as a son. . . . Now it is time. Leave me! I am breaking the cord that binds us. . . ." For Oedipus, to return as a man to his mother's womb was to return to the past. In Sophocles the king unwittingly commits the sins of parricide and incest; in Gide the king unwittingly commits the sin of *returning to the past*.[68] This was the horror the gods had in store for him.

Yet on January 15, 1931, Gide noted in his journal that he had attended a rehearsal of a Japanese *No* drama which his longtime friend, Jacques Copeau, had been rehearsing. Speaking of his friend, Gide said: "He frightens me when he declares that he was never closer to achieving his aim than in the Japanese *No* drama he was putting on, which an accident prevented him from presenting to the public, and of which I saw the last rehearsals. . . . A play without any relation to our traditions, our customs, our beliefs. . . ."[69] Traditions? Customs? Beliefs? Can this be Gide speaking—and sounding for all the world like that eternal bourgeois, the French conservative, Monsieur Prudhomme? Then one remembers that he is talking about art, not life, which, for Gide, seems to make all the difference.

---

[68] "Whoever starts out toward the unknown must consent to venture alone. Creusa, Eurydice, Ariadne, always a woman tarries, worries, fears to let go and see the thread break that ties her to her past. She pulls Theseus back and makes Orpheus look back. She is afraid." Gide, *Journals*, II, 403.
[69] *Ibid.*, III, 139.

CHAPTER III

JEAN COCTEAU:
Divine Poetry and the Infernal Gods

I shall teach that the need of a change in art is nothing other than the need of finding a fresh place on the pillow. Put your hand on the fresh spot, it soon ceases to be so; newness is freshness. The need for novelty is the need for freshness. God is the only freshness that does not grow warm.[1]

When Jean Cocteau wrote these words to Jacques Maritain in 1925, he had already been conducting for more than fifteen years a protean revolt against nineteenth-century art—a revolt aimed at poetry, the novel, criticism, drama, theatre, ballet, music, and painting. My primary concerns here are his use of classical myth in drama and the relation of religion to art in his general esthetic; but they cannot be considered apart from his theory of the theatre.

For nearly half a century Cocteau was a leader in the French theatre, which, at the time of World War I, he set out consciously to save. His program was to formulate and practice a theory of the theatre which, for a time and in distinctly individual fashion, placed him in the forefront of the movement known as

[1] Jean Cocteau, *Art and Faith: Letters Between Jacques Maritain and Jean Cocteau*, trans. John Coleman (New York: Philosophical Library, 1948), pp. 65-66.

theatricalism. Pre-war drama, regardless of whether it took its impulse from the naturalism of André Antoine or the symbolism of Paul Fort and Maurice Maeterlinck, had become in his eyes "literary" and stale by divorcing itself from the arts of the theatre. He considered Antoine's realistic staging, with its addiction to the use of real-life objects, "nothing but an old photograph album." [2] The innovations of naturalism had "concentrated on superficial and basically unimportant things." [3] Cocteau held that "it is not a question of living on the stage, but of making the stage live. This reality of the theatre is the poetry of the theatre and is truer than truth." [4] This maxim is, of course, unexceptionable; it does not prescribe the method by which poetry is to be achieved, and is therefore broad enough to encompass any style of stage presentation, realism included. By the same token, it really does not justify Cocteau's theatre as the only kind to achieve it.

The phrase "poetry of the theatre" or "theatre poetry" is probably Cocteau's best-known and most influential slogan. It is anti-literary, refusing to see drama as a literary form, and regarding it instead only as an element of theatre, one part of a whole which is performance. This is the basis for his attack on symbolist drama, which he viewed as literary and, in the bad sense, "poetic." In the popular mind, said Cocteau, the "poetic" stands for all that is soft, imprecise, fuzzy, and vague. The public must no longer be indulged in this corrupt taste; it must be exposed to the truly poetic—that is, to just the opposite of what it liked and expected. Real poetry was hard, sharp, precise, and direct-hitting. Cocteau is a poet who began by hating the "poetic."

Since his ambition was to create "a beauty which can come to life only on the stage," [5] this meant throwing out dramatic literature, regarded as an all-important text to be mounted and animated by performance. Like Gaston Baty, like others at the same time in Germany and England as well as France, Cocteau rejected "Sire le Mot" ("The Word Omnipotent") in favor of the

[2] Jean Cocteau, *A Call to Order* (London: Faber & Gwyer, 1926), p. 8.
[3] Margaret Crosland, *Jean Cocteau* (London: Peter Nevill, 1955), p. 135.
[4] Jean Cocteau, *Orphée: A Tragedy in One Act and an Interval*, trans. Carl Wildman (London: Oxford University Press, 1933). Quoted in translator's Preface, p. v.
[5] Jean Cocteau, *Théâtre*, I (Paris: Gallimard, 1948), 37.

fullest possible exploitation of theatrical resources. The theatre was to be saved by renewing *all* the elements proper to it, and dialogue must therefore be regarded as merely one of its aural elements; for if a new form was to emerge, dialogue must be combined with dance, acrobatics, pantomime, décor, music, and sound effects. When these combinations were freshly made, poetry would result; but it would be *plastic*, not merely verbal.[6]

This implied more than the subordination of dialogue and a greater emphasis on the visual and other aural elements of the theatre. Cocteau's conclusion was that poetry, i.e., verse, does not belong in the theatre. It was a question of perspective: "Poetry in the theatre is a delicate lace impossible to see at a distance. The poetry of the theatre ought to be a coarser lace, a lace made of rigging, a ship at sea."[7] It is one thing to refuse to give language primacy in the theatre; it is quite another to fly in the face of theatrical history by denying that dramatic poetry has, as T. S. Eliot pointed out, proved very durable indeed. Cocteau had obviously overstated his case in laying down "the rules of the game," and he lived to reverse himself and change them. But he wished no word or gesture to be lost on the spectator, as might well happen where dramatic poetry bore the major burden of creating the theatrical experience. And so he wrote: "Every 'Long live So-and-So' involves a 'Down with So-and-So' or be convicted of eclecticism."[8] By 1943, when he had developed his policy of "traditional anarchy" into "successive sincerities," he could reverse himself with equanimity because circumstances had changed. "Is tragedy dead?" he asked. "Then long live tragedy! For many years I fondled this dream: to write a tragedy in verse."[9] At last he felt equipped for what he now regarded as "the great enterprise." He wrote *Renaud et Armide*, a Racinian tragedy in classical alexandrines, and saw himself as saving the French theatre all over again.

Cocteau's aim was to make drama *concrete*; his subordination of dialogue had interesting consequences, the first of which was

[6] Preface, *Les Mariés de la Tour Eiffel*, in Cocteau, *Théâtre*, Vol. I. For an English version of this, trans. Joseph M. Bernstein, see Toby Cole, ed., *Playwrights on Playwriting* (New York: Hill & Wang Dramabooks, 1960), pp. 240-46.
[7] Cocteau, *Théâtre*, I, 45.
[8] Cocteau, *A Call to Order*, p. 8.
[9] Preface, *Renaud et Armide*, in Cocteau, *Théâtre*, II, 215.

to transfer to the plot and the settings those figurative and imaginative functions usually performed by language.[10] This kept the dialogue hard, spare, and functional. It also raised to first importance the *story* of the play and viewed it as events or externalized action. The form of such a structure tended to be linear and episodic, rather than concentrated. From *Parade* (1919) to *Orphée* (1926), says J. J. Khim, the playwright's search was for an objectified drama, one stripped of "ses longues et ses brèves"; in *Les Mariés* he was close to achieving "un théâtre de *montrer pur*," where all is shown rather than related.[11]

Such externalized action has its limits. Beyond a certain point, it is neither possible nor desirable to present things by means of dramatic picturization. If total dramatization, in the strict sense of the word, were possible by visual means alone, if it could present all themes at all levels and with all degrees of complexity, then pantomime would long ago have became a major, autonomous art-form—which it has never done. Obviously, such drama would be deprived of some of its richest effects, for example, contrast between word and deed, and, most important of all, the particular dramatic force of implication. Khim, a fervid admirer of Cocteau, admits that the reduction of drama in this way quickly reaches what he calls "a border-line position" on the frontiers of drama. It is as limiting as it is extreme.

Except in ballet proper, however, Cocteau never dispensed completely with dramatic dialogue. Indeed, the development of his playwriting shows him placing more and more emphasis on dialogue, a fact which is strikingly evident in *The Infernal Machine* (1934). His early efforts to render the fat from drama, so to speak, and leave only its meat, made for a drama stripped of prolixity and almost all verbal ornamentation. In one sense, to reduce the amount of dialogue is to increase its importance. "To suppress ornamentation in this way," says Khim, "is to demand that not a syllable of the text, gestures or staging be missed by the spectator." [12]

Cocteau undertook these reductive experiments in adapting

[10] Jean-Jacques Khim, *Jean Cocteau*. La Bibliothèque idéale (Paris: Gallimard, 1960), p. 119. Khim notes that Cocteau also transfers the metaphors one would expect in his poetry to his *poésie-critique*.
[11] *Ibid.*, pp. 84-87. Khim sees affinities to the "epic" form of Bert Brecht.
[12] *Ibid.*

three dramatic masterpieces: Shakespeare's *Romeo and Juliet* (1924), Sophocles' *Antigone* (1922), and *Oedipus Rex* (published 1928). *Antigone* is discussed later in some detail, as are the treatments of the Oedipus theme. Here it will suffice to point out some results of his double search for simplicity and novelty, his attempts to restore freshness to dramatic classics by "removing their patina." First, externalizing the action led him to omit transitions and to telescope slow developments, making for abrupt transitions and changes of pace. Second, character as well as dialogue was necessarily subordinated to event. Cocteau was not interested in the psychologizing of character that had marked the development of realism; it led to interiorization, to what he called "invisible" theatre. Consequently the best kind of character-drawing for his purposes would be simple and conventionalized, like types and humors, but it could utilize modern psychological *concepts*. Last, myth attracted him, perhaps as offering dramatic elements in just about the proportion he wished. It was nearly independent of the world; it had clarity of outline, simplicity, and also an inviting profundity; it was older than the theatre itself, yet it offered novelty. In short, the poetry of myth was in its action. It was externalized, it could be shown. Of his adaptation of Shakespeare, Cocteau had said: "I wanted to operate upon a drama of Shakespeare, to find the skeleton beneath the ornaments. I therefore chose the most ornate, the most beribboned one." [13] Cocteau was drawn to myth, with its skeleton or structure already showing, because it is the kind of story that can be written on the back of a postcard.[14] Speaking of Cocteau's theory of the theatre, Carl Wildman said: ". . . to realize the full possibilities of the theatre as a medium for poets, the most likely field is that of plays based on known themes, mythological, legendary, religious, or historical, which lend themselves to stage-conventions, the mood of the age, and the fantasy of the poet. This is Cocteau's way. This has been the way of producers of dramatic poetry in all ages." [15]

We shall be able to trace three stages in Cocteau's use of

[13] Cocteau, *Théâtre*, I, 36.
[14] Frank O'Connor, *The Art of the Theatre* (Dublin: Maurice Fridburg, 1947), p. 14.
[15] Jean Cocteau, *The Infernal Machine: A Play in Four Acts*, English version and introductory essay by Carl Wildman (London: Oxford University Press, 1936), translator's Preface, p. xvi.

myth by examining his adaptation of *Antigone*, his dramatization of the Orpheus myth, and his treatment of the Oedipus myth in *The Infernal Machine*, where he combines original writing and a condensed version of the Sophoclean tragedy.

I. *Antigone*

Antigone was an attempt to present Greek tragedy "as seen from the air, a kind of bird's-eye-view" of Sophocles' play that would be appropriate to the modern age of the airplane and speed. Cocteau preserved the integrity of the text much better than he had done in stripping Shakespeare of ornamentation. The play proved to be both dramatic and theatrically effective, and its conception and stage realization illustrate some of the tenets of Cocteau's theatricalism in practice.

The language is terse, colloquial. The Chorus consists of a single voice issuing from a hole in the center of the scenery, as if from a megaphone or microphone; it speaks "very loudly and quickly as if reading a newspaper article." (For the revival of 1927, we read, "five monumental plaster heads of young men framed the chorus," [16] perhaps in order to focus the gaze of the audience when the Chorus spoke to an empty stage.) "The actors wore transparent masks after the fashion of fencing-baskets; beneath the masks one could make out the actors' faces, and ethereal features were sewn on to the masks in white millinery wire." The actors wore their costumes over black bathing-dress. "The general effect was suggestive of a sordid carnival of kings, a family of insects." [17] In the *agon* between Antigone and Creon, Cocteau's stage direction calls for them to "stand close together as they speak to each other. Their foreheads touch." [18]

What explanation is there for this bizarre conception? People seen from a tall building, or from a plane flying low, look like insects; and insects, when they communicate, put their heads together. But an audience in the theatre also sees the actors at closer range. And here they see formalized features on the actors' masks, with the actors' own features visible underneath. It is as if the characters were being viewed from two angles at

[16] Jean Cocteau, *Antigone*, in Eric Bentley, ed., *The Play: A Critical Anthology* (New York: Prentice-Hall, 1951), p. 495.
[17] *Ibid.*, p. 495.
[18] *Ibid.*, p. 501.

once, one of them a distancing angle, or were presenting simultaneous views such as are to be found in the paintings of
Cocteau's close friend and collaborator, Picasso. The patina of
time, says Cocteau, blinds us to the reality in Sophocles' play.
If we are to see it freshly once more, we must see it under a
startling guise. He provides this by substituting colloquial prose
for verse, by making the Chorus a disembodied voice, by presenting the human characters as a carnival of insects.

He employed a further device. The tragic conflict unrolled at
high speed. Claude Mauriac thinks Cocteau used the effect of
speed deliberately as a means of evoking a sense of the supernatural. He noted that everything happens all of a breath, and
that the play has such a rhythm that it skips "all the intermediate
links that connect human actions in ordinary life," thereby abolishing realistic acting: "Gestures and the essential decisions stand
out in relief and spring from one another with a rapidity that
tends toward immobility by its very excess. No doubt Cocteau
would have liked to contract this drama of fraternal love to a
moment of time, not to the mere forty minutes that the performance lasts; but by his pains he contracted it to the limit of
the possible, and the rhythm in which the playing of Dullin's
troupe swept along, accelerated it further." [19]

The play moves toward immobility through extreme rapidity,
the actor is dehumanized, and a sense of the supernatural is
evoked, as if the action occurred in a moment of time. His subsequent treatments of myth retain and vary these characteristics.

In attacking Symbolist drama, Cocteau objected not only to
its use of the "poetic" in a bad sense but also to its reliance on
the thing which gave it its distinguishing feature: symbol. The
theatre, like a poem, was no place for symbols: it was a place
to show things directly. Under its magical illusion, a thing shown
became real; it did not have to be alluded to. A symbol stood for
something else. But the thing shown needed no meaning beyond
itself: it should not mean but be.

He had, to his annoyance, already encountered what he called
the favorite phrase of the public: "I don't see what that's meant
to be." "The public," he said, "wants to understand first and feel
afterwards." He wished the public to feel first—and not look for

[19] Claude Mauriac, *Jean Cocteau: ou, La Verité du mensonge* (Paris: Odette
Lieutier, 1945), p. 127.

symbols. In 1954, more than a quarter of a century later, when he was engaged in writing and producing motion pictures, he still complained of the public's appetite for symbols: "A film is expected to prove something, to convey a *message*." What the public is least prepared to accept is the principle, the fact, of "gratuitousness" in art. His use of the term is different from Gide's, for whom it denoted at first the absence of psychological motivation for an act, and later the irrational or subconscious part of the psyche. For Cocteau, "gratuitousness" is a quality of beauty, the charm of which lies in its unexpectedness; it is to be accepted and enjoyed, not subjected to reason. "It [the public] wants a meaning for everything. Especially for those things whose beauty consists in not having any. People symbolize through passion for logic. For lack of any direct meaning, they make up indirect ones, and reassure themselves by using symbols." [20]

His refusal to admit that his plays contain symbols forced Cocteau into repeated word-juggling. There is a pattern of recurrences in them, however, that is remarkable. If we may not call these recurrences "symbols," they nonetheless make up a theme—"the death-and-resurrection theme." [21] In *Le Boeuf sur le toit* the Policeman is decapitated by an electric fan but eventually recovers his head. In *Les Mariés de la Tour Eiffel* the general is devoured by a lion but reappears to rejoin the wedding party. In *Orphée* the Bacchantes dismember the hero and his head bounces into the room, complaining of his fate; but Orphée is reunited with his Eurydice. In the earlier entertainments and plays, these deaths and rebirths have about them something of the inconsequence of farce, the impersonal perfunctoriness of those to be found in ritual combats or mummers' plays, where they are believed by some anthropologists to relate to vegetative rites or seasonal changes involving the fertility of man and nature. In *The Infernal Machine* the Sphinx dies in her human form and reappears as a goddess, Nemesis; then Oedipus "dies" as a man, to emerge glorified in myth. In *The Knights of*

[20] Jean Cocteau, *Cocteau on the Film: A Conversation Recorded by André Fraigneau* (New York: Roy, 1954), p. 126.
[21] For a discussion of "how much of an obsession the themes of enchantment and its magic, of metamorphosis, of substitution have become for Cocteau," see Jean Boorsch, "The Use of Myths in Cocteau's Theatre," *Yale French Studies*, III, no. 1 (Fall, 1949), 80.

the Round Table Lancelot and Queen Guinevere die, to "return" in their children, Blandine and Sagramore. In *Beauty and the Beast*, of course, the dying Beast is transformed into the handsome Prince. (In *Les Parents Terribles* and *Bacchus*, where realism requires strict plausibility, there is death without resurrection. Hans in *Bacchus* is obviously a ritual victim, but we have no reason to believe that his death renews the community in any way.) All are symbols of renewal, for the idea of renewal is crucial to Cocteau as an artist, to his revolt against a "corrupt" theatre, to his conception of life seen and experienced anew through the freshening power of poetry.

We might, perhaps, call them "stage symbols," not literary symbols, since we see them and do not need to be told about them. Cocteau would say we do not need to conceptualize what we can see. Whatever they may be, he cannot avoid them. And so he can at least explain them, as he does in *The Infernal Machine* and *The Knights of the Round Table*. Perhaps a symbol explained ceases to be one; or perhaps it becomes a "commonplace," like the dove in *Orphée* that represents Eurydice's soul. In any case, we in the audience ought not to analyze it, but simply experience it.

If we find the idea of such "gratuitousness" hard to accept, Cocteau can cite, for example, the transformation in *Beauty and the Beast*, to show us what is a correct response. In pure fairy tale, we, like the poet, accept the marvelous without question. This is to become as a little child, for a child enjoys the action *for its own sake*; he does not "ask what it means." Thus, according to Cocteau, the child responds directly and instinctively to the poetry. This is what he would like the audience to do; but, alas! audiences are corrupt, as the theatre is corrupt: "In the theatre men rediscover the ferocity of children, but they have lost their clairvoyance." [22] André Maurois referred to this in replying to Cocteau's reception address, on the occasion of the latter's election to the Académie Française: "You surround Death with motorcyclists, like those of the prefect of Police; you replace the judges of Hell with bureaucrats in gowns; you receive in code, by radio, messages from the beyond. You obtain in this way some effects of sovereign and secret beauty, that only great works of art produce. They cannot be explained; they

[22] Cocteau, *A Call to Order*, p. 24.

signify simply by their presence. . . . Be reassured, sir; your mysteries remain opaque and you are saved." [23] If Cocteau turned to myth as a way of avoiding symbol, he had recourse to the very thing he sought to escape, for myths are powerful symbols of human experience, concretized in action.

Cocteau has little to say about myth in his *poésie critique*, despite his early use of it. With one exception, the first explicit reference I have found does not occur until 1953, but it indicates that his love of myth dated at least from the early days of his association with Guillaume Apollinaire, whose *The Breasts of Tiresias*, produced the same year as *Parade*, was written many years before.[24] He was probably indebted to Gide, although it would be difficult to assess that debt. Each writer was uncomfortably conscious of the other's presence, and each irritably denied the other's influence.[25] In any case Cocteau was what Gide never succeeded in becoming: a man of the theatre and a successful dramatist; and if he profited from his elder's pioneering efforts—and he could scarcely avoid it—he did so less by following up the psychological clue than by taking Gide's general hint as to the *freshness* to be found in myth as material for drama.

Cocteau was always sensitive to the currents of his time, among which was, in many quarters, a renewed interest in myth. But deeper than any of these influences, I suspect, are his childhood and his love of theatrical illusion. Cocteau had a passion for the theatre long before he was old enough to attend the "matinées classiques" and Sunday performances at the Comédie-Française, where myth was preserved in the masterpieces of Corneille and Racine. But it was Offenbach, the master of light opera, who provided him with what was to become the central myth in all his writings—the myth of Orpheus. One has only to read his grateful tribute to Offenbach, written some years before *Orphée*, to perceive his debt to him. It reads in part: "The spirit of poetry with its accompanying spirit of death, is not only to be found in works of a sad, but also those of a most frivolous nature. But with perfect poets you will find both moods are

[23] André Maurois, *Discours de Réceptions de M. Jean Cocteau* (Paris: Gallimard, 1955), p. 110.
[24] See Jean Cocteau, *Journal d'un inconnu* (Paris: Grasset, 1953), pp. 143-44. His *Mythologie* (1934) is a poem.
[25] Their quarrels belong among the *longueurs* of French literary history.

intertwined like initials carved in the bark of a tree. We may mention straightaway the name of a master of *genre*, the very name which is diminutive: Offenbach. . . . We cannot help giving very high rank to certain [of his] 'operettas'. . . ." [26] The tribute continues with a specific mention of *Orpheus in the Underworld*, "the faded brilliance of which may appeal to a bad conductor of poetry; whereas a good conductor will feel as if he were having old wounds re-opened."

Cocteau's early approach to the poetry of the theatre seems to have been through the decisive influence in his childhood of the world of faëry, which in his case included the ancient myths. With their unquestioning acceptance of the puzzling and mysterious, they seemed to promise a way to short-circuit intellection and appeal directly to the sub-rational, the instinctive emotions of the audience. The myths belonged in the theatre, for theatre was enchantment, to which audiences responded under collective hypnosis. [27]

II. *Orphée*

Orphée is both Cocteau's first original drama and his first independent move toward theatricalist drama, developed according to the dictates of his manifesto. It was written in a period of religious enthusiasm, for he had announced his reconversion to Roman Catholicism in October, 1925, in the letter to Maritain quoted at the head of this chapter; and he tended at the time to confuse, if not actually to equate, poetry and religion. He told Maritain that he longed for a time when "Beauty would gradually become goodness, masterpieces acts from the heart, genius would become sanctity." [28] His enthusiasm had prompted him to write a play on a Biblical theme, but it came to nothing, and in its place *Orphée* was born (1926):

My play *Orpheus* was originally to have been a tale of Joseph and the Virgin, the tittle-tattle they suffered through the activities of the Angel (a carpenter's assistant), the spite of Nazareth about an inexplicable pregnancy, and the way that spite forced the couple to flee the place.

[26] Cocteau, *A Call to Order*, pp. 165-66.
[27] Jean Cocteau, *The Typewriter*, trans. Ronald Duncan (London: Dennis Dobson, 1947), Preface, pp. 5-6.
[28] Cocteau, *Art and Faith*, p. 55.

This plot lent itself to so many misunderstandings that I gave it up. In its place I took the Orphic theme, in which the place of the birth of the divine infant is taken by the inexplicable birth of poetry.[29]

The incident was prophetic. Religion vanishes, to be replaced by a supernatural world that is increasingly of Cocteau's own imagining. The Biblical theme gives way to two themes which in his mind have become one, and a perennial preoccupation with him: the poet and death. The Christian ethos evaporates, to be succeeded both in the plays and in his *poésie-critique* by an esthetic that finally looks like irresponsibility. Cocteau adapted the Orphic myth a second time in transferring it to the screen twenty-five years later; and since in the later version, he retained elements of the original and mixed them with themes from *The Infernal Machine*, we can follow its mutations and his.[30]

The author styles the play *Orphée* a "tragedy in one act and an interval"; his translator calls it a meditation on death that has an "air of happy inconsequence." [31] Written to be staged in modern dress and pointedly unrealistic scenery, it is quite un-Greek in its treatment. As directed by Georges Pitoëff, it was Cocteau's first definite success, and his best integration thus far of drama and theatre. Here was "acted poetry" in "simple language," allegedly devoid of the despised symbolism.[32] Cocteau's specifications for setting, business, and special effects are full and rigid; they must all come off as planned, or the play will not come to life on the stage as the author has conceived it, and the poetry of the theatre will misfire. If adults found it puzzling at times or were not sure what emotions it called for, children responded to it with delight.

As an example of the unusual effects Cocteau hoped to bring off, we may cite one that was particularly successful—the "interval" in this one-act play, which involves the playwright's preoccupation with time. In one of his best-known aphorisms, Cocteau had defined subtlety as "a very simple way of saying

[29] Jean Cocteau, *The Hand of a Stranger (Journal d'un inconnu)*, trans. Alec Brown (London: Elek, 1956; New York: Horizon Press, 1959), p. 31.
[30] The film *Orphée* (Paris: Éditions André Bonne, 1950).
[31] Cocteau, *Orphée*, p. vi.
[32] *Ibid.*, p. x.

something complicated."[33] The complicated thing he had to do was to suggest the relativity of time, giving one rhythm to life in the world and another to life in the Underworld. But his means were truly "very simple" and calculated to impress the dullest in the audience:

The play was announced thus: "Tragedy in one act and an interval". This *interval* is of considerable importance. It occurs just after *Orphée* has plunged through the mirror to find the path to hell. A brief fall of the curtain marks it and two scenes link it which are repeated word for word. A few insignificant phrases, but their exact repetition, their symmetry, are terrifying. We are seized with anguish, precisely as the author intended. He had to make us understand that time was changing its rhythm for Orphée, that between his time and ours there was no longer a common measure. . . . The dialogue exchanged before his departure thus took on its full meaning. . . . In this way Cocteau was making us experience the mystery physically.[34]

Cocteau contrasts his methods with those of his predecessors thus: ". . . What our masters did was to conceal the object under their poetry. . . . What we have to do henceforward is to conceal poetry under the object. That is why I suggest setting traps, quite ordinary ones, for poetry. Who would guess that love, death, and poetry live in that simple object over there?"[35]

Let us retrace our steps for a moment, to examine the background of the play. The myth of Orpheus recounts the life of "the most famous poet and musician who ever lived." He was both a priest of Apollo whose severed head uttered oracles after he was torn to pieces by Maenads because he neglected to honor Dionysus, and the husband of Eurydice, whom he earlier rescued from Hades by the power of his lyre but then lost, because he disobeyed Hades' command and looked back, before they had completed their return to earth, to see whether she was still with him.[36]

The episode of Eurydice thus gives us the sad tale of lovers separated by death, despite the temporary power of poetry and music to suspend its rule. Cocteau combines this segment of the myth with that of Orpheus' death and creates a one-act "tragedy"

[33] Cocteau, *A Call to Order*, p. 115.
[34] Mauriac, *Jean Cocteau*, pp. 127-28.
[35] Cocteau, *A Call to Order*, p. 207.
[36] For the main accounts and variants, see Robert Graves, *The Greek Myths*, I (Baltimore: Penguin Books, 1955), 112-15.

in which the dead lovers are at last joyfully reunited in a heaven of poetry.

"Do we know what is poetic and what is not poetic?" Orphée asks Eurydice at the beginning of the play. His irritated question is Cocteau's warning that he intends to find poetry in surprising ways, such as the interval already described, and in unexpected places. By the time the question is asked, he has already plunged his audience into a strange world that represents both ancient Thrace and a modern city. Orphée, rich and famous, the high priest of Apollo and the "official" poet of Thrace, fears that his life has begun to "stink of success and death." He is infatuated with a mysterious talking horse that taps out messages which Orphée regards as unalloyed poetry. These shock tactics are deliberate: Orphée speaks for Cocteau when he says, "We must throw a bombshell and make a sensation. We must have a storm to clear the air. We are suffocating. We can no longer breathe." [37]

The message that proves prophetic and also brings about the catastrophe is one which Orphée considers "a poem of vision, a flower deep-rooted in death." It reads: "Madame Eurydice Reviendra Des Enfers." When Orphée submits it as his entry in the Thracian poetry competition, his enemy, Aglaonice, leader of the Bacchantes, discovers that it contains as an acrostic the insulting vulgarism *merde*; she uses this as a pretext for the Bacchantes' fatal attack on Orphée. These messages indicate that the action is saturated with the supernatural. Whence do they come? From the horse? No, says Orphée: "Neither he, nor I, nor anyone else. What do we know? Who is speaking? We are knocking against each other in the dark; we are up to our necks in the supernatural. We are playing hide-and-seek with the gods. We know nothing, absolutely nothing." [38] We are to be shown darkness at noon. The journey to the Underworld is to begin and end in this pedestrian apartment, which will later become transfigured as Heaven itself.

Orphée feels that his life now has renewed purpose: "I am discovering a new world. I am living again, I am stalking the

---

[37] Cocteau, *Orphée*, p. 7. ". . . for the great dramatists of the late nineteenth century a play was a bomb to drop on the respectable middle classes." Eric Bentley, ed., *The Modern Theatre*, VI (Garden City, N.Y.: Doubleday Anchor Books, 1960), 286.

[38] Cocteau, *Orphée*, p. 6.

unknown." But this high priest of Apollo is betraying his true source of inspiration. He used to sing the praises of the sun and to abominate Aglaonice's (Dionysian?) cult of the moon that once held Eurydice enthralled; but now, already misled, he says indifferently: "The sun and the moon are all the same to me. There remains night. But not the night of others! My night. This horse plunges into my night and reappears like a diver. He brings back sentences. . . . I would give my complete works for one of those little sentences in which I listen to myself as you listen to the sea in a shell." [39] He is mistaken: He is not listening to himself, to his "night"—but to the devil.

Despite Orphée's irritable assurances that he loves her, his self-absorbed quest for poetry utterly excludes Eurydice. She becomes jealous of the horse and plans to destroy it: "All mystery is my enemy. I have decided to fight it," she says. Husband and wife quarrel over her former association with Aglaonice—"a woman who nearly led you astray," says Orphée, "a woman who drinks, takes tigers out for exercise, turns the heads of our wives, and prevents girls from marrying." Despite Aglaonice's threat of vengeance on Orphée for having lured her away from the Bacchantes, Eurydice obtains poison from her to kill the horse. Aglaonice sends with it a poisoned letter, for she secretly plans to wreak vengeance by killing Eurydice. The unsuspecting go-between in this double intrigue is the angel Heurtebise, who, disguised as a glazier, has become Eurydice's only friend in her loneliness. Eurydice vainly tries to make Orphée jealous of him. When Heurtebise inadvertently betrays his possession of supernatural power, he becomes part of the mystery she hates. She now feels entirely abandoned.

Eurydice dies of the poisoned letter before she can destroy the horse. In her death agony she has a change of heart toward mystery; she begs Heurtebise to fly, if he can, to fetch Orphée. Before he can do so, Death claims her. Death appears as a very beautiful young woman in evening dress and cloak, accompanied by two assistants in surgical uniforms—the angels Azrael and Raphael. When the latter takes a fancy to the horse, Death gives it to him by letting him feed it the poisoned sugar. The horse promptly vanishes. Using terms from radio transmission, Death and her assistants set their mysterious equipment in operation

[39] *Ibid.*, pp. 5-6.

and release Eurydice's soul—a white dove. They translate her body to the nether world.

Death comes and goes through the mirror in the room. This is a good example of the economy and simplicity Cocteau exhibits in choosing ordinary objects to invest with "theatre poetry" and confer a sense of the supernatural on physical reality. "I am entrusting you with the secret of secrets," Heurtebise tells the distraught Orphée. "Mirrors are the doors through which Death comes and goes. . . . You only have to watch yourself all your life in a mirror, and you'll see Death at work like bees in a glass hive." This article of use is commonplace but also freighted with associations and mystery. It will serve, therefore, as the mouth of Hades, and the journey to the Underworld will be accomplished without a change of setting. (Cocteau does not show the journey itself.)

For Cocteau, there is a "modern mythology" which, simply because we are too busy living it, we do not see until he shows it to us. This is what he means when he speaks of "setting traps for poetry" by concealing it under ordinary objects. The mirror is a timeless trap; but Death's surgical robe and radio-like equipment, the car radio which will be used later (in the film version) to transmit code messages of poetry—all these are modern traps. In Cocteau's eyes, it is quite "normal" to combine the very old and the very new in creating a dramatic paraphrase of ancient myth, because "time is a purely human notion that does not, in fact, exist." [40] In the "interval" of the play he found a striking way to show the relativity of time; here his use of old and new in startling juxtaposition is a device for suggesting the simultaneity of time, a further means of capturing theatre poetry and the supernatural.

The quotations used thus far are sufficient to suggest that Cocteau's dialogue, though sharply pared down, is not so bare of figures as his manifesto would lead one to expect. Death working like bees in a glass hive, her lethal apparatus compared to fishing with a gun (another instance of "modern mythology"), are vivid images that charge the mind as much as the poetry of action and setting. And at the climax, in one of the longest speeches of the play, Orphée's death agony is figured in the

[40] Preface to the film *Orphée*. Pages of the Preface are unnumbered.

pains of "the marble from which a sculptor shapes a master-piece."

When Orphée returns to the villa, he is at first furious at his wife because the horse has disappeared. But he, too, undergoes a change of heart when Heurtebise convinces him that she has died: "Ah, The horse is of little consequence! I want to see Eurydice again. I want her to forgive me for having neglected and misunderstood her. Help me. Save me. What can we do? We're losing precious time." [41] The journey to the Underworld is prefaced by "a scene that moves with extreme rapidity." Heurtebise discovers that Death has left her gloves behind: "Death is going to look for her gloves. If you take them to her, she'll give you a reward." Orphée dons the gloves forthwith and plunges into the mirror. There follows the "interval" which has already been discussed.

It is very curious that in a play which exalts the poet, it is not his poetry that moves Death to relent and surrender Eury-dice. Here is a major change, and one that works against the intent of the play. Rubber gloves may fall under the heading of "modern mythology," but they are scarcely an adequate substi-tute for an element of the myth that one would have thought essential to the story, an element especially dear to the heart of Cocteau, at that. It is as if his bold desire to make poetry out of physical objects had deflected him from what is integral, both to the myth and to his own treatment of it. It could, of course, be merely the exigencies of staging which hampered him; and we have seen what dramatic capital he could make out of these practical limitations in devising the "interval." But he has not carried out his avowed purpose of externalizing the action of a crucial scene, of creating a theatre of *"montrer pur"* which would show the poet in action *as poet*. It is more curious still that later, when he availed himself of the full pictorial possibili-ties of the cinema to picture the journey in the nether world, he again omitted the same crucial scene. To include it would have restored the primary importance of the word. Paradox!

Again contrary to the myth, Orphée succeeds in bringing Eurydice back to earth with him. This is the second major change, but this one is actually closer to the personal myth that Cocteau is creating, as distinguished from the ancient myth he

[41] Cocteau, *Orphée*, p. 23.

is dramatizing. "I'm allowed to have Eurydice again," Orphée explains to Heurtebise, "but I may not look at her. If I look at her, she'll disappear." And so the condition is cruelly extended to apply henceforth to their life together. "How dreadful!" says Heurtebise. But Orphée is not discouraged. "It isn't easy by any means, but it can be done." And Eurydice is overjoyed: "I'm the happiest of wives; I, the first woman with a husband bold enough to recover her from the dead."

But, from the first moment of their return, the friction increases; they quarrel first about the horse, then about the Bacchantes. Orphée repeatedly forgets that he must not look at his wife. Within minutes they are quarreling full tilt. Orphée rages: "It's her fault. She would make the dead turn." Eurydice weeps: "It would have been better to remain dead." The situation is intolerable, because both must act as if they had no memory, yet they dare not forget Death's sanction. In a struggle Orphée loses his balance and looks at Eurydice. She vanishes. He thinks she has merely flounced out in anger, and, bullheadedly, he pretends to Heurtebise that he looked at Eurydice on purpose.[42] Orphée discovers an anonymous letter warning him that the Bacchantes are approaching his house, bent on murdering him. He now knows that Eurydice has died. "Eurydice saw aright," he says. "Heurtebise, the horse has befooled me." Heurtebise urges escape, but Orphée refuses: "I am lost."

At this point, there occurs an odd stage direction, one which is an anticipation of a similar climactic moment in *The Infernal Machine*: "The horse's spell is ended," it reads. "ORPHÉE is transfigured." In this unexpected transfiguration, Orphée accepts —indeed chooses—his death: "Things happen as they must. . . . I know what I can still do. . . . Rejoin Eurydice." Despite his pettiness and egotism, the celebrated poet who took love for granted is transformed before our eyes—and in the twinkling of an eye—into a tragic hero. Later, Oedipus will be similarly and magically transformed from a "playing-card king" into a "man" and an imperishable myth.

[42] The situation is ambiguous—made deliberately so, as I incline to think, by Cocteau, as though Orphée's glance was the result of unconscious intent. The ambiguity extends to the play as a whole. It will be recalled that in Offenbach's *Orpheus in the Underworld*, Eurydice is a nagging wife, and Orpheus would gladly have left her in hell, if public opinion had not forced him to rescue her.

Heurtebise objects that even if Orphée finds her again in death, there will still be more scenes between them. But Orphée is in an ecstasy of anticipation: "Not there, where she beckons me to join her." This sacrifice fills Heurtebise with angelic joy. Orphée affirms the necessity of his death by means of an artistic metaphor:

What are the thoughts of the marble from which a sculptor shapes a masterpiece? It thinks: I am being struck, ruined, insulted, and broken, I am lost. This marble is stupid. Life is shaping me, Heurtebise. It is making a masterpiece. I must bear its blows without understanding them. I must stand firm. I must be still and accept the inevitable. I must help and bear my part, till the work is ended. . . . [*some stones break the window and fall into the room* . . .] That's good luck! Luck! I shall have the bust I wished for.[43]

Orphée plunges from the balcony to his death. The Bacchantes hack him to pieces and fling his head into the room. The severed head bemoans its lot and laments its lost Eurydice. She emerges from the mirror and speaks to the dead—and now invisible—Orphée: 'Quiet. Don't upset yourself. Give me your hand. . . . I have your hand in mine. Walk. Don't be afraid. Let yourself go. . . . You can't see me now, and I may take you away." They sink into the mirror.

Here Cocteau uses a device which with slight variation, he will also use in *The Infernal Machine,* when the blinded Oedipus is led away by the ghost of his mother and wife, Jocasta.

The startling change of tone that occurs in the transfiguration —startling because we are totally unprepared for it by any *psychological* development in Orphée's character—is followed by another, equally abrupt and unexpected. Cocteau injects a farce interlude in which, because Aglaonice has lied about Orphée's death, a bumbling and vain Chief of Police charges poor Heurtebise with murder. It is as if Cocteau, convinced that he had achieved the tragedy which he claims for his play, now felt free to insert a satyr-play before concluding with the apotheosis. In this wild scene of cross-questioning and cross-purposes, Orphée's head, placed on a pedestal like a bust, takes active part in the inquiry, while Heurtebise slips through the mirror to join Orphée and Eurydice. The police inquiry ends in utter confusion, capped by the author's intruding his own name and address into

[43] Cocteau, *Orphée,* pp. 34-35.

the proceedings.[44] An eclipse of the sun has brought "a tremendous change of popular feeling in Orphée's favor," and as there is to be a state funeral, the police are embarrassed at being unable to produce a body. They leave, taking with them Orphée's head, which they mistake for a bust.

The search for theatre poetry led Cocteau to break down the traditional categories of drama as one means of achieving surprise and catching the spectator's emotions unaware. One can write a tragedy without being solemn about death; thus the retelling of the Orpheus myth is by turns "fantastic, whimsical, hilarious, grotesque, and somehow moving." [45]

The final scene "changes to Heaven," but of course remains the same room in Orphée's villa where all the action has taken place—the room, so to speak, as reflected in the mirror. As if seeing their home for the first time, Orphée and Eurydice emerge from the mirror, followed by Heurtebise. They resume the lunch that was so disastrously interrupted when Orphée stumbled and looked at his wife. "First of all, the prayer," says Orphée: "O God, we thank thee for assigning us our house and home as the only paradise, and for having opened to us thy paradise. We thank thee for having sent Heurtebise to us, and we are guilty of not recognizing him as our Guardian Angel. We thank thee for having saved Eurydice, because, through love, she killed the devil in the shape of a horse, and in doing so, she died. We thank thee for having saved me because I adored poetry, and thou art poetry. Amen." [46]

Placed at the end of the action, this prayer would seem designed to offer the hint of an explanation as well as a concluding statement. What does it say? Their house is the "only paradise." Then what is God's "paradise"—poetry? Orphée thanks God for having "saved" Eurydice. How? By giving her an appreciation of poetry? Perhaps she now has respect for mystery. If so, we have hardly seen it. And why didn't it "take" the first

[44] Eugene Ionesco, whose anti-dramas, attacks on language and realism, and self-conscious program for saving the theatre remind one of Cocteau's much earlier campaign, copies his mixing of moods, and this device, in *Victims of Duty*: he introduces the playwright Nicolas d'Eu, who proclaims, quite irrelevantly: "We've got Ionesco and Ionesco, that's enough!"
[45] Eric Bentley, *The Playwright as Thinker* (New York: Noonday Press, 1955), p. 193.
[46] Cocteau, *Orphée*, p. 43.

time she died? And why did God save her? "Because, through love, she killed the devil in the shape of a horse. . . ." But she didn't; she faltered. It was Raphael who killed the horse. (And it is rather odd that Raphael, whose name strongly suggests the angel who accompanied Tobias, as Azrael's name suggests the Angel of Death, should take a liking to the devil and not be able to see through his disguise.) As for the horse, we have Orphée's word for it that it was the devil; but it did no more than dupe him with an impropriety, whereas Aglaonice does far more evil in the play, not only in attempting Orphée's life, but also in actually taking Eurydice's. The fault would seem to have been Orphée's, for having looked for inspiration in the wrong place. And how does Orphée regard his own part in the action, beyond admitting guilt for not having recognized Heurtebise as his guardian angel? He lets himself off very lightly: "We thank thee for having saved me because I adored poetry. . . ." But the poetry we saw him adoring is, by his own admission, the work of the devil. All things are forgiven him, evidently, because he loved poetry, since it turns out—luckily for him—that this beneficent God *is* poetry.

Now, in subjecting this beguiling theatre-piece to humorless cross-questioning, one risks acting like the Commissioner of Police who, clearly out of his depth, exclaims: "I don't believe in miracles. An eclipse is an eclipse. A table's a table. An accused man's an accused man." But none of these things is so! And if one counters by saying that Cocteau's entire career, the figure he cut in French literature as seer and diviner, invites one to look for profundities in a tragedy, or at least for a plot and a theme that mesh, it is obvious proof that one has not read the lesson of the master. "It's not a matter of understanding—but of believing," says Heurtebise; and we find an echo of his words in the epigraph to the film *Orphée*: "You try too hard to understand what is happening, my dear sir. This is a grave fault."

But it is not a matter of expecting tidy explanations, so much as it is a sense that the aim of the play is off target, that Cocteau did not dramatize what he thought he was dramatizing, or —which is more likely—that he leads us to think that he is dramatizing one thing when he is actually intent on something else. This last is in accord with Cocteau's dangerous strategy of including in each play a "parade," a sideshow attraction preceding the real performance in the main tent.[47] The ostensible action is the love story, but it wars strangely with the theme of poetry and death and ultimately comes off a poor second. Let us see whether Cocteau's second version of the myth, undertaken a generation later in a medium that can show events and marvels more prodigally than even Cocteau's theatre, can throw light on the question.

III. The Film *Orphée*

In the film the first apparent and major change is that the whole myth has been secularized. God vanishes and poetry reigns supreme in the playwright's concerns. The major theme, voiced by the author as narrator, is now: "The poet must die several times in order to be born." Orphée is a layman, "no longer the high priest that he was"; Heurtebise is no guardian angel, but a young suicide "in the service of one of the innumerable satellites of death." The mysterious poetic messages have a source neither divine nor diabolic; they come from elsewhere, that is, from all the dead poets whose works Cocteau has known, and thus they represent all past literature. Like the devil's messages, they still dupe Orphée because they come from outside him and are therefore false inspiration. "We should speak of expiration, not inspiration," says Cocteau. "What we call inspiration comes from within us, from our night—not from another, so-called divine night outside us." [48] Finally, the afterlife, whether Heaven or Hell, is replaced by the Zone, "a fringe of life . . . a no man's land betwen life and death, that has no relation to any dogma, and where one is neither fully alive nor entirely dead." [49]

Despite all the explanations he now offers, Cocteau still contends that he does without symbols in the film, as in the play. He says, for example, that the beautiful princess does not symbolize Death: "She is *Orphée's death*, as she will decide to be Cégeste's and Eurydice's. She is one of the innumerable functionaries of death. We each possess our own death which watches over us from birth." Her role in the action is to save Orphée by

[47] Cf. Neal Oxenhandler, *Scandal and Parade: The Theatre of Jean Cocteau* (New Brunswick, N.J.: Rutgers University Press, 1957). *Orphée* is discussed in the chapter "Orpheus and Analogy," pp. 85-103.
[48] For a discussion of this, see Khim, *Jean Cocteau*, p. 108.
[49] The quoted explanations are from Cocteau's Preface, pages unnumbered.

losing herself. "Her love for Orphée and his for her signify that profound attraction poets have for all that transcends the world they live in, their desperation to conquer the infirmity that cuts them off from a flock of instincts which obsess us unless we can give them precise form or can act them out." This death seeks Orphée, not Eurydice: "I loved you," she says, "long before our first meeting." And he seeks her. But to lure him, Death, out of jealousy of her, contrives to kill Eurydice in a motor accident. This is contrary to the will of the infernal judges, who therefore permit Eurydice to return to life. Death has performed the deed earlier assigned to Aglaonice. This time it is an infraction of rules that effects Eurydice's reprieve, and not rubber gloves—still less the power of Orphée's poetry. But the changes emphasize the intimacy of the poet and death.

There is a further important change in the myth, dictated by the theme which Cocteau makes more explicit in the film. The Princess is all glamor and mystery, whereas Eurydice is now even more pointedly the very model of a modern "little woman," impervious throughout to mystery—that is, to poetry. She chatters of her pregnancy, of layettes and taxes, while her oblivious poet-husband is bent on discovering new worlds of the imagination. But this time their roles are reversed in one respect: it is she who finds that the condition imposed upon them for their return to earth makes life intolerable, for she rightly suspects that it was not for her sake that he went into the Zone. Heurtebise, who in this version is in love with Eurydice as the Princess is with Orphée, can only say weakly: "If he hated you, he would not have snatched you from death. He will be cited as a model. . . ." Ironic words! For everything in the action supports Eurydice's intuition. The author says: "She had not found Orphée again. She could not bear this return. She wished to rid him of herself, and there was only one way to do it." And so again there is a major change: she *provokes* the glance—the glance which separates them.

When the Bacchantes appear, they are no longer religious orgiasts, but members of the so-called *avant-garde*, skilled in literary feuding and in-fighting. They descend upon Orphée's villa as before. But Cocteau minimizes the transfiguration of Orphée, even though Heurtebise says: "A poet is more than a man." The heroism is muted; for, after all, Orphée is not making a literal sacrifice of his life, nor even seeking Eurydice; he is indulging a death-wish—the longing to be with the princess, his "death." "I found the way to rejoin you," he tells the princess. "I understood you. . . . I was expecting you. . . . I love you."

But their reunion is brief. Death swears him to absolute obedience, then makes the sacrifice by giving him up; that is, she "kills" the already "dead" Orphée in order to restore him to "life," and so she returns him to earth. The author says: "A poet's death must sacrifice itself to make him immortal." The princess and Heurtebise, her accomplice, are then borne off by the minions of the Zone, to suffer unmentionable punishments for having surrendered a life. This time, Orphée and Eurydice are finally reunited, not in Heaven but on earth: "They had to be put back into their dirty water," says Heurtebise. (Cocteau explains that this means simply "brought back to earth.") Orphée embraces his wife, who still adores her "insupportable" husband, and he solicitously, if belatedly, inquires about their baby soon to be born. He professes his love: "Ours is the only love that matters."

Here, on the face of it, is a "happy ending" of domestic bliss appropriate to the cinema, but one which brings us back to earth with a jolt. The myth has been vastly displaced to serve as a complicated allegory of poetic creation; the story is reduced to an account of the difficulties of living with a poet when he is in the throes of "expiration." The Zone can be neither Heaven nor Hell, because nobody really dies. Orphée's "death" is figurative—part of Cocteau's personal mystique of creativity; it is the artist's painful expenditure of himself, the inward "death" that gives life to his works. It was so in the play, too; the film is merely more explicit in revealing the basic theme. It thereby underscores the discrepancy, and consequent friction, between the mythic story and the esthetic theme. The allegory is an inflation which the visual magic of the film finally converts to bathos; and it becomes all the more evident that "the relationships which Cocteau constantly affirms in his poetic universe do not strictly meet the test of analogy." [50] Instead of "tensions of a drama grounded in reality" we have "a reduction of everything to a common denominator of poetic excitement." [51] It

[50] Oxenhandler, *Scandal and Parade*, p. 97.
[51] *Ibid.*, p. 100.

would be hard to say whether Cocteau intends irony here or not, for the contrast between humdrum domesticity and the wild, portentous excitement of Orphée's desire and pursuit of death belies, in every frame of the film, the truth of Orphée's ultimate declaration that replaces the prayer with which the play ends: "Ours is the only love that matters."

From the first Cocteau has been more interested in the creative life of a poet than in the story of a man who reclaimed his wife from the dead, more interested in poetry than in love or God. This is his privilege, though it is certainly introversion to make poetry the whole subject of poetry, and use all the rest of life as a "prétexte." The spectator may be excused if, failing to match the poet's excitement about his own creativity, he would prefer a more flesh-and-blood world where love and spirituality had their own transcendent value. If mirrors are the doorway to death, they should not always reflect Narcissus: "You only have to watch yourself all your life in a mirror, and you'll see Death at work like bees in a glass hive." Eventually, the poet may come to equate poetry with himself.

IV. *The Infernal Machine*

"Surprise me."

With these words, Serge Diaghilev, the famous impresario of the *Ballets Russes*, challenged Jean Cocteau when the latter was a young man in the vanguard of the Parisian art-world. *The Infernal Machine*,[52] produced in 1934, might be regarded as such a surprise, since the view it expresses is diametrically opposed to the religious enthusiasm, the celebration of God and poetry—or of God *as* poetry—that informed the fantasy of *Orphée*. The shock of its contrast comes from the fact that in it Cocteau posits a satanic universe; the epigraph of the play, in Cocteau's own words, reads: "Les dieux existent; c'est le diable." This epigraph is a pun, for it can mean either the wry flippancy, "The gods exist; that's the hell of it," or, perhaps more to the point, "The gods exist; [but] they are devils." With every device of theatre poetry including language, this treatment of the defeat

---

[52] Jean Cocteau, *The Infernal Machine: A Play in Four Acts*, English version and introductory essay by Carl Wildman (London: Oxford University Press, 1936).

of Oedipus and the triumph of myth demonstrates a satanic view of life.

Like Gide before him, Cocteau treats the Oedipus theme by inverting what I take to be the Sophoclean viewpoint. It is as if Gide, implying that the gods had cheated, had shown Cocteau the way by making the self-mutilation of Oedipus a free gesture of defiance against his fate; and Cocteau, pondering the myth in Gide's baleful light, had said to himself: "What a cruel joke the gods played on Oedipus! But what if Oedipus were to turn the tables on the gods?" In seeking to make the trick recoil upon the tricksters, Cocteau found the answer in the existence of myth itself. In *Orphée* he had dramatized the death and rebirth of a poet; now he could dramatize the birth and triumph of a myth.

Actually, it was *Orphée* that was the surprise, just as it was Cocteau who had anticipated Gide, and not the other way round. The seeds of *The Infernal Machine* already existed in *Oedipe-Roi*, Cocteau's free adaptation of Sophocles, written in 1925.[53] As far as any religious or philosophic views are concerned, *Orphée* proved to be a temporary detour, not a permanent change of direction.

In the author's production notes for *Oedipe-Roi* and in the speech he gives to the Prologue, we find further attempts, as in *Antigone*, to conceive new visual terms for the unfolding of this condensed version of the tragedy. We also find the view of the gods as malevolent. Cocteau should be credited with the theatrical conception of a *barbaric* Greece, to supersede the neoclassic view in which Greece was "represented as a white column." Perhaps taking a hint from historical speculation, Cocteau represents Thebes as Egyptian and oriental—a sandy furnace under a wild sky, a place of palm trees, stone, brick, grills, and gutters, a place of small, stuffy rooms where great families in gypsy dress, like insects underground, devour one another. "Ideal spot," says Cocteau, "for gods who love to construct and set snares"; for these Greek gods "have the cruelty of children, and their games cost mortals dear. Without knowing it, Oedipus is in the grip of forces which watch us from the other side of death."[54]

[53] See *Oeuvres complètes de Jean Cocteau*, V (Geneva: Éditions Marguerat, 1948), 99-136. The adaptation was first presented in June, 1937, at the Nouveau Théâtre Antoine, Paris, costumed and directed by the author.
[54] *Ibid.*, p. 104.

The Prologue sketches the background of the myth, that part which Cocteau will dramatize in the later version, and adds:

This Sphinx looks like bait placed there by the gods, as lion-hunters bait their traps.

To guess the riddle! To exterminate the Sphinx! It's enough to turn the head of a young lion and catch him in the snare.

But what is this dark angel that accompanies Oedipus, that first blindfolds and then unbinds his eyes?

It is not a play you are to see, but a torture, a famous case, a trial.

A man at the height of fortune discovers in one day that he was heartlessly tricked by the gods.[55]

Cocteau specifies a theatricalist setting that will bear out the idea of the trap: a platform flanked by walls, and, up center, a third wall which will, beginning with Jocasta's final speech, gradually close in to join the other two. In the center foreground a niche contains the gilded statue of a young man, draped in red and reclining on his elbow, head erect and mouth open. The words of the Chorus are spoken by an actor concealed behind the statue who uses its mouth as a megaphone. The stage lighting progresses from dusk to bright sunlight, reaching its greatest intensity at the moment when the "blind" Oedipus discovers who he is. There is evident here the desire, which is developed further in *The Infernal Machine*, to distance the action by placing it at more than one remove from reality. Such theatricalist handling of event and character suggests that Cocteau is less concerned to dramatize the agony of a man than he is the creation of a myth.

In Sophocles the facts that determine the *circumstances* of the king's fate have already happened before the play begins. The spectator's attention is chiefly engaged by two things: the gradual accumulation of the evidence in the search for the slayer of Laius and, more important, the hero's *agon* as he blindly but surely rushes toward the moment of revelation he seeks to avoid. All but the climax of the myth has already occurred; yet what remains scarcely constitutes "invisible" theatre, even by Cocteau's standards. If ever a play had been stripped of its "longues et brèves," Sophocles' *Oedipus Rex* would seem to be that play; its tightness of *form* would seem to be both more essential and therefore more permanent an element of it, and a deeper analogy of its action, than converging scenery.

[55] *Ibid.*

Consequently the structure of *The Infernal Machine* is a reversal of Cocteau's aim of extreme concision. The play emphasizes event, rather than emotional progression; it keeps its psychology rudimentary, despite a modish use of the oedipal complex. For the three acts preceding Oedipus' recognition of his doom, Cocteau invents episodes to dramatize the antecedent action, then expands and elaborates them. He retains the nucleus of Sophocles' play only as preparation for the climax of his own.[56] Compared to the crisp and fast-moving *Orphée*, it is flaccid and repetitive in making its points and exploiting its effects. Yet this is so only partly because Cocteau places much greater reliance on the written word than formerly. Instead of telling two stories at once by superimposing past action on present, like Sophocles, he prefers direct, episodic action. But he is faced with the technical problem in reverse: he must constantly forecast the future. And he must create, almost from scratch, the supernatural world of "forces which watch us from the other side of death," by embodying them in an appropriate demonology.

These "longues et brèves" are especially noticeable in the first and third acts, where preparation of the audience and ironic foreshadowing occupy him most. Here, instead of exploding a bomb in the spectator's face at rise, he intends to condition his audience, however familiar with the myth it may be, for his extremely exotic treatment of it. The tactic is to inch up on the marvels to come. There is a "bomb," but it will have a long delayed detonation.

As early as *The Infernal Machine*, being careful no doubt to accommodate to the way of the theatre-public an action which, if too starkly rendered, might leave it nonplussed, the playwright consents to interpolate what he came to call much later, in regard to Shakespeare, necessary slow passages [les longues nécessaires]. Thus the whole first act of the play ("The Phantom of Laius") can be regarded as one of these slow movements designed to accustom the spectator to a new atmosphere and enable him to adjust his breathing in preparation for the second act, where the air is rarefied in the extreme.[57]

---

[56] See Joseph Chiari, *The Contemporary French Theatre: The Flight from Naturalism* (London: Rockliff, 1958), p. 106: "The undoing of Oedipus only occupies approximately a tenth of the play; coming after some very amusing chit-chat, it is divested of its emotional context, and is a kind of Parisian drawing-room comedy. . . ."

[57] Khim, *Jean Cocteau*, p. 85.

The Voice, speaking out of time and telling us the whole story beforehand, distances the action. It also emphasizes the fact that Oedipus is beaten before he begins, that the universe of the play is both satanic and determinist: "For the gods really to enjoy themselves, their victim must fall from a great height. . . . Spectator, this machine, you see here wound up to the full in such a way that the spring will slowly unwind the whole length of a human life, is one of the most perfect constructed by the infernal gods for the mathematical destruction of a mortal." [58]

Determinism upsets, if it does not destroy, the balance of conflicting forces that traditionally forms the tension of Western drama. The basic forces consist of "outer necessity" and "inner freedom." If there is to be significant struggle, it is essential that the two be combined. For, paradoxically, it is their balanced combination—not the *omission* of one or the other—that produces a sense of inevitability. How different Cocteau's method is from what we find in Greek drama and also in Shakespeare is emphasized in the following:

Neither here [in *Hamlet*] nor in Greek drama have we anything to do with characters who are puppets in the hands of Fate. In both, we see something of the power of the gods, or the designs of Providence; but these no more override or reduce to unimportance the natural working of individual character than the existence, in the physical world, of universal laws overrides the natural behaviour of natural bodies. It is indeed precisely in the natural behaviour of men, and its natural results in given circumstances, that the operation of the divine laws can be discerned.[59]

But this inevitability, or "fate," is an *esthetic* creation. It is by no means the same as philosophic determinism; rather, it is its antithesis and exists quite apart from it. "Dramatists are committed to the doctrine of free will. They can say they don't believe in it: but they have to write their plays as if they did. (In this they resemble human beings in general, for your most ardent determinist acts on the assumption that determinism is false.) People in plays have to be able to make decisions, and these decisions have got to be both real and influential: they have to affect events." [60]

[58] Cocteau, *The Infernal Machine*, p. 4.
[59] H. D. F. Kitto, "Hamlet and Greek Drama," in *Form and Meaning in Drama: A Study of Six Greek Plays and "Hamlet"* (New York: Barnes & Noble, 1957), pp. 317-37.
[60] Eric Bentley, "The Making of a Dramatist," *Tulane Drama Review*, V, no. 1 (September, 1960), 6.

The point is that determinism is neither an action nor an emotion, but an idea. And I know of no Western drama in which a playwright has succeeded in *dramatizing* that idea, regardless of how much he may require his characters to believe in it or permit them to discuss it for him.[61] But Cocteau made the attempt in *The Infernal Machine* and brought the infernal gods on stage in his effort to show it. The deterministic premise of the action produces results that are technically interesting, but also artistically detrimental to the play taken on its own terms. That it gave Cocteau a maximum opportunity to invent theatre poetry and to experiment with time cannot outweigh the fact that it also involved the sacrifice of suspense and character, deprived the play of a unifying forward action, and ended by developing a self-defeating irony.

This judgment is contrary to the high praise accorded the play in some quarters; hence, one can only examine these opinions from time to time, to see how much their own reservations reinforce it.

Let us begin with the matter of suspense in drama. It is of two kinds, but both involve the hopes and fears of the audience, as well as of the characters, and therefore they imply free will acting under stress. The suspense which derives from the spectator's knowledge of what is to come is esthetically superior; it produces its effects even after repeated viewings. The inferior kind of suspense depends upon withholding knowledge from the spectator, in order to spring a surprise on him: "That which surprises," said Joubert, "does so but once." By telling us the story in full beforehand, Cocteau would seem to be relying on the superior kind; but, as we shall see, the basic point of the play rests upon the other kind. By equating determinism and foreknowledge in the development of the action, however, he robs his characters of the freedom without which they cannot engage the spectator's hopes and fears. Indeed, the deterministic premise leads to curious but well-known psychological reactions which are contrary to the playwright's intention. When circumstances and opposing forces are so loaded against the protagonist that they do not merely bring about his defeat, but rather obliterate from the start any chance of his being able to put up a good

[61] The "scientific determinism" of Büchner's dramas and Zola's *Thérèse Raquin* come to mind most readily.

fight, the action of the play becomes obviously ineffectual, rather than significant, and consequently irritating; and the victim becomes not pathetic but pusillanimous.

All Cocteau's devices have been described as means to slacken suspense and "cool off" the action: use of a familiar myth, stress on explicit foreknowledge (the Voice summarizes and explains events before each act, as well as at the outset), the repeated use of prediction and other ways of foreshadowing within the acts themselves, together with theatricalist staging, which places the action visually at several removes from reality. "This cooling off is a liberation of the spectator, whose attention can now dwell, unbothered, on each scene, the urge to know what comes next being minimized." [62] But in an insistent context of determinism, they serve to cool off the audience's interest instead. And they are, after all, an elaborate blind. The author's prodigal use of pointers shows him to be less concerned to direct our attention to the given moment for its own sake, than to mislead us (as the gods gulled Oedipus)in order to bring off the *coup de théâtre* which he is carefully withholding until the climactic moment: the magical transformation of Oedipus into "man" and "myth." Thus, in tricking the spectator by leading him down the determinist path, Cocteau resorts to the inferior kind of suspense —surprise. And we know that Cocteau values surprise as a trap for poetry.

In Sophocles' tragedy the use of prophecy and its fulfillment gives the play form, because it shapes the plot and guides our expectations. As it works out the pattern that, in part, already exists in the minds of characters and spectators, every step in the forward action gains in importance. The simultaneous development of present action and past action gives the play its powerful dynamic. On the other hand, the forward action of *The Infernal Machine* has no continual through-line; it lacks a "clear line of development and unity," and its "acts are watertight, there are repetitions and abrupt transitions." [63] This may be partly accounted for by the fact that, unlike that of his previous plays, its conception did not come to him as a whole. The theme occupied him for a long time. The second act, "The Meeting of

[62] See Eric Bentley, ed., *From the Modern Repertoire:* Series One (Denver: University of Denver Press, 1949), notes, pp. 402-4.
[63] Cocteau, *The Infernal Machine*, translator's Preface, p. xvii.

Oedipus and the Sphinx," was written before the first, and conceived as a one-act play for Marguerite Jamois and Gaston Baty.[64] It is, incidentally, the one act where language most notably takes stage—literally to weave its spell, in the Sphinx's famous, aria-like speech. The third act was added to the other two; then, a year later, Cocteau decided to add the fourth, which, except for the very ending, had largely been written before all the others, as part of the adaptation of Sophocles. So much Cocteau himself tells us.[65] But he veils the rest of the story in the poetic mystery to which he is so addicted, and does not say "why from Act to Act I hide the seeds of rebirth, why I place Anubis in Greece in the second Act, and the dead Jocasta in the Fourth. A study of this," he concludes, "would take up considerable space." [66] One is reminded of the Sphinx in one of her cross moods: "Why, for example, should you have a dog's head, Anubis? Why have the god of the dead in the shape given to him by credulous people? Why must we have an Egyptian god in Greece and why must he have a dog's head?" [67]

"It is the detestable habit of . . . magnifying myths that makes them seem so remote from us," wrote Cocteau, a few years after the production of the play.[68] The statement indicates his method of conceiving and handling his mythic characters. Since it is a reductive method, it was consonant with his tendency, already demonstrated in the earlier plays, to submerge the human character in the elements of the theatre, and thereby, if unintentionally, to diminish or to depreciate its humanity. Here it seems to be intentional, as a way of bringing the *myth*, rather than the characters, closer to us. And if, at the end, he can succeed in remagnifying Oedipus, as he intends to do, he will have shown once more his virtuosity in "playing at a great height, and without a safety-net." [69]

Cocteau is not interested in exploring the psychology of his characters: this sort of thing he deplores as realism. He gives his

[64] Crosland, *Jean Cocteau*, p. 136.
[65] Jean Cocteau, *Maalesh: A Theatrical Tour in the Middle-East*, trans. Mary C. Hoeck (London: Peter Owen, 1956), pp. 58-59.
[66] *Ibid.*, p. 59.
[67] Cocteau, *The Infernal Machine*, p. 38.
[68] Jean Cocteau, *Round the World Again in Eighty Days*, trans. Stuart Gilbert (London: Routledge, 1937), p. 19.
[69] Cocteau, *Orphée*, Prologue, p. 2.

infernal gods human characteristics, but only that we may glimpse their satanic universe. He uses the oedipal complex as a psychological basis for part of the workings of the infernal machine, but he does not go beyond that. His characters are given, not organic. He sets them before us as recognizable modern types who will re-enact the ancient myth as required. For his preoccupation is not with human nature as revealed in the story, but rather with the outcome of the story—that is, the myth as such. Khim, who describes this two-dimensional characterization as "heraldic," traces it throughout Cocteau's plays, even the seemingly naturalistic ones.[70]

Humor is another of Cocteau's reductive devices for humanizing the myth. It was much in evidence in *Orphée*, where even the lovers' quarrel which snatches Eurydice back to Hades is treated as a "scène bouffe," part of a boulevard comedy. In the mythic context of *The Infernal Machine* humor serves to provide contrast, more than to dissipate solemnity. Jocasta, for example, can be depicted as an amusing cosmopolitan, for the sake of contrast with her awful fate. The Sphinx, presented as a jealous woman who tells her secret out of love and then, out of pique, lets the ungrateful Oedipus meet his fate as planned, is in one sense as unfantastic as possible; thus she is brought close to us. Tiresias, whom Oedipus, not Cocteau, treats as if he were the charlatan out of Gide's play, is allowed to keep his dignity, despite having to wait upon the silly Jocasta and put up with her nicknaming him Zizi. Oedipus is "an ordinary youth, not exceptionally endowed with intelligence";[71] he is immature, egotistical, ambitious. All this serves as contrast to the frame of infinite evil within which the action is set.

With good cause Tiresias warns Oedipus that in his blind arrogance, he may come to pursue "obscure glory, the last resource of the arrogant person who persists in opposing the stars."[72] This arrogance Oedipus shows in Acts II and III, but without any of the characteristics which in Act IV would render plausible his strength and nobility upon discovering his identity, or the tragic dignity he achieves in blinding himself and going into

[70] Khim, *Jean Cocteau*, pp. 87-88.
[71] Cocteau, *The Infernal Machine*, translator's Preface, p. 17.
[72] It is this "obscure glory" which Gide's Oedipe pursues by defying the gods; Cocteau's Oedipus achieves "classic glory" by submitting to his stars.

exile. These changes are "assumed in advance" and accomplished by legerdemain and in the twinkling of an eye,[73] in the same way that Orphée becomes transfigured in contemplating his death. Both anti-heroes act as they do because the myths so dictate, and the theatricalist style permits the arbitrary transformations.

The dead Jocasta's apparition at the end of the play is a similar theatricalist coup, for now all traces of the erotic woman have vanished, and only the maternal woman remains. Her apotheosis has interesting similarities to the ending of H. R. Lenormand's *Man and His Phantoms*, produced ten years before Cocteau's play.[74] This modernized version of the Don Juan theme presents the dying rake, now revealed as a homosexual with a mother-fixation akin to that of Oedipus, as he is comforted at the end by a huge apparition of his mother. She soothes him, accepts all his rationalizations of his misdeeds, and holds him in her arms as he dies. Lenormand's play, like Cocteau's, also contains a satanic element, but one which comes from the evil in Don Juan's character. As for Laius, since we see him only as a ghost in the beginning of the play, he undergoes no transformation; but his ineffectual distress is in marked contrast to Jocasta's serenity at its end, now that the myth has been achieved.

Heraldic characterization notwithstanding, it is necessary to give characters some margin of freedom, if they are to exist at all in the world of the play. From the first Cocteau provides this small margin. How else could the ghost of Laius appear, since he is bent on subverting the will of the gods? All of Act I is devoted to his attempts to warn his widow Jocasta and the prophet Tiresias that his murderer was his own son Oedipus, and that Jocasta must not marry the youth. The very presence of Laius seems to contravene the machine-like efficiency of the infernal system. The Soldier describes the visitation to his Chief:

And once he was visible, he changed his sentences and told us as well as he could that something fearful had happened, a thing of death which he couldn't explain to the living. He spoke of places where he could go and places where he couldn't go, and that he had been where he shouldn't and knew a secret which he shouldn't know, and that he would be discovered and punished, and afterwards he

[73] Francis Fergusson, *The Idea of a Theater* (Garden City, N.Y.: Doubleday Anchor Books, 1953), p. 213.
[74] Henri René Lenormand, "L'homme et ses fantômes," in *Les oeuvres libres*, 41 (1924), 133-206.

wouldn't be allowed to appear, he wouldn't be able to appear any more. . . . "I shall die my last death," he said, "and it will be finished, finished. You see, gentlemen, there is not a moment to lose. Run! Warn the Queen! Find Tiresias! . . ." [75]

But we know that nothing can really interfere with the fulfill-ment of the oracle, let alone alter or prevent it; so his efforts are necessarily unavailing, a fact which is emphasized less by his stammering incoherence than by the soldiers' ability to see and hear him while Jocasta and Tiresias cannot. But, even when speaking to the wrong persons, he cannot say the thing which he came back from death to say—"a thing of death which he couldn't explain to the living." His apparition is doubly pointless.

Two aspects, the thematic and the technical, are involved here. Thematically, the margin of freedom can be seen simply as a refinement of the infernal gods' cruelty, an illusion they permit only because it breeds hope, so as to make the crushing of it the more exquisitely cruel. In Act II there is a momentary de-feat of the infernal plan, when Nemesis-Sphinx gives Oedipus the answer to her own riddle; and in Act III there are the pre-monitions of Tiresias, the "few hints and civilities on the part of destiny" which mother and son are too weary to heed when they are about to consummate their marriage. A character acts, only to have his action undone, or is warned, only to miss the point of the warning. Thus, the technical device on which the entire play is constructed is that of a double reversal, which is auto-matically self-canceling.

In this there is an interesting analogy by contrast to the prophecy in the myth as it appears in Sophocles. The same prophecy was made twice, first to his parents, then much later to Oedipus. In each case an attempt was made to outwit it. The effect was mathematical: two negatives make a positive; and so the separate efforts of parents and son to negate the prophecy ironically insured its fulfillment. Beginning his play when part of the prophecy—the killing of Laius—has already been fulfilled, Cocteau contrives actions which threaten to alter or prevent the trap from closing; but in each case the action is annulled by a counter-action which either returns the situation to its original status or carries it one step further toward its preordained goal. In Cocteau's hands, oftener than not, this creates an impression

[75] Cocteau, *The Infernal Machine*, p. 21.

that negative and positive cancel each other, rather than that two negatives make a positive.

Since Cocteau has humanized the infernal gods immediately involved in the fate of Oedipus, he extends to them, as to mankind, the same margin of freedom; but it proves equally illusory and futile. Their earthly contacts arouse human emotions in the gods, at least when they take human form; and so the Sphinx as a young woman feels a pity for Oedipus that predisposes her to let him go unscathed. But, despite this mortal weakness, her encounter must go off as planned; so Anubis, her "watch-dog," is on hand when Oedipus returns to claim the body of the Sphinx, to see that she fulfills the will of destiny, and the machine continues to unwind inexorably. Even when she reverts to her form as Nemesis, she remembers her pity for man as unbearable: "Poor, poor, poor mankind! I can stand no more, Anubis. . . . I can't breathe. Let us leave the earth."

Nothing can really go wrong among the gods either. For the Sphinx and Anubis are themselves subject to infernal superiors, satellites in an infinite chain of command. Similarly, in the film *Orphée* the Princess—Orphée's "death"—and Heurtebise and Cégeste are only subordinates, operating under military obedience to punitive tribunals in an endless hierarchy. We may note, since the fact applies retrospectively to the climax of *The Infernal Machine*, that although the Princess was able to subvert the rules sufficiently to surrender a life, it was only because it was a *poet's* life, and for Cocteau the creativity of the poet is the only victory there is against death.

In dramatizing these gods Cocteau denudes them of some of their mystery. To offset this, he places them against the background of an impersonal *system* of malevolence that is as infinite as it is implacable. It does the Sphinx no good to rebel:

THE SPHINX: I've had enough of killing, enough of dealing out death.

ANUBIS: We must obey. There are mysteries within mystery, gods above gods. We have our gods and they have theirs. That's what's called infinity.[76]

Individually, the gods are neither omniscient nor all-powerful; but the infernal *system* is. (There is always one exception, of course: the creation of myth.) Like blind humans, the gods must

[76] *Ibid.*, pp. 37–38.

act "without aim, without end, without understanding," because for them "neither Egypt nor Greece nor death, neither the past nor the future has any meaning"; and in seeking the destruction and death of their human victims, they must regard the latter as "no more than noughts wiped off a slate, even if each of these noughts were an open mouth calling for help."

Frightening to contemplate, but even terror is benumbed by the prospect of this dreariest of all possible worlds. Such mindless mystery, infinite absurdity! No wonder the gods, too, rebel. The only good there is, is in man; but even it would seem to be there only so that the infernal system could cancel it perpetually, save, of course, that one unique exception. The sole consolation in this nightmare universe is that man dies his "last death," and so presumably need not contemplate an afterlife of malignant futility.

This play has been called Cocteau's protest against the human condition, against the existence of evil and death: "As a commentary on human freedom, *La Machine infernale* is a protest against the essential nature of the human condition. It is not merely a protest against deterministic philosophies; it goes further than that. It is a protest against the necessity for evil in human lives, against the extraordinary fate that presides over the destinies of men, making the question of free will gratuitous." [77] But this universe is Cocteau's personal invention, itself a demonstration of a deterministic philosophy so reductive of the value of human life that it makes the question of free will indeed gratuitous. It is relevant to ask whether such a blanket indictment of life can provide the basis for a mature art, and whether art alone is sufficient to confer value on life. When Margaret Fuller announced that she had at last decided to accept the universe, Thomas Carlyle said, "Gad! She'd better!"

For the gods neither past nor future has any meaning: "Human time is a fold of eternity," says Anubis. "For us time does not exist. From his birth to his death the life of Oedipus is spread flat before my eyes with its series of episodes." Time being purely subjective, perhaps the theatre-poet can, by his art, raise the

[77] Preface to *The Infernal Machine*, in Oreste F. Pucciani, ed., *The French Theatre Since 1930* (New York: Ginn, 1954), p. 23. It is hard to see how a play that protests against deterministic philosophies can also interpret man's fate as one in which the question of free will is gratuitous.

human spectators to the status of gods and permit them to see —with the gods' superior vision but without their malevolence —their own fates reflected in that of Oedipus. This is Cocteau's technique, to tell his story so that we shall have the illusion of timelessness, of seeing events "spread flat" before us. Past, present, and future shall be exhibited simultaneously, not successively, as from an airplane we should see, in one glance, three widely separate points which, if we passed them on foot, we would only see one after another.

The theatre can do this because, though the fate of Oedipus was sealed long ago, is it not happening here and now before our eyes? As the Voice speaks out of time, so that we know what shall be, so we also know that what shall be has already been. The stage is ancient Greece and the modern city, as it is simultaneously the physical world and the other side of death. Because it is inexorably certain, the whole myth is present in Act I, just as it will be in Act IV. The past (Laius dead) erupts into the present (the ramparts of Thebes) to warn of the future (the marriage of Oedipus and Jocasta). Moreover, Act II, although presented successively, is happening even as we watch Act I: the cock-crow that ends the first act is the same cock-crow that ends the second. The Oedipus whom we see undergoing transfiguration at the end becomes the Oedipus we already knew before the play began. Determinism becomes timelessness. It is Nietzsche's eternal recurrence dramatized, with the mediocre Oedipus transformed by myth into a type of the overman.

Since an audience instinctively attributes freedom of action to the characters in drama, this juggling of times becomes one more means of bringing it up short against the premise. And yet, to the extent that the audience forgets that premise momentarily, Cocteau does not really succeed in creating his deterministic world. His failure has the inadvertent effect of preparing the audience for the unsuspected existence of an escape-hatch through which the action can at last emerge, transformed as myth, when Oedipus achieves classic glory. Logically, this will not hold up under later, cooler consideration: in a predetermined world, the existence of myth would be as much a necessity as the reality of death; but psychologically, in performance, this illusion of a final reversal comes off because it answers, if only momentarily, an instinctive need on the part of the audience for some kind of break-through.

ANUBIS [*holding up the SPHINX'S dress*]: Look at the folds in this cloth. Crush them together. Now if you pierce this bundle with a pin, remove the pin, smooth the cloth till all traces of the old creases disappear, do you think a simple country loon would believe that the innumerable holes recurring at intervals result from a single thrust of a pin? [78]

Each omen, hint, or ironical reversal occurring at intervals in the play is like one of the "innumerable holes," reminding us that the "single thrust of a pin" has already occurred. The play has been described as having four acts, every one of which is a "rational analysis of a *static* situation." [79] To this we might add that each of the four situations is really the same situation; what action there is has not been forward but lateral, so that at the end the spectator realizes that "the story was over before it began." [80] The effort to transcend serial time is in this case, distinct from that in *Orphée*, made at the cost of dramatic progression. Instead of making us experience the mystery physically, it substitutes virtual stasis. In the air, although we can see many places simultaneously, the sense of movement is almost imperceptible; to feel it intensely, we must pass very close to them, one after another, preferably on horseback. A play is an imitation of an action, that is, of a progression. In abolishing time as well as free will, Cocteau has all but abolished the action.

Let us now apply the premise to the climax of the play, where Cocteau changes the rules of the game. It has been Cocteau's assumption that nothing the characters do can affect events. To the extent that their actions are predetermined, they are neither consequential nor real. Necessarily, and most disastrously, this includes Oedipus' acceptance of his fate, his self-mutilation, and his exile. For the infernal machine to inflict total destruction, Oedipus cannot do less; it is all part of the gods' plan. The point of the play lies precisely in the fact that, since man cannot in any way achieve freedom of action, the gods must trick themselves.

We may think we are watching a man being cruelly and irra-

[78] Cocteau, *The Infernal Machine*, p. 57.
[79] Fergusson, *Idea of a Theater*, pp. 213-14 (emphasis added).
[80] *Ibid.*

tionally destroyed; but again, as in *Orphée*, this is mere pretext. What we are really watching is "invisible" theatre: the action of the gods who, as they construct the infernal machine, overreach themselves, so that the irony of their miscalculation recoils upon their own heads. In Sophocles, revelation and reversal are centered in Oedipus the man, and the consequences are dramatically significant to him—and, through him, to us. In Cocteau they are centered in the supreme gods who, so far as the climax of the play is concerned, exist outside the action. No matter how much Cocteau may try to keep it within the play by means of Tiresias' final prediction, their defeat is actually external and adventitious: the audience, although godlike in that it watches the action of the play from the outside, must make an imaginative effort to appreciate its effect. For here the crowning irony consists in the *gods'* realization that it was the very success of their diabolic scheme which has inadvertently created a myth. True, this myth cannot cause their downfall; but it can, for endless generations after Oedipus, survive and grow to be the perfect model of man's *protest* against his helpless existence in a satanic universe. The vehicle of that protest is art, which must then—in the eyes of the gods—be arrogance. Is Cocteau exalting "obscure glory" after all?

Romantic irony is self-defeating. The creation of the myth may have been unforeseen, a cause for ironic laughter against the gods. But it alters nothing. Despite Cocteau, the terms of the premise have not changed. Just as no real defeat is inflicted upon the gods by it, so no real freedom is given man. Of course, the myth of Oedipus may convince man of his moral superiority to the infernal powers, but that is only to increase his agony by increasing his awareness. For an exquisite refinement of cruelty, one could hardly look for a better—even from the infernal gods.

What is the point of all this, if the characters we have watched have a margin of freedom that is more apparent than real, and if the playwright is thereby driven to leap outside the confines of human life to explode the climax of his play, like a bomb, in the face of the gods? In Gide, Oedipe rebelled against his fate and in his rage deprived the gods of their victory. It was at least a human, if perverse, action and a human revenge. In Cocteau, on the other hand, Oedipus *submits out of obedience to the myth*, so as to render the gods' victory perpetually futile. This is scarcely a human action. Nor is Oedipus aware of any revenge. As with the triumph of poetry in *Orphée*, the answer here is that the triumph of myth is simply one more allegory of the transcendence of art in a world of death. Oedipus trans- figured may belong to "the people, poets and unspoiled souls"; but, if we know our Cocteau, we can be sure he belongs to them only by virtue of the poet, on whom he depends not only to perpetuate his myth, but also to confer meaning on his fate by endowing it with form. What meaning? The only meaning of myth is that it is art; and art, remember, is self-justified, gratu- itous; it does not mean, it *is*.

In *A Call to Order* Cocteau had written in block letters: "Do not derive art from art"—and proceeded to adapt classic dramas; when he turned to myth, he did so in order to dramatize art, not life. So far as he exhibits it in his plays, his religion is a religion of art, as Gide's ethics was an ethics of art. Cocteau's later con- victions were, according to Khim, inseparable from those he expressed much earlier in his letter to Jacques Maritain: they "literally assign to the poet in the world of the present, the same role that Christ assumes eternally; and, to his poetry, the same signification that they give to grace and prayer." [81] These stag- gering pretensions remind one of what Heurtebise says in the film *Orphée*: "Nothing is more stubborn than professional bias."

For Cocteau the ultimate realities are the poet and death and the thing the poet makes. This is a diminished view of life, not an expanded one, which rests finally on the mysterious power of art to endure. It makes man a mere occasion for the creation of art, and it confers on art an impossible autonomy. By exalting art as more than human, indeed as supernatural, Cocteau dimin- ishes man and renders his own art unhuman. [82]

[81] Khim, *Jean Cocteau*, pp. 140-41. For Cocteau's personal views, see *La Difficulté d'être* (Paris: Morihien, 1947), pp. 33-34. Trans. Elizabeth Sprigge as *The Difficulty of Being* (London: Owen, 1966).
[82] For a much more sympathetic view of Cocteau's aims and accomplish- ments in the works in question, and one that finds in them far wider thematic significance, see Chester Clayton Long, "Cocteau's *Orphée*: From Myth to Drama and Film," *Quarterly Journal of Speech*, LI, no. 3 (Oc- tober, 1965), 311-25.

CHAPTER IV

ROBINSON JEFFERS:
The Twilight of Man

Another theme that has much engaged my verses is the expression of a religious feeling, that perhaps must be called
pantheism, though I hate to type it with a name. It is the
feeling . . . I will say the certitude . . . that the world, the
universe, is one being, a single organism, one great life that
includes all life and all things; and is so beautiful that it
must be loved and reverenced; and in moments of mystical
vision we identify ourselves with it.[1]

In 1925, the same year that Cocteau rendered *Oedipus Rex* into
prose, the American poet Robinson Jeffers published a dramatic
poem about the House of Atreus, *The Tower Beyond Tragedy*.[2]
This was not an attempt to remove the patina from masterpieces,
but to create an independent work based on a highly individual
interpretation of the classic myth. It contrasts sharply with
Cocteau's ventures in theatre poetry. It relies heavily on language to tell the story, create the characters, and set the action
in a barbaric Mycenae. The barbarism is human, not a matter
of geography or stage-setting; and the characters are real, if excessively violent. The gods in the play are not malign, merely
remote and probably indifferent. This dramatic poem, which

[1] Robinson Jeffers, *Themes in My Poems* (San Francisco: Book Club of
California, 1956), pp. 23-24.
[2] In *The Selected Poetry of Robinson Jeffers* (New York: Random House,
1937), pp. 89-140.

aspires to Aeschylean grandeur of religious spirit, begins in a more than Euripidean disenchantment with life: it refuses to see gods or men as noble. "I can tell lies in prose," said Jeffers.[3]

For his first dramatic venture into classical myth, Jeffers seems to have ignored, if he was aware of them, all the modern play-wright's phantasms about the skepticism of modern audiences as a barrier to communication. He alters, but does not omit, the element of the supernatural; and he uses it with inventiveness and imposing authority. (There is less of it in the later plays, but it is still presented forthrightly.) He also mixes it boldly with a naturalistic conception of mythical figures, who are driven by greed, power, and sexual lust to deeds of unnatural violence beyond anything that the three Greek tragedians imagined in their versions.

Not planned for the stage, the poem has since proved stage-worthy in more than one version. There is no evidence of a wish to create theatricalist detachment; on the contrary, the action assaults the imagination with horrors, both acted and narrated. It rubs our noses in them, so to speak, so that we will imitate its hero Orestes, turn away from the spectacle of human baseness, and seek to transcend its tragedy. Cocteau, like Nietzsche, celebrates a religion of art; Jeffers, who like Nietzsche rejected Christianity and for some of the same reasons, preaches a religion of nature. His pantheism proceeds from a calculated misanthropy, which is intellectual rather than emotional in nature, and to which in 1948 he finally gave the challenging name, Inhumanism.

His doctrine has provoked considerable animosity among critics, so that at times one cannot be certain whether Jeffers is being attacked for his religion because he writes unfashionably explicit poetry, or attacked for his poetry because he has unfashionably repudiated the religion of humanism. In figurative language it advocates "breaking out of humanity" so as to "uncenter the mind from itself." For the individual, as for society, health can come only from detaching the heart and mind from human concerns and human passions, says Jeffers:

There is no health for the individual whose attention is taken up with his own mind and processes; equally there is no health for the society that is always introverted on its own members, as ours be-

[3] Jeffers, "Self-Criticism in February," in *Selected Poetry*, p. 601.

comes more and more, the interest engaged inward in love and hatred, companionship and competition. These are necessary, of course, but as they absorb all the interest they become fatal. All past cultures have died of introversion at last, and so will this one, but the individual can be free of the net, in his mind.[4]

Such detachment is the necessary prelude to a true religious experience which, for Jeffers, is the veneration of the beauty of nature and, at times, mystical communion with it as God. All societies have required religion, says Jeffers, and still do, but each religion is stained with a "private impurity" derived from its human founder. "Why does insanity always twist the great answers?" he asks, and answers himself: "Because only tormented persons want truth." But he is not to be caught by the solipsism that threatens his own "theory of truth":

> Then
> search for truth is foredoomed and frustrate?
> Only stained fragments?
> Until the mind has turned its love from itself and man, from parts to the whole.[5]

The consequences of *not* turning one's love from oneself and from man are the burden of *The Tower Beyond Tragedy*.

I. *The Tower Beyond Tragedy*

The dramatic poem re-enacts Clytemnestra's murder of her husband, King Agamemnon, after his victorious return from the Trojan War; her queening it in Mycenae with her paramour Aegisthus, the king's cousin; the subsequent murder of the pair by Clytemnestra's fugitive children, Electra and Orestes; the latter's resulting madness and remorseful flight, leaving Electra in turn to queen it in Mycenae. This short summary indicates what Jeffers has retained of the myth, but without suggesting the alterations and additions that make his version highly distinctive for its day.

The changes within the traditional framework are many.

---

[4] See Radcliffe Squires, *The Loyalties of Robinson Jeffers* (Ann Arbor: University of Michigan Press, 1956), pp. 33-34; also S. S. Alberts, *A Bibliography of the Works of Robinson Jeffers* (New York: Random House, 1933), pp. xv-xvi. The logical contradictions of Inhumanism as a philosophy and religion are well examined by Frederic I. Carpenter, *Robinson Jeffers* (New York: Twayne, 1962), Chap. 4, pp. 109-35.

[5] Jeffers, "Theory of Truth," in *Selected Poetry*, p. 615.

Agamemnon speaks but few words living, many dead. The prophetess Cassandra is left alive by the queen, to suffer for years as an outcast—and act as *raisonneuse* to span the gap of years until the children grow up and return to avenge their father's death. When Orestes goes mad after killing his mother, Cassandra, who in her own character is as vengeful against all Myceneans as Electra is against her father's slayers, urges the deranged youth to kill his sister. Instead, he kills her, then wanders into the mountains alone. There his madness leaves him, and he undergoes a mystical communion with nature. When he returns to the palace, it is to say farewell. Electra uses every plea to persuade him to share the throne. Incestuously desiring her brother, she offers herself to him: "O my brother / You are Agamemnon: rule: take all you will: nothing is denied you. The Gods have redressed evil / And clamped the balance."

Sustained by his vision, Orestes conquers his own desire for his sister and rejects both her and the throne: "I will not waste inward / Upon humanity, having found a fairer object." Electra tries the moral blackmail of threatened suicide, but this also fails to shake his newfound purpose. Orestes goes into exile, indifferent now to humanity, to life itself, because he has "fallen in love outward"; he has "climbed the tower beyond time, consciously, and cast humanity, entered the earlier fountain."

In Aeschylus the fated chain of crimes could be ended only by the establishment of impersonal human justice. Man was delivered at last from the burden of blood-feuds by joining with his fellows in a pact of mutual dependence, and this human ideal was ratified by the gods. When the play was first performed, Athens celebrated in it the founding of the Court of the Areopagus, then a fairly recent and major event in human history. For Aeschylus it signified the victory of reason over passion, a feat that the gods must approve. But two milleniums later, this will not suffice Jeffers. In this, however, he is not unlike other modern playwrights who have reworked the myth. *The Oresteia*, especially in its third part, *The Eumenides*, is a kind of touchstone on which they bark their shins. In the way they stop short of it, leap over it, or avoid it, they reveal a good deal about their own beliefs. For most of them, the degree to which they depart from its ending indicates the gap between Aeschylus' classic faith in a moral law, together with the worth of human justice based on it, and their modern despair. But though he differs from Aeschylus, Jeffers does not despair.

In Jeffers' view man's continuing preoccupation with his own affairs has not even made him godlike in the classic sense. Men are still the "sick microbes" that lusted and killed in ancient Greece; and their gods are scarcely better:

. . . when they look backward they see only a man standing at the
  beginning,
Or forward, a man at the end; or if upward, men in the shining bit-
  ter sky striding and feasting,
Whom you call Gods. . . .
It is all turned inward, all your desires incestuous, the woman the
  serpent, the man the rose-red cavern,
Both human, worship forever . . . .[6]

Like Orestes, man must leave all that and fall in love outward if he would enter the "earlier fountain" and become one with God.

Incest is the plot element that Jeffers uses to embody the dramatic action necessary for so radically different an interpretation of the myth. He is the first among the modern dramatists I know to present the fraternal love of Orestes for Electra, and hers for him, as becoming incestuous, and this corruption as a direct result of their revenge. If we may judge by the modern collations of the myths, none of the accounts from classical times does so.[7] The only suggestive source for it in Greek drama is Euripides' *Electra*, which, rather than Aeschylus, appears to be the play that most influenced Jeffers. Because it depicts Electra as a woman whose sexual frustration reveals itself as a "subtle streak of nymphomania," it might with effort be made to yield such an interpretation.[8] Freudian psychology assisted the effort. Jeffers had known some of the works of both Freud and Jung for more than a decade before writing *The Tower*: "The use of incest as a symbol is no doubt connected with those dream-studies."[9]

[6] Jeffers, *Selected Poetry*, p. 138.
[7] Robert Graves, *The Greek Myths*, 2 vols. (Baltimore: Penguin Books, 1955), and C. Kerenyi, *The Heroes of the Greeks* (London: Thames & Hudson, 1959).
[8] The quoted phrase is Emily Townsend Vermeule's in David Grene and Richmond Lattimore, eds., *The Complete Greek Tragedies*, IV (Chicago: University of Chicago Press, 1959), 392.
[9] Quoted by Squires, *Loyalties of Robinson Jeffers*, p. 73.

The theme of incest is a major addition to the myth and one whose significance was to prove fruitful for later dramatists. Witness the way Eugene O'Neill develops its implications (as well as Jeffers' use of repetition) in shaping action and theme in *Mourning Becomes Electra*; and the way Jean-Paul Sartre in *The Flies* obliquely exploits its sensational possibilities for putting all traditional morality in question. In *The Tower* it is explicit and integral. The violence of the play dramatizes the "racial introversion" which Jeffers abhors, with incest as the logical outcome and climactic expression of it. Its symbolic antithesis and Jeffers' solution to the ills of mankind are partly embodied in Orestes' rejection of his sister's love.

The action of the plot is designed to show that murder begets more than murder: it brings other crimes in its train. In Euripides "Electra never realizes, Orestes only dimly, that they are committing the same atrocity for which they want to punish their elders." [10] Jeffers changes this. His Electra becomes as unnatural as her mother, because she kills as her mother killed. She is neither horrified nor daunted by her incestuous desires: "It is known horror unlocks the heart, a shower of things hidden"; so that for her, "all that our Gods require is courage." Here she echoes the attitude of her mother who, triumphant in revenge, went on to plot the murder of her own children to prevent retaliation.

Aegisthus had objected fearfully: "It is a thing not to be done: we'll guard them closely: but mere madness / Lies over the wall of too-much." Even as her nature struggles with her resolve, Clytemnestra silences him; she counters by reminding him that he is the child of his mother Pelopia's union with her own father, Thyestes: "See, dearest, dearest? They love what men call crime, they have taken her crime to be the king of Mycenae." They will ratify what she intends to do, these gods, as they ratified what she did. All that is needed is courage.

When Agamemnon's ghost enters the body of Cassandra and speaks through her to his treacherous wife, we have another startling addition to the myth: a ghostly rape—her "last defilement," as the seeress calls it—that is also a variation of the in-

[10] Vermeule in Grene and Lattimore, *The Complete Greek Tragedies*, IV, 392.

cest metaphor in less literal but more horrible form. As an unusual figure of the "demonic parody of marriage, or the union of two souls in one flesh," [11] it is appropriate to the tone and intent of the poem. The device enables the dead man to disclose to the people of Mycenae and to Agamemnon's own troops the murder which Clytemnestra would have hidden and lied about. The ghost exhorts the soldiers to avenge his death, and Clytemnestra must justify her crime and face down her enemies.

The device is also preparation for Jeffers' own possession of poor Cassandra, when he later uses her to prophesy the fate of the audience as well as that of the characters. And one suspects that her function as the author's mouthpiece does more than any logical dictates of plot to motivate Clytemnestra to spare her life. Her long monologue bridges the lapse of eight years until Electra and Orestes, now grown up, return to avenge their father. It presents a cyclical view of history, derived by analogy from the growth and decline of nature and civilizations, reflected in the play's pattern of recurrent action. Cassandra predicts the Roman Empire, American civilization, and modern warfare. Recalling the great Ice Age, she foresees the inevitable doom of man which will at last leave the earth "clean." Speaking in her own character (but with something of Jeffers still within her), she prays to the Godhead to

. . . cut humanity
Out of my being, that is the wound that festers in me,
Not captivity, not my enemies: you will heal the earth also,
Death, in your time; but speedily Cassandra.[12]

As in the myth, her prophecies are ignored; and Jeffers, too, who sees himself as a latter-day Cassandra, expects his message to go unheeded, even if he speaks it to full houses as Cassandra does to an empty stage. He believes his warnings will go unheeded by the public, and only a very few will adopt his doctrine. Having forecast mankind's doom, he does not say, "But if you heed me, you can avert it." The introverted race of man is inescapably lost; there is hope only for the individual man:

But for each man
There is real solution, let him turn from himself and man to love

[11] Northrop Frye, *Anatomy of Criticism: Four Essays* (Princeton, N.J.: Princeton University Press, 1957), p. 149.
[12] Jeffers, *Selected Poetry*, p. 115.

God. He is out of the trap then. He will remain
Part of the music, but will hear it as the player hears it.[13]

Jeffers' assumption that his message will be disregarded only
emphasizes the moral imperative under which he acts, while
making its source the more puzzling.[14] This, for me, further ac-
centuates the unlikeliness of drama as an effective means of
communicating it. But I postpone discussion of this point until
the other plays have been considered.

With Aegisthus away in the mountains, Clytemnestra plays
desperately for time. In this prolonged scene Jeffers, like her,
takes dramatic risks that make the action teeter now and then
on the edge of "too-much." The queen deliberately inflames her
people's hatred, then at a pitch of scorn taunts them with her
beauty, exposing her body bit by bit, to convert their hatred into
lust. This calculated striptease dramatizes the metaphor of incest
in another form, that of the ruler enticing her subjects to a public rut. But, having bared her breasts to provoke their desire,
Clytemnestra will not so easily move us to pity later, when she
bares them before Orestes to plead mercy for the mother that
suckled him. The playwright spares us none of her monstrous
baseness; but, in so doing, he reveals her strength, courage and
resourcefulness, so that she dominates the play as its most fully
rounded character. Even after eight years of ruthless power
have left her exhausted and frightened, she puts up a good fight
against her vengeful children and vows to become the pursuing
Fury that will drive Orestes to beg for death as she begged for
life. The moment she dies, his madness begins.

Thereafter, the intensity of the action declines, except for
Orestes' insane killing of Cassandra. This further change in the
myth emphasizes the wanton heedlessness of the House of Atreus
and also points up Electra's similarity to her mother, since she
took advantage of her brother's insanity to provoke him to the

---

[13] Robinson Jeffers, "Going to Horse Flats," in *Such Counsels You Gave to
Me and Other Poems* (New York: Random House, 1937), pp. 90-91.

[14] "When the human mind presupposes that what it has to say will be disregarded, it will cease in large measure to attempt to please an audience,
although it will not cease to try to please itself. The very isolation may,
indeed, be source of aristocratic pleasure. . . ." Squires, *Loyalties of Robinson Jeffers*, p. 138. Jeffers may not try to please an audience, but his subsequent plays clearly reveal that he has worked hard to *write for* an audience
by coupling his dramatic instinct with an improved technique that is entirely of the theatre.

second killing. Electra, like her mother, says: "I have learned strength." She proves it, but she cannot match her mother's strength dramatically because she is not given scenes of comparable power.

Orestes' transformation of character—his recovery from madness and his mystical identification with nature—occurs offstage, and we learn of it later when he resists Electra's enticements. But the last scene between them is, dramatically speaking, almost gratuitous. It is made to bear the burden of an explicit statement of the theme, and to exemplify Jeffers' solution to racial introversion. Yet, once Orestes had undergone his conversion, there is no very good reason for his return. The conflict between brother and sister that ends the play is weakly motivated and one-sided, if not factitious: Orestes' temptation is more apparent than real. He has already climbed the tower beyond tragedy and cast humanity. The scene serves only to confirm the reality of an offstage action.

If madness has released the sexual ferment in Orestes, it also serves to juxtapose the images of death and life, blood-letting and sexual aggression, "the sword and the fountain," and thus to stress by imagery the theme of incest. In killing Clytemnestra he invaded the source of his being. What is the difference between "the serpent and the rose-red cavern" on the one hand, Jeffers is asking, and "the sword and the fountain" on the other, since the one leads to the other, and vice versa. There is no purely *human* solution to this perpetual worship of the human by the human, only an eternal recurrence of crime. The play, says Harold Clurman, "is an expression of a desire to transcend the pain and violence of ordinary humanity so as to become one with the moral impassivity of nature's eyeless forces." [15]

But that desire, extreme in itself, is prompted by events equally extreme. At times, they are presented as virtually unique in their horror; as Orestes, by slaying his mother, feels he has done "Something not done before in the world." Cassandra, who should know, regards Clytemnestra with the words, "I have ranged time, and seen no sight like this." But there is an inconsistency here. The author, as narrator, regards these horrors as

[15] Harold Clurman, *Lies Like Truth: Theatre Reviews and Essays* (New York: Macmillan, 1958), p. 40.

merely the senseless ruck of life; the stones of Agamemnon's palace have seen as bad or worse:

. . . These also are a foam on the stream
Of the falling of the world: there is nothing to lay hold on:
No crime is a crime, the slaying of the King was a meeting of two
    bubbles on the lip of the cataract,
One winked . . . and the killing of your children would be noth-
    ing. . . .[16]

As a dramatist, Jeffers is committed to the importance of these violent actions; as a philosopher, he undercuts their dramatic significance by a change in perspective and scale that amounts to a cosmic indifference, an indifference characteristic of his God of nature. Yet in developing his religion Jeffers came to regard his God of nature as a suffering God, and man as a participant in these cosmic sufferings. They are therefore necessary, but—paradoxically—unimportant. This is because man is unimportant, except insofar as he exists to serve the ultimately inscrutable purposes of God. In his writings Jeffers proceeds by a method which Squires describes as "negative didacticism." Even if we grant him his method, it is difficult to see how a dramatist can effectively present an action in the theatre as simultaneously important and unimportant, unique and all too human, a matter of horror and shock and also a matter of indifference. But let us assume that we have seen mankind at its worst. We realize very quickly that we have not seen it at its best, or anything like its best. Evidently we cannot be shown it, because the best in humanity does not dwell among men but, like Orestes, only far from their habitations.

Whatever the relationships among human beings, their bases are either sexual lust or blood-lust. The incestuous circle is complete. Orestes' slaying of his mother—"entering the fountain"—is an ironic parallel to his action in casting humanity; for by this latter act he achieves communion with the God of nature; he enters "the earlier fountain." The incestuous imagery is carried to the highest level and then subverted. This is so because what his soul seeks is so remote from mankind, so different from the Olympian gods, that it is, we may say, wholly other. For Jeffers all that is (including humanity), is God; but this God is not a divine person making men in His image, nor does He ever be-

[16] Jeffers, *Selected Poetry*, p. 112.

come man. This God is wholly other in its nature, as in its beauty; and *therefore* it must be loved.

II. *At the Fall of an Age*

Jeffers' second explicit dramatization of Greek myth, *At the Fall of an Age* (1933), stands in contrast to his use of such a major and frequently adapted myth as that of the House of Atreus. For here he combines two minor, little-known segments from the aftermath of the Trojan War: Polyxo's murder of Helen of Troy to avenge her husband, King Tlepolemus of Rhodes, who died at the siege of Troy; and Helen's ravishment by the ghost of Achilles.[17]

From the *Iliad* and Proclus' *Chrestomathy* he took the story that Achilles, after "rising from the dead for love of Helen," was translated to the White Isle of Leuke, where he enjoyed a kind of immortality only inferior to that of the gods and Herakles on Olympus. The less familiar account of Polyxo's vengeance he found in Pausanius' *Description of Greece*, which tells how the widowed queen sent some of her serving women, disguised as Erinyes, to hang Helen. Jeffers kept the revenge motif, discarded the device of the serving women, and developed in a distinctive and very characteristic way the implications of Pausanius' statement that after Helen's death, the people of Rhodes worshiped her as the tree-goddess Dendritis, "Helen of the Tree." [18] His fragmentary sources gave Jeffers much opportunity to invent freely. He composed a taut, concentrated action, thematically more complex than its predecessor and structurally better sustained and resolved. The play is dramatic from first to last, yet critics and producers alike have ignored it.

Its production admittedly would involve technical difficulties: it requires a formal chorus, turbulent crowd scenes, and the protracted hanging of Helen on stage, but even this last, the most daunting problem of all, might be solved by ingenious stagecraft. At the least, the intense emotional power of the play invites platform reading or recorded performance.

Critics, as well as producers, might profitably study this

[17] *Ibid.*, pp. 485-504.
[18] J. G. Frazer, trans., *Pausanius's Description of Greece*, 6 vols. (London: Macmillan, 1913), I, 165.

densely textured tragedy of only 20 pages as an illustration of what Antonin Artaud termed "the theatre of cruelty," not for its grisly violence, but for its statement that life is inherently cruel.

I think its greater complexity of action and theme reflects an increased awareness on Jeffers' part of the need for a more complex view of life than he expresses in *The Tower Beyond Tragedy*. He does not abandon the Inhumanist view of life; he expands and deepens it to encompass a mystery: how the suffering that nature requires for life's continuance results in the creation of nature's beauty, its "transhuman magnificence." This is like Nietzsche's Dionysiac vision of perpetual creation and destruction.

At the Fall of an Age also represents an advance for Jeffers in that it treats more compassionately than does the earlier poem man's part in the vast, perpetual cruelty which Jeffers sees as the law of life and which he was to dramatize at closer range in *The Cretan Woman* (1954). Within a darkly oppressive atmosphere of doom and an age's end, he again aspires to the same religious exaltation as in *The Tower*; but now his more inclusive view forces him to accept unending violence and death as the dark side of nature's incessant beauty, instead of seeking to avoid them through the self-imposed isolation of an Orestes. He sees man as caught in nature's trap, as well as his own—and in both instances it may be an unwilling involvement. Here is the fable Jeffers made by grafting the two myths.

To Polyxo's palace in Rhodes, where for nearly 20 years after the fall of Troy the aged and childless widow has mourned her warrior husband and nursed her hatred for the woman whose surpassing loveliness led to his death, comes Helen, still divinely beautiful. She is escorted by strange guardsmen who might be either her subjects or her captors. Exiled by the sons of Menelaus who inherited his kingdom, Helen seeks refuge with her childhood friend Polyxo. If Polyxo refuses her, the guards will take her with them, home to their sepulchre on the Asian foreland. ("We are charged / To keep this woman whom our Lord has enjoyed intact of any less lover until she dies.") For these are the Myrmidons of Achilles who rose from their graves at their dead master's command, stormed the palace at Therapnae, and held it against Menelaus and his men while Achilles possessed

Helen. ("The wild male power of the world / Was mated with the perfect beauty.")

But it is revealed that Achilles, after ravishing her, abandoned her: he left her in charge of some of his Myrmidons and sailed with the rest to the island of Leuke, never to return, "For there one is free of death's / Dreams as of life's"; and there he will find peace, "The peace . . . that even the most beautiful woman never can give."

Freed now of fear that Achilles might avenge Helen, Polyxo pretends to offer sanctuary and then holds her captive. Her long-nursed hatred moves her to humiliate Helen before the island people and to have her hanged naked from the tree before the palace. To hold off Helen's ghostly guard, she calls forth her spearmen, trusted soldiers of Tlepolemus at Troy. But the Myrmidons, strangely, stand aloof and offer no resistance. Instead, they thirst for Helen's death, saying:

At the fall of an age men must make sacrifice
To renew beauty, to restore strength.
We say that if the perfect beauty were sacrificed,
The very beauty that makes our death-cleansed eyes
Dazzle with tears, would be spread on the sky
And earth like a banner.
All men would begin to desire again, and value
Come back to the earth, and splendor walk there. . . .
Beautiful blossoms of battle again and forever unfolding
Star the earth, but we dropped petals of one
Shall endure peace, not even to behold them again nor to hear them,
In the quiet places, in enormous neutrality.
Oh perfectly beautiful, pain is brief, endure to be sacrificed.
This great age falls like water and a new
Age is at birth, but without your pain it could never be beautiful. . . .
Mycenae is down in corruption but Athens will stand instead,
The Dorians will make Laconia a land of helots.[19]

It is the islanders, stirred by Helen's divine beauty, who revolt: "Evil is planned," says the fisherman Calcho. "Shall we let the most beautiful woman in the world fall into a trap, while we stand idle? . . . Can we endure this?" As Helen is stripped and strung up before the demoralized crowd, Polyxo tries to exult in her triumph, but she cannot, because vengeance fulfilled turns to ashes. The queen dies under the blow of Calcho's trident

[19] Jeffers, *Selected Poetry*, pp. 496, 501.

fish-spear, leaving the throne of Rhodes without an heir. The Myrmidons turn and go back the way they came—to their black ship and their final voyage to the grave:

All is accomplished. . . .
Seed has been planted in Asia, seed in Therapnae.
High in the dark, seed for the white eagles of dawn. . . .
Clash, bronze; beat, shields; beauty is new-born.[20]

On the surface the action of the play is like that of *The Tower*. Polyxo, a lesser Clytemnestra, is motivated by hatred and revenge which bring about her own death; Achilles' voluntary return to death on Leuke is like Orestes' decision to cast humanity and seek God. But the differences, including the new poetic formulation of Inhumanism, are greater than the similarities, not only in motives and atmosphere, but more important in the sense of doom, in the cycle of suffering, death, and rebirth, and in the meaning of the supernatural elements. The latter were scarcely more than expedient allusions in *The Tower*; here it is suggested from the start that the gods have a hand in all events and that therefore the pattern of human destiny parallels the pattern of nature. The first words of the play, spoken by a shepherd to his little son, who reluctantly leads a noosed lamb to sacrifice, are: "The gods get hungry like you and me, so it has to die . . . the gods want perfection. . . ." And the appearance of the Myrmidons, "masked identically, moving like one machine," and constituting the formal chorus, removes the action to a dreamlike, ritualistic level even before it is revealed that they are dead. The supernatural is literally restricted to their presence and to the events narrated, not enacted: Achilles' resurrection, his ravishment of Helen, and his final voyage to Leuke. But the ensuing human action is henceforth seen as involving and affirming a supernatural power at work. The duel of the antagonists, Helen's fear and shame, and her desperate but unavailing struggle for life take on a more than human meaning. They are figures in a transhuman process, that is, a natural process that fulfills a divine will.

The revenge action in *The Tower* remained almost at the level of naturalism. It suited Jeffers' purpose to handle it so: he wished to make the violence as revolting as possible, in prepa-

[20] *Ibid.*, p. 504.

ration for Orestes' mystical discovery and conversion. What was
done was none of the gods' doing, but done rather in defiance
of the true wisdom revealed to Orestes. This concentration on
the purely human, despite the use of a supernatural *coup de
théâtre*, had an important result: it hid the pattern of ritual sacrifice which is latent in the Orestes myth and implicit in Aeschylus'
version.

At the Fall, by contrast, finds both its content and its form in
that same pattern, which has been held traditional to Greek
tragedy. Its first foreshadowing comes in the shepherd's words
and in the Myrmidons' choral refrain: "They planted wild seed
in Asia who buried Achilles." It prepares us for the immolation
of Helen, who bears within her Achilles' seed, "The wild male
power of the world." The choral chants explicitly present Helen's
death as a necessary sacrifice and affirm its accomplishment as
fulfillment of the hungry gods' will. The Myrmidons assume
Helen's deification, now that she is one with nature in her fearful death:

They have planted wild seed in the air who lifted God's
Daughter on high, wavering aloft, blessing the new
Age at birth with the beauty of her body. . . .[21]

Far from expressing the hopes and fears of a human community, the Myrmidons constitute an unusual kind of Greek
chorus. These ghostly warriors see with "death-cleansed" eyes,
they speak from beyond the grave; what they say, being privileged utterance, enables them to transcend their particular identity in a specific dramatic situation. They speak for Jeffers.

About death, they tell the islanders: "Our trade was death.
And now we have known it, it is nothing evil"; and to Helen
they say that, between life and death, "there is nothing to choose.
We know them both, and their beauty is beyond them, their
beauty is the value, / As yours is your beauty. We also were
sacrificed." They and their leader defied the gods that he might
enjoy Helen; but he left her for what he came to know as a
greater beauty, the peace of death, and they will do so too.
The Greek myth conferred immortality on Achilles: here he rejects it. Not for him the impersonal bliss of Olympus nor mating
of wild male power with perfect beauty, and still less, the sun-

[21] *Ibid.*

less half-life of the underworld. It is enough for him to be joined in death to the beauty of nature that he knew in life. He finds extinction preferable. So do his Myrmidons, who, impatient to be gone, urge Helen to accept her lot in the creation of that beauty: "It is beautiful to see men die by violence, but to watch a woman / Killed, is the crown. Oh Queen, die boldly."

Since for Jeffers there is neither memory nor consciousness after death, this is a knowledge that the inhumanist can have only while he is *still alive*. That is to say, it is a faith. Even so, if one recalls Orestes' mystical communion with God while alive, the question arises: how could extinction be preferable to that? If there is an answer, it must lie beyond stoical resignation. And this brings us again to the tragic pattern of ritual sacrifice that gives the play its substance and its shape.

When he published his "Excursus on the Ritual Forms Preserved in Greek Tragedy," Gilbert Murray identified certain tragic events as Dionysian elements that embody "the original drama of the Death and Rebirth of the Year Spirit."[22] These elements usually, though not always, include the following, and normally, though not necessarily, occur in this sequence: *agon, pathos, messenger, threnos, anagnorisis*, and *theophany*. Together, according to Murray, they constitute a pattern inherited from religious ritual immemorially performed to insure the perpetuation and fecundity of crops, herds, and man. It is his further hypothesis that the esthetic object we know as Greek tragedy derives from this ritual pattern. Jeffers, well-versed in classical learning, must have known Murray's thesis; like Frazer's *The Golden Bough*, it was part of the intellectual and literary ferment of his youth. In view of Murray's explanation of the elements in the pattern, Jeffers' choice of the ritual sequence and the extent of his adherence to it are significant.

1. "An *Agon* or Contest, the Year against its enemy, Light against Darkness, Summer against Winter," says Murray. *At the Fall of an Age* gives us the literal contest between Polyxo and Helen against a background of Achilles' parallel contest with the gods: his death, resurrection, and return to death. The central contest widens to ally the Myrmidons with Polyxo against Helen,

---

[22] Included in Jane Ellen Harrison's *Themis: A Study of the Social Origins of Greek Religions* (London: Merlin Press, 1963), pp. 340-63. First published at Cambridge in 1912. For the quoted passages, see pp. 343-44.

the people of Rhodes with Helen against their queen. At the figurative level, the aged Polyxo suggests Darkness and Winter, Helen, Light and Summer. But Helen and Polyxo both die, as if both were sacrificial victims.

2. "A *Pathos* of the Year-Daimon," says Murray, "generally a ritual or sacrificial death, in which Adonis or Attis is slain by the tabu animal, the Pharmakos stoned, Osiris, Dionysus, Pentheus, Orpheus, Hippolytus torn to pieces." Polyxo publicly attributes to Helen all the crimes of the Trojan War, decrees her death as an act of justice, and has her stripped to humiliate her. This is the equivalent of the Pharmakos stoned. "While I avenge Tlepolemus the gods are here / Avenging all," says Polyxo. This speech contains dramatic irony, because it anticipates her own imminent death at the hands of Calcho. In Jeffers' scheme of things, hers is a ritual death, too.

3. "A *Messenger*. For this Pathos," says Murray, "seems seldom or never to be actually performed under the eyes of the audience." If we except the Myrmidons' account of Achilles which is preliminary to the central *pathos*, there is no messenger. Jeffers here disregards completely the decorum of Greek tragedy, as he does in *The Tower*. Both Helen's death and Polyxo's occur in full view of the chorus, the people, and the audience.

4. "A *Threnos* or Lamentation. Specially characteristic, however, is a clash of contrary emotions, the death of the old being also the triumph of the new," says Murray. The emotions in the play are orchestrated for maximum contrast with ironic effect. Helen fights fearfully for her life, while her guards urge her toward death; Polyxo suffers desolation at the moment that her defeated enemy is elevated to godhood, and so on. But I think Murray's idea of the *threnos* applies less to this sort of thing, or to the reversals contained in the emotional through-line of an individual character—such as Polyxo's passage from exultant triumph to anguished defeat—than it does to the conflicting feelings one might expect to find within a Greek chorus (in this case, the Myrmidon band), as it reacts to the suffering and death of the hero-victim.

This ambivalence, which Murray regards as "specially characteristic," and which seems to me unique among the dramatic elements of the ritual pattern because of the dual nature of the Year-Daimon's conflict, is notably lacking in the chorus (which is Jeffers' spokesman) and hence in the play. Its absence may be seen as marking the difference between Inhumanism and the classical Greek concern for man.[23]

The emotions of the Myrmidons, living dead men, are in obvious contrast to those of Helen or Polyxo; indeed, they are remote from all the human considerations that agitate the other characters and that might be expected to agitate a conventionally human chorus. Instead, the Myrmidons lament the passing of a great age, "the time of the heroes . . . When glory gathered on Troy. . . . Then men were equal to things, the earth was beautiful. . . ." Life had splendor then, a value it has now lost.

Now all is decayed, all corrupted, all gone down.
Men move like mice under the shadows of the trees,
And the shadows of the tall dead.
The brightness of fire is dulled,
The heroes are gone. . . .
The sun is crusted and the moon tarnished,
And Achilles has chosen peace.[24]

They long for life to be reborn in a new age, to recover its value. Their faith is paradoxical: the price of such resurrection is death —extinction for the individual person. But their emotions do not vacillate, because they have no human love for Helen, only admiration for her peerless beauty and then veneration of it as "the one perfection to be poured out. . . ." They do not lament her loss; they wait eagerly for her death, that they may worship her deified and welcome the new age it will bring. Then they can go content to their barrows, knowing that the glory that is Greece will succeed the corruption of Mycenae.

5 and 6. "An *Anagnorisis*—discovery or recognition—of the slain and mutilated Daimon, followed by his Resurrection or Apotheosis, or in some sense, his Epiphany in glory. This," says Murray, "I shall call by the general name of *Theophany*. It naturally goes with a *Peripeteia* or extreme change of feeling from grief to joy."

We might expect to find this *anagnorisis* happening to Helen, as she faces death, or Polyxo, as she savors her revenge. But

[23] Except for the *pathos*, when it is represented as in some way involving a "ritual or sacrificial death," all the other elements, and especially the recognition and peripety, can easily be appropriated by drama in general, without retaining any suggestion of a ritual substratum or origin.
[24] Jeffers, *Selected Poetry*, p. 496.

Helen, who is never less than noble, dies dreading death and affirming her own life as she lived it:

. . . I have lived and seen the great beauty of things, and been loved and honored.
If now I must die, it is come. Nothing on earth nor in ocean is hatefuller than death; at least I have not
Wasted my life like this gray murderess, fouling with age, lying twenty years in the pit of time
Grinding the rust on a knife.[25]

Polyxo, as she recognizes the futility of revenge, undergoes extreme changes of feeling, but not from grief to joy. Dead, Helen still overwhelms her with her beauty:

. . . Where is my triumph, has the wind snatched it?
There is no woman on earth so happy as I am, having slain my pain: yet it seems that all present things
Slip away down hill, and I could weep for them.[26]

She shows at last a dim apprehension that Helen has in some way triumphed, but none that she has become more than mortal. And her people mill about in darkness and confusion, also unaware of the meaning of what is happening. Only the Myrmidons know, as they have known from the beginning; and they salute Helen deified. It is the *theophany* of which Murray speaks. But we should note that there is no single discovery or recognition by a principal character that constitutes the central meaning of the play. We are to interpret what happens to each, in the light of the Myrmidons' view of the rise and fall of ages, allied to the process of nature. In this view, victim is victor, scapegoat and god are somehow one and the same. This fusion of the sacrificed with the god to whom the sacrifice is made has overtones of that version of the Year-god story to be found in Euripides' *The Bacchae*, where King Pentheus and the god Dionysus are in some sense ultimately the same.[27]

[25] *Ibid.*, p. 502.
[26] *Ibid.*, p. 503.
[27] See Richmond Y. Hathorn, *Tragedy, Myth, and Mystery* (Bloomington: Indiana University Press, 1962), pp. 122-29, 257-58, n. 39.
   Hathorn defends Murray's thesis, which has long been under attack. What is involved in the controversy over the ritual forms of Greek tragedy is not a question of esthetics, but of historical fact. For views opposed to Murray's see H. D. F. Kitto, "Greek Tragedy and Dionysus," published originally in *Theatre Survey, 1960,* and reprinted in John Gassner and Ralph G. Allen, eds., *Theatre and Drama in the Making* (Boston: Houghton

Murray's ritual-sacrifice theory was an attempt to define the Dionysian spirit in Greek tragedy; the essence of that spirit is expressed in the pattern of suffering, death, and resurrection, in the fulfillment of which there takes place a mystical union with the divine.[28] What is strikingly absent from the tragic pattern in Jeffers' play, and from his thought generally, is a personal resurrection, human immortality. Achilles and the Myrmidons achieve it, it is true, but only that they may the more persuasively reject the idea of its desirability. Their real function is to serve as personifications of an inhumanist faith, to tell us what the dead might tell us if they could speak. Helen dies, and there's an end of it. Yet her deification is not meant as a heartless irony that underscores her extinction and nature's indifference. Her beauty is an expression of the divine, as her death is assimilated to the purposeful workings of nature. It is beauty that is to be worshipped, not her person. Achilles, after the disillusionment of his rebellion, *chooses* extinction. Since nature, which is the face and the will of God made manifest, demands total sacrifice —death without resurrection—virtue consists in man's freely accepting his fate, even longing for it in a spirit of *self*-sacrifice. Though man himself cease to be, let him endure pain and death in the certainty that his body will be at one with nature and hence a part of that beauty which is the ultimate value of all existence.

If, in the playwright's developed view, nature achieves its purpose, not despite the ugliness of human violence but partly by means of it, it follows that man has a place and a use in that plan—a dignity not accorded him in the earlier play. Jeffers

Mifflin, 1964), pp. 6-20; also Gerald F. Else, *The Origin and Early Form of Greek Tragedy* (Cambridge: Harvard University Press, 1965).

What remains unquestioned, at least by dramatists, is the superlative effectiveness of the ritual pattern as the basis of a dramatic action.

Francis Fergusson's judgment of Murray's "Excursus" is that "the general notion—that the ritual enactment of struggle, suffering, sacrifice, and the appearance of new light and life, is at the root of the tragic form— is an insight of the first importance." See his Introduction to *Aristotle's Poetics*, trans. S. H. Butcher (New York: Hill & Wang, 1961), pp. 36-41, especially p. 39.

[28] These three elements, says Mircea Eliade, constitute a schema that occurs in all mysteries of initiation: the ordeals lead to the initiate's spiritual death to an old life, then resurrection to a new life. By analogy, physical death is the last rite of passage. See Eliade, *Myths, Dreams, and Mysteries*, trans. Philip Mairet (New York: Harper & Row, 1967), p. 226.

finds justification for tragic humanity because he sees it now as a necessary partner in the tormented strainings by which nature mysteriously moves toward its transhuman ends. Moreover, nobility is now possible to man, if only he will put by "death's dreams"—the longing for immortality or the remembrance of mortal life—and "endure to be sacrificed."

Jeffers rejected the Christian doctrine of the Atonement, repelled by its elements of pity and mercy and its promise of life everlasting. In its place he developed his own nature-religion. But such a religion, if it cannot account for, let alone justify, the presence of man on this earth, is at best incomplete. How can it ignore man's long record without suffering the imputation of being mindless and evasive? Without man, nature has no history. And so he grafted to nature a cyclical view of human history that reflects and repeats, in the rise and fall of cultures and ages, the seasonal cycle of renewal through death and rebirth; and he did so by means of the ritual pattern. Civilizations, like people, are born, flourish, and die, but all are a part of nature, which is eternal.

This is a resolution of Jeffers' thought that he held to until the end of his life. Fifteen years after *At the Fall of an Age*, we read, in his long didactic poem "The Inhumanist," an old man's meditation:

Retreat

is no good, treachery no good, goodness no good.
But still remains the endless inhuman beauty of things; *even of humanity and human history*
The inhuman beauty—and there is endurance, endurance, death's nobler cousin. Endurance.[29]

Endure to be *sacrificed*.

III. *Medea*

In adapting Euripides' *Medea* for the modern stage, tailoring it it to the acting talents of Judith Anderson, Jeffers proved his increased command of the stage.[30] Perhaps no other play con-

---

[29] Robinson Jeffers, *The Double Ax and Other Poems* (New York: Random House, 1948), p. 81 (emphasis added).
[30] Robinson Jeffers, *Medea* (New York: Random House, 1947); also in John Gassner, ed., *Best American Plays*, Third Series, 1945-1951 (New York: Crown, 1952), pp. 395-414. My references are to the latter edition.

sidered here has proved so certain in its appeal to general audiences or been seen by so many people since its opening performances in 1947. Jeffers enlarged the title role at the expense of the others, further reduced the function of a nearly redundant chorus, muted the element of magic in the plot, confining it to two effects, one offstage, one on, and substituted his own imagery for Euripides'. But the inhumanist author's changes in "freely" adapting the Greek original are less interesting than his ambivalent attitude toward the play and its heroine.

At the risk of belaboring the playwright with his own stick, I stress again that Jeffers is a religious writer and that this fact is one of the most interesting aspects of his work. Yet here he has made a secular drama out of what was a religious one.

. . . The distinction between religious and secular drama is not a mechanical one. There is religious drama in which gods do not appear and secular drama in which they do. There are no gods in the *Medea* or *Hecuba* for example, yet these plays must be regarded as religious drama: treated as tragic character-studies they fail, more or less disastrously; they make good sense only when we see that the real Tragic Hero is humanity itself.[31]

It is certainly not all Jeffers' fault. Today one must take it on faith that the original *Medea* was religious in essence, and so regarded by the Athenians. We have lost the key to the Greek world-view; and the action, even with the element of magic in the original and the adaptation, does not adequately imply, or supply us with, a cosmology and theology that will place its violent events in a religious context and evoke from us the correct response.[32]

Medea is an example of passion unchecked by reason; the vehemence of her emotions, her cunning for evil, and her recourse to black arts, make her witchcraft almost a force of nature. She could teach Clytemnestra to suck venom.

[31] H. D. F. Kitto, *Form and Meaning in Drama* (New York: Barnes & Noble, 1957), p. 231.
[32] After having seen the Piraikon Theatron perform Euripides' *Medea*, I would have to qualify this judgment, which was based on having read Euripides and seen Jeffers' version. Despite my ignorance of the language, Medea, played by E. Vergi, was certainly larger than life; the aura of the play was certainly religious, largely because the chorus conveyed great spiritual intensity; and the whole ceremonious production by D. Rondiris impressed me as a ritual. The result was closer to Kitto's view of the play, given below, than I would have thought possible.

Medea is no character compounded of good and bad, in whom what is bad tragically brings down in ruin what is good, and we certainly cannot fear for her as for one of ourselves. . . .

Medea on the other hand is certainly not all villainy; she loves her children, loved Jason (if that is a merit), and was popular in Corinth; but it is the essential part of this tragedy that she was never really different from what we see her to be. Euripides could easily have represented her as a good but passionate woman who plunges into horrors only when stung by deadly insult and injury. There was no need for him to rake up her past as he does—except that this is his whole point. She never was different. . . .[33]

What Jeffers gives us is a woman whose deeds are the horrible consequences of the betrayal of a trust. It is trust that binds society together, beginning with the bond between man and woman; and in the play the breaking of that faith brings about four deaths—two of them filicides—and the ruin of a man's life. The play lacks, for example, the ironic framework which Shakespeare provides in *Richard III*, whereby we see the villainous Richard become the scourge of God, the instrument of divine punishment for the sins of the treacherous nobles. And so the morally equivocal stand of the play is further confused by the playwright's ambivalence: Medea wavers between being "a good but passionate woman . . . stung by deadly insult and injury" and a monster whose hatred and violence are the products of her own nature and past actions.

When Jason throws Medea over for the sake of an advantageous marriage and political advancement, her love turns to hate, and her hate begets revenge. "Love blows away, hatred remains," says the First Woman of the chorus. Jeffers states here a conviction implicit in his view of human nature, i.e., its capacity for hate exceeds its capacity for love, as its actions for evil exceed those for good. This it is to live among men: there is no health in it.

The pathos of Medea's abandonment, the shame of her rejection, the bitterness of her betrayal, the plight of a lone woman against the world—these ought not to outweigh the horror of her deeds. If we identify ourselves with her, it can only be by giving in to sentimentality. For the things she did in the past, out of love of Jason, were as devastating as those she does against

[33] H. D. F. Kitto, *Greek Tragedy: A Literary Study* (Garden City, N.Y.: Doubleday Anchor Books, 1955), pp. 197-98.

him out of hate. The only crime she has not yet committed is that of murdering her own children. The same struggle occurs within her, more fiercely fought, as did within Clytemnestra. The opposition of the natural and the unnatural is seen awry as mother love and wifely hate. In Jeffers' view hatred is as natural as love; it is excess of either he objects to, and a love as consuming as Medea's is bound to produce an opposite excess.

Images of fire recur through the play, built up from one line in Euripides: "Shall I set fire to the bridal mansion?" They represent the fierce passion of love that leaves only destruction in its wake, and they point to the literal fire with which Medea destroys Creon and his daughter.

FIRST WOMAN: God keep me from fire and the hunger of the
sword. . . .

SECOND WOMAN: A little love is a joy in the house,
A little fire is a jewel against frost and darkness.

FIRST WOMAN: A great love is a fire
That burns the beams of the roof.
The doorposts are flaming and the house falls.[34]

Jeffers does not omit Medea's account of her past crimes, performed for love of Jason, nor does he let her vengeance go unopposed by the Women of Corinth:

MEDEA: You are wise. Anyone
Running between me and my justice will reap
What no man wants.

FIRST WOMAN: Not justice; vengeance.
You have suffered evil, you wish to inflict evil.

MEDEA: I do according to nature what I have to do. . . .

SECOND WOMAN: I dreamed that someone
Gave good for evil, and the world was amazed.

MEDEA: Only a coward or a madman gives good for evil.[35]

But Jeffers judges by inhumanist standards and not, despite the Second Woman, by those of Christian charity. There is no charity in nature. Medea should represent all that is reprehensible in man, judged by Inhumanism: she is obsessively preoccupied with herself and her relationships; wildly immoderate in love, then even more so in hate; deceitful, vengeful, cruel—voluptuously,

[34] Gassner, ed., *Best Plays*, p. 404.
[35] *Ibid.*, p. 410.

sadistically, demoniacally cruel; and murderous toward her own children, out of spite for her husband: "I have done it: because I loathed you more than I loved them." Yet she has traits which the inhumanist must applaud. She is independent and fearless; she despises the sociable, privacy-invading Greeks with their petty concerns, self-congratulation, and inordinate ambitions. She is a fighter who single-handedly (but with the help of magic) and successfully takes on the might of Corinth and destroys it. She has strength to endure. Finally, she is pitiless, or makes herself so, and thus extirpates a human flaw. (Jeffers, who finds no pity in nature, despises it as an emotion that holds men in trap; it was one of his reasons for rejecting Christianity, as it was one of Nietzsche's.)

Medea, for whom Euripides apologized by saying that she behaves as no Greek woman would, in Jeffers' treatment becomes the primitive par excellence. . . . She is a woman of primeval passions—Jason is worldly ambitions; and the tragedy develops from the contrast between her warmth and his coldness; her naturalness, his opportunistic realism; her primitive spirit and his civilized urbanity. Where Euripides apologizes, *Jeffers reveres*. And so the play unfolds as the triumph of the primitive spirit over civilization.[36]

Despite this, Medea is a strange choice as an inhumanist heroine: she does all the things, and worse, that Jeffers most reprehends in Clytemnestra, Electra, and Polyxo; and she remains defiantly impenitent. How, except by inversion, can her deeds possibly serve as examples of the inhumanist doctrine in action? If her scorn of humankind stamps her as a true inhumanist, are we to assume that, by doing violence to her deepest human urge, motherhood, she transcends her own humanity? We look on, so appalled that we should be hard put to it to regard her magical escape, not as flight from the consequences of her crimes, but as a symbolic rejection of the despised human race; as we should be equally hard put to it to contend that saying no to man is saying yes to life. It is a strange act of repudiation that outdoes the enormities it repudiates. Medea's excesses end in paradox: here Inhumanism contradicts itself.[37]

[36] Squires, *Loyalties of Robinson Jeffers*, p. 115.
[37] Dame Judith Anderson, for whom Jeffers prepared his version of *Medea*, knew him well. Interviewed in 1967 on the television program *The Creative Person* (NET Playhouse), she spoke of the violence there must have been in Jeffers. She said it was never apparent in the man—quite the contrary —only in his work.

Her departure with the bodies of her dead sons, although it should be quite different in spirit as in circumstance, is curiously like that of Orestes, for it has something of the author's same approval of the course of action taken:

> Now I go forth
> Under the cold eyes of heaven—those weakness-despising stars:—
> not me they scorn.

IV. *The Cretan Woman*

Between any modern version of Euripides' *Hippolytus* and the original, there stands the masterpiece of Racine's *Phaedra*—one of the most successful examples in dramatic literature of the transmutation of a pagan myth for the audiences of a Christian culture. Despite the impeccable austerity of its verse, the play appalled—and conquered—its auditors by the vehemence of its passion. In 1954 Jeffers published his last play, *The Cretan Woman*, based on Euripides' original. One wonders what would have been the reactions of the audiences in Louis XIV's reign to its vehemence, brutality, and plain-speaking. Yet in boldness of technique, economy of means, and theatrical effectiveness, *The Cretan Woman* stands as an accomplished use of classic myth in modern drama.

In Racine's *Phaedra* the characters of the tragedy, arrayed in the court dress of the Grand Seigneur, duly allude to the gods of Olympus. Theseus petitions his father Poseidon to destroy Hippolytus, his son. The sea-god, duly observing neoclassic decorum, complies with an offstage death. Artemis, goddess of chastity, no longer figures in the cast, because Hippolytus is not her devotee but the lover of her father's enemy, Aricia. And, although the play is a tragedy of love, Aphrodite has been similarly banished: she is a symbol of amorous passion who exists only in the allusions of the great poetry. The gods do not provoke this tragedy: it is set in motion by the device of the false rumor of Theseus' death. The gods are little more than a classical inheritance, decorative furniture from the world of myth. The foreground of the action involves men and women whose passions spring from within themselves to upset the balance of mind, heart, and will in human relationships. When that balance is tipped, as it is by the report of Theseus' death, passion over-

whelms reason in Phaedra and brings on the disaster. Racine, as
a Christian dramatist, employs mythology to disguise a Christian
ethos, and so contemplates it at a distance. His tragedy focuses
on the conflict between the passions, anarchic in fallen man, and
the reason-guided will. His characters speak as if Christianity
had never been; but their moral standards are Christian. He
retains the gods for their traditional weight and perhaps also
as a protective coloration; but he locates the center of tragedy
within man.

Jeffers, like his characters in *The Cretan Woman*, also speaks
as if Christianity had never been; he treats the myth within the
truly pagan world of the Greek tragic dramatists and philoso-
phers, where he has belonged since his youth.[38] He restores
Aphrodite to the cast of characters and uses her as his philosophic *raisonneuse*. She personifies Love, which is here represented as the ruling power of the universe. He does without the
goddess Artemis, apparently because he can find in nature no
chastity as an elemental force opposed to love. He does without
Poseidon, too, for in this play the sea-god answers no prayers,
whether for good or evil; he does not exist. As in Racine, the
center of tragedy is within man, and Jeffers has found striking
ways to vary the order and emphasis of elements from the Greek
tragedy to drive the point home. Despite the changes, *The
Cretan Woman* seems closer in spirit to Euripides than it does
to *Phaedra*, and yet by far closest of all to its contemporaries,
from which, despite its sense of desolation, it diverges so sharply
in its underlying beliefs. Jeffers has put his own stamp on his
version of the Greek, as surely as Racine did his.

Imagine that Orestes, still holding the inhumanist belief, returned to the world of men as Hippolytus. Quite unintentionally, he inspires overwhelming physical desire in his stepmother,
Phaedra, and, by scorning her advances, turns her love to hatred.
She accuses him of rape in her husband's absence and provokes
Theseus to kill him. Why compare him to Orestes? Because, in
every respect except that of living apart from men, Hippolytus
is an inhumanist; and his detachment does not save him. The play
is a statement in full dramatic terms of Jeffers' religion of pantheism and the indifference of nature to man's suffering.

[38] Robinson Jeffers, *The Cretan Woman*, in *Hungerfield and Other Poems*
(New York: Random House, 1954), pp. 25-92.

We recall that the mind, for its health, must turn "from itself and man, from parts to the whole," and seek God in the beauty of nature. Beauty is to Jeffers at once the proof of God's existence and its abiding manifestation in the natural world. Man is himself a part of the creation which is God, but his existence is ultimately tragic. It is tragic, however, not necessarily because he has incestuously concerned himself with human affairs and wrought his own destruction, but because he is also a victim of his god, which operates as surely in the destructiveness of the passions as in the grandeur of rock, sea, and sky. To flee the society of men is no guarantee of protection for the inhumanist: his lot is to endure—with detachment. Man is unimportant, death is the only peace, and annihilation alone offers absolution for all. Such is the groundwork of this tragedy, which does not offer the easy, if mythic, flight from men that ended *The Tower Beyond Tragedy*. It is more pessimistic than the earlier play; it affirms, not man's freedom to "fall in love outward," but the overwhelmingly destructive power of nature.

The gods of Olympus are even more of a dramatic convention—and convenience—for Jeffers than they were for Racine. He uses the convention boldly in *The Cretan Woman*: despite her physical presence, Aphrodite is not a person but a personification.

As the play opens, three women of Troezen, beggars at the door of Theseus' palace, pass near Aphrodite's altar. Suddenly, all three feel the presence of a superhuman force. One says, "Something divine is here. There was such a dizziness at my heart suddenly. . . ." A second says, "I feel my eyes dazzle and my knees tremble." And a third: "There is a divine anger in this place: like the glaring eyes of a wild beast." It is not simply the fact that these women believe in the gods that establishes the stage reality of the invisible force, but their reactions to it. Concerned about other things a moment before, they all respond at once to Aphrodite's presence. And so, when she appears and addresses the audience, we accept her.

Aphrodite lays direct claim to her dominion: ". . . So I have come down to this place, / And will work my will." As she plays with a spray of fruit blossom she carries, she says: "I make the man / Lean to the woman. I make the huge blue tides of the ocean follow the moon; I make the multitude / Of the stars in the sky to love each other, and love the earth." It is she who makes trees flower and bear, birds mate, and "hot whirling atoms" cling together. She sustains the universe; without her, "all life / Would gasp and perish. But love supports and preserves them: *my saving power.*" Here is the basic irony of the play. The power that moves the sun and stars (but is not Dante's Love) and preserves all nature from bursting into chaos, is the same force that causes man to destroy himself and others.

The Cretan Woman, although perhaps not the best exposition of his doctrine, is Jeffers' best play. Structurally, its plot is more tightly unified than its Greek model. Like *Phaedra*, it avoids anticlimax and disunity by prolonging Phaedra's life beyond that of Hippolytus, placing both his death and her suicide quite close together at the end of the play. This Phaedra has no children, so there is no palace revolution or struggle for succession to the throne. Jeffers dispenses with the false rumor and with the waiting-woman as go-between, because he wishes to depict Phaedra's desire for her stepson as directly and as unsparingly as possible. Of the three playwrights, he enjoys the freest stage; so he reverts to Euripides' original version, which the Athenians objected to as unseemly, and has Phaedra herself solicit Hippolytus.[39] This concentrates the action, makes Phaedra's rejection more humiliating and her hatred all the more believable; it also dispenses with the waiting-woman's remorseful suicide.

Unhampered by the conventions of decorum in regard to violence also, Jeffers shows two brutal killings on stage. He intensifies the horror of Hippolytus' death, not only by showing it directly but also, and more important, by having Theseus himself stab his beloved son—and in Phaedra's presence. Then he turns round and achieves the reverse effect: when Hippolytus' friend, Alcyon, tries to save him, Theseus' brutal bodyguards perfunctorily stab him to death.

Since lack of understanding is one of the themes of the play, there is no protracted reconciliation between father and son before Hippolytus dies or any consolation of the youth by Artemis. He lives only long enough to tell Phaedra, "I despise you," and to say tenderly to Theseus, "My poor father." Jeffers prolongs the intensity of the remainder of the play by having Phaedra,

[39] See David Grene, Introduction, *Hippolytus*, in Grene and Lattimore, *The Complete Greek Tragedies*, III, 158-60.

shocked out of her lust, taunt Theseus cruelly in order to provoke him to kill her too. But she fails, and we are spared further brutality. She dies offstage by hanging herself, as in Euripides.

All the ends of the tragedy are now come upon the aging hero Theseus, adventurer, lover, and man of blood. Jeffers treats him not with the admiration of a Gide, but with an inhumanist's moral scorn; and yet he gives him dignity and pathos, this old bull who had to kill his son and indirectly cause his wife's death before waking to the reality of his own nature. Some of Jeffers' most scornful lines have been written about pity. It was the pity implicit in the teachings of Christ that helped to turn him from Christianity. He finds no pity in nature. Yet in this play he evokes pity and obviously intends to do so. Furthermore, he has Theseus, in his recognition scene, realize that it was his lack of understanding and pity that contributed to Phaedra's tragedy. The pitch of pathos is achieved when Theseus calls upon Poseidon to restore his son's life:

THESEUS:

                    O God of the Sea: *my* God,
My foster-father, Cod of the high and shining and leaping Sea: you promised me
You'd answer three prayers of mine, whatever they were.
    I pray you all three at once:
Make my son live! *Make my son live. Make my son live.*

FIRST WOMAN:

                                 You would
    have to pray to the God of Death, Theseus,
Not to the Sea. He has no power in this matter.

SECOND WOMAN:

                            And as to Death:
    those gray stone lips
Have never answered a prayer. His ears are stone: men never pray to him. His cold gray hands implacably
Hold what they take.[40]

This is a major alteration in the myth, and one well conceived to communicate the theme of the indifference of nature to the happiness or unhappiness of man. It makes its point, whether or not the spectator is familiar with the myth or with the earlier versions.

Equally effective, to my mind, is another alteration, which in-

[40] Jeffers, *Hungerfield,* p. 87.

volves one of the thornier problems of the Greek version: the use of a chorus. We recall that in *The Tower* Jeffers omitted a chorus and substituted Cassandra. He retained the Women of Corinth in *Medea* but with something of the awkwardness of the original. When they wished to flee in terror, Medea had to dominate them by sheer force of will to make them stay and hear the results of her revenge. Racine simply did without a chorus. Jeffers retains it, reduced to the Three Women. He solves the principal objection made against its use in Euripides by giving the women an original motivation and permitting them at times to function as individual characters. These begging women now play a decisive role in the action instead of a passive one. They provide background exposition, a slight sense of community, and lyrical statement and music as needed. As a formal device, they break down into individualized attitudes as well as speeches. And they do not have the burden of stating the explicit theme of the play: that falls to Aphrodite.

At the beginning, the women's hunger for food serves as thematic link and contrast to Phaedra's hungry passion for Hippolytus. Though love is an accepted part of life to them, the chief business of living is filling their own bellies and providing for their families, whereas Phaedra is so sunk in the fury of desire that she rejects all food and has not eaten in days. The women cannot imagine any crisis intense enough to make one indifferent to the task of keeping life in the body.

When Phaedra solicits Hippolytus, they are present, as in the Greek version, and later are sworn to secrecy by the waiting-woman. "Above all do we have to refrain from asking why the chorus, despite its oath, allows Hippolytus to be destroyed when a hint of the truth would at least make Theseus pause awhile," says Kitto, in reference to Euripides.[41] He assumes, of course, that the chorus would wish to help Hippolytus. Jeffers solves the problem by making the opposite assumption. Thus, the oath does not neutralize the trio in the action, but makes the women accomplices in Phaedra's scheme to destroy her stepson. Their silence first becomes an accusation against Hippolytus. When Theseus threatens them with a whipping, they give false testimony in support of Phaedra's charge. Hippolytus' earlier words recoil on his head; for he had told them that, before his father,

[41] Kitto, *Greek Tragedy*, p. 215.

they could witness to his innocence and Phaedra's madness, and he had told his father the same.

The women keep silent not because they are bound by oath, but because they sympathize with Phaedra, whom they saw scorned and humiliated. Then their guarded words, chosen to protect her, are twisted by her and the nurse to reinforce the baseless accusation. The women instinctively consent to this perversion of the truth, because they regard the chaste Hippolytus as homosexual and therefore a natural enemy. The development whereby they become involved in Phaedra's lie, and then uphold it, creates strong suspense and dread; it makes the helplessness of his plight much more immediate than would a report, after the fact, of his death offstage. The women's deep antipathy to him, never directly stated but powerfully implied, underscores the theme of the play; their presence is no longer passive and awkward, but active and meaningful. Although they consented to Hippolytus' death, Jeffers can, without inconsistency, also permit them something of the same remorse that Phaedra and Theseus feel. When they pronounce his eulogy, they seem less arbitrarily converted into a stage convention than, for example, Aufidius, who conveniently pronounces the requiem for his enemy in *Coriolanus*.

Hippolytus was happy.
He had his youth, he did no evil, suddenly he died.
The pity of these things has broken my heart.[42]

Then Aphrodite, laughing, reappears on the altar, and the women gaze at her. She stresses the indifference of nature to the woes of men: "What we desire, we do. . . . I am the power of Love." Then she points the moral, warning the audience that men will one day become so powerful through science that they will think they control the world: "Let them beware. Something is lurking hidden. There is always a knife in the flowers. There is always a lion just beyond the firelight." Then she vanishes, and the play ends. The beautiful spray of blossoms she leaves behind contrasts with the other manifestations of love the play has presented. With great authority, Jeffers has used the supernatural, in which he does not believe, to command belief.[43]

[42] Jeffers, *Hungerfield*, p. 90.
[43] Margarete Bieber considers *The Cretan Woman* as a "distorted version of Euripides' *Hippolytus* mixed with Senecan frenzy, calculated revenge,

Man *is* important, and the theatre exists as proof. Moreover, drama is anthropocentric: "The subject of the theatre is man," says Robert Speaight.[44] And for its realization, theatre requires a communal response, being by nature man-centered, social, and public. It is man regarding man—almost a symbol of that racial introversion which Inhumanism opposes. Yet Jeffers' career in the theatre shows him trying successfully, if not to please an audience, at least to improve his dramatic technique. One consequence of this has been that he has increased the objectivity of the form he uses. His philosophy is essentially undramatic, but his plays increase in drama. It seems to me that this occurs because his method of "negative didacticism," together with the increased objectivity, prevents him more and more from communicating the central tenets of his doctrine. Jeffers' God of nature is a suffering God, and yet indifferent to the sufferings of men, who are a part of Him. Aphrodite, effective as she is, does not convey this: "We are not extremely sorry for the woes of men. We laugh in heaven. . . . What we desire, we do." The effect, because of the personification, is not that of suffering and indifference, but of heartless cruelty and even malice.

It is curious to use the peculiarly heightened consciousness that the theatre evokes to tell men that the God of nature is barely conscious, a sleeping beauty, and that annihilation is best, because man in unimportant. It is curious, too, to spend a lifetime creating cautionary stories for men, and preaching to them year after year—if they are unimportant. Again, it is a sort of obsession with one's own kind—almost racial introversion.

---

and modern adulterous passion. Jeffers interprets the Greek myth with ludicrous prejudices." See her *History of the Greek and Roman Theater* (Princeton, N.J.: Princeton University Press, 1961), p. 260. Dr. Bieber appears to prefer accurate translations of the Greek dramatists to adaptations and to be least sympathetic to independent treatments of the *myths*, just as she prefers historical accuracy to artistic freedom in costuming and décor. See Chap. XVI of her *History*, "The Influence of the Ancient Theater on the Modern Theater," pp. 254-70.

[44] Robert Speaight, *Christian Theatre* (New York: Hawthorn Books, 1960), p. 140.

CHAPTER V

EUGENE O'NEILL:
The Family as Furies

[*Dynamo*] is really the first play of a trilogy that will dig at the roots of the sickness of today as I feel it—the death of an old God and the failure of science and materialism to give any satisfying new one for the surviving primitive religious instinct to find a meaning for life in, and to comfort its fears of death with. It seems to me that anyone trying to do big work nowadays must have this big subject behind all the little subjects of his plays or novels, or he is simply scribbling around on the surface of things and has no more real status than a parlor entertainer.

Mourning Becomes Electra, by Eugene O'Neill, is one of the major attempts in modern drama to present materials from classical myth in terms congenial to realism, the dominant theatrical style between the two world wars. Performed with great success in 1931, this ambitious trilogy about the House of Mannon parallels in many ways the *Oresteia* of Aeschylus; yet it is set quite circumstantially in a definite historical period, no more than a century ago, 1865-66, and in a particular place, a New England seaport. By putting his tragedy back in time a few generations, O'Neill sought to distance the action, so as to give it perspective and also to avoid the complexities of contemporary life. He wrote it in a style of selective realism and took enormous pains to achieve a careful verisimilitude. For it was to be, before all else, "really an essentially modern psychological drama"; [1] that is, all supernatural elements of the Greek myth were to be eliminated.

Here is irony, if not paradox. Of all the English, French, and American plays that used classical myth in these decades, *Mourning Becomes Electra* is the only one to give an impression of the world and of man that is, if anything, even older than the mythical world of its classical model. Jean Cocteau's *The Infernal Machine* takes place partly in a satanic Never-Land of the playwright's own imaginings, partly in the polytheistic ages of the Eastern Mediterranean, and partly in a modern city; Sartre's *The Flies* depicts a barbaric Greece where the gods of Olympus have superseded the chthonic gods; but it is a land transposed in time to an age of skepticism very like our own. Whereas O'Neill's play, behind its façade of Civil War New England, seems to unfold in a world ruled by the *Manes*, the immemorial religion of the dead which has been called "the most ancient worship among men": "We find this worship of the dead among the Hellenes, among the Latins, among the Sabines, among the Etruscans; we also find it among the Aryas of India. Mention is made of it in the hymns of the Reg-Veda. It is spoken of in the Laws of Manu as the most ancient worship among men. . . . This belief and these rites are the oldest and the most persistent of anything pertaining to the Indo-European race." [2]

In basing a modern psychological drama on "one of the old legend plots of Greek tragedy," O'Neill stated the problem that confronted, in one way or another, all the playwrights whose works utilized classical myth, since the problem involves not only the beliefs of each, but also the beliefs of modern audiences. "Would it be possible," he asked, "to achieve a modern psychological approximation of the Greek sense of fate which would seem credible to a present-day audience and at the same

[1] Eugene O'Neill, "A Note for This Edition," *Mourning Becomes Electra*, in *The Plays of Eugene O'Neill*, Wilderness Edition, 12 vols. (New York: Scribner's, 1934), III, xiii. This edition is used for all quotations and page references. This chapter appeared as a two-part study in the Winter and Spring, 1967, issues of *Drama Critique*. The quotation at the beginning of the chapter is from Barrett H. Clark, *Eugene O'Neill: The Man and His Plays*, rev. ed. (New York: Dover, 1947), p. 120.

[2] Fustel de Coulanges, *The Ancient City: A Study of the Religion, Laws, and Institutions of Greece and Rome*, trans. Willard Small (Boston: Lee & Shephard, 1874), p. 25.

time prove emotionally affecting?" [3] This is a tactful statement of the problem to which he gave a plainer formulation in his earlier "Notes and Extracts from a Fragmentary Diary," kept while he was planning and writing the trilogy. There he posited a modern play based on Aeschylus which "an intelligent audience of today, possessed of no belief in gods *or supernatural retribution,* could accept and be moved by." [4] While using a plot about supernatural retribution, what retributive force could he substitute for the supernatural so as to give a sense of ineluctable fate to an audience which he assumed believed no longer in either?

With this as his starting point, O'Neill made major changes in emphasis and incident, especially in the outcome of the mythic plot. Nonetheless, Whitney J. Oates could say: "The thing about O'Neill's trilogy which has most interested me is the fact that in the first two plays you have almost a one-to-one correspondence with the version of Aeschylus"; adding, of course, that the thing missing from the third play is "theology." [5] The story became Electra's, rather than Orestes'; "its complex human interrelationships and its chain of fated crime and retribution," which were to provide the psychological framework, O'Neill altered here and there and especially in the final play, to make them yield "modern imaginative possibilities." [6] It is in Aeschylus' *The Eumenides,* where the gods appear in order to defeat and mollify the Furies, that the sense of fate as vengeance is weakest. But it is in *The Haunted,* his concluding play, that O'Neill sought to make the sense of fate strongest and the retribution it brings overwhelming. The Greek trilogy has a happy ending; O'Neill's was to end in unrelieved tragedy, as if by tripling the handicap he would outdo the Greeks at their own game. On his own terms he succeeded. But this is not to say that his is therefore the greater play; rather, it is to mark the deep difference of spirit between the two works. It is just this sense of fate, implacably vindictive in its retribution—this doom that makes life a contin-

---

[3] O'Neill, *Plays of Eugene O'Neill,* p. xiii.
[4] Reprinted in full in Barrett H. Clark, ed., *European Theories of the Drama: With a Supplement on the American Drama,* rev. ed. (New York: Crown, 1947), pp. 530-36 (emphasis added).
[5] Quoted in Mark Van Doren, ed., *The New Invitation to Learning* (New York: Random House, 1942), pp. 18-19.
[6] O'Neill, "Notes and Extracts," in Clark, *European Theories,* p. 530.

uing horror, so that extinction is to be preferred to it—that makes the modern psychological drama older in spirit than that of an age which saw the birth of tragedy.

Mourning Becomes Electra is notable in another respect. Among the plays of the period, O'Neill's was the first to attempt the transposition of classical myth into the theatrical style of modern realism. Cocteau gave his *Orphée* a modern sauce of setting and costume; but underneath was a fantasy of the most dream-like improbability, with a talking horse, a flying glazier, Death as a woman in evening gown, and an epilogue in Heaven. T. S. Eliot, too, was to attempt the hurdle of modernity in *The Family Reunion*; but, in a sense, he hedged by retaining the Furies, the chorus, and verse dialogue. Only Jean Anouilh, like O'Neill, accepted fully the challenge involved in mating classical myth and realistic verisimilitude in *Eurydice*, one of his three plays on Greek themes.

Despite all the departures from it made in the time of O'Neill, realism was still the dominant style of drama. Regarded simply as a style of playwriting, it is no better, and probably no worse, than any other. Much is written about its cramping restrictions, in much the same way that Romantic dramatists complained of the arbitrary limitations of neoclassicism; yet it must be remembered that realism, in its turn, came as a liberation from the unrealities of a decadent Romanticism. Playwrights who inveigh against it seem really to be attacking not the style itself so much as a popular preference for little else; and there, of course, they have a point. Modern drama had produced no other definite style to triumph over it and supplant it, however various and insistent the modifications of it had been from time to time. Notably, it was verse dramatists like T. S. Eliot who felt its challenge most keenly, as if they sensed that a new style could be achieved only by first succeeding in, or through, realism itself.

Realism implies accurate, if selective, observation of physical reality; and so plausibility in speech, manners, and psychological portraiture is necessarily one of its criteria. In the hands of all but the most skilled, verisimilitude becomes subservience to *imitation*—imitation of surfaces, as well as depths; imitation of appearances as well as realities, although the true realist would say that appearances are a part of reality, that you cannot have the essence of life without its substance. The attempt to do the latter was the aim—and the limitation—of expressionism. Yet realism, stemming as it did from philosophic naturalism, still retained, however unintentionally, traces of its origins. In drama it proved difficult to give allegiance to the externals of realism while avoiding implications either of determinism through heredity and environment or of materialism. Clearly, this difficulty increases when the playwright derives his materials from classical myth. By definition one would expect mythical stories and themes to prove most refractory when treated realistically. Yet O'Neill, said an English critic, "found, in recent history, a suitable soil for Greek tragedy, which is more than Cocteau ever did." [7] And he did so, as Oates remarked, while modeling his play upon a specifically theological one, whose spirit it directly contradicts: "I think that the essential theme of the *Oresteia* is a theological one. It is Aeschylus's attempt to discover, portray, and express the ultimate power behind the Universe. The nature of that power, its relation to man and also, in addition, what man must do when he faces the brute fact of evil in this world." [8]

In regard to form and craftsmanship, then, though not of language, O'Neill's attempt was important, and his success equally so. The play, in fact, imposes itself with great immediacy and directness; it achieves its undoubted effectiveness without having to rely on the suggestiveness of its parallels or on the enrichment of associative imagery and classical allusions. It is, in this respect, the direct opposite of André Gide's *Oedipe*, and consequently it serves to clarify a problem of esthetics posed by the whole effort to use myth in modern drama. Is a play better for gaining such independence that it can do without these added values of poetic allusion and emotional association, the dividends of basing a modern play on a classical masterpiece and patently mythical characters? Yes: it is the proof that the play creates its own autonomy, that its principal effects spring from itself as source and not from its model. The informed spectator undoubtedly derives from the parallels and associations additional pleasures, but they are surplus values. The mythical archetypes are *in* the play, not merely suggested by it; and, in O'Neill's case,

[7] Laurence Kitchin, *Mid-Century Drama* (London: Faber & Faber, 1960), p. 69.
[8] See Van Doren, ed., *The New Invitation to Learning*, pp. 18-19.

they have been so thoroughly transmuted as to bear the modern playwright's signature.[9]

Analyzing modes in *Anatomy of Criticism*, Northrop Frye says that "the mimetic tendency itself, the tendency to verisimilitude and accuracy of description, is one of two poles of literature," the other of which is myth.[10] Indeed, his spectra of modes, symbols, myths, and genres, each of which rounds upon itself, provide interesting categories against which to range the elements of O'Neill's trilogy. It will be found, for instance, that the content of the plays is highly realistic, so that this mode constitutes its underlying tonality, but the form of the plays is strikingly nonrealistic in its use of irony and repetition. Frye says: "Irony descends from the low mimetic: it begins in realism and dispassionate observation. But as it does so, it moves steadily towards myth, and dim outlines of sacrificial rituals and dying gods begin to reappear in it." [11] We see this happening in *Mourning Becomes Electra*, where pride of family, combined with a puritan conscience, creates a new religion—or re-creates an old one: the religion of the dead.

Again following Frye, we find that O'Neill's realistic tragedy, with its strong sense of fate and retribution but without the supernatural, actually combines two traditional theories of tragedy which Frye calls "contradictory" and therefore "extreme limiting" views of it. They are the fatalistic and the moralistic. The former holds that "all tragedy exhibits the omnipotence of external fate"; the latter, that "the act which sets the tragic process going must be primarily a violation of *moral* law, whether human or divine; in short, that Aristotle's hamartia or 'flaw' must have an essential connection with sin or wrong doing." [12]

It was an acceptable modern equivalent for omnipotent, external fate that O'Neill sought; and yet, when he completed his

[9] "Archetype" and "signature" are Leslie Fiedler's convenient terms for applying to mythic materials the traditional standards of universality and individuality, respectively. See Leslie A. Fiedler, *No! in Thunder: Essays on Myth and Literature* (Boston: Beacon Press, 1960), especially "Part Four: The Theory," pp. 295-328.
[10] Northrop Frye, *Anatomy of Criticism: Four Essays* (Princeton, N.J.: Princeton University Press, 1957), p. 50 *passim*.
[11] *Ibid.*, p. 42.
[12] *Ibid.*, pp. 209 *et seq*.

trilogy, he had also created in Lavinia Mannon a heroine as blind as Oedipus to the true meaning of her actions. From the viewpoint of moralistic tragedy, her flaw was to assume that, in dealing out revenge, she had acted purely as an instrument of justice. Her recognition, or anagnorisis, consisted of discovering at least the impurity of her motive; it is this realization that brings about her defeat so that, as in the classic fashion of *Oedipus Rex*, her recognition and her catastrophe exactly coincide. This is a formal virtue of the play that has not, so far as I know, been recognized and appreciated—perhaps because of the great length of the trilogy, by contrast with the taut brevity of Sophocles' play. The nature of this recognition is such as to prepare one for an ending that will put the play in the tradition of idealistic, rather than realistic, tragedy; but Lavinia's doom is to be implacable, and, with a final turn of the screw, O'Neill provides one that even Zola would have approved.

O'Neill's "Notes and Extracts" are full of his wrestlings to derive from his material, or inject into it, an inexorable fate. In order to accomplish it, he resorted to Freudian psychology, self-destructive guilt, a puritan inheritance as a family curse, and characters that speak self-consciously about their fate. The New England setting he regarded as the "best possible dramatically," because it provided the "Puritan conviction of man born to sin and punishment—Orestes' furies within him, his conscience. . . ."[13] But it is quite clear that, despite his considerable powers of invention, none of these things alone, nor even all of them together, would have accomplished his purpose convincingly, without the *form* into which he cast them. Indeed, given the form he used, it is conceivable that he could have succeeded as well with a different plot and different "fatalistic" trappings, because, in the last analysis, it was the highly patterned action which yielded the mythic grandeur and sense of fate he aimed at. It is not too much to say that in *Mourning Becomes Electra* form *is* fate.

Before dealing in detail with the form of the play and examining the dramatic technique by which it is adapted to realism, I shall summarize the plot and consider the dynamics of its motivation for its bearing on the shape of the action.

[13] Clark, *European Theories*, p. 531.

The "curse" on the House of Mannon has, it should be noted, a human and dramatic origin in the family past. The Mannons are the richest and most powerful family in the town. "They've been top dog around here fur near on two hundred years and don't let folks fergit it," says Seth Beckwith, caretaker of the family name and secrets, as well as of the estate. Abraham Mannon became head of the family in its rise to affluence. He built his inheritance into a huge shipping fortune in the days of the clipper ships, working in partnership with his brother David. When the latter seduced Marie Brantôme, a Canuck nurse girl employed in the house, and married her to legitimize her child, Abraham dealt with the scandal by disowning David and cheating him out of his share of the business at forced sale. He also tore down the homestead to expunge the shame and built on its site a white-pillared mansion, the present House of Mannon.

David and his wife led a life of poverty and wandering. He took to drink and hanged himself. Marie became a seamstress and supported their child Adam. The boy ran away to sea, neglected his mother, and became a ship's captain. He took the name of Brant, derived from his mother's surname, as a repudiation of his father and the Mannons. Marie turned for help to Ezra Mannon, who had succeeded his father Abraham as head of the family, but Ezra never answered her appeal. Returning from a voyage to find his mother dying, Adam swore on her corpse to revenge her death on his heartless cousin.

Ezra, a professional soldier before his father's death, left the army, took over the shipping business, and married. He also studied law and became a judge, went into politics, and became mayor of the town. His wife Christine bore him two children, Lavinia and Orin. When the Civil War began, he rejoined the army and rose to the rank of general. Orin, too, joined the army, serving in his father's regiment.

Such is O'Neill's version of the background to Aeschylus' revenge plot. The quarrel between Abraham and David resembles that between King Atreus and his brother Thyestes; but it is significant that the crime which occasioned it was not, as in the older play, adultery with a brother's wife, but a scandal that involved the family name. Marie Brantôme is O'Neill's invention, but her son Adam, Ezra's first cousin, is the equivalent of Thyestes' son Aegisthus. The Civil War obviously is the Trojan War;

Ezra, with his military career, Agamemnon; Christine, Clytemnestra; and their children Lavinia and Orin, Electra and Orestes. There is no Iphigenia, as there is no Cassandra; in place of the daughter Agamemnon sacrificed to insure a safe voyage, O'Neill economically substitutes the circumstance that Orin was goaded by his father and sister into enlisting, thus depriving Christine of her son and favorite.

The parallels, with variations, continue into the direct action of the play when Adam, to insult Ezra and avenge his mother, seduces Christine. But Adam ends by falling in love with his cousin's wife. To conceal their clandestine relationship, which began in the last year of the war and in the absence of both Ezra and Orin, Christine has had Adam visit the house, ostensibly to court her daughter. Although much attracted to Adam, Lavinia suspects her mother's infidelity, follows the lovers to an assignation, and confirms her suspicions.

The first play, *Homecoming*, begins on the day the town receives news of Lee's surrender. Lavinia, determined to protect her father and the family name, confronts both Adam and Christine with their guilt and, in turn, learns the full story of the family past. She demands that Christine give up her lover or suffer exposure and disgrace at her husband's hands. Christine counters by conspiring with Adam to murder Ezra. In the last act Ezra returns. But his homecoming is ironically different from Agamemnon's. On the battlefield this grim judge, puritanical husband, efficient businessman and soldier, underwent a conversion. In the midst of death, he discovered life, whereas all his life before he had been filled with a puritan preoccupation with death. That life-denying inheritance had blighted his marriage by making sexuality sinful and disgusting, so that Christine had secretly grown to hate him; but now he is eager, indeed desperate, for life, and he hopes to renew with Christine their long-dead love. The contrast with Agamemnon, who returned as a proud conqueror with his concubine in tow, to commit the sin of pride before his murder, could hardly be greater and yet still retain its suggestive parallels. Ezra is a truly pathetic figure, longing to throw off his repressions but unable to do so, and hoping to begin life anew at the very moment that his wife has resolved upon his death.

When Christine lies with her husband that night, she contrives to increase his self-disgust; she deliberately brings on an attack of his heart ailment by taunting him with the failure of their marriage and disclosing her adultery with Brant. When he calls for his medicine, she substitutes the poison Adam had procured for her. Ezra lives only long enough to accuse Christine cryptically before Lavinia. Christine denies the charge but collapses; and Lavinia obtains the remainder of the poison as proof. She denounces her unconscious mother: "You murdered him just the same—by telling him! I suppose you think you'll be free to marry Adam now! But you won't! Not while I'm alive! I'll make you pay for your crime! I'll find a way to punish you!"

The second play, *The Hunted*, begins with the return of Orin on the eve of his father's funeral. Orin is a war casualty, suffering from a head wound. In contrast to his father, he can think only of death. He is quickly drawn into the duel between his mother and sister. Christine tries to win him to her defense by forestalling Lavinia's charges. Lavinia discloses to him Christine's adultery in order to enlist his aid in avenging their father's death. When Christine, in desperation, flees to Boston to warn Adam, Lavinia and Orin follow them aboard his ship and spy upon them. After his mother has left, Orin, now completely under his sister's domination, shoots and kills Adam on board, making the murder appear to be the work of thieves. When Orin reveals to Christine that he has killed her lover, she shoots herself.

This scene on shipboard—the only one in which the locale is shifted from the Mannon house—O'Neill regarded as the "center" of the trilogy. There the act occurs which destroys not only Adam but Christine as well, and which makes brother and sister partners in a crime of revenge and sharers of a secret guilt. This is the central hinge of the action, where Lavinia, mistaking her jealousy for justice, kills the man she loves.

In the *Oresteia*, years elapsed between the killing of Agamemnon and the return of Orestes, grown to manhood, as avenger; and more years passed between the murder of Clytemnestra and Aegisthus and Orestes' final deliverance from the remorse of blood-guilt. In *Mourning Becomes Electra* it was necessary for O'Neill's purpose that the story begin with Lavinia and Orin fully grown, and as a result, the action of the first two plays is virtually continuous. But important changes in character result from the crime of Lavinia and Orin; and so O'Neill lets a year elapse, beginning the third play, *The Haunted*, upon the return of brother and sister from a long voyage to the South Seas, undertaken for Orin's health.

Physically, as well, the two have altered markedly. Lavinia, more than ever the dominant sister, has filled out and become very attractive, just as she has come to terms with life and achieved peace. Orin has grown thin, haggard, yet soldierly in his bearing. Where Lavinia has returned home eager for life, Orin has come back to a house haunted with the ghosts of his guilt. She would like to marry Peter Niles, who had courted her before her father's death, but she fears to do so until Orin is well again. She would also like Orin to marry Hazel Niles, but he is not really interested and is instead afraid that Lavinia will leave him. His morbidity increases. To prevent Lavinia's marriage, he undertakes a history of the family crimes, which he gives to Hazel for safekeeping, to be read in case he should die —or Lavinia should marry Peter. The fear of exposure chains Lavinia to Orin as Christine had been chained to Ezra. Lavinia forces Orin to recover the incriminating confession. Orin is now driven by the urge to confess publicly and urges her to join him, as the only way to find peace. Lavinia prevents this by driving him to suicide as he had done his mother. Once more there is a funeral in the great house.

Lavinia hopes that at last she can marry Peter, go away, and forget the past and all the Mannon dead. She finds, however, that her guilt is already beginning to infect Peter and corrupt his happiness, as Orin's guilt had driven away Hazel. Trying to stifle her fears, she begs Peter to marry her: "Take me in this house of the dead and love me! Our love will drive the dead away! It will shame them back into death!" Frantically and passionately, she kisses Peter, and these words escape her: "Want me! Take me, Adam!" Her suppressed love for her mother's dead paramour has finally betrayed itself. She had all along convinced herself that, in hounding her mother and killing Adam she acted only in justice; now she sees that jealousy and her love, turned to hatred, had driven her to her crimes. "Always the dead between! It's no good trying any more!" She accepts her defeat: she gives up Peter and becomes a recluse in the House of Mannon, immured from the light of day and cut off from converse with the world. The ghosts of her dead have the rest of her life in which to punish her.

This summary of the plot, even while it stresses the differences between the two trilogies, gives little indication of the *pattern of motives* underlying the parts that most resemble the *Oresteia* and the divergent final play.

Early in O'Neill's jottings there occurs the phrase, "drama of murderous family love and hate. . . ." No matter how many revisions he made thereafter, the playwright held to this conception of the *family* as breeding a triad of love, hate, and murder. Since he could not rely upon his audiences' sharing a common history, religion, or philosophy, O'Neill was reduced to finding in man alone—that is, in his psychology—the sense of inevitability or fate that had formerly been ascribed to the gods, to chance, to society. In the last version of *Days Without End*, O'Neill, speaking of the *subconscious*, called it "the mother of all gods and heroes." [14] Here it provides the means whereby man creates his own punishment, since his actions spring from its contrary impulses of love and hate, and these impulses center in the family. As a dramatic mechanism, the subconscious is self-contained and *self-sufficient*: it prompts to crime and punishes its own promptings, thus providing a dynamics which, because it is introverted and repetitive, O'Neill could apply to the story of the Atreides.[15] As used in the trilogy, it may be summarized as follows:

Love begins and ends with the family, so that all love is basically incestuous. (The resemblance of this to Robinson Jeffers' view in *The Tower Beyond Tragedy*, which O'Neill almost certainly knew, is plain. But Jeffers' likening of man's obsessive concern with his own kind as incestuous is rather a philosophic statement made by means of a poetic figure. O'Neill's use of incest is both psychological and quite literal.) Jealousy is consequently unavoidable. Each man is his father's rival for his mother's love; each woman is her mother's rival for her father's love. In loving a woman other than his mother, a man is seeking her image in that other; in loving a man other than her father,

[14] Quoted by Doris V. Falk, *Eugene O'Neill and the Tragic Tension* (New Brunswick, N.J.: Rutgers University Press, 1958), p. 152.
[15] For O'Neill's possible sources, see Falk, *ibid.*, p. 136. O'Neill cited his own observations of life as his sources.

a woman is seeking his image in that other. We are simultaneously torn by love and hate, for we love the one parent and hate
the other as our rival. And so the family, because it is the center
of love, is also the center of hate.

These incestuous impulses may not be recognized and expressed, because society will not permit it (why it will not is
never explained); so the person suffers a sense of guilt because
he must regard these impulses as wrong. Yet, if he suppresses
—or represses—them, he suffers frustration and mental pain.
The depth-psychologists may devise emotional escape-hatches
in the form of human relationships and activities which are forms
of sublimation, acceptable substitutes; but O'Neill, because he is
concentrating on the tragic aspects of life, will have little to do
with them. He suggests them, particularly in the persons of
Hazel and Peter Niles, but only so that he may show their impossibility for the puritan consciences of Lavinia and Orin, rid-
den by guilt. It is an ironic insight into O'Neill's independence
as a dramatist that, writing in a period when Freudian doctrine
was popularly regarded as the last word from Mount Sinai and
the source of the new deliverance, he should have used its dynamics to motivate one of the grimmest dramas of stature ever
to be written in this country.[16] Lavinia's immurement is simply
the stage symbol of the implications O'Neill has drawn from his
scheme: the self as jailer and jailed, the tortured and the
torturer.

In the following it is my contention that O'Neill's determination
to eliminate the supernatural entirely and to rely solely on a
psychological system of unconscious compulsions has had the
ironic effect of driving him back to the supernatural by way of
the *demonic.*

To show that this interpretation is not an unsupported private

[16] "Now, when Freud's doctrine began to be widely propagated in the
nineteen twenties, its publicists and popularizers were, at best, only familiar
with his earlier work [that "concentrated on those factors in neurosis which
stemmed from abnormal repression of the instinctual drives, the forces of
the id"]. They were the spokesmen of a cultural revolt which sought to
discredit the moral prohibitions of the past, and they presented an often
garbled version of Freud's early findings as a scientific justification of the
cult of uninhibited 'self-expression.'" Peter B. Neubauer, M.D., "The Century of the Child," *The Atlantic,* CCVIII, no. 1 (July, 1961), 85.

judgment, it will be instructive to assess the trilogy against an objective critical system. This will also serve to bring into relief the tensions that result from treating mythical structures realistically.

My critical yardstick is Northrop Frye's *Anatomy of Criticism* [17] mentioned earlier, which in four essays presents four theories—those of modes, symbols, myths, and genres. My concern is with the first and third, to be dealt with in some detail. In the first, as I noted, he proposes four narrative *modes* that apply equally well to prose fiction and drama. They are: myth, romance, high mimetic, and low mimetic. Since they are tendencies rather than fixed categories, they may be schematized as four areas on a spectrum—but a spectrum that rounds on itself. Myth is at one extreme, low mimetic at the other, corresponding respectively to extreme nonrealism and naturalism (or, in theatrical terms, to the conventional and the illusionary). When regarded as form or style, myth is "an abstract or purely literary world of fictional and thematic design"; as narrative, it is "the imitation of actions near or at the conceivable limits of desire," and hence concerns itself with gods or demons. At the other end of the spectrum, low mimetic represents the concrete treated with utmost verisimilitude or plausibility; it is "human experience skillfully and consistently imitated," or "representative to life": hence, extreme realism, or naturalism. But naturalism, when followed to its limits, tends to round on itself toward myth again, stressing *demonic* aspects in the process.

The vast area between these two limits Frye defines as romance, which includes the "high mimetic." In romance he finds "the tendency to displace myth in a human direction and yet, in contrast to 'realism' to conventionalize content in an idealized direction." Frye gives the name "displacement" to the use of all devices intended to solve the problems of plausibility created by the presence of a mythical structure in realistic fiction, and states: "The central principle of displacement is that what can be metaphorically identified in a myth can only be linked in romance by some form of simile: analogy, significant association, incidental accompanying imagery, and the like." Consequently, the further toward naturalism the treatment of myths tends, the more deeply buried its metaphorical structure is likely to be.

[17] See Frye, *Anatomy of Criticism*, pp. 136-37, 206-23, 147-58.

Analysis makes it evident that O'Neill has been forced to invoke the central principle of displacement, and that, although what he finally produces is not romance, he has had recourse to the forms of simile named. On the other hand, while the metaphorical structure of the trilogy, which I take to be that of fate in the form of the system of unconscious drives, turns the effects of the action inward upon the consciences of the characters, it yet becomes increasingly apparent in the action as *design*.

Mourning Becomes Electra has the virtue which Frye finds in most popular fiction— that of a "good story," by which he means "a clearly designed one." It is "realistic enough to be plausible in its incidents and yet romantic enough" to have a clear and satisfying shape. His first example of this applies directly to the Electra myth. "The introduction of an omen or portent, or the device of making a whole story the fulfillment of a prophecy given at the beginning, is an example. Such a device suggests . . . *a conception of ineluctable fate* or hidden omnipotent will. Actually, it is a piece of pure literary design, giving the beginning some symmetrical relationship with the end, and the only ineluctable will involved is that of the author." [18] O'Neill cannot use Cassandra and her prophetic powers, for there can be no place for them in a design which resolutely eliminates the supernatural. And so the need for displacement is evident at the outset. He uses instead the effective, although relatively weaker, devices of prediction and expression of intention. But the whole process of thorough-going displacement has ironic results. The more firmly O'Neill moves away from myth and toward the low mimetic, the more surely he ends by approaching the demonic, which is to the mythically ideal as Hell is to Heaven.

In making form the embodiment of fate in the plays and in emphasizing the clear design of the action, O'Neill works against his own realistic tendencies. Highly patterned action is by definition nonrealistic. Hence, the plays fall into both the romantic category and the realistic; for the former exhibits "the tendency to suggest implicit mythical patterns in a world more closely associated with human experience," and the latter, "the tendency . . . to throw the emphasis on *content and representation* rather than on the *shape* of the story." [19]

[18] *Ibid.*, p. 139 (emphasis added).
[19] *Ibid.* (emphasis added).

The artistic success of the play lies, I believe, in O'Neill's ability to control and exploit contrary tendencies at their point of maximum tension. His strong emphasis on action works against "abstractly mythical" elements which ordinarily produce a clear design and which more readily respond to *thematic* treatment. The solution he found was "abstraction in character-drawing," a sacrifice in part of his realistic objective but one which served the psychological system on which the action is based, while permitting him to utilize sparse but convincing realistic detail. The patterns of character development complement the correspondingly symmetrical form of the action. The realistic elements of historical period, recognizable locale, and sordid crimes associate the plays with the category of "ironic" literature, which "begins with realism and tends toward myth, *its mythical patterns being as a rule more suggestive of the demonic than of the apocalyptic. . . .*"[20] But in themselves these realistic elements are not sufficient to account for the result. That must be sought in the playwright's outlook, his "tragic view," if you will: ". . . Eugene O'Neill has exhibited the tragic significance of a world in which character has given way to the powers of subconscious mechanisms, complexes, and compulsions which give human fate the cruel significance of animals trapped by forces within themselves over which they have no control. It is not only the multiplicity of his instances but the courageous acceptance of the implications of the scientific world-view that give O'Neill's trilogy its effect of tremendous tragedy."[21]

The "organizing design" that O'Neill chose to provide the sense of fate was that of interlocking *repetitions*, within which operate ironic reversals so arranged as to produce further, or contrasting, repetitions. In this dynamics, qualities turn into their formal opposites; as indicated above, love, for example, becomes hate, and people come to resemble the objects of their hate—Lavinia like her mother, Orin like his father. Ironically, and this I take to be another indication of the demonic drive of the plays, the characters do *not* become like the objects of their love.

In his third essay Frye applies his revolving categories to a

[20] *Ibid.*, p. 140 (emphasis added).
[21] Fred B. Millet and Gerald E. Bentley, *The Art of the Drama* (New York: Appleton-Century, 1935), p. 154.

"theory of myths," as a basis for "archetypal criticism." Here he uses the term "myths" to represent "four narrative pregeneric elements of literature" which he calls "*mythoi* or generic plots," because these four narrative categories are "broader than, or logically prior to, the ordinary literary genres." He defines them as tragedy, romance, comedy, and irony (or satire); and relates them to the cycle of the seasons and the ritual death of the old Year-Daimon. Again resorting to schematism, we find tragedy situated opposite comedy on the circumference of the circular spectrum, as romance is opposite irony; therefore tragedy is between romance and irony. Tragedy is "the Mythos of Autumn," as irony (or satire) is "the Mythos of Winter." The relationship of tragedy to its adjacent categories is indicated by the analysis of tragedy into six phases, three of which find their analogies in romance and three in irony: "The phases of tragedy move from the heroic to the ironic, the first three corresponding to the first three phases of romance, the last three to the last three of irony."

When measured against these six phases, *Mourning Becomes Electra* is seen to have affinities with all six, but especially with the last three that relate by analogy to irony. Archetypal criticism sees in tragedy "a mimesis of sacrifice," says Frye, adding that the *ritual* analogies of sacrifice to tragedy "are more obvious than the *psychological ones, for it is irony, not tragedy*, that represents the nightmare or anxiety-dream." [22] It is important to note this at the beginning not only to indicate the direction of the ironic goal, but also to stress the fact that, despite the literal violence in the trilogies, O'Neill emphasizes the psychological aspects of the action; and that, in the case of his protagonist Lavinia, whose punishment is to be psychological rather than physical, the tragic and ironic elements that Frye catalogues will be present, not literally but analogically.

The first phase applies but slightly, since it usually involves the infancy of the hero, whose qualities are dignity, courage, and innocence. Dignity and courage Lavinia has. Her innocence is more ambiguous, as later treatment will show. The second phase concerns itself with the tragedy of innocence of the young, in the sense of inexperience; in this type, the central character often survives, "so that the action closes with some adjustment to a new and more mature experience." The third phase throws strong

[22] Frye, *Anatomy of Criticism*, p. 214 (emphasis added).

emphasis "on the success or completeness of the hero's achievement." In the beginning Lavinia is twenty-three years old. She
lacks experience of life and love. She has been attracted to Adam
Brant. But she has already learned that he is her mother's lover
and soon learns that he is her cousin. Both family loyalty and
close blood-ties force her to stifle her love. But in repressing it,
she incurs a guilt of which she is unaware. O'Neill's assumption
of unconscious motivations, together with the taint of puritanism,
makes the distinction between innocence and experience ambiguous indeed. Lavinia survives, certainly, and in the end she
makes an adjustment to a new experience—the discovery of her
true motivation; but whether it is a more mature adjustment is
an important question. Here we may add one of Frye's general
comments on the tragic hero: he is usually "an imposter in the
sense that he is self-deceived or made dizzy by hybris. In many
tragedies he begins as a semi-divine figure, at least in his own
eyes, and then an inexorable dialectic sets to work which separates the divine pretense from the human actuality." Lavinia
made herself the instrument of justice and committed her crimes
in its name; in the end, however, when this divine pretense has
been separated from the human actuality, she realizes she was
self-deceived. As for the third phase, we cannot speak of the
success of her achievement, only of its dreadful completeness;
the principle of irony operates so strongly here, actually reaching its grimmest point in the climax of the trilogy, that her success becomes her downfall.

The fourth phase has, in part, already been anticipated. It
involves "the typical fall of the hero through hybris and hamartia" and the crossing of "the boundary line from innocence to
experience which is also the direction in which the hero falls."
As indicated, O'Neill has provided Lavinia with both hybris and
hamartia. Her repressed love for Adam, turning to hate, reinforced her hatred for her mother and her determination to avenge
the family honor. But her recognition of her loss of innocence is
long delayed, occurring only a few minutes before the end of
the third play. And O'Neill has even built up her pride for a
further fall by first permitting her to achieve an illusory sense
of peace and innocence during her long voyage to the South Seas.

"In the fifth phase," says Frye, "the ironic element increases,
the hero decreases, and the characters look further away and in

a smaller perspective." The ironic element increases as Lavinia, convinced now that all will be well, finds she is chained to her brother, whose guilt represents a constant threat of exposure. It may be true to say that in *The Haunted*, the heroic decreases, at least as compared to the first two plays, but hardly that the characters look further away and in a smaller perspective: what happens is that the scope of the action narrows. The ironic perspective common to tragedy of this phase, says Frye, is "attained by putting the characters in a state of lower freedom than the audience," that is, by showing the characters as "moving according to the conditions of a law . . . from which the audience has been, at least theoretically, redeemed." The conditions of this "law" are hard to separate. They consist of family loyalty, unconscious drives springing from sexual desire, the blight of intrenched puritanism and its concomitant, an overriding sense of guilt—in Orin, if not yet in Lavinia. Perhaps puritanism ought not to be separated from family loyalty and sexual desire. Is it not the product of the guilt resulting from desire in conflict with the family and society?

It is by no means clear whether O'Neill would regard the members of the audience as even theoretically redeemed from the conditions that bind the Mannons. After all, he sought a *common ground* with his audiences: hence his emphasis on motivations formed by psychological, rather than external, pressures. He might regard members of the audience as individually emancipated from the strictures of family loyalty and perhaps less guilt-ridden than the unhappy Mannons; but the picture of life which his works present is not one of liberation from these same unconscious drives. Most of the characters in *Mourning Becomes Electra* try to oppose the conditions of the law that binds them, insofar as it is represented by puritanism or family loyalty; but the conditions according to which they *wish* to move are determined by those drives. They promise bliss, but they deliver hell. The result is checkmate. As for the heroic scale of the characters, Lavinia and Christine, being both highly volitional, put up such a fierce struggle to achieve their desires that the very intensity of their combat lifts them to a state of higher freedom than the audience. At the end of the play, of course, we find that their freedom was illusory. The problem of scale and freedom is not simple: "It is clear . . . that [O'Neill] hoped to give the *dramatis personae* a Titanic, Aeschylean grandeur. But whereas the Titanism in Aeschylus creates an impression of freedom transcending nature or at least material causation, O'Neill's characters are at once larger than living men and less free. On stage *Mourning Becomes Electra* had a mythical eminence . . . and the final effect was one of awe. . . . [But later] one finds that its personages have shrunk. Now, these obsessions and compulsions seem not so grand as in former time." [23]

Tragic action in the fifth phase occurs in a "world of adult experience," characterized for the most part by "lost direction and lack of knowledge," by strong suggestions of fatalism, and the raising of *"metaphysical or theological questions rather than moral ones"* (emphasis added). As might be expected, this phase best describes the last play of the trilogy. Lavinia, now fully mature as well as steeped in blood, has become the image of her mother. But she cannot escape from the family toils into a normal marriage, nor does she know how to control the increasingly haunted Orin. She loses direction and drives her brother to suicide, to insure that the family honor shall stand unblotted before the world. Watching this backlash of crime, this inevitable dissolution, our moral horror deepens instinctively; but the mind, appalled at the cycle of love, hate, violence, and guilt, asks rather if there is any possible *escape* from this circle of doom.

In the sixth phase, says Frye, we enter "a world of shock and horror in which the central images are images of *sparagmos*, that is, cannibalism, mutilation, and torture"; hence, "sixth-phase tragedy shocks as a whole, in its total effect." Shock, "the specific reaction . . . appropriate to cruelty or outrage," is for me the cumulative effect of the trilogy. The final play contains *all* the elements of *sparagmos* described. Instead of literal physical mutilation, we have its psychic equivalent in puritanism, which wounds and twists its victims, finally preventing them from achieving any respite, let alone happiness. We have *self*-torture in Orin and later in Lavinia, both victims of a law in which punishing oneself is the only means of expiation. And, finally, we have cannibalism, represented in the self-devouring family and by the parody of resurrection that turns them into the pursuing dead.

[23] William G. McCollom, *Tragedy* (New York: Macmillan, 1957), pp. 231-32.

At the end of this phase we reach what Frye describes as "a point of demonic epiphany, where we see or glimpse the undisplaced demonic vision, the vision of the *Inferno*." Since the first play we, like the characters, have been increasingly aware of the portraits of the Mannon dead on the ancestral walls. For O'Neill, just as they did for Ibsen in *Rosmersholm*, they represent the ineluctable grip of the past. As the crimes succeed one another, O'Neill emphasizes these portraits more and more. The dead take on a kind of life, baleful and increasingly vindictive. They guard the family mansion like demonic lares and penates, hoarding its guilty secrets by devouring the living—even Lavinia, who killed to honor and to appease them. The house becomes Lavinia's prison, thus providing one of the chief symbols of the sixth phase, as the dead become ghosts ("instruments of a torturing death"). "The crimes in Aeschylus are open; those in O'Neill are concealed, and therefore infinitely more sordid. . . . This is inevitable; for now that public justice has been long established, murder implies subterfuge. [By the same token] the Furies are within the characters. . . ."[24]

Despite all the overt action of the three plays, the drive of the action has been steadily inward, to the piling up of a mountainous guilt, and it reaches its goal in the haunted mind of one person, Lavinia. The "strong element of demonic ritual" which Frye says tragic and ironic myth exploits is not, therefore, to be found in "public punishments and similar mob amusements." Resolute to the last, Lavinia will do nothing that betrays the family honor, least of all make a public confession. And so the demonic ritual is "private," in the ceaseless punishment of guilt and the "mob" amusement, in the vindictive relish of the onlooking dead. There is one final characteristic of the last phase to be found in the end of the third play, and it is "the horror of being watched, [which] is a greater misery than . . . pain." But Lavinia seems to look forward to their unabating stare.

Frye's abstract of demonic *imagery* further supports the conclusions derived from his analyses of *structure*. In O'Neill, however, imagery is much more often to be found in structural analogy and stage picture than in the dialogue, which is realistic but undistinguished. The action of the plays develops in a "demonic

[24] Ormerod Greenwood, *The Playwright: A Study of Form, Method and Tradition in the Theatre* (London: Pitman, 1950), pp. 102, 103.

human world," that is, "a society held together by a kind of molecular tension of egos, a loyalty to the group or the leader which diminishes the individual, or, at best, contrasts his pleasure with his duty or honor."

In *Mourning Becomes Electra,* not only does the family inhibit the individual and flatly oppose duty to pleasure, it also upholds a conception of family honor that is akin to secret guilt and ultimately the source of the individual's destruction. The two poles of this "sinister human world," says Frye, are "the tyrant-leader, inscrutable, ruthless, melancholy, and with an insatiable will, who commands loyalty only if he is egocentric enough to represent the collective ego of his followers," and "the *pharmakos* or sacrifice victim, who has to be killed to strengthen the others." Lavinia is clearly the tyrant-leader, whose conflicts spring directly from her resolve to command the loyalty of the others in preserving the Mannon name; and it is to "strengthen the others" —the family—that she causes the deaths of Adam, Christine, and finally Orin. "In the most concentrated form of demonic parody," says Frye, "the two become the same." O'Neill achieves this by making Lavinia the tyrant-leader and the last victim of family loyalty, as well. For Frye, "the ritual killing of the divine king . . . is in literary criticism the demonic or undisplaced radical form of tragic and ironic structures." This element O'Neill has not so much displaced as he has intensified it by a cruel inversion that is worse than literal death. Lavinia, like the others, had sought "life-in-death"; she must, throughout a long life, suffer a "death-in-life."

In the "apocalyptic conception of human life," contrary to the demonic conception, three kinds of fulfillment are possible, says Frye: they are "individual, sexual, and social." None of these is possible in the world of the Mannons, with its nightmare of sexual compulsions, love that turns to hate, and hate that can never give way to love. Therefore: "The demonic erotic relation becomes a fierce destructive passion that works against loyalty or frustrates the one who possesses it. It is generally symbolized by a harlot, witch, siren, or other tantalizing female, a physical object of desire *which is sought as a possession and therefore can never be possessed.*" [25] Christine's passion, for example, drives her to break her marriage vows and betray family loyalty,

[25] Frye, *Anatomy of Criticism,* p. 149 (emphasis added).

but it ends in frustration. She, in turn, is "a physical object of desire" for her husband, for Adam, and also for Orin. At one point, both Orin and Lavinia regard their mother as a harlot. Later Orin turns the charge against Lavinia, too, when she has become like her mother. With two exceptions, the loves these characters exhibit are the desire for possession, and hence doomed to frustration. The first exception is Ezra's love for his wife which, however, he achieved too late. The second is Lavinia's for Peter. But the demonic stains even this last, for it is revealed as a substitute for her passion for Adam, who was always beyond her grasp. Her love for Adam is "a fierce destructive passion," for when it turns to hate, it confirms her in her resolve to kill him as well as Christine. When she stands over his corpse, her first words are: "How could you love that vile old woman so? But you're dead! It's ended!" Only then does she pray "coldly, as if carrying out a duty": "May God find forgiveness for your sins! May the soul of our cousin, Adam Mannon, rest in peace!"

In the third play there comes, now in its most explicit as well as commonest form, "the demonic parody of marriage, or the union of two souls in one flesh"—incest:

ORIN: Can't you see I'm now in Father's place and you're Mother? That's the evil destiny out of the past I haven't dared to predict! I'm the Mannon you're chained to. So isn't it plain—

Later the desire takes possession of him:

There are times now when you don't seem to be my sister, nor Mother, but some stranger with the same beautiful hair—
    Perhaps you're Marie Brantôme, eh? And you say there are no ghosts in this house? . . .
    How else can I be sure you won't leave me? You would never dare leave me—then! You would feel as guilty then as I do! You would be as damned as I am! [26]

Extended to the inorganic world, the demonic imagery of the play is associated with buildings and fire but not with water. The temple-like mansion of the Mannons is a demonic parody of "the temple or One Building of the apocalypse," for it is "the prison or dungeon, the sealed furnace of heat without light, like the City of Dis in Dante." And the "world of fire" is "a world

[26] The previous quotation and this one are found in *The Haunted*, Act II, p. 273, and Act III, p. 293, respectively.

of malignant demons like the will-o'-the-wisps, or spirits broken from hell"—in this case, the Mannon dead. Whereas in demonic imagery "the world of water" is "the water of death . . . above all the 'unplumbed, salt, estranging sea,'" the sea in *Mourning Becomes Electra* becomes the source of apocalyptic imagery. One is reminded of O'Neill's attachment to the sea and the important part it plays in many of his works. The sea is Adam's dream of freedom, never achieved; along with the South Sea islands, another example, it is Orin's pathway to the Blessed Isles, where he would live alone with his mother, whom he identifies with both: ". . . finally those Islands came to mean everything that wasn't war, everything that was peace and warmth and security. I used to dream I was there. . . . There was no one there but you and me. And yet I never saw you, that's the funny part. I only felt you all around me. The breaking of the waves was your voice. The sky was the same color as your eyes. The warm sand was like your skin. The whole island was you." [27] To this may be added the "rolling river" of the chantey "Shenandoah," with its romantic yearning and pathos of unfulfillment, which runs through the plays like a leitmotif, up to the death of the seafaring Adam Brant, to recur again only at the very end.

Since the sixth phase of irony is very similar to the sixth phase of tragedy, it would be repetitious to assess the trilogy against it as well. We may note, however, that irony and satire attempt to give *form* to the "shifting ambiguities and complexities of unidealized existence." The last phase "presents human life, in terms of largely unrelieved bondage," and it "brings us around again to the point of demonic epiphany" which is "a world without pity and without hope. . . ." In the following Frye has Dante's *Inferno* in mind, but what is said applies also, with ghastly appositeness, to the end of *Mourning Becomes Electra:* "Tragedy and tragic irony take us into a hell of narrowing circles and culminate in some such vision of the source of all evil in a personal form." O'Neill centers his vision not in Satan but in the human psyche, moved by a love which in the very nature of things, it seems, must become hate and ultimately vindictive self-hate.

Examination of demonic elements in *Mourning Becomes Electra* has already, if indirectly, raised the question: how free are O'Neill's characters? And the opinions quoted—that they

[27] *Ibid.,* Act II, p. 157.

are "larger than living men and less free," and that they are "trapped by forces within themselves over which they have no control"—assume that the world of the plays is deterministic. (They remind us of Jean Cocteau's *The Infernal Machine*, which is clearly both deterministic and explicitly demonic.) The characters in O'Neill's plays are almost as limited in their motivations as are Cocteau's; and indeed, repetition of those motivations, with variations, constitutes the basic design of O'Neill's action. There is, however, a difference: his characters—even the weaker ones—are highly volitional. They seem much freer, so long as they act, and they act a good deal. No matter how tight the band of determinism a playwright would put upon his characters, he undermines the effect of determinism if he gives them strength and permits them to act decisively. With the Mannons, we witness acts and their consequences, not the creation of a myth. It is this which tells in the theatre, rather than a playwright's assumptions, whatever they be. There is, for instance, a far greater sense of determinism surrounding the bums in the naturalistic *The Iceman Cometh*; but this may be as much because they are inactive in their defeat as because the play explicitly preaches a philosophy of hopelessness.

In the trilogy, moreover, O'Neill clings to the possibility of idealistic action: he gives such action to both Orin and Lavinia. In each case, it follows a moment of recognition, with the effect of ratifying the character's freedom. In *The Haunted*, before he shoots himself, Orin achieves the act of forgiveness. It is against every instinct of his nature, "as if he were retching up poison." He addresses Lavinia, who has been taunting him for his cowardice, as if the ghost of his mother were speaking through her:

Yes! It's the way to peace—to find her again—my lost island—Death is an Island of Peace, too—Mother will be waiting for me there—

Mother! Do you know what I'll do then? I'll get on my knees and ask your forgiveness—and say—[*his mouth grows convulsed, as if he were retching up poison*]

I'll say, I'm glad you found love, Mother! I'll wish you happiness —you and Adam! [*he laughs exultantly*]

You've heard me! You're in the house now! You're calling me! You're waiting to take me home! [28]

Here, as in Lavinia's recognition already referred to, the idealism

[28] *Ibid.*, Act III, p. 295.

is not clear and unmistakable, because of the context of the scene. Lavinia is trying to drive him to commit suicide, and there is no trace of pagan nobility in his response to the idea of death. Moreover, it is as if *Christine*, whom Lavinia for the moment embodies, were demanding his suicide as payment for her own: an act of eye-for-an-eye justice. Even so, he sees that death will be a way to peace and reunion with his mother, only if he begs her forgiveness—which forgiveness can only be obtained by his first forgiving her. This is the meaning of the speech and the reason that it convulses him: he is purging himself of the jealous hatred that his love for his mother had become.

As for Lavinia, her recognition results in the same kind of Mosaic justice. Having recognized that she, too, was motivated by hatred instead of disinterested justice, she sees that it is not enough to relinquish Peter—and with him the hope of happiness. She regards her crimes as too great to be expiated by anything less than a lifetime of punishment—and this is what the ghosts of her dead, who have taken possession of her conscience, will exact to the last breath.

"When the play ended, and the last Mannon was gone into the house, the door shut, I felt in a full, lovely sense that the Erinyes were appeased, and that the Eumenides, the Gentle Ones, passed over the stage." With this (to me) astonishing statement, Stark Young concluded his review of *Mourning Becomes Electra*.[29] His response clearly attests to the finality of the play's form and also, perhaps, to the restored balance of Mosaic justice. But the critic's serenity of feeling seems to me achieved at the expense of the implications of the ending. If the ending looks toward the final release of death, that release is only to be won after a lifetime of remorse.

Idealistic tragedy frequently presents, despite outward defeat and even death, the consoling irony of the protagonist's inner victory; his agony leaves him spiritually whole and undivided. There can be no such consolation here: the irony is replaced by defeat without *and* within. Lavinia is left alive and strong, so as to endure the self-punishment of a soul riven with guilt and self-hatred. But such punishment is meaningless, if it has

[29] Stark Young, "Eugene O'Neill's New Play," in *Immortal Shadows: A Book of Dramatic Criticism* (New York: Scribner's, 1948), pp. 132-39.

no term, or any earnest of real absolution. It is a foretaste of hell.

For whether it carries in the theatre or not, O'Neill's intention is explicitly clear in the text. Lavinia submits to, even welcomes, precisely the kind of vindictive justice, inflicted by her conscience, that we saw her inflict on her kin. She has seen her own sinful flaw, but her spirit is unchanged: it has not revealed to her any higher conception of justice.

Through all the acts of violence, the Furies have slowly gathered in pursuit: Christine first, then Orin. Now they drop for the kill on Lavinia. The departure into idealistic tragedy, with her renunciation of Peter, was momentary; the play does not end with that saving doom, but goes remorselessly on. "I'm bound here—to the Mannon dead," says Lavinia. "I'll live alone with the dead, and keep their secrets, and let them hound me, until the curse is paid out and the last Mannon is let die!" Then (says O'Neill) she adds, and *"with a strange cruel smile of gloating over the years of self-torture"*: "I know they will see to it I live for a long time! *It takes the Mannons to punish themselves for being born!"* [30] These proud words, with their unmistakable stage direction, confirm Lavinia's decision. "Lavinia, who remains, will punish herself. But even the freedom intimated by her willed identification with justice is undermined by the spirit of her decision." [31]

Regardless of the agent or instrument, says Northrop Frye, "The righting of the balance is what the Greeks called *nemesis,*" and "the essential thing is that *nemesis* happens, and happens impersonally, unaffected, as *Oedipus Tyrannus* illustrates, by the moral quality of human motivation involved." [32] But here it does not happen impersonally; and it is consistent with O'Neill's basic premise that it cannot. His final point is that it must be entirely personal and self-imposed, for the self is both the torturer and the tortured.

Less exhilarated by the ending of the trilogy than Stark Young, the late Richard Dana Skinner nonetheless expressed a similar view. But to do so he had to ignore the playwright's words: *"But above and beyond the words of the poet's description,* there is the feeling of deepest introversion, of a turning back of the

[30] *The Haunted,* Act IV, pp. 315-16 (emphasis added).
[31] McCollom, *Tragedy,* p. 231.
[32] Frye, *Anatomy of Criticism,* p. 209.

feminine soul into its innermost depths, as if to discover in death to herself, the one last chance of a new life. . . . Lavinia, the woman, unlike the frightened child-men who turned back to the maternal past, may discover the secret of living with fears until they are tamed, of opening her eyes to truth instead of mocking shadows, of finding tenderness in place of the sinister giants that seemed to block the agonizing path to maturity and peace." [33] Skinner's hope of redeeming the play from the diabolic horror of its close led him to an interpretation of the ending "so different from the mask of self-torturing words that clothe it" that he was forced to base his conclusion on evidence outside the play —specifically, on its two successors, *Ah, Wilderness!* and *Days Without End.* He wrote his study in the belief that O'Neill's theatre, taken as a whole, showed at that time a development pointing to the playwright's resolution of his doubts and a return to the Catholic faith. Unfortunately for O'Neill, as Skinner had no way of knowing then, the quest ended not merely in doubt, but in nihilistic despair.[34]

As O'Neill frankly said, *Ah, Wilderness!* was wish-fulfillment —a picture of the author's life as he would have wished it to be; and not, as in *Long Day's Journey into Night,* his life pretty much as it had been. In the latter play O'Neill went beyond pity, which he had always had, to a forgiveness of "all his dead Tyrones"; and one is reminded painfully of Orin. But in *The Iceman Cometh,* written long after the autobiographical play, he reached the nadir of despair, rejecting life and mankind as seemingly worthless and irredeemable. The barflies in Harry Hope's saloon are weaklings who, lacking any vein of iron pride, take refuge in dreams and drink; whereas Lavinia summons her considerable strength to welcome a doom as hopeless as theirs and, because of her very courage, more horrible. Yet *Mourning Becomes Electra* is free of the author's vast disgust which permeates the later play; it is spared the rejection and contempt; and the author is more detached, perhaps, than he ever had been or would be in his works. It is not he, but Lavinia, who rejects life.

[33] Richard D. Skinner, *Eugene O'Neill: A Poet's Quest* (New York: Longmans, Green, 1935), pp. 225-26 (emphasis added).
[34] This refers only to O'Neill's beliefs as inferred from the plays. Up to now, biographical data give us no reason to think things ended otherwise for him in life, but the final state of a man's mind and soul is, mercifully, beyond literature and biography.

Her self-entombment isolates her from humankind and marks the
end of the Mannon line. Her acceptance is the victory of puritanism, and it is made in a puritanical spirit. Thus, it is the antithesis of the life that her father, for whose sake she first killed,
had rediscovered on the battlefield.

But the entire trilogy must be read as a story of the effects of
puritanism, and not as an allegory of all human life, for taken
on its own terms it does not offer a general and inclusive statement of the human condition. (We recall O'Neill's love of ecstatic
generalities, but they are not to be found here, where all the
dramatic elements are subordinated, fused into the action.)
O'Neill put into the three plays forces which work against any
such comprehensive judgment. I do not refer simply to the Mannons' dreams of an uncorrupted life on the Blessed Isle or
even to the existence of the earthly paradise in the South Seas,
but to the direct presentation of other characters and their
meaning for the plays. The chorus of townspeople, although one-
dimensionally portrayed and scarcely providing an attractive
picture of human nature in its communal aspects, seems nonetheless free of the Mannon curse of pride and self-hatred, as
well as of the unconscious motivations that bedevil their betters.
More importantly, the characters of Hazel and Peter Niles provide deliberate contrast, as being both free of the Mannons' besetting sins and superior to the other townspeople in their genuine goodness. They, like the other townspeople, figure in the
action from first to last, so that there is no mistaking the importance of their function. The curse on the house is puritanism,
and its agent is the incestuous triangles formed through self-love
and self-hate. It comes out of the past, it is true; but it has its
origin, as I have already said, in a human and dramatic action,
too specific and operative to be interpreted as original sin. The
Mannon household is surrounded by a life that is larger than
its self-devouring puritanism. And because it holds, however
faintly, the possibility of an existence different from the Mannons', both happier and better, Lavinia's rejection of it for a
lifetime of proud suffering is a form of frustrated suicide, a prolonged death-in-life.

This conclusion is directly contrary to that reached by Doris
V. Falk in *Eugene O'Neill and the Tragic Tension*, already referred to. This study of a "single, complex pattern" in the plays

of O'Neill—the neurotic pride-system exhibited by so many of his characters—applies particularly to Lavinia Mannon and the self-hatred she exhibits: "If the hero does not know himself, fate will force the knowledge upon him. And with self-knowledge comes self-criticism: that evaluation of motives which results in guilt and responsibility. For the neurotic, self-knowledge may reveal the subconscious self-hatred which generated the illusory self-image in the first place; then on a conscious level the hatred can be satisfied, the self can be punished and finally accepted; justice can be accomplished and the protagonist can find peace at last." [35]

The above is from the chapter entitled "The Trapped," which is especially relevant to the trilogy. My contention is that the form of punishment the self-hatred consciously adopts is itself a product of puritanism, as is the view of "justice" Lavinia has; and together they render void the possibility of peace. Lavinia has not escaped from the blight of puritanism, and her withdrawal from the world confirms the fact.

But the pursuit of meaning in the plays requires a more direct consideration of means than I have so far made.

The world of the plays ended by becoming demonic, but O'Neill began with a naturalistic premise and hoped to attain realistic results. Hence, the choice of a modern, but not contemporary, setting; psychic, not supernatural, fate; real, not mythical, characters. Yet in the conception and the writing, realism was the end, not the beginning, of a long process of testing and discarding nonrealistic devices of dramaturgy.

O'Neill made his name as a playwright of realism. He wrote his best works in that style. Yet he belongs to the rise of theatricalism, because of his repeated attempts to transcend realism through formalistic devices. He sincerely desired to "liberate" the stage, as Cocteau wished to "save" it; and he had such fondness for the devices he used that it was all the more unlikely that he should at last decide to do without most of them and moderate the others to fit the realism of his dialogue and setting. As one follows the account of his many revisions, the sureness of his dramatic instinct becomes plain. It finally resisted all the

[35] Falk, *O'Neill and the Tragic Tension*, p. 141.

temptations to neglect action, character, and clear dramatic form for the sake of novel and striking devices. In the process O'Neill recapitulated most of the stages he had gone through up to that time. In the early plays of the sea, he had aspired to a naturalistic formlessness within a thematic and atmospheric unity. Then he tried the formal balance of contrasts in the careers of the two brothers in *Beyond the Horizon,* and the fates of the consumptive lovers in *The Straw. The Emperor Jones* and *The Hairy Ape* teemed with the theatrical effects of expressionism: distorted scenery, mechanically dehumanized crowds, masked figures, and the like. The controlling metaphor of sea and fog was chosen to lift *Anna Christie* above its drab realism. *The Great God Brown* experimented with masked principals and multiple personalities. *Lazarus Laughed* employed vast choruses, lyric speeches, and an endless proliferation of masks. The otherwise realistic *Strange Interlude* imitated the novel by incorporating formal asides of such length that they became soliloquies expressing a kind of stream of subconsciousness. O'Neill subjected his audiences to all these, and they accepted them as new and broadening experiences. So his contribution to the American theatre in this respect is historically important.

But from the point of view of artistry and of craftsmanship, these devices were too often an artistic indulgence, a temptation to convey the drama through stage directions, rather than through character, dialogue, and underlying structure. The plays often succeeded despite O'Neill's inability to control and shape his material, although what was most fully communicated was sometimes not so much the drama as the author's personal urgency, his doubts and anguish: "The stage becomes O'Neill's lifeless megaphone. Nothing stands between the audience and O'Neill shouting his views." [36]

Yet there was no tendency, in all this experimentation with form, to recast classical myth. The closest he came to it before *Mourning Becomes Electra* was the use of mythical symbolism in *The Great God Brown,* where we have a Gidean confrontation within one man, Dion Anthony, of ascetic and orgiastic tendencies: Dionysus versus St. Anthony, with the prostitute Sibyl as an emanation of the earth mother, Cybele. But these

[36] Francis Fergusson, "Eugene O'Neill," in Morton D. Zabel, ed., *Literary Opinion in America,* rev. ed. (New York: Harpers, 1951), pp. 513-21.

are no more than associations with myth; the plot, modern in setting and highly expressionistic in treatment, and the characters are O'Neill's own.

Encouraged by these experiments, and perhaps attracted by the formal aspects of Greek tragedy as well as by its content, O'Neill conceived the characters of the trilogy as wearing half-masks, and speaking in the long asides he had used in *Strange Interlude*. These, he wrote, "will aid me to get just the right effect—must get more distance and perspective—more sense of fate—more sense of the unreal behind what we call reality which is the real reality!" [37] (One is reminded of Cocteau's theatre poetry, which was to be "truer than truth.") O'Neill had earlier declared that "the use of masks will be discovered to be the freest solution of the modern dramatist's problem as to how he can express those profound hidden conflicts of mind which the probings of psychology continue to disclose to us." [38] He undertook to include both asides and traditional monologues: "The unrealistic truth wearing the mask of lying reality, that is the right feeling for this trilogy, if I can only catch it!" [39] He would be highly selective in giving his characters a realistic basis: "Exclude as far as possible and consistent with living people, the easy superficial characterization of individual mannerisms—unless these mannerisms are inevitable fingerprints of inner nature —essential revelations." [40] The intermittent chorus of townspeople should be almost lay-figures, differentiated only by exterior characterization. Peter and Hazel, foils for Lavinia and Orin, were to be treated similarly.

Then the theatrical devices, at first purely external, began to graft themselves to the action. O'Neill conceived of the masks as a means of establishing a chain of resemblances among the characters of the two generations of Mannons as their relationships altered. Retaining the idea of *resemblances*, he transformed the masks into a Mannon characteristic, the hypocritical or secretive defense of his principals when "in repose." Now it was part of the theme, needing only make-up and the actor's co-

[37] "Notes and Extracts," in Clark, *European Theories*, pp. 532-33.
[38] Quoted in Croswell Bowen, *The Curse of the Misbegotten* (New York: McGraw-Hill, 1959), p. 157.
[39] Clark, *European Theories*, p. 533.
[40] *Ibid.*

operation to serve as "a dramatic arresting visual symbol of the separateness, the fated isolation of this family, the mark of their fate which makes them dramatically distinct from the rest of the world. . . ." [41] The pattern of resemblances expressed the character transformations appropriate to the psychological system he had adopted. It is fortuitous that Christine should resemble her lover's mother, Marie Brantôme (though not that Adam should love Christine because of her resemblance to his mother), but quite consistent that Lavinia, who at first resembles and imitates her father, should come to look like her mother. Such changes were integral to action and theme.

The mask, symbol of the Mannon inheritance through which the individual passions appear and withdraw, was extended from the characters to the setting of the house. O'Neill's stage directions specify an act curtain that shows the Mannon house at a distance. The actual setting of the façade and steps of the house brings us closer: we see it is a "whited sepulchre"—a "pagan temple front stuck like a mask on Puritan gray ugliness!" as Christine says. Then the action of each play is so planned as to begin outside the house, setting up a rhythm of advance and return. Used structurally and thematically, the mask device does not call attention to itself, but to the significance of the action; thus it can work directly upon the spectator's emotions, without obtruding or causing such confusions as plagued it in *The Great God Brown*. It is an example of how O'Neill could work for "unreal realism" without violating the convention of life-likeness.

A good deal of O'Neill's experimentation may have been an attempt to hide the "bare melodrama of the plot," to convert "the unavoidable entire melodramatic action" into a compelling "working out of psychic fate from [the] past," if his essentially modern, psychological drama was to attain tragic significance. In any case, after finishing the second draft, he began to reverse himself. Out came the superflous asides, which were suited only to the depiction of the "modern, neurotic, disintegrated soul," and not to "characters of strong will and intense passions." Out came the half-masks, too, as we have seen; for they introduced "an obvious duality of character symbolism quite outside my intent in these plays." For the time being, he kept the soliloquies, even rewriting them for greater formalization. Then they also had to

[41] *Ibid.*, p. 535.

go, because they halted the rush of action and contributed nothing that could not be "shown directly or clearly suggested in . . . pantomime or talk."

These experiments proved instructive: O'Neill gained "new insights into characters and recurrent themes"; but now the task was "to get all this in naturally in straight dialogue—as simple and direct and dynamic as possible." He realized that in his experiments he had been "doing things to these characters, instead of letting them reveal themselves—in spite of (or because of!) their long locked-up passions, I feel them burning to do just this!"

As in Aeschylus, the key to action and theme, to the sense of inherited fate, lay in the idea of *recurrence;* and that became the basis of the architectonics of the plays: "Repetition of the same scene—in its essential spirit, sometimes even in its exact words, but different characters." [42] This revealed enormous possibilities of dramatic recall: variation, overtone, and echo. He elaborated the Aeschylean plot by inventing incidents, relationships, and motifs that could be combined, recombined, altered, and varied, so as to convey a sense of repetition that took on heightened significance through recurrence in new combinations. In other words, O'Neill, deprived of the convenient authority of prophecy or a premonitory chorus, achieved coherence and form by exploiting to the full that device which is the reverse of foreshadowing—"dramatic recall": "[Dramatic recall] has a peculiarly gratifying emotional result; it furnishes on the affective level instances of expectations gratified, and goals achieved, which the denouement as a whole exhibits on the sides of plot and characterization. . . . Like the device of foreshadowing, it is a . . . device of coherence, serving to tie up neatly ends of motifs that otherwise might seem untidy and frayed; it assists in making the play seem an efficient structural unity." [43]

It was clever of O'Neill to fuse a plot of recurrent murder to a system of psychic recurrence. But nothing in his previous dramaturgy prepares one for the extent to which he then went on to elaborate their variations in overt action, transformation of character, dialogue, and setting, while driving the plot forward, and all without loss of clarity or blurring of form. So much ad-

[42] *Ibid.*
[43] Millet and Bentley, *The Art of the Drama,* p. 199.

verse comment has been directed at O'Neill's inadequacies of language, as if language were the whole story, that critics have largely ignored the really astonishing structural merits of the trilogy. It is a feat of sustained dramaturgy unparalleled by any of the playwrights then using myth; in O'Neill's theatre, no play before or after *Mourning Becomes Electra*, with the possible exception of *Long Day's Journey*, is so well designed.[44] Plotless subjectivity in drama may be left to those who like that sort of thing. *Morning Becomes Electra* is an achievement of genuine artistry because its form is so completely the expression of its meaning.

Certain repetitions in the plays, such as the sea chantey and the references to the South Sea isles, are obvious, though nonetheless effective for that. What is less obvious is the intricate maze of cross-references, the complexes or clusters of minor motifs, which to chart would be an impossible task. To show O'Neill's use of repetition and variation in creating dramatic recall, it will be sufficient to cite one example carried through the three plays. Courage and cowardice are important in an action where family pride is one of the main driving forces, and Lavinia is the embodiment of courage and family pride from first to last. In *Homecoming*, ironically, the charge of cowardice is first made against her by Brant, when he seeks to tell her the unsavory truth about the Mannon past, which involves her beloved father: "You're a coward, are you, like all Mannons, when it comes to facing the truth about themselves?" Lavinia will endure no word against the family, but Brant is mistaken in attributing cowardice to her. There is a double irony in his speech, for he also is a Mannon, however much he may wish to deny it. When Lavinia seeks to wring from him an admission that he has become her mother's paramour, in order to revenge himself on her father, she uses the same tactic as he did: "And I suppose you boast that now you've done so, don't you?—in the vilest, most cowardly way—like the son of a servant you are!" This hits

---

[44] An example of brusque dismissal on the grounds of language is to be found in George Steiner's *The Death of Tragedy* (New York: Knopf, 1961), p. 327: "O'Neill commits inner vandalism by sheer inadequacy of style. In the morass of his language the high griefs of the house of Atreus dwindle to a case of adultery and murder in some provincial rathole." This literary judgment flatly contradicts numerous accounts of the effect of the play in performance.

home: Brant seduced Christine by stealth, while Ezra was away at war. Then, when Christine enlists Brant's help in her plot to murder Ezra, his first reaction is "Poison! It's a coward's trick!" And now Christine, quite unconsciously, echoes both Brant and Lavinia, lover and enemy, as she prods him to consent: "It must be the Mannon in you coming out! Are you going to prove, the first time your love is put to a real test, that you're a weak coward like your father?"

The Hunted gives us a repetition of situation—the plotting of murder; but this time Lavinia and Orin are involved, instead of Christine and Brant, and it is now Brant, instead of Ezra, who is to be the victim. Again the charge of cowardice is used to force consent to murder. Lavinia says to her brother: "Then if I can't make you see your duty one way, I will another. If you won't help me punish her, I hope you're not such a coward that you're willing to let her lover escape!" The murder of Ezra not having gone as planned, Christine warns Brant that they are in danger because Lavinia suspects them. Brant says dejectedly: "It serves me right. . . . It wasn't that kind of revenge I had sworn on my mother's body! I should have done as I wanted —fought with Ezra Mannon as two men fight for love of a woman! I have my father's rotten coward blood in me, I think! Aye!" After the murder of Brant and the suicide of Christine, Lavinia flings the charge at Orin again, this time because, unable to bear the guilt on his conscience, he has written a confession exposing the family crimes and is attempting to spirit it out of the house: "You—you traitor! You coward! Give it to me! Do you hear? . . . You can't do this! You're a Mannon!" And the charge proves to be the means whereby Lavinia drives her brother to suicide in order to remove the threat of exposure. Orin begs her to go with him now and "confess and pay the penalty for Mother's murder, and find peace together!" Lavinia refuses: "No! You coward! There is nothing to confess! There was only justice!" Then she becomes frantic with rage and hatred: "I hate you! I wish you were dead! You're too vile to live! You'd kill yourself if you weren't a coward!" The moment that Orin realizes her intent, he sees her as the instrument of his mother's justice: "Another act of justice, eh? You want to drive me to suicide as I drove Mother! An eye for an eye, is that it?" And the scene proceeds to his death. In the last moments of the play, when Lavinia recognizes her doom, the theme recurs more subtly, again associated with the deaths of Christine and Orin. Old Seth, frightened by Lavinia's manner as she turns for the last time to enter the house, exclaims: "Don't go in there, Vinnie!" She replies: "Don't be afraid. I'm not going the way Mother and Orin went. That's escaping punishment. And there's no one left to punish me. I'm the last Mannon. I've got to punish myself!" Acceptance of doom is in her eyes an act of courage that a Mannon can take pride in.

"The mother of all gods and heroes. . . ." This was what O'Neill called the subconscious mind. In it he grounded the psychic fate of his trilogy and discovered its form. It is this which makes his "modern" drama seem older than those of classic Greece. It takes us back unimaginable ages to a time, if ever there was such, of truly unaccommodated man—man before he peopled the world with the Olympians and other sky-gods, and instead worshiped and placated his ever-present dead. When O'Neill recasts the ancient myth of Orestes and Electra and abolishes the Olympian gods and all supernatural fate, however, the result is unexpected paradox: the subconscious becomes the mother of *demons*, the dead become the pursuing Furies, and man goes inward to a hell of his own devising.

CHAPTER VI

JEAN GIRAUDOUX:
In Tune with the Finite

The play is the only form of moral or artistic education of a
nation. It is the only evening course available for adults and
the aged, the only means whereby the most humble and least
literate members of the public can find personal contact with
the highest conflicts, and create for themselves an undenomi-
national religion, a liturgy and its saints, sentiments and passions. Some people dream, but for those who do not dream
there is the theatre.[1]

This statement attests to two things about Jean Giraudoux: his
love of man and his love of theatre. What it omits is his love
of nature and his dislike of all religion. He was a humanist who
held "an excessive pantheism, a politeness toward creation," [2]
but at the same time distrusted the supernatural with which nature seemed to be permeated. And yet, in the latter half of his
life, he wrote plays which teemed with angels, archangels, on-
dines, ghosts, personifications, and the Olympian gods. Three
of his plays rework classic myths: *Amphitryon 38* (1929), *La
Guerre de Troie n'aura pas lieu* (*The Trojan War Will Not Take
Place*) (1935), and *Electra* (1937).

[1]Jean Giraudoux, quoted in Frederick Lumley, *Trends in Twentieth Century Drama*, 1st ed. (London: Rockliff, 1956), p. 40.
[2] Quoted in Wallace Fowlie, *Dionysus in Paris: A Guide to Contemporary
Theater* (New York: Meridian Books, 1960), p. 60.

Beginning with *Siegfried* (1928), he achieved a theatre that made him the foremost playwright of France between the two world wars. His first play, an enormous success, was felt to mark a new epoch in French theatrical history: it brought back language as the pre-eminent dramatic value, and with it the long speech and the pleasure of rhetorical virtuosity.[3] He achieved the restoration of Sire le Mot, whom Cocteau had tried so hard to banish in favor of a *poésie du théâtre*. This was a wry turn of events not only because Cocteau himself later decided it was high time to change the rules of the game, but also because Giraudoux had obviously taken an "evening course" in Cocteau's theatre and learned from his plays many of the advantages of theatricalism and the uses of classical myth which he then applied to the creation of his own theatre poetry. The acknowledgments are there, plain to see, especially in the plays based on myth; the results, except for Cocteau's subordination of language, are a vindication of his theatrical concepts.

I. *Amphitryon 38*

If Cocteau would let himself go, Gide had said, he would write boulevard comedies. Giraudoux let himself go in his first venture with classical myth, *Amphitryon 38*, and the result was such a boulevard comedy, but a comedy that also sounded some of his major themes: the divided nature of man, his relation to the world, and the closeness of love and war. Moreover, in the seduction of Alcmena by Jupiter, Giraudoux found a myth that demonstrated clearly one of his deepest convictions about man: "Nothing in Giraudoux suggests atheism, but nothing suggests religious fervor either. Discreetly silent on the question of a Christian God . . . hostile towards the God of the Jews, and impatient with all matters of cult, he would have us turn our eyes away from the gods to dedicate ourselves to this world, to fellow men, to the here and now." [4]

Giraudoux's God is undramatizable, because he is the Unknown God, impersonal and indefinable, who sees the world quite differently from the way men do and who does not inter-

[3] Laurent LeSage, *Jean Giraudoux: His Life and Works* (University Park: Pennsylvania State University Press, 1959), pp. 66-68.
[4] *Ibid.*, p. 157.

fere with the affairs of men; instead, totally remote from man, this God of German idealism is preoccupied with the esthetic of the world—that is, he contemplates esthetically the Great Whole, the superior harmony of the cosmos.[5] But there is a contradiction in man, a discord between his desire to transcend himself and the harmony that should obtain between man and nature. Man should respond to the solicitations of nature, in order to achieve a proper harmony with it; but in the act of doing so, he may encounter powers which endanger his humanity. The appearance of the Olympian gods, Jupiter and Mercury, in *Amphitryon 38* marks both the appearance of the supernatural in Giraudoux's work and the onset of the tragic. In one sense, then, they mark "the climax of what one could expect of the Giralducian esthetic: the dream of a union with the non-human, and, more exactly, the communion between beings of unlike natures"; the theatre provides, in a way the novel could not, for a fraternal mingling of men and supernatural beings. And so one might expect the gods to symbolize "the cosmic life that man ignores and neglects by turning in on himself too much." But after *Amphitryon 38*, and even there by implication, the Olympian gods

appear not only as strangers, but as hostile, dangerous, malefic: the creation of a new notion carries no solution for the internal conflict of the Giralducian morality, it serves on the contrary only to develop the ambiguities and deepen the contradiction in them. The "gods" [become] a formal notion, purely dramatic, in fact—which he will endow with all meanings. . . . Thus the gods are sometimes presented not as beneficent union with the non-human, but as a madness and a perilous disorder. . . . His heroes are men who betray their fellows in favor of the supernatural. . . .[6]

Such is the drift of the tragic development in Giraudoux's thought, as evidenced in *The Trojan War* and *Electra*. The gods are useful symbols of fate or destiny; or they represent the beliefs of men about the nature of the divine, and in this way, too, lead to tragedy. Man's primal sin was his creation of a division between himself and the more-than-man, and he has lost the key to the gates of Paradise. He endangers himself, now, if he attempts to find it. The best he can do is to try to strike a balance

[5] René-Marill Albérès, *Esthétique et morale chez Jean Giraudoux* (Paris: Librairie Nizet, 1957), Chaps. 21-23, pp. 332-79. I have appropriated Albérès' terminology where convenient.
[6] *Ibid.*, pp. 347, 350 (my translation).

and live in harmony with the world about him, cultivating a purely human wisdom and "a politeness toward creation."

But Giraudoux is saddened that men do not appreciate and fulfill their own humanity. And so he writes a play to celebrate their humanity at its most humanly perfect, utilizing a plot which deals with the invasion of human privacy by the gods.

Plautus' *Amphitryon*, with which the ancient Romans annually honored the father of the gods (to the great scandal of the philosopher David Hume), is a "tragi-comedy" of mistaken identities and cross-purposes that derives its piquancy from the fact that Jupiter, in his latest amorous adventure among mortals, decides that he will lie with Alcmena and, in thus cuckolding her husband Amphitryon, give her a son, Hercules. He conquers Alcmena's chastity by assuming the guise of Amphitryon, much to the latter's discomfiture until the confusion is cleared up, and triumphantly arranges matters so that Hercules shall have a twin brother, who shall be Amphitryon's son. When Jupiter departs, all the mortals involved feel honored.

For his adaptation, Giraudoux altered the myth to make Alcmena the principal character and decided that Jupiter should come a cropper. It was the mortal Alcmena, the perfect wife, symbol of female fidelity, who should triumph.

Jupiter succeeds in his deception by creating a war that General Amphitryon must go off to, and in his absence assumes Amphitryon's mortal guise and lies with Alcmena. As a result of this union, she conceives Hercules. But Jupiter so enjoys the liaison that he proposes to repeat it, this time not in disguise but in full panoply. Alcmena discovers the deception, to her horror. She turns for help to Leda, whom Jupiter had once ravished in the guise of a swan. She persuades Leda to act as substitute for her in secret. Meanwhile, the real Amphitryon returns from battle (Jupiter has called off the war), but he is mistaken for Jupiter himself by Alcmena. The upshot is a double adultery, involving both husband and wife, but in both cases they are ignorant of the true circumstances, and innocent of any intent to be unfaithful.

Jupiter, not to be gainsaid, arrives in state with all of Thebes on hand to welcome him. Alcmena, the perfect wife, is equal to the occasion. She offers him friendship, induces him to accept it, and so fulfills the impossible divine decree: to wit, that she should give herself to Jupiter and that she should remain faithful to Amphitryon.

At the level of boulevard comedy, it is wittily ironic that Alcmena should come off victor by offering friendship. Jupiter, first of the gods, symbol of the world's incessant fertility, seducer and ravisher, the divine Don Juan of countless ingenious *amours* —to be palmed off with friendship? What a comedown! And that he should accept it willingly—what a joke on the gods!

But isn't it also a letdown? At that level, yes. But at a deeper level the irony is seen to lie elsewhere. Throughout the play we have been concerned with connubial love, which Jupiter's interference has turned into unwitting adultery. Suddenly, friendship comes to the fore, seeming at first a slightly lame solution to the plot. But the idea of friendship throws a revealing light, retrospectively, on the marriage of Amphitryon and Alcmena. The way Alcmena handles Jupiter tells us how she handles her marriage. In both cases the clue is friendship. Further, the respect which Jupiter comes to have for her casts light on the mutual respect of husband and wife.

They are the perfect married lovers because they are also perfect friends, with all that friendship bespeaks. In Alcmena we see what is for Giraudoux the perfection of natural humanity; but its crown is not sexual love, it is friendship. Sexual love, after all, is something man shares with the animal kingdom; and for him, too often, it is merely a matter of the reins, instead of the heart and mind. As Jupiter, disguised as a beggar, in the later play *Electra* says: "Fraternity is the mark of human beings. Beasts know only love . . . cats, parrots, et cetera, they only recognize fraternity by the hair. To find brothers they have to love men, to turn to men. . . ." [7]

Man cannot claim sexual love as uniquely his: it is the necessary basis for the natural world of which man is only a part. Also, as Giraudoux knows, Eros was born of Aphrodite and Ares: war and desire. On the other hand, the bond which cements, instead of dividing, the specifically human world is friendship. It is that which is uniquely man's. (A charming idea, but an inaccurate one, as many accounts of animal friendship attest.)

[7] Jean Giraudoux, *Electra*, trans. Winifred Smith, in Eric Bentley, ed., *The Modern Theatre*, I (Garden City, N.Y.: Doubleday Anchor Books, 1955), 243.

Giraudoux is not here opposing eros to agape, a love that aspires to friendship with the divine. Quite the contrary. The friendship he exalts is a purely natural love with nothing of the divine in it; but in his view it is to be anything but despised on that account. For Giraudoux, the fact that it is purely human is quite enough; precisely there lies its distinctive virtue.

It is her human capacity for friendship that makes Alcmena the perfect mortal, the perfect wife, and thus superior to her divine lover. The gods themselves do not possess friendship, nor do they possess its components or attendant virtues of gentleness, fidelity, and devotion. Thus, its presence marks the limits of their power in the human world, just as its lack marks the flaw in their supernatural perfection. They cannot tamper with it, except by guile. It is, above all, the one thing they cannot *exact* from men. Human beings may fear the gods or flout them; they may worship them, endure them, or freely surrender to them; but *they do not respect them as friends.*

Yet Alcmena did so. She offered Jupiter the very thing which made her superior to the gods. She confers it upon him; and, although she is careful to hide the fact out of respect for her new friend, her relationship to Jupiter as a god is that of a superior being bestowing a gift upon an inferior one. When he leaves the earth to return to Olympus, Jupiter's regrets are an admission of all that the gods are deprived of in not having human friendship. He should feel pleased, indeed honored, at receiving such a gift, and so he does.

By these means, the playwright reverses the order of things to celebrate humanity. When human beings love their fellows as friends, they are at their human best; and that is better than anything the gods have to offer, says Giraudoux, the confirmed humanist.

II. *The Trojan War Will Not Take Place*

Giraudoux's second venture in dramatizing classical myth was *The Trojan War Will Not Take Place* (1935).[8] It deals with the efforts of Hector to prevent a conflict with the Greeks by induc-

[8] Jean Giraudoux, *La Guerre de Troie n'aura pas lieu*, trans. as *Tiger at the Gates* by Christopher Fry (New York: Oxford University Press, 1955). All quotations are from this version.

ing his countrymen to return the ravishing, but scarcely ravished, Helen to her husband Menelaus, close the Gates of War, and live in peace. As it proves, we are on the very eve of a war which we know took place. The interim is devoted to Hector's increasingly desperate tactics to control the warlike propensities of the Trojans by puncturing their sophistries and exposing their belligerent pride as false, and to induce the parties most closely concerned—Paris, Helen, and Ulysses as Greek ambassador—to act as if nothing had happened. The issue is raised the moment the curtain rises:

ANDROMACHE: There's not going to be a Trojan War, Cassandra!

CASSANDRA: I'll take that bet, Andromache.

ANDROMACHE: The Greeks are quite right to protest. We are going to receive their ambassador very civilly. We shall wrap up his little Helen and give her back to him.

CASSANDRA: We shall receive him atrociously. We shall refuse to give Helen back. And there *will* be a Trojan War.[9]

From a dramaturgic point of view, nothing could be fairer than that. The plot is summarized precisely at the outset. The things the two women say in the third and fourth speeches are contradictory and yet true. We are already exposed to the dialectics of the play's development: we are to have a disquisition on the origins of war and an action that demonstrates them.

I mentioned earlier what seems to me Giraudoux's considerable indebtedness to Cocteau in learning the possibilities of mythic material and theatricalist techniques for his particular kind of imaginative theatre. It is the more interesting, then, to discover that the basic dramaturgic problem he faced in this play is very similar to Cocteau's in *The Infernal Machine*, staged the year before: to make drama out of an attempt to prevent what we know will happen. For me, Giraudoux succeeds where Cocteau fails. It is not a question of skill, since each succeeded in doing what he wished. And so, either my judgment of the earlier play is wrong and my position inconsistent, or else it is possible to attack the same problem and obtain different results by using different techniques and, no less important, a different outlook on life. Obviously, the same problem faces all the dramatists who work from well-known mythic materials, as it does

[9] *Ibid.*, p. 1.

those who deal with historical themes. It stands out in these two plays, however, because each is so insistent: Cocteau's in showing that fate cannot be avoided; Giraudoux's by asserting in its very title what we know to be false.

Both men assume the myth and rely on the audience's knowledge of it as the basis for the play. But there are differences. Cocteau dramatizes segments of a given myth, Giraudoux, only an action that the myth implies. That is, Giraudoux infers that the repercussions among the Trojans to the rape of Helen must have resulted in councils of war; he will show us a council of peace. Where Cocteau mostly embroiders upon given instances, Giraudoux invents an entire action to fill a lacuna. He is careful, within certain qualifications, not to go beyond it and dramatize known incidents from elsewhere in the epic. Although the subsequent fates of many of the characters are known to us, this confining of the action makes the myth less intrusive. By restricting himself in this way, Giraudoux actually gains greater freedom, since nothing within the action has to conform to more than the single outcome: the declaration of war. I say "within the action" because, until the end of the play, Giraudoux is careful not to invent incidents that conflict with our knowledge of subsequent events. He cannot, for instance, have Priam, instead of the invented Demokos, die in the quarrel with Hector. For Priam must be preserved in order that he may perform later the deeds recorded of him in the *Iliad*. But there is an exception: the death of Ajax, offstage, in the rush of the denouement. Ajax, whether he is Great Ajax, son of Telamon, or Little Ajax, son of Oileus, did not die before the war had begun.[10] But we do not notice this discrepancy, because the focus is on stage, on Hector, Andromache, and Cassandra, and the opening of the Gates of War.

Perspective figures here, too. Cocteau took us behind the scenes, so to speak, and showed us eternity as well as Thebes; in every way possible, he gave us a godlike omniscience. Giraudoux mainly sticks to the limited viewpoint of human reason, but he shifts the angle from which we see the action. The *Iliad* is a Greek epic, seen through Greek eyes, that exalts Greek heroes and involves Greek national pride. Giraudoux forces us to

[10] See Robert Graves, *The Greek Myths*, 2 vols. (Baltimore: Penguin Books, 1955), II, Chaps. 165, 168.

readjust by choosing the Trojan point of view. This is a simple change, organic to the theme: to see both sides of a situation is to understand "the enemy" better. The approach robs the Greek participants of their traditional nimbuses. But Giraudoux does not then succumb to the opposite temptation, that of idealizing or sentimentalizing the Trojans, who are going to be the losers. That would defeat his purposes.

It is true that he exempts Hector and Andromache and the women in general (even Helen) from this deflationary treatment. He spares the women because it is part of his theme that they are by nature less bellicose than men; having a truer instinct for living, they can fulfill themselves best when the land is at peace. He ennobles Hector, but not his warlike qualities. He makes this storied hero (whose courage is unquestioned) foreswear his own past victories and love of battle to fight barehanded for peace. Hector is not entirely disinterested: his own happiness is bound up in the struggle, as are his wife's and children's. But so is the true happiness of everyone else in Troy, and it is this which he must make the Trojans see. He is a hero to Giraudoux because he represents the spirit of brotherhood allied to right ends, and we know that Giraudoux gives to fraternity the ultimate human value. And he is exemplary not only because he shares the playwright's beliefs, but also because he exemplifies them in action. When we see how silly and self-delusive the Trojans are about the rape, who will condemn him for countering with equally specious assertions to prove that Helen is still chaste and that no one's honor has been insulted nor anyone's rights infringed?

Giraudoux's emphasis is defined in this statement: "The subject of *La Guerre de Troie* is not the arrival of war, but the hesitation of the world between war and peace. . . ."[11] Consequently, he does not harp upon inevitability, either within the action or outside it. This is contrary to Cocteau's practice. But Giraudoux *creates* a convincing semblance of inevitability, first through his plot, then his characters, and finally through his own attitude.

That attitude is, of course, anterior to the play it pervades. It

[11] Jacques Guicharnaud and June Beckelman, *Modern French Theatre from Giraudoux to Beckett*, Yale Romanic Studies, Second Series, 7 (New Haven: Yale University Press, 1961), p. 31.

succeeds in suggesting a life of peace that is profoundly desirable, not only because it is beautiful in itself, but mainly because it would enable admirably human people like Hector and Andromache to fulfill their enormous gifts for living. The physical beauty of life, which vibrates throughout the play with the touching fervor of Giraudoux's love, is evoked through concrete, but generalized, detail that provides an idealized setting for Hector's dream of peace. This attitude, which is also one of restraint, strikes a balance between our sympathies for Hector's valiant fight for peace and our intellectual stimulation at the witty interplay of conflicting ideas and manners. Thought is a passion with Giraudoux, despite his disclaimers, as it is with Shaw, so that he need not cool off the audience or the action because he can stimulate both our minds and our emotions. Giraudoux obviously cares deeply about peace; it is the indispensable condition for achieving that harmonious relation of each person to his world, which is, to him, the highest good. Quite simply, his choice of theme is more universal and important than Cocteau's introverted meditations on art. Giraudoux is the last person to feel that life is demonic or that art is its only compensation.

The plot that Giraudoux invents is arranged to evoke our mixed emotions of hope and fear (the classic definition of suspense), regardless of whether or not the outcome is known. We are in suspense not because we are ignorant of the outcome, but because we care about it. Giraudoux does not mislead us by creating a fool's paradise and then shattering it at the last moment; rather, he imagines something very much worth saving and then places it in jeopardy. For example, he foreshadows the end in one of the best-prepared and most ironic entrances in modern drama: Hector's entrance upon his return from war. Cassandra speaks to Andromache of war as a sleeping tiger which is being prodded awake. This image is developed and counterpointed at some length, leading up to the following:

CASSANDRA: Today is the chance for peace to enthrone herself all over the world. The tiger licks his lips. And Andromache is going to have a son! And the horsemen have started leaning from their saddles to stroke tom-cats on the battlements! The tiger starts to prowl.

ANDROMACHE: Be quiet!

CASSANDRA: He climbs noiselessly up the palace steps. He pushes open the doors with his snout. And here he is, here he is!

(HECTOR'S voice: Andromache!)

ANDROMACHE: You are lying! It is Hector!

CASSANDRA: Whoever said it was not?

[*enter HECTOR*] [12]

The unexpected juxtaposition of the tiger image and Hector is borne out by the climax of the play. Driven to frenzy in his efforts to secure peace, it is Hector himself, the man of peace, who kills Demokos with a spear-thrust and brings about the war he strove to prevent.

In a close reading of the play [13] one critic has demonstrated conclusively how little success Hector has in persuading to his convictions person after person—Paris, Priam, Helen, Busiris, Ajax, and Ulysses; how he is therefore reduced to using tactics to wring from them reluctant concessions, and so is moved repeatedly to voice his own distrust of his apparent success: "They have all given in to me. . . . And yet I can't help feeling that in each of these apparent victories I have been defeated." And again: "I will win every round. But still with each victory the prize escapes me." In this interpretation the reason offered is that only actual experience of the kind Hector had in his last battle can convince; anything else leaves the soldier a prey to the illusions of godlike power and pity as he stands over his enemy, or leaves the civilian a prey to the intoxication of beauty that is Helen's, or to the desire to risk life so as to savor it more intensely or to risk it to confer on it a value that it does not otherwise have. Confronted with these diverse reactions, which place their possessors on the side opposite Hector, we are as uncertain as he is. But the more unsure he becomes, the more desperately he struggles, until at last his hope, and ours, makes him (and us) think that the hazardous moment has passed, saving the day for peace. That, of course, is the precise moment that Demokos, protesting wildly the surrender of Helen, enters and provokes Hector into striking him with his spear. Then comes the reversal. Dying, Demokos shouts a lie—that it was *Ajax the Greek* who killed him. The cry is taken up over Hector's shouts of denial, and the crowd kills Ajax. Hector takes Andromache's hands: "The war

[12] Giraudoux, *Tiger at the Gates*, p. 3.

[13] Eugene H. Falk, "Theme and Motif in *La Guerre de Troie n'aura pas lieu*," *Tulane Drama Review*, III, no. 4 (May, 1959), 17-30.

will happen." The Gates of War open to reveal Helen in the
arms of young Troilus. This points back to the scene where Andromache pleads with Helen: "Love Paris! . . . Then the war
will only be a scourge, not an injustice." But as the curtain falls,
we see that Andromache was right, that the most famous of
all ancient wars, and "the splendor and calamity of the age to
come," are alike "founded on a trivial adventure between two
people who don't love each other. . . ."

Giraudoux reduces the role of the gods and the supernatural
to such an extent that they could be eliminated entirely without
loss or distortion of the play's statement. He concentrates instead
on humanizing his characters. Cassandra, for instance, denies her
prophetic powers: "I prophesy nothing. All I ever do is to take
account of two great stupidities: the stupidity of men, and the
wild stupidity of the elements." After the Tiger of War scene,
she plays only a subordinate part. She has a brief scene with
Peace, discussed below, but does not prophesy again until the
end: "The Trojan poet is dead. And now the Grecian poet will
have his word." This takes us back to the myth, with the intima-
tion that we have seen the true version and that Homer's account
will be false because it justifies the Greeks and glorifies war.

Giraudoux contributes a new touch when he effectively transfers to Helen Cassandra's prophetic powers. Hector can dimly
see the future in her eyes: Paris dead, Andromache weeping,
Troy burning. Helen says she only imagines the future, some
parts of which are vivid to her and others drab; but she admits
even the brilliantly shining parts sometimes fail to come true:
"No one is infallible." This transfer adds to the mystery of Hel-
en's personality, and the attraction of her beauty for others.

When Peace appears to Helen and Cassandra, we have one of
those fanciful Giralducian scenes which, given the proper setting, can be both charming and sadly funny, but which seems
quite out of place in what Ulysses calls "the weight of this incor-
ruptible, unpitying air of these coasts and islands." Then, just
before the private meeting of Hector and Ulysses and in the
presence of rulers and people, Iris appears in the sky with messages from the gods, and again we have a jarring intrusion. Her
messages from Aphrodite and Pallas Athene are flatly contradictory. The command of Zeus is equally ambiguous: "The decision
he gives to Hector and Ulysses, is to separate Helen and Paris

without separating them. . . . Or else—he swears to you: he swears there will be war." In the interpretation cited above, this is regarded as Giraudoux's "sneer" of dismissal at the "mysterious powers of destiny" and a way of emphasizing that war is born of man's illusions: it is they that constitute chance and fate.

The conundrum the gods propound to the disputants reminds us of Jupiter's wish that Alcmena should give herself to him and still remain faithful to Amphitryon. Perhaps it is a conscious echo of the earlier play. We saw how Alcmena succeeded in meeting Jupiter's apparently irreconcilable command: she gave him her friendship. And if men could realize Giraudoux's—and Hector's —ideal of fraternity, the Trojan War would not take place. Ulysses interprets the message thus: "They have merely given us full powers . . . to stand above the catastrophe and taste the essential brotherhood of enemies." To Hector, this remark is a profanation of fraternity, as Helen's attitude was a profanation of love. I incline to think that Giraudoux, with his ambivalence toward nature and the universe, has let the final answer stand in mystery, but that he has also shown us enough to make us feel that man, if he were to achieve brotherhood, might in good heart take his chances with the unknown.

It is only partly true to say of *The Trojan War* that "the dénouement of a Giraudoux play is one familiar to the spectator, after he has been led to expect almost anything else." [14] There may be a trick involved, but it is only that which relates make-believe to the multi-consciousness of an audience; and Giraudoux has not dealt unfairly with us. Paradoxically, he makes us forget the outcome by keeping the possibility of it before our eyes in the shifting uncertainties of the action; he does this by engaging our emotions. He makes the finality of the past into a contingent (and therefore perturbing) present. This is, after all, the playwright's job. If he does it, and sustains it, he can play as much as he wishes with planes of reality and "the acceleration of time"; they will increase our perspectives, and thus our understanding, of that present.

Ingenious and sound as it is, the plot would not succeed without the creation of characters that give it conviction and illuminate its alternations of hope and fear:

[14] Guicharnaud and Beckelman, *Modern French Theatre*, p. 32.

They are drawn, it is true, with psychological art and are real enough with their motives and emotions to fit into a story. But they are above all the vehicles of certain qualities admired by the ethical sensitiveness of humanity whose spokesman Giraudoux makes himself. . . . Hector with his sense of brotherhood . . . all of them are very human and yet a little more than human, endowed by the abstracting imagination with an eloquence of person and function that derives not from themselves but from the human faith of their creator.[15]

In *The Infernal Machine*, it scarcely mattered *what* Cocteau's characters were like, so little influence did they have upon events. Here, their humanity counts because their activities count. Hector acts and defeats himself—but would not have done so without the maddening resistance, beneath their apparent capitulation, of all those about him. Giraudoux succeeds in convincing us that character is destiny, and that inevitability—or, if you will, fate—can best be created by showing men in action.

III. *Electra*

Two years after his play on the Trojan war, Giraudoux presented *Electra* (1937), noncommittally offered as "a play in two acts," but having the same tragic pretensions as his play *Judith*.[16] Again, as in that excursion into Biblical themes, the tragic figure is a young girl, and again she is tricked by fate.

In dramatizing the Electra myth, Giraudoux proceeds by deception and arabesque; that is, he deceives the audience about the myth by changing it and concealing the changes under arabesques of incident, emotion, and language. His ultimate deception is ironic, for these interlacing patterns do lead us back to the myth, as D'Indy's musical composition begins with the variations and ends with the theme. True, the play is titled *Electra*, and we recognize its initial situation from Sophocles and Euripides: the impending marriage of Electra to a peasant at the behest of her mother Clytemnestra and the regent Aegisthus. But very early on we cease to be sure of much else; we wonder how, or even whether, Giraudoux will reconstitute the myth.

The play develops like an ill-starred party. Electra's wedding

---

[15] Ronald Peacock, "Public and Private Problems in Modern Drama," *Tulane Drama Review*, III, no. 3 (March, 1959), p. 66.
[16] *Judith*, a full-fledged tragedy, had failed and closed after six weeks. See Donald Inskip, *Jean Giraudoux: The Making of a Dramatist* (London: Oxford University Press, 1958), p. 64.

is the occasion, but the guests are as much or more concerned with their own affairs. While the guests wait for the ceremony, the conversation piece creeps along amid growing uneasiness. Then the party gets out of hand. A gate-crasher appears and makes everyone uncomfortable. Guests begin to upbraid one another and speak home-truths. The wedding is postponed. Shocking disclosures are made. Finally, the son and daughter of the house murder the host and hostess.

When, halfway through the slowly gathering action, the forlorn bridegroom informs us on the highest authority that the marriage never took place and quits the play for good, he leaves us quite uncertain as to what further liberties Giraudoux will take with the myth. This is like Cocteau's use of surprise. The style being theatricalism, there are no predictable limits to the directions the playwright's fancy can take, nor to his independence of the myth either. The earlier play stated in its title, as if in flat defiance of the myth, that the Trojan War would not take place; but we knew that it had done so—and in the action of the play it did. By similar feints, Giraudoux nearly convinces us that Agamemnon's death will not be revenged; but at last it is—and just at the moment when the *fact* of the king's murder is being established for us in all its particularity.

Giraudoux not only alters and adds to the myth, he also applies to it the retrospective method and seeking action of *Oedipus Rex*; and he adds to that an Ibsenite method of gradually disclosing the reality beneath appearances. The conversation-piece opening is a mask for the slow uncovering of past events through Electra's seeking action: to find the slayer of Agamemnon and the motive for the murder, and to exact justice therefor. Since few know there was a murder and no one admits it, let alone talks about it, the approach is tortuous and oblique, building up dramatic pressure through the effort to divine the truth and communicate the unexpressed.

Knowledge of the myth is some help to the spectator in following the action, but it may also prove a hindrance, because of the changes Giraudoux has made in the story and his highly idiosyncratic manner of writing. It is only at the end that we realize the basic situation remains the same, and that the appearances are superficial changes that provide a present façade for the realities of the past: adultery, regicide, and usurpation. But the seeking action, until it discovers what the realities of the present circumstances are, cannot determine what is true of the past.

This technique of equivocation is best seen in the device of the Eumenides, represented as three little girls, cheeky and macabre, who grow up during the action until in the last scene, they become the Furies, "of exactly the same height and figure as Electra." I suspect that Giraudoux hit upon the device after meditating the passage in Euripides' *Orestes* where Electra tries to restrain her guilt-maddened brother, when he is seized by a fit. "*Let me go!*" he screams. "I know *you*. You're one of my Furies too!" (ll. 263-65). The playwright's originality lies in having converted the idea into a theatrical image and developed it visually to reinforce Electra's responsibility for the tragedy and for the consequences thereof to Orestes.

The little girls make a premature appearance, escorting Orestes on stage at rise; they explain the occasion of Electra's wedding and play grisly games of make-believe. As one of them says, "We lie, we slander, we insult." And their lies lay a smokescreen not dissipated by the fact that at times they also tell the truth. Their games reveal, but also distort, the truth, as their presence foreshadows disaster. They are as unorthodox in conception as they are original, and their effectiveness comes from their being pretty and funny, instead of physically monstrous. It is both more horrifying and more pointed to have them, at the end, come to look like Electra: "We've taken on your age and your shape—to pursue him," they tell her, as they set out after Orestes. "Good-bye! We'll not leave him until he's been driven to madness or suicide, cursing his sister."

Perhaps Giraudoux's basic change in the myth is to assume that this most notorious of mythic murders could be kept secret and palmed off as an accident. (The Eumenides do not belie the Gardener when he tells Orestes that "our king, Agamemnon, coming back from the war, slipped into the pool, fell on his sword and killed himself." Instead, one makes the ambiguous comment: "He took his bath after his death. About two minutes after. That's the difference.") On this clever assumption, he builds a deceptive structure of events that occurred during the previous decade; his method is akin to that of Clytemnestra and Aegisthus, who have succeeded in their elaborate pretense that all is well, fair in fact as in seeming. Aegisthus usurped the throne, Clytemnestra apparently retired to an inactive widow-hood, and life in the kingdom went on peacefully and prosperously.

The second assumption the playwright makes is that, Clytemnestra's infidelity with the then young Aegisthus having been kept as well hidden as the murder, it could also come to an end quietly with no one the wiser. Aegisthus is a notorious libertine, and his present dalliances actually help to deflect suspicion from their past liaison. Clytemnestra seems to regard his loose life with merely frigid disapproval. If she feels more than that, she can do nothing, because the bond of secret guilt between them checks her; and, indeed, her love seems to have died, too. Obviously, this change in plot involves a corresponding change in Clytemnestra's character which adds to the deception.

No one has challenged the regent's usurpation of the throne for twenty years, the length of Orestes' absence. "Her mother sent him out of the country when he was two," the Gardener tells the unidentified Orestes, "And he's not been heard of since." (In his presence the Eumenides talk about Orestes but address him directly only as "this stranger.") After two decades of peace, to use detective story terms, the murder of Agamemnon looks like the perfect crime. Orestes' return seems to involve only the issue of usurpation, not something else; yet usurpation is not spoken of either. The technique shows Giraudoux's skill in presenting certain facts, without explanation, as simply given.

There are even conflicts between the queen and the regent to mislead us. After having agreed to Electra's marriage to the gardener, Clytemnestra reneges. The regent may have ordered the marriage for reasons of expedience, but Clytemnestra's objections are those of a mother, not a ruler. Moreover, the conflicts between the queen and her daughter seem to have no bearing on the secret facts of the case (of which Electra is for much of the time ignorant): they appear to arise from Electra's deep-seated antipathy, caused by her obsessive love for her dead father and her sexual jealousy of Clytemnestra. At the same time, curiously, her hatred is nourished by an instinctive conviction that her mother's love for her husband was less than her own. In their open quarrels they obsessively rehash an incident from the past that seems entirely irrelevant: once, when carrying both children, Clytemnestra let Orestes fall. But this is another disguised hint pointing to the past, where the truth of things lies; the Beggar, the mysterious interloper at the wedding who is really a god in disguise, drops the hint in his Act I curtain speech. Clytemnestra had contended that Electra was responsible for Orestes' fall, because she had pushed him, and Electra denies it. The Beggar debates the case and decides that Electra did not push her baby brother:

So Electra didn't push Orestes! That makes everything she says legitimate, everything she undertakes irrefutable. She's unadulterated truth, a lamp without a wick. So if she kills, as looks likely, all happiness and peace around her, it's because she's right. . . . For the young girl is the guardian of truth; she has to go after it whether or not the world bursts and cracks down to its foundations, whether innocents die the death of innocents to let the guilty live their guilty lives.[17]

And buried in this long monologue, which reaches such important conclusions on the basis of a seemingly superfluous detail, is a clue about Clytemnestra's character that hints at the motive of the murder, and it, too, comes from the business about letting Orestes fall:

Anyway, seeing the child capsizing, in order to hold him she need only free her arm of little Electra, throw little Electra off on the marble floor, get rid of little Electra. Let little Electra break her neck, so the son of the king of kings be unhurt! But she's an egotist. For her a woman is as good as a man, she's a woman; the womb as good as the phallus, and she's a womb; she wouldn't dream for a second of destroying her daughter to save her son, so she keeps Electra.[18]

Giraudoux employs the Ibsenite method again when he includes a subplot—the discovery by the President, a minor official, of his wife Agatha's unfaithfulness. It is subtly handled to forestall Electra's suspicions and ours, and yet foreshadow the disclosure of Clytemnestra's perfidy. Agatha is a featherbrain married to a vain fool whose vanity she must always feed at the cost of her own freedom. We know that she is cuckolding him, and we take her reasons for granted. But behind her infidelities is a hatred of her husband so deep that they become her way of revenging herself on him for her bondage. The parallel throws

[17] Bentley, ed., *The Modern Theatre*, p. 242.
[18] *Ibid.*

us off the track because it is not exact. No comparison seems possible between Agatha and Clytemnestra; if we look for its counterpart in the present action, instead of in the past, there is none. There is no suggestion that Clytemnestra and Aegisthus are lovers. Aegisthus, however, *has* been Agatha's lover. He is one of her many infidelities, as she is one of his many conquests on which the queen looks with silent disdain. This makes a liaison with the queen still more unlikely. The parallel is there, if inverted, but it points to the past, not the present, and to Clytemnestra's own sexual hatred for Agamemnon.

Further deception is to be found in the character and treatment of Electra. Here Giraudoux has largely adopted Cocteau's methods: application of modern psychological concepts to mythical characters, and "heraldic" treatment of character within a theatricalist style. Cocteau gave Oedipus an Oedipus complex and made the character somewhat conscious of his own quirk. Giraudoux gives Electra a full-blown Electra complex but does not let her recognize it for what it is. She is far advanced in her obsession; it is the psychological drive behind her implacable demands for absolute justice, and it has become the mainspring of all her thoughts and actions, the motive, purpose, and meaning of her life.

Much beyond this we probably should not go; for while she may be a clinical case for psychology from one point of view, Giraudoux does not treat her clinically. Instead, he makes her one of his ideal characters or essences—in this case, the instrument of fate, the human embodiment of justice. And he has done so in the modern manner, that of mixing and synthesizing disparate elements—myth, depth-psychology, anachronisms, laughter, terror, detective story, conversation piece, and tragedy of fate—all served up with poetical language, witty common sense, and theatricalist décor.

Dramatically speaking, Electra is so single-minded as to be extreme, a sure source of disruption, if not tragedy; like Medea in Euripides' play, she is almost a force of nature. But here again, Giraudoux ironically plays us false. In the first act she has so little to support her intuition and motivate her undefined suspicions and search that these seem merely the products of her obsession. Perhaps Giraudoux felt it necessary, for this reason, to bring on the divine Beggar and have him speak in her behalf out of his omniscience. It is only in the last part, as the variations are drawn back into the theme, that we see her suspicions were justified despite all appearances to the contrary.

We should add to the playwright's deceptive tactics, as to his clever way of taking questionable situations for granted, Electra's incestuous love for Orestes, which he returns. Its relevance to the theme is not clear to me; it seems introduced for dramatic reasons—as a means of assuring Orestes' espousal of her case against Clytemnestra, as well as his own case against Aegisthus, and as a further means of insuring Electra's tragic isolation at the end, when she has not only lost Orestes but also become the image of his torment and object of his curses. The Furies goad her when Clytemnestra and Aegisthus have been killed by Orestes, for the regent's death makes certain the destruction of the city by the invading Corinthians. "Satisfied, Electra? The City's dying." She replies: "I'm satisfied. I know now that it will be born again," and adds: "I have my conscience, I have Orestes, I have justice, I have everything." But the Furies show her that she is now as guilty as her mother, and that Orestes has fled to madness or suicide. All she can say now is, "I have justice, I have everything." Were it not for the fact that the dawn breaks and life still goes on renewing itself, we should feel that in gaining justice she was left with nothing.

Her love for Orestes may come from the fact that this green plant that grew straight because it was always in the shade has had no love, parental or other, through all her life, and this despite her tremendous love for the memory of her father. She is surely the victim of Clytemnestra's infidelity and murderous hate. But that love is stained with her own hatred for her mother: it seems to have its origin partly in sexual jealousy: "Take your life from me, Orestes, not from our mother." Perhaps Orestes' love for her may be interpreted in the same way, since he also is a victim of his mother's crimes.

At the end, we see that Clytemnestra had for her husband, the king of kings, the same deep hatred that Agatha had for the President, and that her infidelity with Aegisthus was simply her earlier revenge upon Agamemnon. The answer to the question of Clytemnestra's motive is shown to be pure sex-hatred, so complete that it seems to lose within it, as if it were a detail, her hatred of him for having sacrificed Iphigenia. Here is where the schematism of the play becomes clear. Electra follows her intuition out of sexual jealousy, and what she uncovers is sexual hatred. That is, the basis of the present action is sexual jealousy: woman vs. woman; the basis of the past action is sexual hatred: woman vs. man. In loving her brother so completely and in wanting to cut her hated mother out of Orestes' life, Electra may have been affirming her complete contrast to her mother. But Giraudoux's final irony is that, whatever Electra's motive, however twisted it may have made her nature, her intuition was right; and she would not have followed it up so implacably without the powerful urge of her jealousy. And look what it led to—the defeat of the army, the sack of the city, death and destruction for thousands. It is an amazing demonstration of the premise that the most private and secret hatred can have the most public and remote consequences, that over a lapse of years justice will work itself out by the most tortuous and seemingly most irrelevant means. In the action of the play, justice proved the most deceptive thing of all, for all concerned. Giraudoux's deceptive method is an analogue of his theme and action.

In regard to character-drawing, the play is less successful than *The Trojan War*. There are several reasons for this. The first lies in the conception of Electra, who needs all our understanding and sympathy if we are to put up with her absolute demands and their destructive consequences. But for much of the time we have as little to go on as she and therefore cannot fathom her hatred. In a sense, because of the background of myth in which it is based, it is both too willful and too readily assumed. When we see, and can share, her defeat at the last, it is too late to reconstruct our attitudes and change our emotions accordingly. Second, in trying to humanize his Electra, Giraudoux emphasizes her love for Orestes in such a way that we are repelled, despite his efforts to induce us to accept this also as given, by offering it without explanation. Third, his theatricalist treatment of character robs, or threatens to rob, the characters of human consistency or equally human inconsistency. Aegisthus, purely for the playwright's ironic purpose, is totally altered in character in the second half of the play. Like Jeffers' Orestes, he undergoes an offstage conversion. As an idea, this has its brilliance; as a stage reality, it may or may not come off; but its effect is to undermine our faith in the humanity of the characters.

"The characters of Giraudoux's *Electra* do not live, or at least they do not live consistently in such a way as to grip the audience through the human quality and truth of their actions and fate." [19]

Many of the characters in French plays based on myth are conscious of the fatality assigned them by the myth; that is, they are self-consciously playing a role in "life" according to the dictates of the myth, which they know but should not. This gives them a *theatrical* awareness that detracts from the contingent humanity we expect them to exhibit and makes obtrusive their obedience to a foreordained plot. This may be intellectually diverting but seldom emotionally stirring. One is inclined to think that plot, dialogue, and setting can withstand the most extreme theatricalist treatment and still "carry" in the theatre, but that character is the dramatic element most resistant to such treatment, and that the playwright theatricalizes it at his peril.

Giraudoux's "primary conception of the theatre was that of originality of treatment rather than of subject." [20] Not all his plots are derived, but one can imagine the pleasure a playwright intent on creating theatre poetry would take in his own ingenuity as he reworks a plot used many times before to see what new treatment he can give it. The myths, of course, invite this approach. When Giraudoux transferred to the stage the whimsical fancy of his novels, it was the "free," the imaginative, the theatricalist stage of Cocteau that he chose to write for. Thus, his addiction to the supernatural, to abstractions, to devices like the acceleration of time, sometimes leads him to excesses. He is rather like the comic opera singers in *Ondine* who appear, whether sent for or not, and immediately burst into song. Supernatural characters have great advantages, as the Beggar in *Electra* proves. He is eerie, sinister, unpredictable; he charges the already tense atmosphere. And it is doubtful whether Giraudoux could have told his story in the dramatic form he chose, even *within* the theatricalist style, unless he had the help of the Beggar to speed up destiny. But he is by definition a privileged character, whereas the human characters ought to exist within more definite and reliable limits. And, having supernatural characters, Giraudoux is tempted to use them to play with

[19] Inskip, *Jean Giraudoux*, p. 88.
[20] *Ibid.*

startling effects. In *Electra* all the action builds to Orestes' killing of his father's murderers. It occurs offstage, as the Beggar
describes it for us. This is well enough, but Giraudoux cannot
leave well enough alone: he lets the Beggar's omniscient account
outrun the event itself, turning what should be a tragic moment
into a theatricalist *truc*.[21] The truth is, it seems to me, that theatricalism, by its nature, cannot impose a decorum in these matters; it is up to the playwright to do that. The greater the freedom of the stage, the greater the playwright's restraint should
be in availing himself of it. Consistency is a virtue, even in
theatricalist art. Where Giraudoux exercised restraint, as in
Amphitryon 38 and most of *The Trojan War*, he succeeded in his
efforts. At other times he, like Cocteau, could not decide how
much audacity is really too, too much.

Giraudoux's writings, and especially his plays, says François
Mauriac, "contain a magnificent little catechism for humanists."
But in Mauriac's view the playwright fights a losing battle, because that "small, earthy catechism" must eventually be destroyed
through time and use: "The cutting edge of Giraudoux's mind
collides with a hard stone against which Greek thought before
him blunted itself, the stone that we call original sin; he puts
his trust in Nature and does not know that she is flawed." [22]
    Mauriac was speaking principally of *Amphitryon 38*, where
the perfection of man on earth, if only he be true to himself
at his best, is hopefully and gaily hymned. But the following two
plays, as I see them, show the results of that collision on Giraudoux's mind. Hector the ideal man crashes against the perversity
of life, as if that ultimate flaw were still outside man; yet
Giraudoux is already embodying it in men, and even, in the form
of classic rashness, in Hector himself. And in *Electra* the flaw in
nature is shown to be as much in man as anywhere, so that man
is tragically defeated, even in victory; we are brought to a tragic
awareness of the ambiguous nature and consequences of absolute demands when they issue from human motives.

[21] For a discussion of this device and of Aegisthus' transformation of character, see John Gassner, "At War with Electra," *Tulane Drama Review*, III,
no. 4 (May, 1959), 49.
[22] François Mauriac, *Second Thoughts: Reflections on Literature and Life*
(Cleveland: World, 1961), p. 128.

Giraudoux's love of humankind is for me one of the most moving things in modern drama, and it does not become less so as his hope for its self-achieved perfection grows more hopeless. In order to draw his ideal portraits, he had to turn aside from the experience of one world war, only to be increasingly oppressed by his prophetic fear of a second. The second came, bringing with it the possibility of still a third, and perhaps of total destruction. Thus, in his *Sodom and Gomorrah*, where man's deep division is now symbolized by the war between the sexes (the bitter opposite of that friendship that was to fulfill their natures so splendidly), the two warring factions of the human race no longer heed the archangel's, and the dramatist's, warning.

Giraudoux may have despaired of man at last, though one hopes this was not so; but in his desperation he did not cease to love him. It was for this reason that Mauriac could say of his "miraculous" little catechism: "Even when pulverized by the other, its débris would be precious and useful to the sons of men."

CHAPTER VII

T. S. ELIOT:
The Subjective Correlative

This historical sense which is a sense of the timeless as well as of the temporal and of the timeless and the temporal together, is what makes a writer traditional. And it is at the same time what makes a writer most acutely conscious of his place in time, of his contemporaneity. . . .[1]

When he wrote his famous review of *Ulysses* in 1923, T. S. Eliot proposed to the writers of his generation James Joyce's use of classical myth as "a method which others must pursue after him." But that method—the manipulation of "a continuous parallel between contemporaneity and antiquity"—is one that Eliot has not followed in his plays, even fitfully. Indeed, when we examine his own uses of classical myth, we find them so remote from Joyce's example that they never come to grips with the genuine difficulties which their use in modern drama entailed for playwrights like Gide, Jeffers, Cocteau, O'Neill, Giraudoux, Sartre, and Anouilh.

For Eliot, in conceiving and writing his plays, myth seems to serve him as private guide or referent as he tries to impose order and form on his own creation. But the myth itself is not apparent in the plays as dramatic experience, and therefore it provides no point of vantage in the theatre. Whether it be the myth of

[1] T. S. Eliot, "Tradition and the Individual Talent," in *The Sacred Wood* (London: Methuen, 1920), p. 49.

Alcestis in *The Cocktail Party*, or that of Ion in *The Confidential Clerk*, or that of Oedipus at Colonus in *The Elder Statesman*, we do not find it substantially reconstituted in the plot and characters of the play. Nor, I may add, do we find the Orestes legend in *The Family Reunion*, although Eliot and others have assumed for years that, because of thematic resemblances, it is there. He does not manipulate the myth, except to depart from it drastically in every case.

Of course, he is entitled to do so—and without even being inconsistent, since in the *Ulysses* review he carefully left the way open for such handling of myth as would suit his own purposes. The point is this: Eliot, in sharp contrast to the playwrights mentioned above, is specifically a Christian dramatist, intent on imbuing his plays with Christian vision and Christian values. It is not odd that he should choose his subject matter from pagan myths; but it is genuinely regrettable that he should then so far displace them that they are, by all reasonable standards, no longer recognizable in the theatre. What resemblances remain, therefore, become more properly a matter of literary exegesis than of performance, for in the theatre nothing is so bootless as a footnote. Eliot did not attempt, let alone achieve, a Christian interpretation of pagan myth comparable to what Henri Ghéon did in his tragedy *Oedipus; or, The Twilight of the Gods*, where the events, treated at much greater length than in Sophocles, adhere closely to the received myth.

Let us suppose something like the following. Eliot may feel, let us say, an attraction to the story of Alcestis. Something in it strikes an emotional chord in him or teases his mind with its psychological implications. But the play, when finished, is altogether different from its source. Naturally, we should expect it to be different from Euripides: its individuality, its "signature," will be Eliot's, and that is quite as it should be. But the play, in its situation, characters, and ensuing action, will also be quite different from the myth itself.

The mythic "archetype" from which *The Cocktail Party* derived, for example, has disappeared. Edward and Julia are *not* Admetus and Alcestis, because the situation they inhabit and the actions they perform are not to be found in the myth. Neither of them could, so far as one can tell, perform the deeds their archetypal characters performed. Julia's disappearance is not a death, but only the rupture of a marriage that had, from the start, little reality and no love. That Edward gets her back, and that they both begin again as quite changed persons, is merely to stretch the symbolism of death and resurrection to its uttermost. What we have not seen, even as refracted through the dramatist's imagination, is the myth of a man under literal sentence of death; a wife who loves him enough to spare him by dying in his stead; and his consequent relief, shame, or sorrow —all brought on himself by accepting his wife's offer. We have, instead, such a radical displacement of plot that the mysterious figure of Sir Henry Harcourt-Reilly, cutting across the action to reunite the couple as Hercules did to snatch Alcestis from death, cannot restore true similarity. It is not a matter of the *subject* of the play: Euripides' version concerns itself with what a man does when faced with certain death and how those around him respond to his plight. It is only one possible subject: many others might be derived from it, even when the same set of circumstances is retained, along with characters capable of performing at least the basic actions.

So with *The Elder Statesman*: we do not find the last phase of the Oedipus myth inhering in the play as its visible archetype. (It is odd to see Eliot making a secularized story of a myth that definitely illustrates supernatural election, thus foregoing his favorite theme.) There are only the most general resemblances: a man who feels that death is imminent; a daughter devoted to him in his last days, as Antigone was to Oedipus; a son who seeks his father's help and then quarrels bitterly with him, as did Polynices. Oedipus' expiatory suffering for guilt he did not knowingly incur and will not accept becomes, in Lord Claverton, secret guilt which he will not acknowledge. But Lord Claverton's past is not that of Oedipus, and so, regardless of the details by which the dramatist individualizes his character, Lord Claverton will not be a man capable of doing, or having done, what Oedipus did. Thus, the old peer's death under the beech tree will have only the force of a literary allusion to Oedipus' miraculous translation in the sacred grove.

Certainly, transmuting a Greek myth to fit a Chrisitan ethos would require some displacement: Greek fate, even at its noblest expression in the *Oresteia*, is not the same as Divine Providence. But the changes Eliot makes seem to me prompted less by such

considerations than by his view of what is appropriate or acceptable to modern audiences. This view comprises three things that
deeply affect his treatment of mythic materials: first, his preoccupation with realism, despite his aversion to it; second, his lack of
confidence in the ability of contemporary audiences to respond
to the forthright dramatization (not discussion) of religious
themes; and last, his nearly fatal tendency to internalize action
—his reliance on words as, so to speak, the *subjective* correlative
of drama.

"I only want to write plays of contemporary life," said Eliot,
after *Murder in the Cathedral*. "For me, at least, a play set in
the past, or in some fictitious place or time, would be an evasion
of the immediate task." He would seem to have taken this position because he was primarily concerned with the problem of dramatic verse in a contemporary idiom. This position, although it
need not have done so, committed him to a perpetual struggle
with realistic drama—the type for which, I suspect, he had least
affinity or aptitude. His refusal to evade the immediate task as
he saw it is admirable; it may well have been dictated by that
consciousness of his contemporaneity which he spoke of in "Tradition and the Individual Talent," quoted at the head of this
chapter. Evidently he envisaged subjects relevant to modern
audiences as necessarily involving modern characters in a modern
milieu. Fortunately for them, the French dramatists cited above
permitted themselves more freedom. Yet Eliot's intention was to
modify—and leaven—this realism by verse dialogue and make
it yield a treatment of religious themes in terms acceptable to
general audiences. Such was Eliot's compromise with realism,
and he was remarkably faithful to its conditions.

When Donald Hall interviewed him in 1959 for *The Paris Review*, Eliot described his working methods. He gave a clear
picture of the transformation the myths underwent that he examined for his initial inspiration. Nothing was said of realism,
but its unseen presence can be felt:

But I wouldn't like to refer to my Greek originals as models. I have
always regarded them more as points of departure. That was one of
the weaknesses of *The Family Reunion*; it was rather too close to the
Eumenides. I tried to follow my original too literally and in that way
led to confusion by mixing pre-Christian and post-Christian attitudes
about matters of conscience and sin and guilt.

So in the subsequent three I have tried to take the Greek myth as a sort of springboard, you see. After all, what one gets essential and permanent, I think, in the old plays, is a situation. You can take the situation, rethink it in modern terms, develop your own characters from it, and let *another plot* develop out of that. Actually, you get further and further away from the original.[2]

The direction Eliot takes is away from the overt action of the myth and from its externalization of the supernatural toward a surface realism. The Eumenides in *The Family Reunion*, physically present and visible to the audience, were his first and last attempt at such externalization in a realistic milieu. In *Poetry and Drama* he said of them: "But the deepest flaw of all was in a failure of adjustment between the Greek story and the modern situation. I should either have stuck closer to Aeschylus or else taken a great deal more liberty with his myth. One evidence of this is the appearance of those ill-fated figures, the Furies. They must, in future, be omitted from the cast, and be understood to be visible only to certain of my characters, and not to the audience. . . . They never succeed in being either Greek goddesses or modern spooks."[3]

One consequence of Eliot's increased theatrical experience in the realistic mode was that he reduced the "poetry" in his plays over "a long period of disciplining [it], and putting it, so to speak, on a very thin diet in order to adapt it to the needs of the drama. . . ."[4] Those who miss the vivid imagery of his lyric poetry deplore this development. But it enabled Eliot to find a verse form suitable to his purposes—the goal he always sought. In his study of Eliot's plays David E. Jones describes that form as "a line of varying length but a fixed number of stresses, normally three, with a caesura coming after the first or the second stress."[5] This was a major accomplishment for the verse dramatist. If the form proves as flexible as Eliot believed, if others find that they also can use it to advantage, it will mean that the ghost of Elizabethan blank verse has been laid at last.

Now no one is more unsparing of his plays, or wittier on the subject, than Eliot himself. But even as he points out shrewdly

[2] Donald Hall, "The Art of Poetry: T. S. Eliot," *The Paris Review*, XXI (Spring-Summer, 1959), 61 (emphasis added).
[3] In Toby Cole, ed., *Playwrights on Playwriting* (New York: Hill & Wang Dramabooks, 1960), pp. 256-57.
[4] *Ibid.*, p. 258.
[5] David E. Jones, *The Plays of T. S. Eliot* (Toronto: University of Toronto Press, 1960), p. 85.

their shortcomings as drama, he often sounds as if the problems of his plays, and indeed of drama in general, begin and end with prosody, idiom, and imagery. He had been willing, but slow, to learn the first principle, laid down years ago by Lady Gregory when she said that the dramatic poet will have to learn that "poetry must serve the theatre before it can again rule there." [6]

That Eliot continued to write a kind of symbolist drama of modified realism shows how firm was his rejection of the other nonrealistic movements in the modern theatre, of which he was well aware. As early as "A Dialogue on Poetic Drama," [7] he has B., one of the speakers, refer to "Cocteau, who is a real playwright. . . ." The French theatricalists were pre-eminently the group using classic myth in ways closest to that which he had prescribed, yet their work seems to have left him largely unaffected. I regard *Murder in the Cathedral* as his most successful play, not least because he effectively combines in it the formalistic devices taken from Greek models and a theatricalist freedom which he may well have learned from the continental dramatists. The Knights' speeches are comparable to the farcical interlude in Cocteau's *Orphée*, yet entirely original in effect. They go beyond Cocteau's own practice in their acknowledgment of the audience.

To return to "A Dialogue," another speaker, D., proposes a way of establishing "some constant relation between drama and the religion of the times": "When the age has a set religious practice and belief, then the drama can and should tend towards realism, I say *towards*, I do not say arrive at. The more definite the religious and ethical principles, the more freely the drama can move towards what is now called photography. The more fluid, the more chaotic the religious and ethical beliefs, the more the drama must tend in the direction of liturgy." [8] I doubt that Eliot, after writing that, believed religious and ethical principles were becoming more definite in Western society. His own handling of religious themes within the realistic mode seems so oblique as to belie it. Yet if D. speaks for him, that is the impli-

[6] Quoted by Maurice Browne, *Too Late to Lament* (Bloomington: Indiana University Press, 1956), p. 117.
[7] T. S. Eliot, "A Dialogue on Poetic Drama," with John Dryden's *Of Dramatick Poesie* (London: Etchells & MacDonald, 1928).
[8] *Ibid.*, pp. xvii-xviii.

cation of his continued adherence to realism. The warm reception accorded Eliot's liturgical play, on the other hand, would seem to prove D.'s position and disprove Eliot's subsequent efforts at realistic drama for a secularist world; it would indicate that he took the wrong turn.

This brings us to the second point affecting Eliot's handling of myth. I suggest that he lacks confidence in the ability, or the willingness, of modern audiences to respond to the direct dramatization of religious themes. Unlike some of his French contemporaries, Eliot wishes to depict grace, not the gratuitous. He believes in the supernatural as that which infuses all life and gives it transcendent meaning. But the only kind of supernatural that interests him, or at least the only kind that he appears to feel modern audiences will accept, is that which remains hidden behind and beneath our workaday life and takes the form of conversion in souls touched by grace.

In this connection it is well to remember that Eliot had concerned himself in the debates raised by I. A. Richards in *Practical Criticism* over the problem of belief when writer and reader do not have a common creed. When it is a matter of play and audience, however, this problem seems to me substantially altered. Eliot uses the terms "philosophical belief" and "poetic assent," and Richards the terms "emotional belief" and "intellectual assent." Richards' first term applies to the kind of enjoyment involved in imaginative literature, and, for theatrical purposes, it seems to me nearer the mark than Eliot's "poetic assent." Eliot himself says belief is irrelevant to the grasp of meaning; what is necessary is *knowledge* of the belief to enhance poetic assent: "It is a matter of knowledge and ignorance, not of belief or skepticism. If you can read poetry as poetry, you will 'believe' in Dante's theology exactly as you believe in the physical reality of his journey; that is, *you suspend both belief and disbelief*." [9] In reading Dante Eliot may suspend both belief and disbelief; but he evidently does not trust the ordinary theatre-goer to do the same when he attends a play. And the reason seems to me characteristic of Eliot: he is really concerning himself with intellectual assent, when he should be letting that take care of itself while he concentrates on obtaining emotional belief. His primary

[9] T. S. Eliot, *Selected Essays* (New York: Harcourt, Brace, 1950), pp. 218-19.

concern should be the urgency of the *action*, not the credibility of the creed: in short, drama, not doctrine.

Eliot had spoken in "Religion and Literature" of a type of "religious literature" that he placed under the heading "Propaganda": "I mean the literary works of men who are sincerely desirous of forwarding the cause of religion." [10] Whether Eliot thereafter found himself "preaching" to the converted or to the unconverted, I think this describes the intent of his own plays. It is an entirely legitimate aim. But, given such intent, it seems to me mistaken to proceed diffidently, exhibiting a well-bred air that is not quite one of apology. In the theatre diffidence is fatal.

Yeats is quoted as telling young playwrights: "You must never keep a secret from your audience." [11] This is good advice that Eliot seems never to have learned; for he even withholds from his audience as long as possible the real subject of his plays, which is precisely the religious experience. He resorts to the most elaborate disguises and indirections, further complicated by the need for verisimilitude in the realistic style, to woo the spectator, who, he seems to fear, will be uninterested or skeptical or both. The result is emotionally so restrained that the experience comes across, if at all, as something both attenuated and esoteric. Surely, by way of contrast, part of the vigor and theatrical color of his play about Becket derived less from Eliot's conviction than from his directness, his unself-consciousness, in presenting religion.

This is not to underestimate the difficulties of his task, which are both genuine and considerable, but to stress that they are basically *dramatic* rather than psychological or doctrinal. Eliot's practice strikes me as just the opposite of dramatic. To use the terms of Frank O'Connor, Eliot acts as if the theatre were an "art of persuasion" instead of an "art of mass-illusion" that invokes the "collective imagination of the audience" to produce a "weight of mass assent." Within the style of modified realism Eliot must calculate probabilities, possibilities, and even improbable possibilities; whereas, as O'Connor says: "The fact is that in the theatre there are no degrees of probability; merely degrees of the skill and taste with which improbability is used, for improbability is the raw material of drama, and it is im-

[10] *Ibid.*, p. 346.
[11] Frank O'Connor, *The Art of the Theatre* (Dublin: Maurice Fridburg, 1947), p. 14.

probability, shaped to an imaginative pattern, which gives us that extraordinary feeling of spiritual liberation, that sense of pure, unconstrained activity, which is the greatest joy the theatre has in store for us." [12]

Myth, which implies if it does not explicitly contain the supernatural, was raw material that Cocteau and Giraudoux, for example, found liberating. Eliot merely begins with myth, transforms it beyond recognition, and then tries to use the residue realistically, even surreptitiously. Perhaps the chief difference is that Cocteau and Giraudoux see the theatre as a place to *show* things. They use the real stage to create a stage reality which tells us something about life without imitating it; they dramatize that which is "truer than truth" by externalizing it; they employ the supernatural variously, often spectacularly, and always without apology or hesitation. They can do this because they regard reality as something they must dissolve before they can re-create it in drama. Eliot sees reality as something to be imitated, short of reproducing the "desert of exact likeness," and the supernatural as something to be suggested rather than shown. The stage is not for him, as it is for them, a place of freedom that invites improbabilities of action as the natural consequence of make-believe. And so, when he comes to religious themes, he is tentative and lacking in confidence.

These combined tendencies drive Eliot to create his own curious approximation of Cocteau's "parade"—a kind of misleading sideshow diversion. The drawing-room comedy or drama must be worked out with as much surface plausibility as verse will permit, so that the religious theme will emerge from it convincingly. That emergence usually takes the form of didactic speeches of explanation or self-discovery, from which, moreover, all overtly Christian references have been carefully removed, as if Eliot feared to lose his audience's assent if he ventured beyond a natural theology couched in largely psychological terms. Eric Bentley, in *The Dramatic Event*, has dubbed this strategy "crafty godliness," and noted that when it fails it does so mostly because Eliot's chief weakness is his inability to create realistic characters and an organic plot, both essential to successful realism. [13]

[12] *Ibid.*, p. 13.
[13] Eric Bentley, *The Dramatic Event: An American Chronicle* (New York: Horizon Press, 1954), pp. 230-33.

Eliot, the daring innovator in modern poetry, is cautiously traditional in the theatre.

His handling of the theme of religious vocation in *The Confidential Clerk* will show how his circumspection risks defeating his ends and even falsifying the play's statement. He has reversed the direction of the myth, so that Colby, leaving the world that Ion enters, ends as Ion began: "You'll be thinking of reading for orders," says Eggerson, who speaks with the authority of Chorus, at the end of the play. This is what Eliot has been aiming at from the first, of course, but only dares to bring out now, amid the general excitement of discoveries and reversals. And yet it comes with the air of one trying to slip something past us. Why? Because Eliot has concealed his purpose behind an elaborate analogy between art and religion. Sir Claude's contemplation of pottery and Colby's love of music are metaphors for that which Eliot will not name directly: the longing for genuine religious experience.

Colby, a second-rate organist and composer, desires a religious vocation. He is one of the elect, although he does not know it until the end; but the others have sensed it and responded to it. There is something "different" about him. Eggerson defines and confirms the difference: it is priesthood. In the case of Lady Elizabeth, Eliot has dared to deal more openly with religion, but only because she represents a travesty of it—the restless sampling of exotic religious fads. By satirizing her indulgently, he can advance the religious theme without seeming solemn. Dramaturgically, however, he must resort to the same evasions of true religious experience as send her racketing about the continent in search of novel substitutes.

Long ago in "A Dialogue" he—or one of his speakers—objected to the use of literature (and, by extension, all the arts) as a substitute for religion. He held that to confuse art and religion could only result in debasing both. Yet in using art as a metaphor for religion in the play, he risks confusing general audiences as to his own quite clear hierarchy of values, and thus of frustrating his own intention. For one of the things most characteristic of our day is the tendency to substitute art for religion and make of it a worship devoid of doctrine, liturgy, and church. (Cocteau will stand as an example of the artist's part in this substitution: the artist as priest.) The same tendency is widespread among art-lovers, who constitute, as it were, the faithful. Philip Rieff, in *Myth and Mythmaking*, describes the transvaluation that takes place:

The cultured of this era strive to relate themselves to art as a way of recapturing the experience of the divine in which otherwise they no longer believe and cannot feel participant in, even indirectly. Through the mediation of [the artist], the art work is experienced as a thing in itself, bracketed and raised above the ordinary workaday world, and yet related to that world as revelation is related to that which is revealed—superior and saving. The work of art becomes that *wholly other*, present and yet inviolate, through which the cultivated may escape, for the time of the relation, their self-isolation. Thus, for significant numbers of people in contemporary culture, the aesthetic relation takes on religious import.[14]

Finally, Eliot's theme of religious conversion takes a curious form that is characteristic of his third problem in his dramas: it is that of releasing the elected person from association with characters with whom he had little or no real connection to begin with. Where the action of his plays should be centripetal, bringing people together in conflict, it seems mostly to operate centrifugally, flinging them apart after an association in which there has been no real communication or contact of spirits.

In Eliot's plays the struggle is characteristically within the hero, not between the persons of the action. And the crucial scenes of discovery come not as a result of conflicts, but as the result of exchanges with a "confidant"—as with Harry and Agatha in *The Family Reunion*, or Sir Henry and Edward and Lavinia in *The Cocktail Party*. The isolation of the individual person is a legitimate theme of modern drama, but it is not dramatized by showing characters who have nothing in common. It is, however, a theme which Eliot has often and movingly expressed in his poems. Such verse is likely to be lyrical or to constitute "dramatic poetry"—but not drama. We may add to this that Eliot avoids consequential action or, when he is displacing a myth, goes so far as to blur it beyond recognition. Myth as plot, and as character capable of enacting it, has all but vanished. Hugh Kenner calls Eliot "the invisible poet." Cocteau, looking at an excessively verbalized rather than dramatized play like *The Family Reunion*, might call it "invisible theatre." Where

[14] Philip Rieff, "A Modern Mythmaker," in Henry A. Murray, ed., *Myth and Mythmaking* (New York: George Braziller, 1960), p. 269.

Cocteau strove for a theatre of *"montrer pur,"* which quickly led him to employ classical myth, Eliot, in using myth only as a point of departure, must fight against creating a theatre of *"parler pur."* Too often the objective correlative he seeks escapes him, because he seeks it in words instead of drama.

CHAPTER VIII

JEAN-PAUL SARTRE:
Myth and Anti-Myth

God is dead, but man has not for all that become atheistic.
Silence of the transcendent joined to the permanence of the
need for religion in modern man—that is still the major thing,
today as yesterday. . . . God is silent and that I cannot deny
—everything in myself calls for God and that I cannot forget. . . . As a matter of fact, this experience can be found in
one form or another in most contemporary authors: it is the
torment in Jaspers, death in Malraux, destitution in Heideg-
ger, the reprieved-being in Kafka, the insane and futile labor
of Sisyphe in Camus.

Theatre is a great collective, religious phenomenon, capable of
awakening in the recesses of the spirit the things which all men
of a given epoch and community care about. It explores the
state of man in its entirety and presents a portrait of him, his
problems, his hopes, and his struggles. It is austere, moral,
mythic, and ceremonial in aspect. It attempts to show the public
the great myths of death, exile, love. Its characters are people
of flesh and blood whose tragic experiences are complete in
themselves; and yet they are mythical in the sense that their
experiences can serve as the embodiment of all similar experiences. The greatness of the theatre derives from its social and,
in a certain sense, religious functions; and thus, even as it
speaks to the spectators of themselves it does so in a tone and
with a constant reserve of manner that discourages familiarity

and increases the distance between play and audience; for theatre is, and must remain, a rite.

The foregoing might fairly stand as a description of the intent and achievement of tragic theatre in classic Greece. It is actually a description of a theatre for modern man, one condensed without quotation marks from Jean-Paul Sartre's notes, written in 1946, on his theatre of moral commitment.[1] His own plays, he said, and those of Jean Anouilh, Albert Camus, and Simone de Beauvoir, exemplify it. There is a conscious return to a tradition, the Corneillean drama of situation, in his early plays, *The Flies* (*Les Mouches*, 1943) and *No Exit* (*Huis Clos*, 1944). This tradition he regarded as the most serviceable, because in it "the systems of values, of ethics and of concepts of man . . . are lined up against each other."[2] It entails the rejection of realism and symbolism as theatrical styles having no intrinsic value, and also the abandonment of the creation of unique characters by means of detailed psychologizing. Sartre's conviction as a playwright, then, is that "if it is to address the masses, his theatre must speak in terms of their most general preoccupations, dispelling their anxieties in the form of myths which anyone can understand and feel deeply." This mythic theatre that stresses situation would enable the playwright to create his own public, because it would provide the best means of fusing into a single unity the atomized audiences of today.[3]

If he sought the form and emphasis of *The Flies* in French neoclassic drama, Sartre, like Giraudoux, Eliot, and O'Neill, turned for his subject matter to the classic myth of Orestes and Electra. The hero of this myth has been called by Gilbert Murray the most representative figure of Greek tragedy: "He is . . . the most central and typical tragic hero of the Greek stage; and he occurs in no less than seven of our extant tragedies. . . . "[4] It is evident from the play that Sartre intends his Orestes, despite his unusual dilemma—even because of it—to be no less repre-

---

[1] Jean-Paul Sartre, "Forgers of Myths," in Toby Cole, ed., *Playwrights on Playwriting* (New York: Hill & Wang Dramabooks, 1960), pp. 116-24 *passim*. The quotation at the beginning of the chapter is from Wilfred Desan, *The Tragic Finale: An Essay on the Philosophy of Jean-Paul Sartre* (Cambridge: Harvard University Press, 1954), p. 179.
[2] *Ibid.*, p. 120.
[3] *Ibid.*, p. 121.
[4] Gilbert Murray, *The Classical Tradition in Poetry* (Cambridge: Harvard University Press, 1927), p. 206.

sentative to modern audiences. Orestes' experiences are to serve as the embodiment of all similar experiences, and more: Orestes is Everyman. The calculated result is paradoxical. Sartre, the self-styled "forger of myths," dedicates his play to destroying myths which he regards as inimical to human freedom, and the means he uses is myth itself.

His particular introduction to theatre and playwriting was aptly symbolic: it ocurred in prison. While interned in Germany (1940-41) Sartre wrote and staged what was ostensibly a Christmas play. But the Biblical story was simply a veneer of "simple symbols" to fool the prison-camp censor: the point of the play was aimed at making Sartre's fellow prisoners aware of their state, and its effect showed him the power of theatre: ". . . when I suddenly saw them so remarkably silent and attentive, I realized what theatre ought to be—a great collective, religious phenomenon."[5] In prison, too, he made his personal discovery of what he believes to be the true nature of liberty.[6] Upon his release and return to Paris, Sartre taught classes in Greek drama at Charles Dullin's acting studio. In the light of all this, it is not surprising that he should have turned to playwriting, that his theme should be freedom, or that he should choose for his story a myth from Greek tragedy.[7] His Christmas play was covertly addressed to his fellow prisoners; *The Flies*, at the time it was first produced (June 3, 1943), was similarly addressed to his countrymen, fellow victims of the German occupation. These special circumstances, although they appear to have influenced what Sartre wrote, are incidental. The play is really addressed to every man, for it is Sartre's first attempt to reach an immediate and popular audience with his revolutionist philosophy of existentialism.

Contrary to the impression created in the United States after World War II, *The Flies* was neither a critical nor a popular success. It did not fare well, despite its courageous bootlegging of a subversive call to freedom under the very nose of the German censor, who was to be no more alert in 1944 when he passed Jean Anouilh's *Antigone*. There was controversy: attacks from

---

[5] Sartre, "Forgers of Myth," p. 121.
[6] Philip Thody, *Jean-Paul Sartre: A Literary and Political Study* (London: Hamish Hamilton, 1960), p. 71.
[7] *No Exit* takes place in prison, a Second Empire drawing-room in hell, as *The Flies* unfolds in the prison-city of prehistoric Argos.

anti-Semites, communist-inspired disturbances in the theatre. Maurice Rostand praised it. But it did not become the rallying cry of the Resistance that Sartre hoped it would be.[8] *Antigone*, although not without its own ambiguities, fitted the situation better because the issue of resistance was more simply stated. In Sartre's play the Paris audiences had to find the call to defy their conquerors under a Nietzschean demonstration that God is dead.[9] When revived in a cut version in January, 1951, the play fared slightly better but did Sartre's reputation as a play-wright no good.[10] By then its topicality had dwindled, and the wider meaning of the play could stand free. At this remove, we can afford to ignore Orestes as the war-time symbol of the un-committed French intellectual, Aegisthus as the German con-queror, and Clytemnestra as the French collaborator.[11] Philip Thody says: *"The Flies* is certainly better if judged as an ex-ample of literature taking sides than as an expression of moral and philosophic ideas in convincing dramatic form." [12] But it is as the latter that the play has been produced elsewhere in Europe, England, and the United States. It must make its ap-peal and be judged on the basis of its human drama and the relevance of its philosophical statement.

In using the myth of Orestes, Sartre takes advantage of both the principal ways open to the playwright. For much of the ac-tion he retains the story, if only in its barest outlines—the murder of Clytemnestra and Aegisthus by Orestes and Electra. Then he departs from it and radically changes its meaning. It is possible for him to do this, partly because here the plot is the cloak of the drama, rather than its soul. The limits of the action are those

---

[8] The accounts are contradictory. Béatrix Dussane, in *Notes de théâtre 1940-1950* (Paris: Lardanchet, 1951), emphasizes the deep appeal of the play: "But what is certain is that a whole generation of youth recognized there its own excitement, and clearly heard the appeal that was made to it." Quoted by Harold Hobson, *The French Theatre of To-day* (London: George C. Harrap, 1953), p. 43.

[9] Confusion resulted again, in June, 1951, with *Le Diable et le Bon Dieu:* ". . . most audiences . . . thought they were seeing an attempt to prove that God does not exist, while Sartre himself said that the play suggested the unhappy position of Europe poised between the U.S.A. and the U.S.S.R." Hobson, *The French Theatre*, pp. 77-78.

[10] Thody, *Jean-Paul Sartre*, p. 77.

[11] "It is highly probable that . . . he used these myths principally because of the need to get past the censor." *Ibid.*, p. 78.

[12] *Ibid.*, p. 77.

of Aeschylus' *The Libation Bearers*, with the murder of Agamemnon providing the occasion for a double killing that is not
committed as revenge but as a gesture of defiance against all
authority, the necessary prelude to the achievement of human
freedom. This last is the heart of the play. Sartre thus uses the
spectator's knowledge of the myth and the tragedy both to
arouse his expectations and then, by departing from the story,
to defeat them. That is to say, he "helps himself to a powerful
legend, which is clustered with all sorts of valuable emotional
overtones that he finds convenient to his dramatic purpose," [13]
then alters it to underscore the change of meaning he has conferred upon it. As in O'Neill's trilogy, the third part of *The
Oresteia* is necessarily omitted because the meaning of the story
is now as contrary as possible to Aeschylus' conception. There
is no court of Areopagus because Orestes will be judged by no
court, human or divine; there are no Kindly Ones to be honored,
only Furies to be dreaded until man somehow reaches the far
side of despair; there is no God or Fate to be reconciled because
for Sartre neither exists.

Orestes, only recently informed of his true identity by his
tutor-slave, returns to Argos after an absence of fifteen years, on
the anniversary of Agamemnon's death. He is a young cosmopolitan, without roots or purpose in life, and curious to see again
not only his homeland, but also his mother and his sister, neither
of whom he remembers. He is ignorant of his father's murder by
Clytemnestra and Aegisthus, the latter's usurpation of the throne,
and their subjugation of his sister Electra. He finds the city a
tyrant's prison, the people cowed by remorse for their compli-
ance in the late king's murder. The place is infested with a
plague of flies, visible signs of the guilt which haunts them and
their queen. These flies (like the little girls in Giraudoux's
Electra) will grow into the avenging Furies.

Longing for commitment, to enter into his kingdom and claim
his family and his subjects, Orestes looks on in disillusionment
and angry disgust while the city and its rulers abase themselves
in an orgy of public repentance on the Day of the Dead. Only
Electra, who has dreamed for years that her brother will return
to kill her father's slayers, refuses to accept guilt for their crime.
Heartened by her encounter with Orestes, who is still incognito,

[13] Hobson, *The French Theatre*, p. 118.

she defies Aegisthus, who condemns her to exile on the morrow. Inspired in his turn by her defiance, Orestes reveals himself to her, and, despite her reluctance to involve him, together they plot to slay the tyrants. When confronted by his accusers, Aegisthus offers no resistance to Orestes and dies. Orestes also kills his mother, but without Electra as witness. Brother and sister seek sanctuary in Apollo's shrine; but when they wake next morning the flies, now grown to ravenous Furies, lurk round them ready to pounce.

Now, for all that she had dreamed of it until it was her only motive for living, Electra is horrified at the finality of their deed. In revulsion she repudiates her part in it, refuses to flee with Orestes, and begs forgiveness for her sin so that she may be spared by the Furies. Orestes speaks to his people and asserts that the killing of his mother and her paramour is neither a sin nor a crime but his glory and his life's work. Accordingly, he denies any guilt. Although he has earned his throne by the bond of blood between him and his subjects, he relinquishes it, takes upon himself all their guilt and remorse, urges them to begin life again, this time in freedom, and goes into exile with the curbed Furies at his heels.

Such, in outline, is the story Sartre tells. Except for Electra's open defiance and her repudiation of the crime, it seems little different from the tale as told by Aeschylus. Yet it is possible, and the fact is significant, to recount it while omitting all mention of the second most important character in the play—the god of gods, Zeus. Despite the curious nature of his role in the action, Zeus's importance in the *meaning* of the play is indispensable to Sartre's intention, which is the complete inversion of the myth as used by Aeschylus, in order to "expose" religious belief as falsehood and civil order as tyranny, and to announce in their stead a revolutionist doctrine of man's absolute freedom and solitary self-sufficiency. Aeschylus, celebrating the fulfillment of the divine will in the establishment of human justice, brings to the stage Athena, Apollo, and the Furies, but not "Zeus, whose will has marked for man / The sole way where wisdom lies. . . ." [14] To make his point, Sartre writes *his* play with Zeus on stage, embodied as the Old Man, eavesdropping, tempting,

[14] Aeschylus, *Agamemnon*, in *The Oresteian Trilogy*, trans. Philip Vellacott (London: Penguin Books, 1956), p. 48.

passing miracles, all for the purpose of keeping men in ignorance of the fact that they are free and that he himself does not exist except as men believe in him.

The play is not a tragedy, although Sartre's Orestes is evidently a hero meant to evoke Corneillean admiration. It is a verbal duel, punctuated by "big" scenes and spectacular effects: a melodrama, retarded by debates on the ultimate nature of existence. In the light of Sartre's theatre of moral commitment, the dilemma of Orestes, torn between Apollo's command to avenge his father and the deep human aversion to matricide, would, in its agonizing choices, provide a myth apt to his purpose. Here is universality, because the alternatives confronting him run counter to the deepest human ties. But Sartre chose it for quite different reasons. He needed a sanction for the act of cold-blooded matricide, and he felt he could find none credible enough outside the body of Greek drama. "Mythology alone, in his view, could provide a sufficiently horrible action, for if he had invented the story of a son who killed his mother and then proclaimed that it was his duty to do so, no one would have believed it." [15] But this is not quite the point. Aeschylus' hero suffers because the divine command requires an act that revolts him—the murder of his mother, and so ". . . in *The Libation Bearers*, duty becomes repulsive." [16] The avenger's anguish is thus intensified, and for a sound dramatic reason: the play must demonstrate the great need for human justice to replace blood-feuds. In *The Flies* the situation is much different. Orestes' mother is to him a stranger for whom he has neither love nor hate; his killing of her is an ideological act. He is not revolted, not torn by conflicting duties, not filled with anguish. He feels no compunction before the deed, as he feels no guilt or regret afterward. He kills both tyrants as a gesture of commitment to the people of Argos that will make him one with them and justify his claim to the throne. It is this which is hard to make credible, let alone palatable, to an audience. Yet Sartre intends that Orestes' conversion to freedom and his deliberate assumption of responsibility for his action, with all its consequences, shall be admirable, even exemplary—the mark of a truly free man.

[15] Thody, *Jean-Paul Sartre*, p. 71.
[16] Richmond Lattimore, Introduction, in David Grene and Richmond Lattimore, eds., *The Complete Greek Tragedies*, I (Chicago: University of Chicago Press, 1959), 28.

The effect is to lower considerably the dramatic pressure which Aeschylus was at pains to build to the point of hysteria by incantation and the release of primitive emotions, and to replace them, through different motivation, by an anguish that has an entirely different source: the discovery of one's existential freedom.

The other major difference, which involves Zeus more directly, is that virtually all sense of fatality has been removed from the world of the myth. Characters speak of evil to come—Electra, for example, of the curse in the blood of the Atrides, the doom upon their house; but such talk is at best half-hearted. It echoes the myth out of habit and expediency, not conviction, as beliefs to be disproved. Blood begets blood, but for such different motives that the fateful repetition, the sense of "the third, completing draught," has all but vanished. The idea of a curse is irrelevant to Sartre's purpose; he mentions it only to dispose of it, by inference, as false. To give it a central function, a dramatic reality in the play, would be to admit the supernatural, in however baleful a guise; Sartre has difficulty enough in dramatizing the supernatural powers of Zeus, while simultaneously demonstrating them to be weak, inconsiderable, and irrelevant to the life of free man. And so, in ironic contrast to our expectations, the whole course of the action is made to run directly counter to the will of Zeus. In his freedom man triumphs over the god who made him free, and Zeus is defeated, as he knew he would be: "Well, Orestes, all this was foreknown. In the fullness of time a man was to come, to announce my decline. And you're that man, it seems." [17] (This suggests the Promethean myth but is clearly in opposition to Aeschylus' affirmation of Zeus as eternal Good and eternal Law.)

Again the effect is to diminish the emotional pressure, because the removal of fatality slackens the suspense that comes from foreknowledge—the same foreknowledge, born of the spectator's familiarity, that determined Sartre's choice of the myth in the first place.[18] But this is a necessary sacrifice if Sartre's attack

[17] Jean-Paul Sartre, *The Flies*, trans. Stuart Gilbert, in John Gassner, ed., *A Treasury of the Theatre*, rev. ed., II (New York: Simon & Schuster, 1956), 494.
[18] The compensating advantage is stated by Thody: "Moreover, the traditional insistence on the theme of fatality in the Orestes legend enabled him, by contrast, to bring out the importance of his idea of liberty." *Jean-Paul Sartre*, p. 71.

on man's religious belief is to succeed, and the doctrine, not of free will, but of existential freedom, is to stand as the crux of the play.

There is a further result, a basic structural change in the plot which shifts the crisis from Orestes' decision to revenge his father to the discovery of his freedom. The traditional decision is now a consequence of that discovery and a means of asserting it. In the myth as transformed, Electra devotes a long scene to dissuading Orestes: she urges him, as had his mother and his tutor earlier, to flee from Argos—again in direct opposition to the course of *The Oresteia*.[19] Orestes prays to Zeus for guidance:

O Zeus, our Lord and King of Heaven . . . this you know: that I have always tried to act aright. But now I am weary and my mind is dark; I can no longer distinguish right from wrong. I need a guide to point my way. Tell me, Zeus, is it truly your will that a king's son, hounded from his city, should meekly school himself to banishment and slink away from his ancestral home like a whipped cur? I cannot think it. And yet—and yet you have forbidden the shedding of blood. . . . O Zeus, I beseech you, if meek acceptance, the bowed head and the lowly heart are what you would have of me, make plain your will by some sign; for no longer can I see my path.[20]

Zeus obliges with a sign—and thereby makes his mistake. Orestes does just the opposite of what the god intended: "So that is the Right Thing. To live at peace—always at perfect peace. I see. Always to say 'Excuse me,' and 'Thank you.' That's what's wanted, eh? . . . The Right Thing. *Their* Right Thing. . . . From now on I'll take no one's orders, neither man's nor god's."[21] This is quite a reversal: it not only forces Orestes' resolve to slay the tyrants (although not out of vengeance) and foils Zeus's will, it also abolishes all objective considerations of right and wrong and elevates individual judgment to a general moral principle. Each man must decide for himself, no one else can; this is the consequence of his freedom.

The decision to act in perfect freedom has awful consequences, worse than the anguish of conflicting desires or commands and

[19] This scene (Act II, Scene 1) includes the "recognition" of Orestes and Electra, accomplished here without the lock of hair and the matching footprints of *The Libation Bearers*. The recognition is skillfully prolonged, so that not until Orestes convinces her his resolve is firm will Electra acknowledge him as truly her brother.
[20] Gassner, ed., *A Treasury of the Theatre*, p. 483.
[21] *Ibid.*

worse even than the remorse that overtakes the traditional Orestes, for whom the Furies are retribution. When freedom "crashes down" on Sartre's hero, "out of the blue," all life changes. What was "warm and living" round him, "like a friendly presence," dies, to be replaced by "endless emptiness, as far as eye can reach!" Orestes' youth vanishes. Life is robbed not only of nature's subtle preachments about the goodness of Zeus, but of all purpose, all excuse for living. Freedom isolates man from the fold: it ends in exile: ". . . I knew myself alone, utterly alone in the midst of this well-meaning little universe of yours. I was like a man who's lost his shadow. And there was nothing left in heaven, no right or wrong, nor anyone to give me orders." [22] Such is the tragic pathos of the Sartrian hero when he does the real Right Thing and achieves his freedom.

Sartre capitalizes on this fundamental change to alter the meaning of Aegisthus and his death. It will be recalled how Giraudoux with bold theatricalism arbitrarily transforms Aegisthus into an admirable, even heroic, defender of Argos. Sartre does the same, in a way, but motivates the rehabilitation with psychological plausibility. The tyrant, who for fifteen years has maintained the pretense of remorse for his crime and forced his people to share his public penitence, reaches the edge of despair. He is drained of desire to live, filled with nausea at the perpetual sham which is the price of power. When Zeus warns him that Orestes plots his death and urges him to imprison both brother and sister, Aegisthus foreshadows Zeus's defeat as well as his own; he knows that the game is lost. Orestes overhears this exchange:

AEGISTHUS: Are they so dangerous?

ZEUS: Orestes knows that he is free.

AEGISTHUS [*eagerly*]: He knows he's free? Then, to lay hands on him, to put him in irons, is not enough. A free man in a city acts like a plague-spot. He will infect my whole kingdom and bring my work to nothing. Almighty Zeus, why stay your hand? Why not fell him with a thunderbolt?

ZEUS: . . . Aegisthus, the gods have another secret. . . . Once freedom lights its beacon in a man's heart, the gods are powerless against him. It's a matter between man and man, and it is for other men, and for them only, to let him go his gait, or to throttle him.[23]

[22] *Ibid.*, p. 493.
[23] *Ibid.*, p. 487.

But Aegisthus, like Orestes, refuses the bait. He wills his death as a deliverance and, although he dies cursing his assassins and predicting their punishment by the Furies, does not resist the sword. This is because he suffers, as prisoner of his own inauthentic power maintained by the force of a lie, a deep disgust with life. Paradoxically, his disgust is very like Orestes' nausea, born of "dreadful freedom."

Sartre does not observe neoclassic decorum: Aegisthus' death occurs on stage in a very brutal, prolonged assault. Clytemnestra, however, dies out of our sight. Sartre does not even risk that part of the terrible confrontation of mother and son which, in Aeschylus, rises to her scream: "Beware the hounding Furies of a mother's curse. . . . My dream—O Gods! Here is the snake I bore and fed." [24] In other words, Sartre seeks the sanction of Greek myth to render the killing credible but does not chance alienating his audience by showing them a killing which it is nonetheless expected to find admirable rather than revolting. He substitutes a cover scene in which, as Electra stares at the body of Aegisthus and experiences the difference between her dreams and reality, we see the beginning of her disillusionment, her first falterings at the consequences of the deed. Sartre has left Electra, as well as us, to imagine the killing of Clytemnestra, and, in the final act, makes excellent use of this to feed her morbid imagination and growing sense of remorse. At the shrine of Apollo, Electra dreams luridly of her mother's death, shrinks from Orestes upon awakening, and falls prey to the vile promptings of the Furies which serve to drive a wedge between brother and sister:

ORESTES: Do not listen.

FIRST FURY: Away! Away! Make him go, Electra; don't let him touch you! He's a butcher. He reeks of fresh, warm blood. He used the poor old woman very foully, you know; he killed her piecemeal.

ELECTRA: Oh no! That's a lie, surely?

FIRST FURY: You can believe me; I was there all the time, buzzing in the air around them.

ELECTRA: So he struck her several times?

FIRST FURY: Ten times at least. And each time the sword squelched in the wound. She tried to shield her face and belly with her hands, and he carved her hands to ribbons.

ELECTRA: So it wasn't a quick death. Did she suffer much?

[24] Vellacott, trans., *The Oresteian Trilogy,* p. 137.

ORESTES: Put your fingers in your ears, do not look at them, and, above all, ask no questions. If you question them, you're lost.

FIRST FURY: Yes, she suffered—horribly.[25]

Dramatically—and not merely because of the lurid scene conjured up by the words of the First Fury—this is one of the best moments of the play. There is an intense, three-way struggle among brother, sister, and the Furies, in which the latter's enticements to remorse perfectly embody Electra's vivid imaginings and imminent collapse. At the same time, Orestes' appeals to Electra fall on deaf ears. He can do no more than tell her how to achieve freedom: she must find her own strength to meet the crisis. As he makes his appeal, our imaginations attribute to him a burden of memories that we should find intolerable. Yet the Fury may be deceiving Electra. We cannot be sure, however, because, like her, we did not see the killing; we can only imagine, in the light of what we saw Orestes do to Aegisthus, how it might have been. The tense complexity of this scene, where the imaginings and suspicions of the audience contribute directly to the ambiguity of effect, is in direct contrast to the lack of complexity in the rest of the play. Mostly the action is a two-way conflict rather than a three-sided one, linear rather than triangular in its development; it substitutes dialectics, the ironies of which hardly compensate for the fact that they often accompany the action instead of growing out of it and influencing it in their turn.

Zeus carries the burden here. Because of the meaning and function Sartre has assigned him, the logic of the thesis requires the god to show his hand repeatedly and injudiciously. Dramatically, his effect is dissipated in argument, whereas Orestes' is conserved, because much of the time the latter need only rebel and, by acting, seize the dramatic initiative. The defect lies in this: that Zeus is not God. If he were, then the struggle could determine the extent of man's freedom in a God-ruled universe, and what reprisals Zeus might take against the rebel he had created, and whether and in what way rebellious man might triumph in the teeth of his creator. Instead, Zeus is only man's *belief* that there is a God; the question turns upon the power of this belief over man's actions—or man's power to rule, rather

[25] Gassner, ed., *A Treasury of the Theatre*, p. 490.

than be ruled by, his own beliefs. Even this is not all; for, in Sartre's atheistic view, Zeus is really society—society being interpreted as the combination and organization of those traditional beliefs and conventions which man accepts and institutionalizes. What is presented as a Promethean struggle against Zeus is really Rousseau's and the Romantics' revolt against society and its institutions as inherently evil. It is society which is the villain of the piece, and man's subservience to it, the thing that corrupts him. This beclouds the conflict and makes it difficult to respond to the play, since one must continually adjust the meanings he ascribes to Zeus and, therefore, to the nature of Orestes' rebellion. God? No, He doesn't exist. Man's religious beliefs? Partly. The Church? Yes, but more than that. Society? Yes! But Society is so comprehensive an abstraction that we must begin to enumerate its components: government, law, family, customs, morals, ethics, and so on and on. But none of these can exist without others besides the individual. People, then, as well? We shall return later to Sartre's treatment of this uncomfortable question.

Whatever the total weight of meaning Sartre finally ascribes to Zeus, it is his religious connotations that carry most forcefully in the play. And Sartre, to illustrate his thesis, must clearly delimit the power of religious belief for which Zeus is, among other things, symbol and spokesman. That power evaporates before the strength of a free man resolved to live his freedom: men are free, but they do not know it. By definition, then, Zeus is a myth, a useful fiction, a vital lie—yet not so vital that he cannot be vanquished. But in the present instance, Zeus as antagonist is little better than a straw man, although perhaps he need not have been. This defect is emphasized by Sartre's employment of Zeus as mouthpiece as well as agent at points in the play where he badly hampers the action. Harold Hobson noted this as one of the chief weaknesses of *The Flies*: "But the fact that Sartre felt it necessary to expound these ideas through the mouth of Jupiter is a confession that he failed to make them spring spontaneously out of the action." [26]

When Zeus makes his last appearance and appeal, he promises Orestes and Electra the throne, if they will repudiate their crime

[26] Hobson, *The French Theatre*, p. 88.

and reinstate the public mourning which Zeus, in alliance with tyranny, demands. Zeus both wins and loses: his offer hardens Orestes' obduracy but completes the capitulation of Electra, who pleads: "Help! Zeus, king of gods and men, my king, take me in your arms, carry me from this place, and shelter me. I will obey your law, I will be your creature and your slave, I will embrace your knees. Save me from the flies, from my brother, from myself! Do not leave me lonely and I will give up my whole life to atonement. I repent Zeus, I bitterly repent." Now the Furies cannot make her their kill because she is under the god's protection; they will dwindle to flies once again. And Electra will become the copy of her mother, aged and raddled by remorse. Here, as in the parallels drawn between Orestes and Aegisthus and in Zeus's proposal that brother and sister succeed the murdered tyrants, the patterns of repetition suggested resemble those that round off O'Neill's trilogy. There, of course, it was Orestes who was weak and Electra who was strong. But the nightmare of endless recurrence is only for the weak; it will not do for Sartre and his Orestes. The action must open out in a new direction—and it takes the path of exile.

Orestes confronts the people of Argos who, roused by the screams of their dying rulers, have surounded the palace: "So here you are, my true and loyal subjects? I am Orestes, your king, son of Agamemnon, and this is my coronation day." He will not let his crime enslave the city, as did Aegisthus': "My crime is wholly mine, I claim it as my own, for all to know; it is my glory, my life's work, and you can neither punish nor pity me." He claims kinship with them, although they fear his ruthless daring: "There is a bond of blood between us, and I have earned my kingship over you. As for your sins and your remorse, your night-fears, and the crime Aegisthus committed—all are mine, I take them all upon me. Fear your Dead no longer, they are *my* Dead. And, see, your faithful flies have left you to come to me" (Act III). Yet, because it was Zeus that had offered him it, he rejects his victims' throne, to become "a king without a kingdom, without subjects." He urges his people to begin life anew, repudiating the past entirely; and he leaves them, the whimpering Furies in tow, to begin his own new, strange life—a life of perpetual exile in which to bear the burden of his freedom.

The superficial resemblance of this ending to *The Libation*

Bearers only underscores its total change of meaning and tone. There, the people of Argos bless Orestes and pray for his deliverance in the hope that Apollo will cleanse him of his deed; and Orestes flees, crying out: "You can not see them, but I see them. I am driven / from this place. I can stay here no longer." [27] In Aeschylus there is no guilt upon the Argives and no vicarious atonement that Orestes makes for them. Orestes' exile is the will of the gods, whereas the Sartrean hero's is self-imposed, and illustrated—although not explained—by Orestes' telling his people the story of the Pied Piper of Hamelin, here transformed as a legend of a plague of rats in Scyros.

This is a curious turn, as if Sartre, either beguiled by the romantic figure which his exile cuts or determined to steal some of the emotional force of the Christian act of atonement, forgot the logic of the action. The positive ending would have been to enter his kingdom, Zeus or no Zeus, and hasten the end of Zeus's reign by liberating the people from their superstitions and getting down to the business of ruling a city dedicated to the liberty of man. This would have been the defeat of myth by anti-myth, consistent with the inversion of myth which is the basis of Sartre's method and with his revolutionary doctrine. (A king is, however, an awkward person to represent the drastically anti-authoritarian viewpoint of Sartre which is so thorough-going as to oppose law and restraint in any form. But Sartre is stuck with Orestes, the king's son, not only because of the myth, but because his kingship is represented as the basis on which Orestes seeks to belong to his people.) Instead, as if he had reached an impasse, Sartre introduces a counter-myth—the wandering exile as self-elected scapegoat. It is a way to break the pattern of repetition and guilt in Argos, to insure that no taint of Aegisthus' power-lust and rule by deception attaches to the hero. All the same, the counter-myth is unexpected and, as critics have noted, risks producing anti-climax and confusing Sartre's thesis. There seems to be no logic in the action or in any of the play's dialectics for Orestes' astonishing gesture: "As for your sins and your remorse . . . all are mine, I take them all upon me." This idea, totally inconsistent with Sartre's philosophy, will be developed later.

Apart from this, however, the recurrent theme of *The Oresteia*

[27] Aeschylus, *The Libation Bearers*, in *The Complete Greek Tragedies*, I, 131.

can still stand when applied to *The Flies*: "The doer must suffer. By suffering man learns." [28] Yet not only has its context entirely changed, but the face of life itself has altered beyond recognition. I have pointed out already that Orestes does not achieve freedom by slaying the tyrants; he achieves it when he rejects Zeus and decides for himself. Freedom is a necessary *precondition* of the slaying, and the slaying, aside from ratifying Orestes' freedom, accomplishes nothing but the utter enslavement of Electra and the total alienation of Orestes.

Although his purpose is obviously didactic and persuasive, Sartre cannot be accused of making freedom speciously attractive; quite the contrary. Aeschylus' hero suffered intolerable anguish from violating his instincts. Perhaps in existentialist psychology the attribution of instincts is inadmissable, as assuming man to have an essence preceding his existence (that is, his creation of his own nature through acts). But although Sartre's hero delivered himself from remorse by his dedication to freedom, he did so only to grapple with an anguish far more crushing than anything suffered by the Greek dramatist's more *human* avenger. We are forced to keep reminding ourselves that Orestes suffers not because of the action which the myth requires but because he is *free*, and that his freedom, which preceded the killings, continues thereafter. It is a constant. The action effects no change in the nature of that freedom: it can promise no human relief. For this, says Sartre, is what it is to be a man. The upshot is confusing, even defeatist, and, dramatically speaking, dangerously close to being pointless. Plot and theme have not fused, they accompany each other. And this state of affairs is reinforced by the curious fact that Orestes' commitment leaves him humanly so detached, so unaffected emotionally, that it neutralizes the private anguish of his alienation and renders it barely credible.

This brings us to a consideration of Sartre's characters in a play where theme and plot tend to command the greater interest, as is usually the case in thesis drama. Sartre, as we remember, deliberately eschews the creation of unique characters by means of detailed psychologizing. Now the strict subordination of character to the demands of plot, although it is in accord with

[28] Formulated by Vellacott in *The Oresteian Trilogy*, p. 22.

the model of tragedy he has chosen, will not explain their reduction of stature to something far below what the Greek dramatist, working from like assumptions, achieved. Such characters, although they can often be extremely powerful, seldom change or grow. Yet Sartre, in trying to demonstrate moral commitment, finds himself obliged to attempt just this with Orestes and with Electra, too, where the counterpointing of her weakness with her brother's growing strength requires the dramatizing of her dissolution.

Within the rather narrow compass of the action, Orestes must be brought from the aimless detachment of a young dilettante to a mature man's total commitment to his freedom and its realization through action.

For Sartre, man creates his nature by his deeds; he becomes what he does. The analogy to drama is evident: characters are created by action; they are what they do, and nothing more; they have no existence previous to their actions in the play and none thereafter. This was true before the introduction of realistic —or, for that matter, existential—psychology to the stage, and is still so.

Sartre prepares his hero's development by making him young, untested, but already weary of his rootlessness. His situation calls for anonymity and disguise, for remaining passive while he sizes up people and events. Thus he can meet Electra and his mother and come to know them without declaring himself. Others can characterize him for us, by attributing to him qualities he has not yet demonstrated as does Zeus when he says: "Do you wish to enforce your rights? Yes, you're brave and strong and spirited. I can see you as a captain in an army of good fighters"; or Electra, after her unsuccessful defiance of Aegisthus: "You deceived me. . . . Yes, it was your eyes that made a fool of me. . . . I don't know what you're after, but this I know: that I mustn't believe you. Your eyes are too bold for my liking"; or Clytemnestra, regarding him as dangerous: "Leave this place. I feel you are going to bring disaster on us." For a time his presence acts as a catalyst, but he himself does little. His first show of passion is a flare-up at Aegisthus, who invokes Agamemnon's name at the ceremony for the Dead. Orestes impulsively draws his sword and exclaims, "I forbid you to drag my father's name into this mummery." But Zeus silences him, and Aegisthus, apparently uncomprehending, is at that moment distracted by the dramatic entrance of Electra, clothed in white so as to deny her share in the public guilt and to defy the tyrant.

Yet when Aegisthus banishes Electra, Orestes' first resolve is to flee with her. She, however, will not go; she is still waiting for her brother to come and avenge her. Her contempt for cowardice forces Orestes to reveal himself; his loneliness as a stranger, his wish to belong—not any passionate urge to avenge his father's death or any love or hatred for his mother—prompts him to stay and take up his sister's cause. Then when Zeus answers his prayer with the sign meant to weaken his resolve, his commitment becomes total. He will slay the tyrants, yet he can say truthfully: "The gods bear witness that I had no wish to shed their blood."

So far, the advantage of myth in priming our expectations is evident. When the characters act in accordance with the myth, they need do only the minimum to fill in the outline in the spectator's mind and so strengthen their dramatic reality. At the end of Act II, Scene 1, Sartre, by the aid of myth, induces us to accept Orestes' resolve, despite the fact that he acts under no divine compulsion, no strong sense of family ties or familial duty, no love or hatred for the tyrants, but principally because of his defiance of Zeus's miching falsehoods and because of our revulsion from the state of things in Argos. Sartre has done his best to make Orestes' assertion of his manhood believable by shifting the whole emphasis from blood-guilt and revenge to the clash of slavery and liberty, one man's fight against society, tyranny, and belief in God, and by representing the realization of liberty as a deeply transforming experience in itself. But this is still an idea only; it has yet to be proved; and, as indicated above, when the time comes to do it by killing his mother, Orestes' passionless commitment must face the test not only of the action demanded, but also of the spectator's acceptance. Mark Schorer said of *Wuthering Heights* that "the book sets out to persuade us of the moral magnificence of such unmoral passion." [29] It might be said of *The Flies* that it sets out to persuade us of the moral magnificence of such passionless morality. From the point of view

[29] "Technique as Discovery," in James E. Miller, Jr., ed., *Myth and Method: Modern Theories of Fiction* (Lincoln: University of Nebraska Press, 1960), p. 90.

of drama, the result is paradoxical: Orestes is morally committed but humanly uninvolved. Changing the myth to yield a new theme, one linked to a new rationale, entails changing the character to its dramatic detriment.

Sartre's hero murders his mother, and experiences no regret. This lack of feeling, this absence of any revulsion of affection, this disregard of the Western recoil from acts of blood, instinctively affronts the conceptions of what is just and even natural that have been built up during two and a half thousand years in European civilizations. Yet it is precisely this that Sartre finds admirable. The whole play is conceived and written so that, at the end, Orestes may issue this flagrant and triumphant denial of traditional values.[30]

To succeed in inducing an audience to consider, let alone accept, a moral system so at odds with its own, one would expect Sartre to be at pains to embody that system in as *human* a character as he could possibly create. But Sartre proceeds in a diametrically opposite direction, depriving Orestes of human motivations other than a moral fervor that overrides all other considerations. Its claim is so extreme that it takes on the quality of the perverse: it becomes, not unexpectedly, Gide's "gratuitous act" in a new guise.

Electra, in her emotional reversals, can be effectively depicted without the risks that attend Orestes' development. Her progress is psychologically plausible, because her desires for revenge are represented as a young girl's compensatory daydreams that will not survive the test of reality. They do not disrupt the myth because her disavowal of complicity in the revenge and her repudiation of Orestes do not deflect him from his path, but only add to his final alienation. But she is tainted by the theme of incest which Sartre, perhaps taking his cue from O'Neill's trilogy and Giraudoux's play, perversely introduces, as if to fill the emotional vacuum created by his doctrinaire treatment of Orestes, or else to show that, as with matricide, no morality attaches to incest. She is drawn to Orestes, not knowing him to be her brother. And after the killings it is only natural that she should instinctively seek shelter from the horror of them in her brother's affection. But the scene has erotic overtones, given it by the earlier scene quoted below; we remember how blood-lust and sexual

[30] Hobson, *The French Theatre*, p. 90.

lust are associated at the outset of the play in the dialogue between Zeus and the Old Woman:

ZEUS: Yes, but you left your window not quite closed, so as to hear [Agamemnon's screams] the better, and, while you peeped behind the curtains and held your breath, you felt a little tingling itch between your loins, and didn't you enjoy it! . . . And when you went to bed that night, you had a grand time with your man. A real gala night [Act I].

His ambitions charged by his decision to kill the king and queen, Orestes vaunts his strength before Electra:

ORESTES: . . . You are *my* sister, Electra, and that city is *my* city. *My* sister. [*he takes her arm*]

ELECTRA: Don't touch me. You're hurting me, frightening me—and I'm *not* yours.

ORESTES: I know. Not yet. I'm still too—too light. I must take a burden on my shoulders, a load of guilt so heavy as to drag me down, right down into the abyss of Argos. . . . Come, Electra, look at our city. There it lies. . . . It fends me off with its high walls, red roofs, locked doors. And yet it's mine for the taking; I've felt that since this morning. You, too, Electra, are mine for the taking—and I'll take you, too [II, 1].

The text is no more explicit than that, but then it need not be; the subsequent action is not conclusive, beyond the following, which occurs after the killings:

ELECTRA: Take me in your arms, beloved, and press me to your breast. How dark the night is! I never knew such darkness; those torches have no effect on it. . . . Do you love me?

ORESTES: . . . We are free, Electra. I feel as if I'd brought you into Life and I, too, had just been born. Yes, I love you, and you belong to me. Only yesterday I was empty-handed, and today I have *you*. Ours is a double tie of blood; we two come of the same race and we two have shed blood.

In his desire to "belong," brotherly affection for Electra would in itself strengthen Orestes' motivation to stay in Argos and destroy the tyrants. It is understandable that he should seek her praise, rather than the scorn she showed him earlier. But these passages link the two of them thematically to the offensive atmosphere of Argos: a pall of craven remorse, sexuality, and bloodshed. Electra, it is true, succumbs to this atmosphere out of hysterical fear, but Orestes does not; and these scenes do not seem intended to suggest that he is in any danger of doing so

—quite the contrary. They make more definite the final break between brother and sister at the end of the play. But beyond that, the incestuous bond, like Orestes' remorselessness in slaying his mother, seems deliberately gratuitous, as if to show that man may do all things so long as he is "free." Or else it is deliberately designed to shock, as if Sartre would affront not only our taboos against matricide but also those against incest. Does he find this, too, admirable in his hero? Is Orestes like a proper existentialist, improvising his moral code as he goes along, and must that code, as a continual assertion of freedom, oppose conventional morality in every respect? If so, one is reminded of William Arrowsmith's comment about Euripides' *Orestes*, with which this play has curious affinities of tone and outlook in depicting a world of nightmarish absurdity: ". . . slowly, inexorably, all moral terms are either inverted or emptied of their meaning." [31]

Enough has been said about Aegisthus' final rebellion against Zeus to indicate why and how Sartre has given his character prominence as a precursor of Orestes. Clytemnestra is put to similar use, in foreshadowing what her daughter will become for having cravenly capitulated; in her case, Sartre's reworking of the myth has meant her reduction both in stature and in importance. She is anything but a brazen adulteress, dominating her paramour and ruling her kingdom; instead, for his purposes, she is a woman with dead eyes, aged and ravaged by remorse, a creature given to self-castigation in public for her "inexpiable crime." Her remorse has become a monomania. It is sincere. Yet she upholds Aegisthus' invention of the fable of the Day of the Dead, fabricated to impress his subjects, only to see him, on the eve of her death, become momentarily the dupe of his own invention, so that he spurns her with the name of "whore" because he thinks Agamemnon's dead eyes are upon them. Remorse has destroyed her life, as the hypocrisy of power has all but destroyed Aegisthus'. In the early scene where she encounters Orestes without recognizing him, there is a conflict between Electra and her that is reminiscent of Giraudoux's treatment of the relationship; we know that she half fears, half hopes, her son is still alive to return some day. But she is almost entirely passive. She fills out the picture, little more, and at the appointed time she serves as the necessary victim.

[31] Introduction, *Orestes*, in *The Complete Greek Tragedies*, IV, 189.

Zeus is a symbol for all that engages Sartre's deepest hatreds. And so one might expect that he would make him a redoubtable character, a worthy opponent for Orestes, so that Orestes' victory would be all the greater. But Sartre has not found a way to hedge his divinity so as to give it substance and definition while at the same time granting him stature or grandeur, however evil. The Zeus we are shown is an eavesdropping sleight-of-hand artist, a most immoral old scoundrel who created the world and man and says, "I am Goodness," but never exemplifies that goodness. His will is the law of the universe, but it is strangely impotent when confronted by his creatures, once they have discovered the secret that he made them free. (And why did he?) A god ought to be able to generate conflict instead of indulging in disputation. He stands for so much in Sartre's eyes, and all of it evil; yet the character the playwright has given him merely trivializes what might have been monstrous and awesome.[32]

Our final consideration of Sartre's use of classical myth concerns its adequacy as a vehicle for a popular statement of his philosophy of existential freedom, or, what is slightly different, the alterations his philosophy may undergo when *dramatized* in the familiar terms of myth.

That philosophy proceeds from two postulates: first, that life is absurd, and second, that man is free. From these proceed the assertion that each man *is* his own freedom (Zeus, says Orestes, has "no power to make me atone for an act I don't regard as a crime"), and its corollary, that each man must assert that freedom for himself, because no one else can do it for him (". . . every man must find out his own way," says Orestes). In the play this last is dramatized by contrast in Electra's breakdown, of which Orestes can only say: "She is dearer to me than

[32] This is to take the play at its face value and assume its seriousness of method as well as purpose. Two comments by Eric Bentley suggest that a different approach (whether intended by Sartre or not) is the right one:

"Here is a play in which Greek myth is material for French conversation. The legend is not, properly speaking, redramatized; it is taken for granted. . . . The more one sees this play, the more one realizes how much Sartre the playwright owes to Giraudoux; his Zeus is no god, he is Louis Jouvet." *In Search of Theatre* (New York: Vintage Books, 1954), p. 137.

"When *The Flies* is played ponderously, every fly an elephant, you realize that the play lives by the one quality such a production lacks: lightness of touch. Sartre's rhetoric, always on the verge of the false, is often redeemed by a kind of irony in which the audience is asked not to take the whole thing too seriously." *Ibid.*

life. But her suffering comes from within, and only she can rid herself of it. For she is free."

This is Orestes' message to the Argives and, by extension, to the audience. Its application discloses a gap between Sartre's picture of man when he speaks as a philosopher and that which he presents as a playwright. It also makes clear his difficulty in using theatre as a collective rite in which to subvert the collective religious, moral, and social beliefs of his audience. His effort, like his philosophy, may be compared to that of a man who, to lift himself by his own boot-straps, pulls the rug from under his feet.

If we apply these postulates, some regrettable conclusions result. First, if existence is absurd, then so are you and I. To another man, whose existence we are part of, we are society and are therefore simply elements in his contingent existence that threaten his efforts to assert his total freedom. We are, in fact, "the others." Consequently, regardless of how well-intentioned we may think ourselves, we possess a sinister character, because, sooner or later, we will seize our chance to limit his freedom in order to extend our own. (If we are bourgeois, we will of course do so sooner.) But we have each only to turn the tables, to place him among "the others," and regard *him* as a sinister threat to our respective freedoms. "All the world is mad save me and thee. And sometimes even thee—." With subjectivity rampant in this maddest of all possible worlds, every man's hand is against his fellow.[33]

Sartre's analysis of existence leads him to a nihilistic conclusion which he tries to avert by appealing to man to create himself out of his own freedom, like a craftsman trying to make the best of very shoddy materials. Harold Clurman has concisely stated Sartre's position in a way to point up the clash between his distrust of man and his compulsion to exhort him to assert his freedom:

Sartre believes that the individual must develop the independence to free himself of all taboos, whether they be religious, philosophical, social or political. At the same time, Sartre has little confidence in the

[33] "In one of the unpublished notebooks of Rilke there is an unpublished phrase which might be our text: '. . . if you're not one up (*Blitzleisch*) you're . . . one down (*Rotzleisch*).'" Stephen Potter, *Some Notes on Lifemanship: With a Summary of Recent Researches in Gamesmanship* (New York: Henry Holt, 1951), p. xiv.

existence of a general "human nature," or even an individual psychology. There is no innate goodness in man and perhaps no innate evil. Each man may achieve freedom only through an action that his own vigorous consciousness of the possibility of such action will prompt.[34]

Love itself is infected with this absurdity—indeed, perhaps love most of all, because it provides a deceptive means for one immitagably self-seeking person to use another while pretending to sacrifice himself for the beloved or to share a common good. Love of God is pointless self-delusion, of course, because God does not exist and even if He did, it would make no difference.[35] (Perhaps herein lies the explanation for Zeus's unsatisfactory character as antagonist.) Love of one's fellows is equally deluded, a disguise for the exploitation of others. In Sartre's *No Exit*, hell is not the absence of God; it is the presence of others. The prison whose three inmates endlessly get at one another is Sartre's picture of life at its worst. It dramatizes a basic finding of Sartre's psychology which is also a tenet of his phenomenology: the presence—the stare—of others. This is society. It is in *The Flies*, too, symbolized by the blood-smeared statue of Zeus, "god of flies and death," with its white, staring eyes; by the invisible dead that return one day a year to increase the remorse of the living by staring at them; by the presence of Zeus himself, who watches and eavesdrops; by the remorseful Clytemnestra, who wills herself to feel fixed upon her the stare of the Agamemnon; by the flies that buzz and settle. We are reminded of Frye's analysis of the demonic in its final phase, "the horror of being watched," which is "a greater misery than . . . pain."

In this world-view, which Sartre contends is "optimistic, a doctrine of action," the last thing we should expect to find is genuine altruism. Yet, next to his courageous independence, altruism is Orestes' cardinal virtue and his only motive. Or rather, altruism is the expression of Orestes' desire to belong, to be com-

---

[34] Harold Clurman, *Lies Like Truth: Theatre Reviews and Essays* (New York: Macmillan, 1958), p. 209.

[35] "There is no universe other than a human universe, the universe of human subjectivity." J.-P. Sartre, *Existentialism*, trans. Bernard Frechtman (New York: Philosophical Library, 1947), p. 60.

"Existentialism is nothing else than an attempt to draw all the consequences of a coherent atheistic position. It isn't trying to plunge man into despair at all. . . . Rather, it declares that even if God did exist, that would change nothing." *Ibid.*

mitted to something outside himself. And it may well be that Sartre, to make sure no taint of self-interest sullied that altruism, was forced to retain the myth by sending Orestes into exile. Orestes is, nonetheless, a perfect exemplar of Sartre's doctrine: he asserts the absurdity of life, he asserts his total independence, and he translates his "dread" into obligation to others. Sartre says: "In fact, anguish, as I see it, is the concurrence of the complete absence of justification and responsibility toward others." [36]

This altruism, this "love" for his people (to use Orestes' own word for it), is to give the ending of the play an exaltation that will compensate for the defeat implied in his rejection at the hands of the Argives and in his exile. Whence does it come? Certainly not from God, for Zeus says, "I've no use for love. I love nobody"; and insofar as Zeus is also society, certainly not from society either. And not from man's essential nature either, because for Sartre there is no such thing. Man has only an existential nature, that is, one which he creates for himself; and goodness is not innate. Altruism, or responsibility toward others, then, is a datum, a postulate of Sartre's philosophy which, as an axiom, he would have us take for granted. We are free, and *therefore* must obligate ourselves. It is a paradox: a gratuitous obligation.

The slaying of the tyrants, therefore, serves a double function: it asserts Orestes' freedom, and it fulfills his obligation toward others. This is its specific, literal meaning; viewed in this light, it makes sense. When the idea of it occurs to him, however, Orestes speaks of it in misleading—because figurative—terms. "I must go down into the depths, among you. . . . I must take a burden on my shoulders, a load of guilt so heavy as to drag me down . . . supposing I take over all their crimes. Supposing I set out to win the name of 'guilt-stealer,' and heap on myself all their remorse. . . ." But when Electra asks, "So you wish to atone for us?" he replies confusingly: "To atone? No, I said I'd house your penitence. . . ." His point is that, with the king and queen out of the way, the remorse and guilt they fostered will vanish of themselves, since they were no more than useful lies perpetuated by the tyrants. But at the end, in the speech to the Argives already quoted, he says again: "As for your sins and your remorse, your night-fears, and the crime Aegisthus committed—all

[36] *Ibid.*, pp. 65-66.

are mine, I take them all upon me." And he reinforces this speech visually by taking the Furies with him into exile. His exit has all the appearance of the scapegoat sacrificing himself for his people, to achieve for them a vicarious atonement. It is the special virtue of the drama to suggest, by means of what is seen, that which is unseen; but the unseen is not the same as the non-existent. And for Orestes, as for Sartre, sin and crime (except possibly the crime of tyranny?) have no objective existence; guilt, penitence, and remorse have, therefore, no reason for being. Orestes' assertion of freedom was simply to prove the slavery of other men false. The very logic of the existentialist ethic, which holds each man responsible for his own actions, as it holds him responsible to himself alone, makes nonsense of the idea that a man can assume the load of another's guilt, heap on himself another's remorse, and take upon himself all that other's sins and crimes; and it makes of Orestes' words and action windy rhetoric and empty gestures.

This, we may say, is nothing but a poetic statement, a theatrical symbol, whereby Sartre tries to dramatize the meaning of what Orestes has done. But such reductive phrases as "nothing but" are not to be used lightly in considering drama as an art; they make poor excuses. Sartre helps himself to a symbol "clustered with all sorts of valuable emotional overtones that he finds convenient to his dramatic purpose," but he does not alter it to underscore the change of meaning he has conferred upon it. But this time the overtones are borrowed from Christ's crucifixion as vicarious atonement for the sins of men. This is jarring, even shocking, not only because the symbol is inappropriate to the action, but also because the entire play is a repudiation, in the deepest sense, of the very doctrine it apes. It is a parody of it, just as Zeus's attempt to make Orestes submit to him before the spectacle of "the firmament, spangled with wheeling stars" is, besides being the god's argument from design in nature as proof of his own existence, an inversion and travesty of the gospel account (Matthew 4:8-10) in which Satan tempts Christ with the kingdoms of this world: "All these will I give thee, if falling down thou wilt adore me"; and just as Sartre's essential message, propounded with messianic conviction, is—again in the deepest sense—an echo and a repudiation of the words of Christ: "You shall know the truth, and the truth shall make you free."

The discrepancy between the playwright's philosophy and the myth as dramatized would seem to reflect a basic inconsistency in the philosophy itself, in which Sartre tries to make existentialism revolutionary. The strong moral impulse behind it is the desire to achieve an authentic existence, despite his assertion that sincerity and good faith are equally impossible of achievement, since they are posited as ineradicable constants of the human condition. Leslie A. Juhasz, in a critique of Sartre's works, points out that the main thesis of his metaphysics negates the possibility of the authentic, that this possibility appears as no more than a footnote in *Being and Nothingness,* and yet that in *Existentialism* "he suddenly jumps to the conclusion that good faith exists and he implicitly identifies good faith with authenticity." [37] Hence, says Juhasz, "It is highly significant that Sartre has never defined philosophically how authenticity could exist and in what it would consist." [38]

But without such a possibility the only alternatives for a moralist like Sartre are self-defeating nihilism and futility—no bases for a program of action, let alone one designed to attract adherents in the theatre. Sartre, although he is as obsessively oriented to the future as Nietzsche, did not make Nietzsche's mistake of assuming that disciples would spring up of themselves; he saw just in time what was needed, and his play shows it. But our allowing even for this about-face—or last-minute development—in his ontology still does not resolve his contradictions. He posits man's total freedom and his responsibility to improvise his acts. "Yet," says Juhasz, "all of his works implicitly affirm the existence of a moral order over and above his acknowledged principles. This second, implied code condemns brutality, cruelty and aggressiveness; it rejects the institution of the scapegoat; it censures the maltreatment of the weak by the powerful; it reproves the suppression of the poor, the ostracizing of any segment of society on the basis of racial or other prejudices. In Sartrean theory, there is only one notion: that of responsibility, in the defense of these implied values." [39]

Sartre defined theatre as a rite, a religious phenomenon, and

[37] Leslie A. Juhasz, *The Major Works of Sartre* (New York: Monarch Press, 1965), p. 81.
[38] *Ibid.*
[39] *Ibid.,* p. 12.

attributed its greatness in part to its religious function. As we have seen, however, the intent of his play is so clearly anti-religious that the terms of his esthetic are ambiguous, if not contradictory. Once more we may be excused for feeling that "terms arc either inverted or emptied of their meaning." For it is man's incorrigible proneness to religious worship that the play attacks. Nor will Sartre permit man to substitute himself for God, as the object of his own worship.

The existentialist will never consider man as an end because he is always in the making. Nor should we believe that there is a mankind to which we might set up a cult in the manner of Auguste Comte. The cult of mankind ends in the self-enclosed humanism of Comte, and, let it be said, of fascism. That kind of humanism we can do without . . . man will fulfill himself as man, not in turning toward himself, but in seeking outside of himself a goal which is just this liberation, just this particular fulfillment.[40]

Yet religious rites presuppose a collective belief to which they serve to give collective expression. Sartre's announced purpose was to line up systems of values, ethics, and concepts of man and pit them against one another in dialectical conflicts precipitated by carefully chosen dramatic situations. *The Flies* exemplifies his method: myth is made to contradict, and thus to subvert, itself. Further, a mythology is used to discredit a theology. Sartre pits his philosophy against traditional religious belief, intending the disadvantage of the latter. The purpose is to dispel the anxieties of modern man "in the form of myths which anyone can understand and feel deeply." Here, of course, Sartre refers to the myths which the playwright creates by reshaping or transforming the classical myths. By virtue of its very unexpectedness, his choice of the myth of Orestes is strategically shrewd; *The Flies* is a logical, indeed an indispensable, starting-point for his theatre, because God must first be gotten out of the way.

This is where the play, already ironic in conception, reveals a double aspect. It intends not only to show this riddance happening in the action but actually to bring it about in the theatre itself.[41] Thus it resembles a magical rite: an action designed to

[40] Sartre, *Existentialism*, pp. 59-60.
[41] Sartre's reverse English on the myth reminds one, by contrast, of the chorus in Sophocles' *Oedipus Rex*, which questions the point of its ritual dance if the oracles are not proved true:

bring about the very thing enacted. Each new spectator is to be initiated as a literal participant in a rite of collective *un*belief, a parody of religious ritual in that the death of a god is to be followed by the birth of free man. Man is to believe in himself alone: "Freedom with negation of all the rest: that is the choice of Sartre. The rest is tragic isolation."[42] With his sight thus cleared by a true belief, man is now ready to contemplate "the great myths of death, exile, love." This is the meaning, for modern man, of Sartre's version of the Orestes myth.

"The situation and future of two individuals [Oedipus and Jocasta] has become a test of divine power: if they are right, sings the chorus, 'why reverence Apollo's Delphi, the center of the world? Why join the choral dance?' . . . and with this phrase the issue is brought out of the past into the present moment in the theater of Dionysus. . . . If the oracles and the truth are not equated the performance of the play has no meaning, for tragedy is a religious ritual. This phrase is a tour de force which makes the validity of the performance itself depend on the denouement of the play." Bernard Knox, "Sophocles' Oedipus," in Cleanth Brooks, ed., *Tragic Themes in Western Literature* (New Haven: Yale University Press, 1955), pp. 18-19.

[42] Desan, *The Tragic Finale*, p. 184.

CHAPTER IX

JEAN ANOUILH:
Pièces Pures et Sales

Every serious character in Anouilh sooner or later is a victim of his own lack of faith—in love, in life, or simply in himself. There is no question anywhere of faith in God. Hopelessness and mistrust reign through the serious plays and all is reduced to a world of individual despair. The hero does not believe in anything any more in the later Anouilh—save his own guilt and loneliness.[1]

Between 1929 and 1959 Jean Anouilh wrote nearly 30 plays. Three of them, written during the German occupation and just after the liberation of France, redramatize classic myths: *Eurydice* (1941), *Antigone* (1942), and *Medea* (1946). The first two belong to what Gabriel Marcel has called the "central range" of Anouilh's work,[2] but after the third we do not find him resorting to myth. A disciple of Claudel and Giraudoux, both of whom he eventually forsook to develop independently, Anouilh has created a distinctive theatricalism that bears a closer relation to the *commedia dell' arte* and the tradition of Molière than it does to the *poésie du théâtre* of Cocteau and Giraudoux. His efforts at dramatizing myth seem both less instinctive and

---

[1] Edward Owen Marsh, *Jean Anouilh: Poet of Pierrot and Pantaloon* (London: W. H. Allen, 1953), p. 180.
[2] Cited by Leonard Cabell Pronko, *The World of Jean Anouilh*, Perspectives in Criticism Series, 7 (Berkeley: University of California Press, 1961), p. 21.

less characteristic than theirs. Myth is almost a redundancy for him: he has found his own method of abstracting and generalizing. Besides, when he reached the 1940's, he had already created his own obsessive myth of Innocence and Experience in a world totally corrupt and almost totally corrupting, and redramatized it in every play. It is abundantly evident and has the stamp of his own sufficient theatricality.

Anouilh began writing in the realistic tradition, but theatricalism emerged through his comedies, the *pièces roses*. It developed as a mixture of the tragic and comic, the serious and the grotesque, the pathetic and the farcical, which fusing of genres he has made peculiarly his own. All three of the plays based on myth are tragic—*pièces noires*; though the first two contain humor, it is hardly prominent and is used sardonically to add bitter contrast through its callous tone. *Eurydice* is set in a modern, urban milieu of deceptive realism, *Antigone* in a neutral, timeless, and impersonal Thebes, and *Medea* in an equally indeterminate locality and time. Anouilh uses realistic details of speech and manners only partly for plausibility; he does not regard himself as a realistic writer but seeks instead "a poetic and imaginative interpretation of reality."[3] It has been pointed out that one of Count Tigre's speeches in *The Rehearsal* might stand as Anouilh's *ars dramatica*.[4] In it we find Cocteau's esthetic objective reaffirmed, even to the phrase "plus vrai que le vrai": "The object of art is precisely to give [life form], and through all possible artifices to create something that is truer than truth."[5]

Anouilh found no new themes in the three famous myths; rather, he adapted them to support recurrent themes from his earlier "black" plays: the isolation of man's consciousness from his fellows, and even from himself, in an empty and absurd universe; the dread of age, which necessarily implies corruption; the mutability of love; a puritanical horror of sex as the most degrading manifestation of life's bondage, coupled ambivalently with a sentimentalized view of love as a transcendent but doomed experience; and death as the only means of realizing one's illusions or regaining the true "purity" of self—that childhood innocence inevitably lost in growing up.

[3] Quoted in *ibid.*, p. xix.
[4] *Ibid.*, p. 129.
[5] *Ibid.* (Pronko's translation).

I. *Eurydice*

Eurydice appeared five years after 1936, the year that Anouilh says marked a change in his dramaturgy: "I realised that the dramatist could and should *play with* his characters, with their passions and their actions. . . . To 'play' with a subject is to create a new world of conventions and surround it with spells and a magic all your own. . . ." [6] In thus reanimating and playing with a great myth, it is very much to Anouilh's purpose not to show us a deathless love in a timeless past, but to show us the death of that love when the myth is applied to life in the present. Since the action moves toward disillusionment, Anouilh reconstructs the everyday reality in which it takes place to show it as drab, tedious, false, and sordid. Rather than a deathless love, we have a love that can only be preserved in death because (says Anouilh) even the greatest love cannot withstand the erosions of life.

The play is like Cocteau's *Orphée*, especially in its ending. Orpheus "looks" at Eurydice when she returns from the shades, loses her because he disobeys the conditions laid down, and decides in the end to rejoin her in death. But it is a play about love and "purity," not poetry, and their inability to withstand corruption—Anouilh's synonym for life. Orpheus is a young musician, saddled with a parasitic father; Eurydice is the daughter of an aging actress in a theatrical touring company. Her widowed mother is the mistress of Vincent, one of the members of the company. Eurydice herself has been the mistress of the company impresario, as well as of various other men to whom she capitulated out of kindness, or pity, or the desire to avoid a fuss. Boy and girl meet in a railway station between trains and fall instantly in love. Orpheus deserts his father; Eurydice, her mother and the company. They run off together and consummate their love in a squalid hotel room. The innocent Orpheus looks forward to a life of happiness; the experienced Eurydice, although she knows this to be the true love of her life, fears that she will not be able to live up to the idealized picture which Orpheus has of her. She has already made some admissions but cannot bring herself to tell him the whole truth. She feels stained by all her past affairs. When she receives a letter from the impresario, threatening

[6] Quoted in Marsh, *Jean Anouilh*, p. 189.

to expose her unless she rejoins the troupe, she panics, flees, and dies in a bus accident.

Through the offices of M. Henri, the agent of death, Orpheus is permitted to see Eurydice again. Their meeting takes place at night in the eerily deserted railway station, and at first all seems well. But inevitably the demanding Orpheus must "look" at her, must know the whole truth about her even if it should cost him his love: "All the words haven't yet been said. And we must say them all, one after the other," he tells her. "We must go now to the very end, word by word. And there are plenty of them. . . . Now I've got to look at you." She pleads with him: "I may not be the woman you wanted me to be. The one your happiness invented that wonderful first day. . . . I shall give you all the happiness I can. But don't ask of me more than I can give. Be content. Do not look at me. Let me live. . . ."[7] Orpheus shouts his refusal: "Live, live! . . . Oh no. I love you too much to live." He rejects compromise: it would simply make them like her ridiculous mother and her lover, or like his seedy father who still tries to seduce chambermaids. In time they would see the death of their love and like their elders settle for shabby substitutes. Orpheus demands the truth because he will have love on none but absolute terms. He *must* look at her.

When he does, Eurydice, knowing she has lost him, makes her full confession: vignettes from her life are relived, showing Orpheus that her promiscuity was the result of good intentions. She vanishes. Orpheus is left to mourn her. His father appears. Listening to his prattle and self-deceptions, Orpheus sees what life will make of him too. M. Henri offers him death as the means of recovering Eurydice, "a Eurydice of the genuine features that life would never have given you." Orpheus struggles weakly against the allurements of death, then gives in and commits suicide. In the hotel room Orpheus' father wakes to find him gone. Alarmed, he is questioning M. Henri as Eurydice enters, leading Orpheus.

EURYDICE: Will he be able to look at me?

M. HENRI: Yes, without ever being afraid of losing you.[8]

[7] Anouilh, *Eurydice*, trans. Kitty Black, in Jean Anouilh, *Five Plays* (New York: Hill & Wang, 1958), pp. 55-120. Produced in England as *Point of Departure*, in the United States as *Legend of Lovers*. Quotations are from this version.
[8] *Ibid.*, p. 120.

The lovers embrace. Neither the father nor the hotel waiter can see them, only M. Henri can do that. Death is the true climate of love.

John Masefield said long ago, "Love is an active passion." Certainly it ought to be in drama if it is to have much reality. We see the lyrical scene of the lovers' meeting and another after they have consummated their love. But we do not see them realize their love for each other in any *action*. At first Eurydice fights —lies—to preserve that love by hiding her past, but she quickly turns tail and runs away to inadvertent, but fated, death. We do not have, as in *Romeo and Juliet*, a perfect love destroyed by outside forces. The seeds of dissolution are within it from the start, in Orpheus' insistence on the perfection of his ideal and in Eurydice's cowardice about her promiscuous past. Most important, perhaps, we do not have characters whose will to live is intensified by their love, so that they are moved to struggle greatly for its preservation. This would add to, not detract from, the poignancy of a young love cut off in the flush of youth; and it would give it dramatic rather than lyrical intensity.

There is a striking contrast between what the characters say and what they do, as there is between the roles assigned them by the myth and the kind of people the playwright has made them. At their first encounter, before they even know each other's names, there is this exchange:

EURYDICE: . . . How strange it is! Here we are, the two of us, standing face to face, with everything that's going to happen drawn up ready and waiting behind us. . . .

ORPHEUS: D'you think much is going to happen?

EURYDICE [*gravely*]: Everything. All the things that happen to a man and woman on earth, one by one. . . .

ORPHEUS: Gay things, sweet things, terrible things?

EURYDICE [*gently*]: Shameful things and filthy things. . . .

ORPHEUS [*taking her into his arms*]: How wonderful! [9]

And at the end of Act I, when Eurydice's most recent paramour, Mathias, has thrown himself under a train out of unrequited love, the lovers stand pressed against each other; and the mythic framework of the action is stressed:

ORPHEUS: Our story is beginning. . . .

[9] *Ibid.*, p. 66.

EURYDICE: I'm a little afraid. . . . Are you good, or wicked? What's your name?

ORPHEUS: It's Orpheus. What's yours?

EURYDICE: Eurydice.[10]

All this has a poignant irony, because Orpheus forgets his joyful anticipation of *living*—"all the things that happen to a man and woman on earth"—as soon as he begins to encounter the "terrible, shameful and filthy" things in Eurydice's past. His love clashes with his ideal of love which makes him desire the truth about his beloved; and the truth wins. It wins again when they meet in the ghostly station after Eurydice's death. The idealist in love (Innocence) proves less capable of living that love than Eurydice (Experience). This would be a valid point, but it is not what Anouilh is saying in the play and is therefore canceled by the underlying statement.

By the time Orpheus has looked at Eurydice and lost her, Anouilh has proved his case for the mutability of love—at least for *these* characters, performing *these* actions, under *these* circumstances. If he had wished to show simply what sort of thing can destroy love, this action would have sufficed. And Orpheus' tragic realization would drive home the point of his loss. But this would imply that, had Orpheus taken his beloved on her own terms, or been less exigent, their love need never have died. The drama would have developed its own inevitability—which is what we would prefer it to do—instead of having followed a priori assumptions. As it is, the outcome is a foregone conclusion, imposed by the playwright, of course, as it would be in any case, but not emerging necessarily from the combination of characters and situation.

But this is because Anouilh will not admit the possibility of love's survival in life. The other "black" plays show the same pattern: love cannot survive life. And the "rose" plays emphasize by their insistent theatricality that durable love is a theatrical formula, not a fact of life.

The hypothetical ending suggested above follows the myth rather than Anouilh's alteration; it is significant that it could be dramatized without Orpheus' father or Eurydice's mother. In the play as written, strictly speaking, the parents do nothing one

[10] *Ibid.*, p. 83.

way or the other to affect the course of the love affair. They contribute nothing materially to the plot by their acts; they simply are what they are, and that is enough for Anouilh's purpose. For they are on hand simply to show, by their fraudulent vitality and sentimental affectations, what living does to people and their loves. This points to the curious lack of conflict in the structure of the play, which instead gives us contrasts. The juxtaposition of the lovers and their elders is, then, vital to the theme or statement of the play, not to its action. Anouilh depicts condition more than action; and for the inevitability of drama he substitutes the inevitability of "life."

Lest we should miss the point, M. Henri is there to spell it out to Orpheus: his love will be compromised by living, and he will settle for a delusive happiness.

As the attendant of death, M. Henri is the one supernatural character in Anouilh's three mythic plays. He is a kind of Heurtebise in street dress, deftly inserted into the seemingly realistic milieu at rise and kept on stage until it is time for him to drop his inconspicuousness and become oracular. He is an anomaly in the throng of sharply drawn characters in Anouilh's theatre, almost colorless despite his portentous function. He is given only minimal characterization, as if Anouilh wished to draw attention only to what he has to say and not to who or what he is. His solicitations cannot be interpreted consistently as projections of Orpheus' conscience or "death-wish," just as the scene in hell cannot be interpreted as the externalizing of Orpheus' torment or as a dream or such-like evasions: too much is said and shown by M. Henri which Orpheus could not possibly think or know. This is so despite the fact that "in Anouilh the gods have become the conscience itself, the memory of things done in the past."[11] M. Henri is a compromise with the surface realism of the play, and not a successful one; for if we forget the spectral visitant behind the slouch hat, mackintosh, and ever-ready cigarette case, then his soft verbal nudges and hypnotic praise of easeful death fail of their effect.

He speaks to the lovers for the first time, telling them of Mathias' death under the train. As if exchanging the confidences of a stranger, he talks to them of death:

[11] Marsh, *Jean Anouilh*, p. 95.

THE YOUNG MAN: . . . It never hurts to die. Death never hurts anybody. Death is gentle. . . .

EURYDICE: . . . We don't even know you.

THE YOUNG MAN: But I know you. I'm very glad to have met you both. . . . I hope I'll have the pleasure of meeting you again? [12]

He turns up in the hotel room in Marseilles, just after Eurydice has fled, and insinuates himself into Orpheus' life and thoughts, calling himself "M. Henri" ("My name won't mean anything to you").

M. HENRI [*looks at ORPHEUS for a long time, smiling*]: Little Orpheus and Mademoiselle Eurydice. . . . One doesn't get such a stroke of luck every day. . . . I shouldn't have spoken to you. . . . But I couldn't resist the urge to know you better—I don't know why. . . . You must be wondering why I take such an interest in you. . . . I was at the back of the restaurant yesterday when she came to you, as if called by your music. These moments when we catch a glimpse of Fate laying her snares are very exciting, aren't they? [13]

This speech gives a fair example of Anouilh's technique in presenting M. Henri. He is forced to temporize dramaturgically, because the lines are meant to point to the uniqueness of the lovers and their involvement in the myth, and at the same time neutralize Orpheus' naturalistic responses and confine them to his own dilemma.

Having praised death at length, M. Henri goes on to preach Anouilh's philosophy of the two races—the heroic, "pale and tragic," and "the masses, teeming and happy. . . ." He tries to nudge Orpheus toward death, as a pander nudges toward lust:

M. HENRI: . . . Hasn't that sort of thing ever attracted you?

ORPHEUS: Never; and this evening less than usual.

M. HENRI [*going to him and laying his hand on his shoulder; looking at him, almost tenderly*]: It's a pity. You shouldn't believe too blindly in happiness. Particularly not when you belong to the good race. You're only laying up disappointments for yourself. [14]

Then the news comes of Eurydice's death in the bus crash, and M. Henri takes Orpheus to the deserted station for the reunion. There is an apt economy in this choice of hell, for we associate with it all the characters whom Anouilh would have us regard

[12] Anouilh, *Eurydice*, p. 83.
[13] *Ibid.*, p. 95.
[14] *Ibid.*, pp. 95-96.

as walking dead—Orpheus' father, Eurydice's mother and her lover Vincent, Dulac the impresario, and so on—"the masses, people who just live, ordinary people." Before Eurydice appears, M. Henri again woos Orpheus for death, but the youth reiterates his wish for a full life:

ORPHEUS: Whatever she is, I love her still. I want to see her again. Ah, I beg you, give her back to me, however imperfect. I want to suffer and be ashamed because of her. I want to lose her, and find her again. I want to hate her, and rock her gently afterward, like a little child. I want to struggle, to suffer, to accept. . . . I want to live. . . .

M. HENRI [*annoyed*]: Of course you'll live. . . .

ORPHEUS: With the mistakes, the failures, the despair, the fresh starts . . . the shame.

M. HENRI [*looks at him, scornful and tender; murmurs*]: Poor boy. . . .[15]

But the subsequent meeting of the lovers proves that Orpheus had learned nothing, and this picture of himself as accepting suffering, struggle, and all the myriad possibilities of life has no dramatic reality. Anouilh neither gives it any reality nor makes any dramatic capital out of the gross discrepancy between intention and action. We should remember, at this point, that Orpheus is still saying yes to life and no to death. (Anouilh's characters have much more assertive vigor when they rebel against life and say yes to death.) His idealism takes the form of a compulsive self-laceration from which he learns nothing about himself, and almost nothing about love, except that it is not for this world.

In the flashbacks that explain Eurydice's promiscuity to Orpheus, we see her mother and Vincent affecting the grand passion. And now the dead Eurydice joins M. Henri in persuading Orpheus: "You see, darling. We mustn't complain too much. . . . You were right. In trying to be happy, we might perhaps have become like them. . . ." Then, with Eurydice consigned to the shades once more by her lover, M. Henri renews the attack, this time aided by the father's reminiscences of his sexual conquests:

M. HENRI: . . . he's saying what you'll see tomorrow in every eye, if you get up and try to start life again. . . . But Eurydice can be given back to you forever. The Eurydice of your first meeting, eternally pure and young, eternally herself.

[15] *Ibid.*, pp. 103-4.

ORPHEUS: . . . No.

M. HENRI [*smiling*]: Why not?

ORPHEUS: I hate death.

M. HENRI: . . . Life would never have allowed you to keep Eurydice.

ORPHEUS: I don't want to die.

M. HENRI: Then listen to your father, Orpheus. He can tell you about life.[16]

The father, as horrible example, represents the clinching argument. Orpheus accepts death with the assurance that now he will be able to look at Eurydice "without ever being afraid of losing her." Basically, the ending is very like that of Cocteau's *Orphée*: "Orphée is a poet who loses love in the search for poetic truth and finally achieves both in the realm of the dead." [17] Orpheus is an idealist who loses love in the search for the truth about his beloved and he also achieves both in the realm of the dead.

An afterlife is certainly an equivocal device in Anouilh's theatre if it is to represent more than fantasy. But let us grant him poetic license. We still look for poetic justice: what has Orpheus done to *earn* his reunion with his beloved? The answer is nothing, unless we see his insistence upon the truth as tantamount to saying no to life. For Anouilh this defiant gesture is payment enough. Death is the only way for a character to retrieve the purity of his love, as it is to regain the lost innocence of childhood.

When the play was produced in London, Ivor Brown said, with some justification, that it preached a "cult of death." But if we are not to take M. Henri's solicitations literally—and his very presence, together with the use of the myth, discourages that—the question arises as to what the play says. And here there is an interesting division of opinion which seems to be based not on how realistic the play is thought to be, but on how pessimistic each critic thinks Anouilh is. He has written the play many times, with or without myth, both before and after *Eurydice*, and in each of these, the hero (or heroine), whether

16 *Ibid.*, p. 116.
17 Neal Oxenhandler, *Scandal and Parade: The Theatre of Jean Cocteau* (New Brunswick, N.J.: Rutgers University Press, 1957), p. 74.

or not love is the reason for his search, tries to realize himself in this life and fails. The largest group of Anouilh's heroes achieves redemption in death.[18]

A strong admirer of Anouilh's theatre finds that he uses the myth to give a "parable of the futility and sordidness of life . . . all the elements of Greek tragic inevitability," and draws the general conclusion: "Men are born to entertain hopeless aspirations . . . for they are eternally damned by the impossibility of reconciling the baseness of everyday life with the grander qualities of their minds." [19] This critic says further: "Jean Anouilh was not writing propaganda for general suicide in *Eurydice*," but notes that for "those who pursue the ideal," death is the "only solution," for "life maintains incessant war on the ideal"; and so "each play is a modified dissertation on the values of life and death." [20] The implication here is that love is doomed to defeat in this life, and what is worse, to corruption. If death restores and preserves it pure and unchanged, that is surely saying that life cannot.

Quite a different view is offered by another admirer of the play, who rests his case for its "elusive" but "challenging and positive" meaning upon "the order in which it presents its impressions." [21]

The intricate preparation of Acts I and II, the protracted struggles of Eurydice in Act III and of Orpheus in Act IV, convey their belief in an ideal, in a way of life which is real and worth suffering and dying for. Their symbolic deaths are but to emphasize their determination to make the tragic sacrifice to preserve this inviolate. A fictitious impression of the impossibility of purity in human relations is a real statement of the desirability of it. . . . In *Eurydice*, in effect, only ideal happiness is suppressed—because the nature of this happiness is the subject under discussion. We the audience are invited to supply what is missing.[22]

This is to place the play in the category of literature of contrast. But it is totally beside the questions the play raises. One accepts (with the aid of myth) the *reality* of their love and far more its

---

[18] David I. Grossvogel, *The Self-conscious Stage in Modern French Drama* (New York: Columbia University Press, 1958), p. 145.
[19] Marsh, *Jean Anouilh*, pp. 91, 94.
[20] *Ibid.*, pp. 103-4.
[21] J. L. Styan, *The Elements of Drama* (Cambridge: Cambridge University Press, 1960), pp. 217-27.
[22] *Ibid.*, pp. 225, 227.

desirability. What we seek in the play is some indication as to the *possibility* of its survival in life; the "fictitious impression" of that impossibility happens to be by far the strongest impression the play makes—much stronger, for the reasons noted, than that of their love's reality. " 'Pessimistic', any more than 'optimistic', should not be a critical pejorative," adds the critic, in what is to me a highly questionable position; the term is certainly pertinent to the meaning of the play.[23]

The action of the play is precisely the birth of love, its erosion by life, and its restoration in death. The emergence of the myth repeatedly presents (although with dubious effectiveness) the lovers as exceptional and their love as a great love; the known direction of the myth (up to a point) is relied on to give a strong and classic sense of "Fate laying her snares," because life does not permit great lovers, members of the "good race," to escape its trap. By the same token, death's interest in them is explained. M. Henri must be taken as supernatural; the authority of the myth is employed to show clearly that the lovers are capable of tragic action and that it is a *great* love that is going down to inevitable defeat, thus clinching the case. Anouilh's plays, moreover, achieve a strong sense of generalization, of a poetically stated but universal truth.[24]

By fleshing out the myth with two quite imperfect people as his lovers, Anouilh thwarts his purpose; on the one hand the effect is to cast doubt on the ability of a great love to survive, and this achieves his purpose; on the other hand it is to make us feel that he loads the dice against that love, as he does against the older people by painting their lives as unrelievedly and uniformly squalid in their grossness and affectation. Both the lovers lack confidence in the power of love. Eurydice is afraid of its fragility; Orpheus is implacable in his demands on the beloved. The end of the play proves her right, for lack of any acts to the contrary on the part of either. In other words Anouilh depends upon the myth to do the work he has not done—and, moreover, will not do because of his a priori judgment of life. Thus, while his lovers may not be conscious of their mythical status as were other characters we have examined, they are infected with the

---

[23] I dislike taking issue with a work which in every other respect I regard as a genuine contribution to the understanding of drama.
[24] See Marsh, *Jean Anouilh*, pp. 182, 185.

playwright's pessimism, as well as its converse, his defeated idealism. As a result, they are rendered pusillanimous and defeatist. And they are conscious of the erosion of their love, although Orpheus remains blind to those actions of his which help to erode it. Orpheus in hell says: "Why didn't you tell me everything the first day? The first day I might have been able to understand. . . ."

The real conflict in the play is not in the action but in the playwright's attitude toward life; and that attitude is pessimistic.

II. *Antigone*

The première of Jean Anouilh's *Antigone*, based on Sophocles, was held at the Atelier, Paris, February, 1944. Time has given an ironic perspective to what was once an exciting episode of French theatre under the German occupation during World War II. This modern version of the classic struggle between Creon, ruler of Thebes, and his niece Antigone, who resists his edict to the death, became a rallying point for the civilians of Paris in their resistance to their German overlords.

Despite electricity failures, lack of heat, and the danger of air-raids, the crowds at the performances of *Antigone* increased, and the spectators responded with a popular enthusiasm rare in French theatre. Antigone's stubborn determination to give her brother's body religious burial, knowing all the while that Creon would put her to death for disobeying him, became identified in their minds with their refusal to withhold aid from underground fighters or to turn them over to the Germans. Her rejections of persuasion or force, her categorical "No!" to Creon's repeated commands to submit, symbolized for the conquered Parisians their refusal to admit defeat. But it was this interpretation given to the symbol that made the play deeply significant for them, not the playwright's meaning. And by the time the Liberation came, *Antigone* had become a different play: "When I took friends to see it who had recently come back to Paris, I was astonished to feel no longer the same tension between stage and audience. . . . The explanation is that with the Liberation the tension between constraint and clandestinity suddenly vanished. It was now necessary to sympathize with *Antigone* by an intellectual effort, whereas formerly one had been in conspiracy with it." [25] Anouilh's attitude toward life—one of nonacceptance, rejection of all established religious and cultural values, permanent revolt—was already familiar to Parisians. What they had actually been responding to, apart from their own attributions of meaning, was not a disguised call to struggle and revolt against their conquerors, but an expression of a total rejection of life, a revolt against the fact of existence itself. Had they responded directly to the burden of the play, they would have provoked their masters to a blood-bath for the sole purpose of asserting their freedom (for Anouilh, the only genuine freedom) to die. One would have thought, speaking in general terms, that life is a categorical yes; but it remained for Anouilh to provide his countrymen the "Sweet, sweet, sweet poison for the age's tooth."

One can imagine the consternation of the American producers of the play when they saw what they had purchased—a "hit play" (more than five hundred performances in Paris) about a heroine who insists upon dying for no ascertainable reason.[26] To protect their investment, they adapted it to stress a political motivation for Antigone's rebellion and thus restored to it something of Sophocles' treatment.[27]

To stress the timeless nature of its protest, the play takes place in a neutral setting; the characters wear inconspicuous modern dress; the prose dialogue, with its colloquialisms, anachronisms, and barracks talk, can be traced back to Cocteau's earlier efforts at modernizing the classics; and so can the formal device of the informal Chorus, who addresses the audience directly as the actors of the drama sit about in frozen attitudes. The Chorus does more than provide exposition. He foretells the action to eliminate all surprise (not suspense) and comments like a novelist, in order to condition the spectator to what is to come. In Greek fashion he talks to the principals, or rather to Creon only; he is very much aware that this is tragedy he is exhibiting, that the action is all preordained, and that it will roll down through time:

[25] The account is given by Béatrix Dussane in *Notes de théâtre 1940-1950* (Paris: Lardanchet, 1951); the translation, Harold Hobson's, in his *The French Theatre of To-day* (London: George C. Harrap, 1953), p. 45.

[26] Anouilh, *Antigone*, trans. and adapted by Lewis Galantière, in Jean Anouilh, *Five Plays*, pp. 1-53.

[27] James H. Clancy discusses the principal changes made and their effects in "The American Antigone," *Educational Theatre Journal*, IV, no. 3 (October, 1954), 249-59.

CHORUS: . . . You are out of your mind, Creon. What have you done?

CREON: . . . She had to die.

CHORUS: You must not let Antigone die. We shall carry the scar of her death for centuries.[28]

And he lectures us on tragedy, sounding like Cocteau's voice out of time:

CHORUS: The spring is wound up tight. It will uncoil of itself. That is what is so convenient in tragedy. The least little turn of the wrist will do the job. Anything will set it going: a glance at a girl who happens to be lifting her arms to her hair as you go by. . . .

And so on. Obviously, this is a different view of tragedy from the Greek. It may be, as the Chorus says, that "inhuman forces" whirl Antigone out of this world, but the world Anouilh presents through his Chorus is not one of inevitability worked out through the laws of the universe; instead, it is a world of pure contingency, where chance sets the infernal machine unwinding, and thereafter, somehow, it is to operate inevitably. It is a world of the absurd; Antigone's protest will be against no specific, concrete action or situation which might be suffered, or prevented, or changed, or even simply understood; it will be against the nature of life, indeed the fact of living. Creon's edict will be for her, as well as for Anouilh, merely a pretext for incurring her death, because she refuses to continue living on life's terms.

The Chorus begins to sound like M. Henri, selling eternal rest:

Tragedy is clean, it is restful, it is flawless. . . .
In a tragedy, nothing is in doubt and everyone's destiny is known. That makes for tranquility. There is a sort of fellow-feeling among characters in a tragedy: he who kills is as innocent as he who gets killed: it's all a matter of what part you are playing. Tragedy is restful; and the reason is that hope, that foul, deceitful thing, has no part in it. There isn't any hope. You're trapped.[29]

Life a kind of theatrical performance, action devoid of moral significance, hope something not even the characters of the tragedy have—these ideas are audience-conditioning for a play built upon absurdity; and so the playwright needs to convince us as much as possible in advance, if he can, in order not only that the action may seem inevitable, but also that the heroine's

[28] Anouilh, *Antigone*, pp. 44-45.
[29] *Ibid.*, pp. 23-24.

rebellion will seem to have for us a basis in reality. It is difficult
to sympathize with what we cannot accept as credible.

Like Cocteau in *The Infernal Machine*, Anouilh seems overly
insistent on the inevitability of the action. Here he adds to the
technique the use of direct theatricality to assist him. To emphasize that this is a play—but a "tragedy," the best kind—to show
us the characters and tell their fates beforehand, to stress that
they have "inevitable" roles to play ("When your name is Antigone, there is only one part you can play; and she will have
to play hers through to the end"): such a priori assumptions
beg the question, borrow their associations, and steal the authority of the past. And at the end of the play, Chorus appears
and says: "And there we are," as if he had offered us proof.
"Quod erat demonstrandum."

He also says, "It is all over. Antigone is calm tonight, and we
shall never know the name of the fever that consumed her."
The name of the fever is Anouilh's pessimism, and it is interesting to see the devices he uses to avoid the suspicion that his
heroine is an hysteric and to make the irrational action both
palatable and seemingly inevitable.

There is first the business of preparing us about certain things
so that we will not be surprised. Say that she is a "tense, sallow,
willful girl whose family would never take her seriously"; when
she lives up to her description, we shall be convinced and even
think that we have a hint of psychological motivation. "Antigone
is young. She would much rather live than die. But there is no
help for it." With this, Antigone must demonstrate her love of
life, yet convince us that she must nonetheless die. This is difficult, because it is mostly her detestation of life that we see in
the play.

Some of the difficulty can be gotten round by beginning the
play *after* she has committed her rebellious act: plunge into the
middle of things, present the spectators an accomplished fact
which can be withheld to come as a surprise, and go on from
there. It is much easier to believe that something has already
happened, or even that it will happen, than that it is happening.
The device has already been used in variant form by Chorus: he
tells us of an action that has already happened, that what we are
about to see is, in fact, already over and done.

To show Antigone's love of life, we have a description of the beauty of the world at dawn; then we see evidence of her love for her old Nurse, from whom her decision to die is already isolating her. Show her as strong and Ismene, her sister, as weak, and regard the matter as settled:

ISMENE: Creon will have us put to death.

ANTIGONE: Of course he will. That's what he's here for. He will do what he has to do and we will do what we have to do.[30]

Show Antigone as having lived intensely. ("Who was it that was always the first out of bed because she loved the touch of the cold morning air on her bare skin? Who was always the last to bed because nothing less than infinite weariness could wean her from the lingering night?") This will not be inconsistent with her pessimism, because in Anouilh's theatre childhood is the time of innocence, when life is very heaven; it is growing up that means corruption and compromise. Show her momentarily weak, suffering at the thought of what awaits her: an audience instinctively responds to suffering and does not stop to ask the why of it. Use pathos: show Antigone concerned for the pet dog she will leave behind. Then show the scene with Haemon, her fiance, in which she makes her farewells. Have her tell him what a devoted wife and fine mother she would have made and that she loves and wishes to be loved. But be careful: don't present these things as good in themselves. After all, they are part of corrupting life; present them instead as things Antigone *wants*—this way, they will be part of her "purity," her imperious demands on life which filthy life is not going to let her have because (we know) she is going to die. But swear Haemon to silence, *so that he may not ask questions*; there must be no need to explain, argue, or defend the indefensible until the big scene with Creon; and so the audience may forget that it is she who elects to die. After all this, finally make the revelation: "You are too late, Ismene. When you first saw me this morning, I had just come in from burying him." With this *coup de théâtre* fired, switch at once to Creon and the guards and involve the audience with that side of the struggle. Once in deeply enough, the spectators may be caught up in the rush of the action, thus preventing reflection. Then show Antigone man-

[30] *Ibid.*, pp. 10-11.

handled by the brutal guards before she engages in the central debate with Creon.

For that, you must appear to give Creon a very strong case. The stronger and more menacing he is, the more he represents not only political and military strength but the full weight of organized society, then the more lorn, lonely, and defenseless Antigone will appear. And so the audience will sympathize all the more, because it always sympathizes with the underdog. Make certain that these attitudes and their accompanying emotions are thoroughly roused before going into the dialectics of pessimistic rebellion. Then:

CREON: My dear, I woke up one morning and found myself King of Thebes. God knows, there were other things I loved in life more than power.

ANTIGONE: Then you should have said no.

CREON: Yes, I could have done that. Only, I felt that it would have been cowardly. I should have been a workman who turns down a job that has to be done. So I said yes.

ANTIGONE: So much the worse for you, then. I didn't say yes. I can say no to anything I think vile, and I don't have to count the cost. But because you said yes, all that you can do, for all your crown and trappings, and your guards—all that you can do is to have me killed.[31]

Then beat down Antigone's resolve with the sordid politics of the civil war and spring the revelation that the bodies of her brothers were indistinguishable on the battlefield, that Creon himself does not know which one it was he gave a state funeral and enshrined as a patriot, and which he left to rot unburied as a warning to subversives. Finally, point out that it doesn't matter in any case, since both Eteocles and Polynices were equally dirty revolutionaries and *both* had conspired against their father's life.

When Antigone seems to have capitulated, begin the slow build on the word "happiness." Present happiness as cowardly compromise, an acceptance of all that is filthy, before you have Antigone scream out her rebellion against it:

ANTIGONE: I spit on your happiness! I spit on your idea of life— that life must go on, come what may. You are all like dogs that lick everything they smell. . . . I want to be sure of everything this very

[31] *Ibid.*, p. 35.

day; sure that everything will be as beautiful as when I was a little
girl. If not, I want to die! [32]

Then present the scene between Creon and his son Haemon,
followed by the prison scene, with Antigone dictating to one of
the guards her farewell letter to Haemon: "And I don't even
know what I am dying for." But we know why she is dying.
Creon diagnoses it correctly in speaking to the Chorus: "Death
was her purpose, whether she knew it or not. Polynices was a
mere pretext. When she had to give up that pretext, she found
another one—that life and happiness were tawdry things and not
worth possessing. She was bent upon only one thing: to reject
life and die." [33]

Any playwright works with such calculation to obtain the
effects he wishes. What is interesting in Anouilh's case is
that his premise forces him to *involve and move* his audience,
whereas Cocteau may have been trying to cool off the action
and permit his audience the maximum in reflective detachment.
And many of the same formal devices—the Chorus, the reliance
on myth, the emphasis on seeming inevitability—are used to
accomplish *opposite* results. It is significant to me that the chief
thing Anouilh avoided was a preliminary scene (like that in
Sophocles) in which Antigone would debate her reasons for
what she was going to do. He was wise to present the fact before the issue, and justified, too, by the character of Antigone,
who acts out of instinct and not reason. Chance, which Chorus
holds up to us as the fuse of tragedy, leads to an explosion only
if the character is one of "pure" instinct, like Antigone; for then,
indeed, anything that violates her desire to live life entirely on
her own terms will set it off.

"We are of the tribe that asks questions, and we ask them to
the bitter end," says Antigone. But the one thing she never questions is her right to demand of life that it shall enable her "to
be sure of everything this very day." This assertion of the instinctive will, this "purity," is for Anouilh sacrosanct, even more
than is love (for love is so ephemeral in a stained world that
the hope of preserving it becomes one of life's strongest de-
lusions); it must hurl the defiance of its "No!" into the teeth of
life "until no tiniest chance of hope remains to be strangled by

[32] *Ibid.*, pp. 42-43.
[33] *Ibid.*, p. 45.

our hands." This is the first question that Anouilh's emotional treatment of the myth is able to suppress from the consciousness of the audience. And the second is related to it: what does a permanent attitude of rebellion, a perpetual no, permit one to do? How can freedom be so negative a thing?

Attending a revival of the play in 1949 after having seen the original production, Gabriel Mercel wrote: "The play holds, undeniably; whether one likes it or not, he cannot fail to recognize that it is one of the strongest and most significant in contemporary theatre. I would freely admit that it is a witness-play, and it is that aspect of it on which I would insist today. Witness to a world utterly degraded; and if the stench that rises from *Antigone* is at times almost intolerable, that is because the author himself does not seem to realize all that this world has lost."[34]

III. *Medea*

When he came to write his version of the Medea myth,[35] Anouilh concentrated it in a one-act "black" play of Strindbergian intensity. The drama is a kind of mythic "Dance of Death"; the story of Jason and Medea is seen as the last hysterical spasms of sexual hatred and warfare between man and woman. Sexual union is presented as the strongest corruptor, and therefore as the deadliest enemy, of "purity" of self. On this battleground rage all the themes of Anouilh's theatre which I listed in discussing *Eurydice*. In the ability of the play to contain them, we have an instructive example of the protean capacity, the multivalence of myth. We do not know the possibilities latent in a myth until a playwright has realized them; once he has done so, it seems almost fated that he should have been drawn to a particular myth as the vehicle that can condense all that he wishes to say. So it is with Anouilh and the myth of Medea.

Anouilh's inspiration here is Senecan, not Greek. But he surpasses the Roman playwright in horror. Seneca's Medea invokes the aid of Hecate, Pluto, demonic ghosts, the Furies, and the chaos of endless night, knowing that, to perform her dreadful

[34] Gabriel Marcel, *L'Heure théâtrale* (Paris: Librairie Plon, 1959), p. 102.
[35] Anouilh, *Medea*, trans. Luce and Arthur Klein, in Eric Bentley, ed., *The Modern Theatre*, V (Garden City, N.Y.: Doubleday Anchor Books, 1957), 180-213.

deeds, she must drive herself to madness. She rejects Jason with the furious threat, "If in my womb there still lurk any pledge of thee, I'll search my very vitals with the sword and hale it forth." Anouilh seizes on this violent image, compounded of sexuality and suicide: his Medea invites total possession by evil; she voluptuously welcomes the devil's embrace. And in all this, she believes—and Anouilh, incredibly, gives every indication of agreeing with her—that by coupling with the devil, by slaying herself as well as her children, she achieves not madness but true self-fulfillment. When Anouilh says, "The object of art is . . . to create something that is truer than truth," is *this* the sort of thing he means?

The piece is bold to the point of recklessness; it is imaginative, admirably economical, thoroughly expert—and I find I cannot believe a word of it. It dramatizes—or reduces—Anouilh's philosophy of the absurd to the last point of its logical absurdity. And the final mockery, for me, is that the playwright himself does not even seem to suspect, let alone fully appreciate, the nature and extent of his accomplishment: to have rendered patently ridiculous his long held world-view.

Neither Euripides nor Jeffers dealt much with the nature of the bond between Jason and Medea; they concentrated on the hatred and revenge of the woman scorned. Anouilh emphasizes the bond, making the encounter between the estranged lovers the heart of the play, as the long duel between Creon and his niece is the heart of *Antigone*. The action, as it explores the effects of that relationship, reveals in detail what their life together was like. This is not a change in the myth, so much as it is simply a new interpretation. But there are changes: first, in the character of Medea, who is disclosed as having been flagrantly unfaithful to Jason in attempting to break away from him; second, in the ending, where Medea triumphs by killing herself, as well as her children, and dying with them in the flames of her gypsy-wagon, to which she sets fire in a final gesture of destruction. This, of course, requires a radically different motivation which, aside from her wish to poison Jason's life further by stamping on his memory her own death throes ("And now try to forget her!"), enables her, by revenge and suicide, to free her "true" self so that it can triumph over her weak self, represented by her wish to return to the past. This "true" self, "demanding and pure," can affirm and realize itself fully only in death. And it is precisely this motivation, offered in all seriousness by the playwright, that renders the play absurd. It is believable that a person should do such things, perhaps believable also that he should rationalize them in such terms—but only if the person is regarded as insane.

Yet the "purity" Medea achieves, however paradoxical it turns out to be, is not something at all new in Anouilh. The difference is simply one of degree. This time it represents total commitment to absolute evil—and Medea herself recognizes it as such:

MEDEA [*alone*]: It is now, Medea, that you must be yourself . . . ! O, Evil! Great living beast who crawls on me and licks me, take me. I am yours tonight. I am your wife. Come into me, tear me, swell and burn in the middle of myself. You see, I welcome you, help you, open myself to you. . . .[36]

I forebear to quote more. This should be enough to indicate the level, intensity, and manner of her achieving true selfhood at last. There is a certain dreadful appropriateness in the scene: Medea is a witch, and this is literally a witch's Sabbath, a calling up of Satan as lover. But what is obviously the utter perversion of her humanity, an imperiously willed damnation, is presented by Anouilh as both heroic and tragic. And the implications of this—that the playwright himself does not stand apart from the demonic nightmare he has created, to judge and condemn it— are even more horrifying than the fictive spectacle of Medea's apotheosis. In the face of such truly appalling perversity (however willing one may be to grant out of charity that it is sincere), it would be gravely, inexcusably remiss to confine oneself to an appreciation of formal and technical excellences. As if they mattered at this point, except insofar as they render the idea persuasive! It is now entirely a question of the use to which these excellences are put; beside that question, esthetic concerns shrink into trivialities. That use is the communication of a profound blasphemy against life.

This play makes even Anouilh's admirers uneasy—an inadequate reaction, at best. But it will not do to regard the play as the dramatist's self-purging of the "last remnants" of a supposed "obsession with death";[37] self-purges need not be published or

[36] Anouilh, *Medea*, p. 208.
[37] Marsh, *Jean Anouilh*, p. 132.

performed. Besides, this is to blink the fact that the play is a masterly synthesis of all Anouilh's previously dramatized themes and standard attitudes of his exigent heroes and heroines; it simply extends to its logical conclusion the rebellion against the world and the hatred of life which can be found more or less in suspension in Anouilh's theatre, up to the time that Antigone opted for the absurd to prove her moral superiority.

Nor will it do to see in the hysterical violence of this play its author's repudiation of his former views, and point to the relatively sympathetic treatment of Creon and Jason as indicating, at long last, his rebellion against rebellion itself. However much one might wish to hold this view, the ambiguities of the work militate against it, as they militated against any affirmative statement in the earlier plays.[38] We are not dealing with logical attitudes in Anouilh but with the emotional attitudes of an "instinctive" writer. The basic inconsistencies of his emotional position are not new to his work, but implicit from the beginning; and they continue to appear in later plays, which do not bear out the hoped-for change of heart.[39]

What is the difference between a character Anouilh obviously

---

[38] Lest my reading of the play should seem a purely private and solitary view, I offer the following evidence:

"The only way she can fulfill herself is by giving herself to the evil that she feels is her most real self. . . . In order to become herself she must destroy her children, which not only are a living testimony of her compromise with Jason, but represent a will to live and be happy." Pronko, *World of Jean Anouilh*, pp. 31, 32.

"There is a fundamental weakness in the heroic revolt of Anouilh's characters, for it is not based upon any universal criterion of what should or should not be. It may stand as a criticism of life and of a universe in which this must be so, in which perhaps there are no universal values. . . . But as a practical solution to man's problems it is not valid. Perhaps this is indicative of Anouilh's belief that man's problem has no valid solution." *Ibid.*, p. 34.

"Anouilh's view of life and man's place in the universe has remained essentially unchanged throughout his career. . . . To be sure, there is a certain development and a shift in focus as the author matures. But it is noteworthy that Anouilh's basic concepts are present from the beginning and have not changed fundamentally in the course of almost thirty years." *Ibid.*, pp. 3-4.

"His view of the world and of human existence has not altered through the years. . . . The constancy of theme in [his] plays gives his work, taken as a whole, the appearance and the forcefulness of an ideology." Wallace Fowlie, *Dionysus in Paris: A Guide to Contemporary Theater* (New York: Meridian Books, 1960), pp. 112, 114.

[39] Marsh, *Jean Anouilh*, pp. 134, 164, 179, 181, 199.

abominates—the Inquisitor in *The Lark* (written seven years after *Medea*), who is insane in his hatred of man—and a Medea whom Anouilh pities and admires for her "purity," although she is equally insane in her hatred of life? Isn't a defiant "no" to man pretty close to saying the same to life? How can one be hateful and the other admirable? How do we discriminate, when both deal out death? If this play is for Anouilh a recantation, how curious it is that it should be in no way different, except in degree, from all its "black" predecessors! Ambiguity at such a time is a vice.

It is ironic that some should see a change of heart in a play where the dramatist has exceeded human tolerance and perpetrated what has elsewhere been called "the abuse of the terrible." At this point, talk about "poetic truth" becomes not only inadequate but irresponsible—as if a poet were not, after all, human like the rest of us, with the same obligation to use his reason as best he can. Art has its limits, though it may be thought indelicate to say so. I propose that to base art upon a philosophy of the absurd is to deprive art of both rationale and meaning, and hence of beauty.

Anouilh is generally admitted to be the most expert playwright in Europe, possibly in the world, today. He seems able to contrive any theatrical effect he wishes: no mixing of emotional tones, no fusing of contrasts, seems beyond his artistry. He is limited only by his view of man and his valuation of life; but these limitations are so extreme as to invalidate his art.

Such enormous technical skill ought to be sufficient proof of his personal detachment from his materials, ought to attest sufficiently to his objectivity, that one could dissociate the man from his work. But when his plays are taken as a whole, his pessimism is so overwhelming that he seems to be writing not out of artistic detachment, but out of a furious hatred of life that would consume him if he could not channel it through art. It is this which prompts critic after critic to make a distinction between content and form in his plays. This, for example: "As a study of human character, it is hysterical and often foul-mouthed. As a piece of dramatic architecture, it is . . . exquisitely gripping." [40] Or this: "The ideological conflict [in many of his plays] is paral-

[40] Kenneth Tynan, *Curtains* (New York: Atheneum, 1961), p. 396. The reference is to *Pauvre Bitos*.

leled in the amazing contrast . . . between a virtuoso's technique
and the gravity of a revolt against human fate." [41] And the general reaction reflects and widens the critical gap: "The plays of
Jean Anouilh are either judged to be important works of art containing the philosophic resonances that are the signs of genius, or
they are dismissed as trivial melodramas in a novel tone." [42]

Because of the acrid bite of his anger, his attacks on hypocrisy,
self-deception, greed, lust, and so on, we assume that the author
is a moralist. Consequently, we try to judge his attitude as ar-
biter toward the dramatic conflicts in his plays. I suggest that
it is a mistake to try to do so, because the plays provide no
reasonable or truly consistent basis from which to judge. Harold
Hobson makes an observation that may explain this grave de-
ficiency: "His plays are not made out of moral categories. He is
an instinctive writer, for whom feeling replaces reflexion and
thought." [43] A morality of feeling is what we ordinarily expect
of a moron or a disturbed adolescent. In this case, the feeling
is frozen into a permanent rage at finding life and people not
what the moralist would like them to be; the inevitable results
are misanthropy and pessimism. It is especially interesting that
some of Anouilh's most objectionable characters, toward whom
he is savage, are moralists; they proceed, however, not according
to feeling but according to their sense of right and wrong. Such,
for example, is Julien in *Colombe*. He is as intransigent and demanding of life as Colombe, his wife, is easy-going and unde-
manding. The play, like *Medea*, and for that matter like *Eurydice*, is a story of estrangement, an X-shaped conflict that
results (we think) from excessive actions on the part of both; the
detached playwright's position must lie somewhere in between.
On the contrary, Anouilh's sympathies are with the loose-living
Colombe. And Julien? "In this odious character Anouilh expresses
his instinctive reaction to people who conduct their lives, not
according to feeling, but to ideas of what is good and what is
evil." [44] These right-wrong moralists are curious projections of
the playwright, who, in his "feeling" morality, is every bit as
exigent as they.

[41] Fowlie, *Dionysus in Paris*, p. 123.
[42] Marsh, *Jean Anouilh*, pp. 17-18.
[43] Hobson, *The French Theatre*, p. 203.
[44] *Ibid.*, p. 205.

But the obverse of his morality of feeling leads not to charity but to sentimentality. No more lethal attacks on sexual promiscuity have been written for the stage of our day than *Ardèle* and *The Waltz of the Toreadors*. How consistent is this moralist of feeling, then, in approving sexual promiscuity in his string of soiled heroines, Eurydice included, in all of whom it is "an admirable thing if only it proceeds from kindness of heart, unselfishness, and the desire not to give pain"? [45] So far, I think, we have been spared the cliché of the harlot with a heart of gold, but only because these heroines have maintained their amateur standing.

I have repeatedly echoed Anouilh's use of the word "purity," but without defining it. "Purity," like "dirty," is one of the key words in Anouilh's works. The desire for, or assertion of, "purity" is what motivates all his heroes and heroines; for each it has a separate meaning. A thorough comparative study of all Anouilh's plays [46] has shown the variant meanings they attach to it: wealth and social recognition; acceptance of the past, together with a rejection of easy habit; rejection of money and an easy life; a flight to maintain spontaneity and fellow-feeling; refusal to accept one's old self; "for Antigone, for Orphée, for Frederic and for Jeanette, purity can be found only in death; for Medée the same is true, with the distinction that she must find death through a return to her real self." But for none of them has it either the traditional meaning of sexual purity or any generally recognized moral meaning: "And the curious, the disturbing thing is that Anouilh perceives no incongruity in this. He does not, like Hardy, defy morality. He does not seem to know that it exists. He has a passion for purity, and he finds it in people who have no more sensitiveness over the sexual act than if they had been brought up in a brothel." [47]

If Anouilh were a cold tactician like Gide, we should suspect that such amphibology was a deliberate effort to darken counsel and so subvert traditional morality. He seems too emotional for that, however, yet without vacillating widely from play to play. But the recurrence of certain attitudes, inconsistent as they may be, eventually defines Anouilh's position: "Moods change, but a

---

[45] *Ibid.*
[46] Pronko, *World of Jean Anouilh*, p. 172.
[47] Hobson, *French Theatre*, p. 203.

man's stable moods correspond to the things he chooses to regard as important." [48]

The only way to achieve consistency is to subsume them all in Anouilh's consistent approval of the person who makes his imperious demands on life in the name of "purity." The social consequences of these violent assertions of will do not concern Anouilh except as they provide dramatic conflict. Why should a character hesitate to get his own way at whatever cost; why should he concern himself with the good of society, when in Anouilh's view it is society itself that corrupts and defeats him? True, responsibility is not entirely cast out—Jason felt it, perhaps Orpheus did also; but the bitch-goddess Life will pervert it as she does everything else, so that it is little more than a forlorn dream.

The summation of Anouilh's "feeling," and thus of his philosophy and morality (if we may stretch these words at the risk of distorting them), is simply the Romantic assertion of the "I" all over again. It is Michelet's "Moi! Ils m'arrachent mon moi!" It is Gide's reckless self-realization, the instinctive and emotional version of the titanism with which we began, here defeated by its own pessimism. The individual Ego is absolute, and the World is absolutely corrupting.

We have moved as far as possible from the religious view that the misfortunes of life constitute trials of the *spirit*, and that the spirit affirms itself and grows through such testing. We are equally far from the moral view that the obstacles of life constitute the rock on which *character* is tested and honed. Gide, with his moral athleticism, would at least have concurred with the latter; his heroes are not prevented from acting for fear of consequences. There is still an important difference between them and the entirely secularized, pusillanimous characters of Anouilh whose defiant "no" has only the appearance of strength, because, being in love with easeful death, they seem masochistically bent on self-destruction.

It is strange indeed that Anouilh's obsession with innocence and "purity" cannot encompass the one thing which belies his hopelessness: the idea, the fact, of sanctity. Perhaps this is because sanctity is something earned through action, and Anouilh,

[48] Hugh Kenner, *The Invisible Poet: T. S. Eliot* (London: W. H. Allen, 1960), p. 266.

as Hobson shrewdly noted, writes *"as if purity were in being and not in doing.* If there is a paradox here, it is one that Anouilh has not perceived." [49] The relevance of this attitude to drama (and to an existentialist view of life) is striking. Anouilh's exigent heroes assert their "purity"; but that is as far as they can go, because if they attempt to do something about it (other than die), they inevitably become corrupted or are defeated. Obviously, then, their purity can be only a state of being, not a form of action; for in this view, the moment you convert being into existence, you have compromised it.

Reviewing *La Sauvage* in 1949, Gabriel Marcel wrote: "But it seems that M. Anouilh is unaware even of the name of Christ. I know of no work to which the thought of the supernatural would seem stranger than it would to his. Thereby it witnesses —with what force! *for* that of which it is unaware." [50] If this is so, there is all the more reason for trepidation when Anouilh twice dramatizes the lives of canonized saints—St. Joan in *The Lark*, St. Thomas à Becket in *Becket; or The Honor of God*. Presumably it was not their sanctity that attracted him; sanctity, after all, has to do with morals, and these he finds repugnant. He ignores it as only one more illusion. And so there are no saints in Anouilh's mythic world, only heroes and heroines who project their desires upon life and call them their "purity." Clearly, the very idea of sanctity is inimical to his personal mythology of Innocence and Experience: it is a datum of that mythology that innocence is only something to be lost, never regained in this life. If it could be regained, perhaps even increased, his faith in the absurd—and with it his theatre—would be invalidated.

At his destructive worst, Gide, I believe, never questioned what was for him the categorical imperative: to live. All his efforts of self-assertion were his fierce determination to live precisely as he wished, regardless of others—but at least to live. It was puritanism he broke from; but in *Oedipe* the rejection of happiness in order to achieve self-transcendence is horrifying precisely because it marks the turning back of his revolt to the very puritanism he despised. There is a dreadful fascination in

[49] Hobson, *French Theatre*, p. 204 (emphasis added).
[50] Marcel, *L'Heure théâtrale*, p. 94.

watching him flee from his fate like Oedipus and—again like Oedipus—encounter in his flight and embrace the very thing he thought he was escaping!

Gide was determined to have his freedom though the heavens fell, and he helped substantially with the razing. But he was activist by temperament, as is Sartre. I doubt that he ever envisioned the wholesale destruction that Sartre would wreak as the logical extension of Gide's own premise. But Sartre's position, in its turn, looks positively optimistic compared to the atheistic pessimism of Anouilh.

Both the younger men took up the theme of the rejection of happiness and made it central to those dramas I have considered. Again I doubt that Gide, with his nineteenth-century faith in progress and science, could have foreseen what they would do with it. For now happiness is not to be rejected when it becomes delusive; it is to be rejected outright, everywhere and always, as delusive in itself. It has become "filthyhappiness"—one word, indivisible. What begins as a repudiation of bourgeois compromise becomes that and more in Sartre, and in Anouilh finally becomes "pure" illusion, all-pervasive, all-corrupting, so that not even an existentialist, having asserted his freedom and achieved the new anti-bourgeois happiness, could justify his indulging in it. Indeed, for Anouilh, not only is happiness dirty and delusive, but so also is hope; it too is one word, indivisible: *salespoir*.

To me, it is anything but accident that these views of happiness parallel in their development the Gidean idea of the gratuitous. This tiny, inexplicable quirk within him fascinated Gide: he saw it first as a kind of leak in the moral universe, a promise of a moral freedom from the stifling puritanism in which he was reared. He saw it next as the revelation of the subconscious self, the key to the emergence of the true self, and he transferred to it the imperious will to self-assertion of his conscious being. That true self must on no account be denied or suppressed, regardless of the consequences to oneself or others. As we saw, this is the motive for Philoctetes, and much more plainly so for King Candaules and Oedipus. They are the ancestors of Sartre's Orestes and Anouilh's Antigone and Medea; Gide's pervasive ideas were certainly an influence on both the younger men—part of the French air they breathed. His example is at the origins of Sartre's doctrinaire revolt, as it is one of the models for the frenetic self-assertions of "purity" among Anouilh's heroes. Gide began by finding the gratuitous in existence; they ended by finding existence gratuitous. And so Gide's ethical muscle-flexing ends in the paralysis of the absurd: happiness filthy, hope filthy, and now life, too. Had he envisioned all this when he imported Nietzsche into France? Poor Gide! Whatever the answers, the question is Man.

However incongruous it may seem, what we return to is a drama of puritanism. All the components are there: hatred of the human condition, widespread guilt, disgust of sex, self-hatred and hatred of others, fear of life, obsession with death, and the devil's own pride (that besetting sin of malcontents and reformers). To this list we may now add titanism, and top it all with a vindictive God—or a malevolent emptiness—that cannot abide to see human beings love and be happy.[51] The Romantic hero, trailing clouds of diabolism, his promethean assertion of self rendered absurd by being turned back upon him by an absurd universe, joins hands with the puritans of old and agrees with them: "We are not on this earth to be happy!"

[51] Of Anouilh's *Roméo et Jeannette*, written between *Antigone* and *Medée*, Marsh says: "From the very beginning Anouilh has been preoccupied with purity and justice, corruption and the sense of sin, without reference to God. Here he paints a picture of a cruel God who is quite indifferent to humanity except in one respect—he cannot tolerate human love and happiness. Lucien's curses at the impossibility of love in this world are frightening in their intensity." *Jean Anouilh*, p. 129.

CHAPTER X

TENNESSEE WILLIAMS:
Orpheus as Savior

About their lives people ought to remember that when they are finished, everything in them will be contained in a marvelous state of repose which is the same as that which they unconsciously admired in drama. The rush [of time] is temporary. The great and only possible dignity of man lies in his power deliberately to choose certain moral values by which to live as steadfastly as if he, too, like a character in a play, were immured against the corrupting rush of time. Snatching the eternal out of the desperately fleeting is the great magic trick of human existence. As far as we know, as far as there exists any kind of empiric evidence, there is no way to beat the game of *being* against *non-being*, in which non-being is the predestined victor on realistic levels.

Tennessee Williams has twice used the myth of Orpheus and Eurydice as the basis of a play set in the modern American South: *Battle of Angels* (1940) and *Orpheus Descending* (1957).[1] These two attempts to dramatize one of the best known Greek myths hold a place of particular interest in his career as a playwright and in our general study of a recurrent problem in drama.

[1] Tennessee Williams, *Orpheus Descending* with *Battle of Angels* (New York: New Directions, 1958). The quotation at the beginning of the chapter is from Williams, "The Timeless World of a Play," reprinted in Horst Frenz, ed., *American Playwrights on Drama* (New York: Hill & Wang, 1965), pp. 84-85.

First, *Battle of Angels*, written at the age of twenty-nine when he had barely begun his work as a dramatist, was Williams' first play to be professionally produced; *Orpheus Descending*, the same work largely rewritten seventeen years later after he had become the most successful playwright of the American stage and an important figure in international theatre, had the advantages of hindsight, maturity, and more than a decade and a half of crowded professional experience. In both cases, moreover, the plays were clearly intended for general audiences and for popular commercial success on the New York stage.

Second, his extremely conscious, even self-conscious, recourse to myth would seem to run counter to his natural talents. Williams, who says "I think I write mainly from my unconscious mind," [2] has done his best work to date as a realistic and comic writer. Reviewing *Camino Real* in 1953, Eric Bentley said: "The genuine element in Tennessee Williams had always seemed to me to reside in his realism: his ability to make eloquent and expressive dialogue out of the real speech of men and his gift for portraiture, especially the portraiture of unhappy women. There is also a spurious element. Sometimes it's his style that is spurious, for when he is poetic he is often luscious and high-falutin'. Sometimes it's his thought; one day a critic will explain what Mr. Williams has made of D. H. Lawrence. Nor are Mr. Williams' reflections on art more convincing than his pseudo-Lawrentian hymns to life; and when he tells you his theory of the Awful, he is awful." [3] He noted further: "Though the solemn speeches remain lifeless in performance, the funny ones gain a good deal." [4] He emphasized Williams' comic talent again in 1967 when he said it was particularly true of him that "The comic element is often the best part of plays that, as a whole, are not considered comedies"—*Cat on a Hot Tin Roof*, for example; and he added that what prevents *The Glass Menagerie* and *A Streetcar Named Desire* from being "unbearably sentimental" is their wit and humor: "Williams has often been ad-

[2] Quoted in Walter Wager, ed., *The Playwrights Speak* (New York: Delacorte Press, 1967), p. 232.
[3] Eric Bentley, *The Dramatic Event: An American Chronicle* (New York: Horizon Press, 1954), p. 107. For a study of what Williams has made of D. H. Lawrence, see Norman J. Fedder, *The Influence of D. H. Lawrence on Tennessee Williams* (The Hague: Mouton Publishers, 1966).
[4] Bentley, *The Dramatic Event*, p. 108.

mired for other, supposedly profounder elements, and when he has been condemned it has been on the grounds that the profundity was spurious. Those who do the condemning should, however, hasten to add that Williams has a fine comic sense and knows how to use it." [5]

But Williams had early and determinedly set his face against realism. After the success of *The Glass Menagerie* in 1945 he said that "truth, life or reality is an organic thing which the poetic imagination can represent or suggest, in essence, only through transformation, through changing into other forms than those which merely present in appearance"; and he advocated "a conception of a new, plastic theatre which must take the place of the exhausted theatre of realistic conventions if the theatre is to resume vitality as a part of our culture." [6] The result has been a theatre characterized by a sentimental lyricism, a complicated theatricalism, and a preoccupation with the tragic aspects of life, presented through the Gothic elements of shock, violence, and horror. We might anticipate, then, that the use of mythic materials would, besides confronting him with the same problems of displacement faced by other playwrights, handicap his natural talents; but we should remember also that myths lend themselves more readily to the kind of "poetic," nonrealistic theatre he desires.

Finally, his two versions are of particular interest, both because they represent—at least at the conscious level—his most personal identification with a Greek myth, and because he frequently adds parallels from the passion, death, and resurrection of Jesus Christ to his modern treatment of an ancient story. This admixture of pagan and Christian elements is not implied but made emphatically overt and explicit; and in this they differ from all the plays so far considered.

I. *Battle of Angels*

Williams termed *Battle of Angels* "a lyrical play about memories

---

[5] Eric Bentley, "Comedy and the Comic Spirit in America," in Alan S. Downer, ed., *The American Theater Today* (New York: Basic Books, 1967), pp. 58-59. In regard to Williams' sentimentality, see also Francis R. Olley, "Last Block on the Camino Real," *Drama Critique*, VIII, no. 3 (Fall, 1965), 103-7.

[6] Tennessee Williams, *The Glass Menagerie* (New York: Random House, 1945), Production Notes, p. ix.

and the loneliness of them." [7] When the Boston try-out ended disastrously for Williams in the Theatre Guild's decision to take the play off the boards, Williams exclaimed in anguish: "You don't seem to see that I put my heart into this play!" The director Margaret Webster answered, "You must not wear your heart on your sleeve for daws to peck at!" But Williams, although he remembered her advice, has always refused to heed it; and so he continued to revise *Battle of Angels*, publishing one revision in 1941, futilely submitting a second to the Theatre Guild, and publishing still another in 1944. In 1957 after he had established himself with a series of extraordinary dramatic successes—*The Glass Menagerie* (1945), *A Streetcar Named Desire* (1947), *Summer and Smoke* (1948 and 1952), *The Rose Tattoo* (1951), and *Cat on a Hot Tin Roof* (1955), but not including *Camino Real* (1953)—Williams found backing for a Broadway production of his *n*th revision, now titled *Orpheus Descending*. The producer, Robert Whitehead, shared the author's conviction that it was his best play to date and formulated its theme as follows: "The poet's life blood is protest, even though when he does protest he is destroyed; yet, he has planted a seed." [8]

Avoiding most of the troubles that attended *Battle of Angels*, the play nonetheless did not win the acclaim its playwright hoped for it. It was taken off after sixty-eight performances.[9] Yet Williams declared himself satisfied and done with it at last: ". . . I believe I have now finally managed to say in it what I wanted to say, and I feel that it now has in it a sort of emotional bridge between those early years . . . and my present state of existence as a playwright." [10] He had held to his stubborn faith, he said, because "nothing is more precious to anybody than the emotional record of his youth, and you will find the trail of my sleeve-worn heart in this completed play that I now call *Orpheus Descending*." [11]

[7] Quoted by Nancy Marie Tischler, *Tennessee Williams: Rebellious Puritan* (New York: Citadel Press, 1961), p. 69.
[8] Quoted by Francis Donahue, *The Dramatic World of Tennessee Williams* (New York: Frederick Ungar, 1964), p. 88.
[9] Tischler, *Tennessee Williams*, calls it "an international failure" also; see p. 241.
[10] Tennessee Williams, "The Past, the Present and the Perhaps," Introduction to *Orpheus Descending* with *Battle of Angels*, cited above. Actually, he had not yet done with it: it was filmed as *The Fugitive Kind*.
[11] *Ibid.*, p. vi.

In most of his other plays, Williams is a creator of "myths," rather than an adaptor of them. It is true that *The Rose Tattoo* derives its plot from Petronius' tale of the Widow of Ephesus, but it does not depend closely on it for its development or outcome; and besides, the famous tale, being entirely worldly, has no pretension to myth. Robert Hethmon has detected the myth of Hippolytus in *Cat on a Hot Tin Roof*, with Brick, Maggie, and Big Daddy as modern counterparts of Hippolytus, Phaedra, and Theseus. He cites dialogue and incidents to underscore the resemblance, but adds: "The manner in which Williams adapts the elements of the myth to his own purposes is a measure of his success as a dramatist. He has much on his mind, however, and the complex demands of his theme exceed the limits of Euripides' story." [12] Henry Popkin sees in most of Williams' plays a basic pattern that suggests the myth of Adonis and Aphrodite: a relationship involving a young man of extraordinary physical beauty as the passive figure and an older woman, aging and somewhat grotesque, as the aggressor. This "favorite archetypal pattern," he says, contains a contrast that prompts two conclusions: "it is better to be a carefree man than to be a worried, married woman"; and "freedom is better than dependence. . . ." [13] Robert Brustein, speaking of the middle group of Williams' plays and their blatant employment of deviant sex, draws an even more specific conclusion: "The real theme of all these plays . . . is incest—and it is a measure of the painfulness of this theme that Williams, for all his sensationalism, has never mentioned it directly." [14] *Orpheus Descending* comes in this middle group, and in both versions it fits to a T the "favorite archetypal pattern" of Adonis and Aphrodite.

Then why is Williams so attracted to the myth of Orpheus? For its hero suggests a man of action as well as a passive poet:

[12] Robert Hethmon, "The Foul Rag-and-Bone Shop of the Heart," *Drama Critique*, VIII, no. 3 (Fall, 1965), 94-102.
[13] Henry Popkin, "The Plays of Tennessee Williams," *Tulane Drama Review*, IV, no. 3 (March, 1960), 3-9. For a differing view, which presents Williams as a radical moralist, see Arthur Ganz, "The Desperate Morality of the Plays of Tennessee Williams," in Alan S. Downer, ed., *American Drama and Its Critics: A Collection of Critical Essays* (Chicago and London: University of Chicago Press, 1965), pp. 203-17.
[14] Robert Brustein, "Sweet Bird of Success," *Encounter*, XII, no. 6 (June, 1959), 59-60. In 1967 in *The Two-Character Play*, presented at the Hampstead Theatre Club, London, he treats incest explicitly.

he initiates the journey to the underworld to rescue his wife and
so moves the heart of Hades by his gift of song as to gain leave
to take her back to earth, on condition that he not look at her
until they have regained daylight; then, at the last moment, he
loses her when his anxiety causes him to turn round to make
sure she is following.

Myths are protean, malleable. Williams will, of course, no
sooner touch the myth of Orpheus than it will begin to change.
Besides accommodating itself to the Adonis-Aphrodite pattern,
it contains the three elements most appealing to his stubborn romanticism, the same that drew Cocteau to it: poetry, love, and
death. For Williams, however, these translate into the artist,
sexuality, and society, the three elements in the playwright's
perennial battle with the world. Society is the poet's declared
enemy. Love is ambiguous, for it is both attractive and dangerous—as the poet is ambivalent, both attracted and repelled, for
the sake of his art. We shall find here, I suggest, why the classic
myth was not enough for Williams, why he had to add Christian
parallels. The answer lies in his belief that the poet, the artist,
is the savior of the world.

Battle of Angels was written and staged in the style of realism.
For that reason the following synopsis omits wherever it can all
the mythological allusions Williams employs, so as to concentrate
on the action. That action, it should be noted, is developed at one
remove. First dramatizing the classical myth in a modern setting
to increase its immediacy and to make a modern comment, the
playwright then distances it by framing it as a flashback between
prologue and epilogue. As action, therefore, it is already over
and done by the time we see it; as myth, it is in process once
again of becoming a new, local legend.

Prologue: Eva and Blanch Temple, the "only surviving relations" of Jabe Torrance, late owner of the Torrance Mercantile
Store in Twin Rivers, Mississippi, now operate the disused building as a tourist attraction; for it is the site of a sensational double
murder that occurred there a year ago, on Good Friday, during
an electric power failure, an unprecedented cloudburst, and a
flood. Eva and Blanch pay the taxes on the dilapidated building,
put down roach powder, and touch up the fading bloodstains.
Now they draw the tourists' attention to "the famous Jesus picture"—a painting of a very good-looking young man; to the dress

Myra (Mrs. Torrance) was wearing and its color—"ecstasy blue"; and to the Conjure Man, a weirdly dressed Negro who is caretaker of the "exhibition" or "memorial" and who, with his soft chuckle and secret smile, seems to know "something that he isn't telling." There are also a snakeskin jacket, prominently displayed, and, off the main store, the Torrance Confectionery that once offered soft drinks and pinball machines and that Myra had had redecorated to resemble an orchard garden that once bloomed across from Moon Lake. For Myra (say the women), the store was "reality, harsh and drab"; but the confectionery was where "she kept her dreams."

Act I: With morbid avidity the Temple sisters, the pregnant Dolly Bland, Sheriff Talbott, and some other townspeople are waiting at the store for the return from hospital of Jabe Torrance, who is dying of cancer, and his wife, Myra. Still others join them: Cassandra Whiteside, member of the district aristocracy, and the sheriff's wife, Vee Talbott, a religious mystic and a primitive painter. Vee brings with her a young man wearing a snakeskin jacket. This is Val Xavier, who is so handsome, virile, and exotic that he at once causes a stir among the women. ("Don't you know," Sandra explains to him, "what those women are suffering from: Sexual malnutrition! They look at you with eyes that scream 'Eureka!'") Vee has befriended this wanderer, as she has many others, and hopes Myra may have work for him in the store. Sandra challenges him provocatively; he responds with antagonism. She causes turmoil, just before Myra arrives, by shooting at a buzzard: "A bird of ill omen was circling over the store."

Myra Torrance, a slight, fair woman of thirty-four, confirms the report that Jabe's operation was not at all successful. Jabe does not appear; he has been carried to his bedroom by the back way. Until the last act, he will be invisible, announcing his presence only by pounding his cane on the floor above.

Sandra lures Val away by asking him to repair her automobile, but he quickly returns to find Myra distraught from nerves and exhaustion: "Oh, oh, oh, I wish I was dead—dead—dead." Val reveals that he slapped Sandra for making advances in a contemptous way. Myra laughs wildly at the idea of a member of the rich Whiteside family being so roughly treated. Val asks for a job and presents a character reference ("This here boy's peculiar but he sure does work real hard and he's honest as daylight.") He has been a garage mechanic, a coal miner, an oil-field worker in his ten-year wanderings, and now he is writing a book; but he has had no experience as a sales clerk. Myra is interested in his story. She seems drawn to him, as he to her, and she ends by offering him a job.

Act II, Scene 1: Val has been working for Myra for a week. His presence attracts the girls and women of the county, including Sandra Whiteside who, although she pretends to be friendly, seeks to even the score with Val. He wishes she would leave: "I want to keep this job. Every place I've gone to it's been some woman I finally had to leave on account of." She points to a resemblance between them: "You—savage. And me—aristocrat. Both of us things whose license has been revoked in the civilized world. Both of us equally damned and for the same good reason. Because we both want freedom." She invites him to kiss her. When he gives in and begins to embrace her, she bites his hand and kicks him in the groin. Myra comes upon this scene and resents Val's involvement with Sandra.

The friction between Val and Myra grows. He has no talent for helping in the store; his attractiveness to other women annoys Myra, who averts her eyes when she talks to him. A quarrel in which he quits and she fires him turns, instead, into an exchange of confidences. Val speaks of his past, of his search for the answer to his question about life: Why? "That was the first word I learned to spell out at school. And I expected some answer. I felt there was something secret that I would find out and then it would all make sense." When he became the lover of a cajun girl on Witches' Bayou, his search was "thrown off the track." He does not know what it was he wanted, for he still has not found the answer, but he knows now that his sexual intimacy with her was not the answer, and he must continue to look. His ten years of restless wandering were lonely. In Texas he settled down for a spell: "But things went wrong. Something happened." He will not say what. "But everything was different after that. I wasn't free anymore. I was followed by something I couldn't get off my mind. Till I came here. . . ."

Now their desire for each other grows. Val says: "It's no use to struggle. . . . You go the way the earth pulls you whether you want to or not. I don't want to touch you, Myra. . . . It wouldn't be right for me to." Not on Jabe's account, he explains, but on hers; for he feels a fatality in himself. "You been good to me. I don't want nothing to hurt you."

Act II, Scene 2: A few hours later, a customer enters: David Anderson. Myra sends Val on an errand, so that she may talk to Anderson alone. Eight years ago, after his marriage, she had ordered him out of the store. Myra had been in love with Anderson; but when crop failures ruined him, he threw her over and married into the Delta Planters' Bank. She tells how well she's done and what she plans to do after Torrance dies: "My life isn't over, my life is only *commencing*." She dismisses him, feeling that she has made a fool of herself by boasting.

Vee Talbott brings a picture she has painted to put with Myra's Easter decorations. It is a picture of the Church of the Resurrection in Twin Rivers which Vee attends. She has painted the church steeple red: "I felt it that way. I always paint a thing the way that it strikes me instead of always the way that it actually is." Vee acts dazed: "Something's gone wrong with my eyes. I can't see nothing." When Val persuades her to try on some shoes, his touch on her feet and thighs leaves her even more confused.

Myra reports that Jabe now accuses her of wanting him to die. "Don't you?" asks Val. But she doesn't: "Death's terrible, Val." Myra voices her dreams: dancing in a dress of *mousseline de soie*, with jasmine blossoms in her hair, on the Peabody Roof in Memphis, admired by a Hollywood talent scout and a Broadway producer, with photographers taking her picture for the society columns and rotogravure sections, and autograph-seekers begging her to sign her name. Jabe's furious knocking on the ceiling stops this lyrical fantasy.

Val suggests she give Jabe enough morphine to kill him. "I'm a decent woman," she objects. "What's decent?" he asks. "I never heard of that word. I've written a book full of words but I never used that one. Why? Because it's disgusting. Decent is something that's scared like a little white rabbit. I'll give you a better word, Myra. . . . Love. . . ." Val persists with the idea of putting Jabe out of his misery, and Myra still rejects it: "Don't! You scare me. Don't talk that way."

Act II, Scene 3: In the next scene, which follows immediately, Val saves a derelict Negro from a charge of vagrancy. He does this by buying the man's guitar and engaging him to give lessons. This incident, in which Val sides with the dispossessed, serves to anger Deputy Sheriff Pee Wee Bland and some of the men who have been drinking. They call Val a "Nawthun radical," a "red-neck peckerwood with a Nawthun edjication," a "carpetbagger," and threaten him. When one of them spits at him, Val knocks him down. The men close in about Val, but the sheriff disperses them.

Val, now under suspicion, decides that he's bad for Myra's business and that it is no longer safe to stay. He confesses to her that he is a wanted man, falsely charged with rape by a woman in Waco, Texas. He also thinks he should go because of his desire for Myra; but she says: "You don't have to leave on account of a reason like that." If he will stay, she will take every precaution to avert suspicion. He agrees, and they become lovers.

Act III: It is Good Friday. The confectionery has been redecorated with imitation dogwood blossoms to look like an orchard in bloom. Myra herself is transformed, happy and glowing. Business is poor because of rainy weather. There is thunder and talk of floods. The lights flicker as the storm affects the power lines. The Conjure Man appears, offering good luck charms. Myra rejects them: "I don't need holy stones to bring me luck." Dolly Bland inquires for the maternity dresses she ordered two months ago. Beulah drops in to tell the latest news: "Excitement! Cassandra Whiteside's come in town drunk as a lord." She has been in another wreck; and, since her license was revoked, she has a black chauffeur. Like Val in his brush with the hangers-on, she has gotten into trouble: "They say she's been ostracized in Memphis . . . and her father has actually received a warning note from the Klan."

Dolly and Beulah are well aware of something between Myra and Val. Eva and Blanch report further news of Sandra: she has just been put out of the Cross Roads Inn; she was at Sunflower Bridge, having the d.t.'s; she was shouting: "Behold Cassandra! Shouting doom at the gates!" Vee Talbott, wearing black nun-like garments for Good Friday, declares she has had a vision of Jesus for which she waited and prayed so long; and now she is able at last to complete her painting of Christ at the Last Supper. The vision came to her in blinding light by the cottonwood tree on the way to church. She believes the red marks on her palms are stigmata. As a further sign, Jesus touched her bosom and thereby delivered her from obscene thoughts that had bothered her. She has brought the portrait for Myra to put on display. She starts to show it when a furious quarrel breaks out upstairs, with Jabe deliriously refusing to take the medicine prescribed for him.

Val attempts to telephone the doctor but cannot reach him. Myra decides to drive to Jackson Spring to find a doctor. Upon seeing Val, Vee suffers shock and tries to flee without showing her picture. The women discover the face in the picture is that of Val Xavier with a halo: the face Vee had seen in the cottonwood tree, the tree which is also called, as they remind him, the lynching tree. Says Dolly: "Exactly where time an' time again you see couples parked in cars with all of the shades pulled down! And what did he do? He stretched out his hand and *touched* yuh!" Dolly takes satisfaction in thus ridiculing Vee and exposing what she regards as her hypocrisy, for her puritanical self-righteousness has been hard to bear for the women who smoke, drink, and play cards.

Now the Conjure Man reappears, meeting Val alone as he had met Myra. Val shivers as if chilled: "Huh? Naw, naw, naw, I don't want it! Sorry but I don't truck with that conjure stuff." As a storm threatens, Cassandra, drunk and disheveled, comes seeking protection: "I'm in danger. . . . Immolation at the hands of outraged citizens of Two Rivers County. They've confiscated the nigger that drove my car and ordered me out of Two Rivers." She had been pouring a libation of rum on her great-aunt's grave, but the vigilantes would not believe her story and warned her to leave.

She has come to ask Val to go away with her. "You an' me, we belong to the fugitive kind." Sandra, too, knows that Myra and Val are lovers: "Oh, you'd better watch out," she tells Val. "It isn't kiss and goodbye with a woman like that! She'll want to keep you forever. I'm not like that. . . . Women will never leave you alone. Not as long as you wear that marvelous jacket." Val asks her to leave, but she insists on offering herself: "You think I ought to be ashamed to say that? Well, I'm not. I think that passion is something to be proud of. It's the only one of the little alphabet blocks they give us to play with that seems to stand for anything of importance."

As Val shoves her away, Myra returns. She could not get over the river because the bridge was out. Sandra says she has come with a warning: "They've passed a law against passion. Our license has been revoked. . . . Whoever has too much passion, we're going to be burned like witches because we know too much." The two women clash over Val. Myra strikes Sandra and knocks her unconscious. She has Val take Sandra to her bedroom.

At that moment, Sheriff Talbott appears with a Mrs. Regan from Waco, Texas, looking for Val on a charge of rape. Myra pretends that Val has quit and gone to Memphis. Mrs. Regan see Vee's painting of Jesus: "Now I'm convinced. It's *him*. I'd recognize it hanging on the moon." Convinced that Myra is lying to them, they leave to search the town: "The place to look is them sporting houses on Front Street." Val emerges and prepares to flee: "I heard her voice but I thought I must be dreaming." Myra says his escape is cut off because Mrs. Regan has already told the drunken stave-mill workers with whom he quarreled earlier, and they are on the street looking for him. Val is distraught: "Oh, God, Myra, I've washed myself in melted snow on mountains trying to get the touch of her off my body. It's no good. . . . You can't understand what it is to be hounded by somebody's hate." But what Myra had seen in Mrs. Regan's face was a "terrible, hopeless, twisted kind of love" that is "worse than hate."

Myra resolves that the two of them must leave Twin Rivers together that night. He cannot dissuade her. She launches into a long, lyrical reminiscence about a barren fig tree in the back of their yard when she was a child, and uses this story to disclose the fact that she is pregnant: "Oh, God, I knew that I wouldn't be barren when we went together that first time. I felt it already, stirring up inside me, beginning to live! . . . So now you see we can't be separated! We're bound together, Val!"

But Val, the wanderer, the fugitive kind, refuses: "I travel by myself. I don't take anything with me but my skin." Her reply is, "I'll never let you get away from me, Val." He says that he'll go to the desert in New Mexico and, in two or three years when the book is finished, send for her. By then the woman from Waco may have forgotten. Val assures her he loves her. But Myra upbraids him: "Love? You're too selfish for love." When she clings to him, he shoves her aside roughly: "You're like the woman from Waco. The way you. . . ." In despair at having surrendered all decency for love and at having smashed her life to pieces, Myra threatens him just as the other woman had done: "If you try to leave here without me, I'll call for the sheriff!"

Jabe appears at the top of the stairs, a gruesome sight, yelling "Buzzards!" Val wants to take his wages and go, but Myra pleads and taunts: "You can't leave me alone with him, would you? . . . You couldn't be such a coward. . . . You've got to stick with me, Val." When he refuses—"Don't have to do nothing. I'm going!" —she confronts Jabe hysterically and tells him that he is going to die, but that she has new life in her womb.

Suddenly terrified at what she has done, she runs back to Val, but he breaks away. "It's finished!" he says. He takes his wages from the cash register. Myra runs to the telephone to call the sheriff and accuse Val of robbery. Jabe loads his revolver, aims at Myra, shoots her mortally in the back, then says he will accuse Val of having shot her while he was robbing the store: "They'll come here and burn you for it! Buzzards!" Jabe staggers out into the storm. Myra is dying, but she tells Val, "Go on, look out for yourself, get away! I don't need anyone now. . . ."

A mob of townspeople is approaching. Val flees through the confectionery. Sandra descends from Myra's room "with a sort of exultation, appearing like a priestess in her long, sculptural white dress." When some of the mob break into the store and head out through the confectionery, they are confronted by the Conjure Man. "Where is Xavier, you niggah?" He answers by elevating Val's snakeskin jacket. Whereupon, *The woman from Waco screams and covers her face. A gong is struck and the stage is drowned in instant and utter blackness.*

Epilogue: Blanch and Eva, displaying Cassandra's dark sunglasses and her bright red cape, reveal that she drowned in Sunflower River, from which her body was never recovered. "She deliberately drove her car into the river," says Blanch, "and drowned, because she knew that decent people were done with her." They say also that Vee lost her mind, the woman from Texas disappeared, and Val fell into the hands of the stave-mill workers, who took him to the big cottonwood tree and carried out their lynching threat with a blow-torch: "Kill him! Burn the son of a bitch. Burn him!" The revolted tourists flee without paying, the Temple sisters follow them, and the old Conjure Man is left alone.

II.

The story Williams tells in *Battle of Angels* could, with the exception of Vee Talbott's vision, pass for naturalism of the most materialistic kind. Even Cassandra Whiteside can be fitted into its scheme: it did not require a prophetess to see that things would not end well at the Torrance Mercantile Store. The story may be incredible, or at best weakly motivated, but it is "realistic."

Why, then, have recourse to myth? First, because the story as it stands does not have the significance Williams would confer upon it. Second, because the tyro Williams, evidently fearing that the action lacked a strong sense of inevitability, felt he had to convince the audience that some of the things he could not show really did happen. The known patterns of myth provide this sense. In case they aren't enough, provide a prologue and epilogue and *tell* the audience. Then, as if that weren't enough, we have unnecessary proliferation of the circumstances contributing to the catastrophe. Part of the trouble is that the action has little forward movement. This is mainly because Val Xavier is passive and resistant, rather than actively volitional. He is a catalyst pressed into service as a protagonist. So the mythical symbols of the play must not only supply additional meanings to the action, which is their proper function, they must serve as substitutes for action—overemphatic pointers toward a long-delayed outcome.

When the climax comes at last, it has the hysterical intensity of Gothic melodrama, with everything happening at once. The play as staged, though lacking the "makeshift devices" of prologue and epilogue, included in its frenetic climax a Wagnerian conflagration.[15]

Let us look at the play in the light of the traditional four-fold method of interpretation, and then see how Williams went

[15] John Gassner, "Tennessee Williams: Dramatist of Frustration," *College English*, X, no. 1 (October, 1948), 4. Gassner, who was in a position to know, believed that Williams was poorly advised in his rewriting, that the version published in 1945 was an unsatisfactory revision of the stage version which was, in turn, inferior to the manuscript originally submitted to the Theatre Guild.

about creating the levels of meaning. At the literal level, there is an illicit love affair between a young man and an older married woman that results in the death of the latter by shooting, of the former by lynching. The deceived husband dies of cancer. The girl who tried to prevent the catastrophe dies by drowning, probably a suicide. The woman who foresaw the end goes mad. At the allegorical level, it is the story of Dionysus, of Attis, of Orpheus and Eurydice, or Persephone and Pluto, or Adonis and Aphrodite, made to parallel at points the passion and death of Jesus Christ. As his archetypal play, with his subsequent plays merely working variations on its obsessive basic action, it uses these myths to represent the awakening (in this case, the reawakening) to life through sexuality. At the moral level, it is the struggle of the rebellious, free individual against the ties and prejudices of the community, as well as of the artist against the lures and distractions of the philistine world. Williams says he himself sees it as "a play about unanswered questions that haunt the hearts of people and the difference between continuing to ask them, a difference represented by the four major protagonists of the play, and the acceptance of prescribed answers that are not answers at all, but expedient adaptations or surrender to a state of quandary." [16] At the anagogical level, although such a term seems utterly inappropriate in relation to Williams' play, the action dramatizes the biological antithesis of life and death.

Traditionally, the anagogical interpretation assumes the objective existence of ultimate truth, a transcendent reality which is God, so that the art work at its highest level of truth must recognize and affirm a divine source toward which all existence tends. By definition, neither Williams nor any of the other playwrights here considered, except the Christian Eliot and the pantheistic Jeffers, could attain this level or validate his dramas there, regardless of how much he, or literary critics like William Troy or Joseph Campbell, might wish to do so. For Williams, Christ is a literary symbol like myth, and little more; life alone is the ultimate reality, death its negation, and sexuality and artistic creation are the two significant expressions of this biological brute fact.

The theme of a "battle of angels," of war in heaven, occurs in Act III when Cassandra imagines a struggle between the

[16] Williams, Introduction, *Orpheus Descending* with *Battle of Angels*, p. vi.

forces of light and darkness: "I have it on the very best authority that time is all used up," she tells Val and Myra. "There's no more time. Can't you see it? Feel it? The atmosphere is pregnant with disaster! Now I can even *hear* it! . . . A battle in heaven. A battle of *angels* above us! And *thunder!* and storm!" And Myra, as she is dying, repeats the idea: "Isn't it funny I should just now remember what happened to the fig tree? It was struck down in a storm, the very spring I hung them ornaments on it. Why? Why? For what reason? Because some things are enemies of light and there is a battle between them in which some fall!" The battle of angels, ordinarily interpreted as the conflict of good and evil, may be so interpreted here only if it is understood that good and evil, in Williams' radical morality, have less to do with any clearly defined moral action than with the basic biological antithesis of life and death. All these levels of meaning, we must conclude, could be brought out only through recourse to myth—principally by means of allusion and attribution.

Here is the symbology of *Battle of Angels* that one can find if he looks for it. The presence of symbols or symbolic intent, however, does not insure dramatic efficacy; for that, the playwright must recreate symbols by making them operative within the dramatic system of his own play. Until that happens, we have borrowed radiance, unearned significance, symbol-mongering.

The time-scheme of the action moves from winter to spring, ending on Good Friday, with the events of Act III coinciding with the hours of Christ's passion and death on Calvary; the storm, flood, and power failure paralleling the darkness over the land and the turmoil of nature, with the darkened store, the mythical Hades in which Eurydice is imprisoned, now standing also for the harrowing of Hell that followed Christ's death and preceded his resurrection. Val's death on the lynching tree repeats the pattern of Christ's death on the cross; his snakeskin jacket is a symbol of resurrection, for to the pagan world the snake was not only a religious and sexual sign, but also its shedding of its skin was held as a figure of renewal.

Temple, the last name of Eva and Blanch, probably refers to organized religion, which is always subject to attack by Williams as being empty and dead, and thus part of the death-in-life landscape of Hell that is Twin Rivers. The women of Twin Rivers are church-going hypocrites, maenads who seek to dismember and devour Val Xavier. The latter's name conspicuously combines Valentine, or love, with Xavier, a play on words suggesting "savior." Williams, following his master D. H. Lawrence, insists on a sexualized Christ such as Lawrence imagined in his short story, "The Man Who Died"; for a religion of sex, such as he preaches, needs a Priapus as catalyst to incarnate the sexuality that is to drive the community to frenzy and to murder. And Myra Torrance is to be associated with the Virgin Mary, as well as with Eurydice, Persephone, and Aphrodite. But her name first suggests Myrrha, the mother of Adonis, who had unnatural love for her own father and was changed into a myrtle tree. This recalls to mind Robert Brustein's comment: "The real theme of these plays is incest." In any case, the playwright is guilty of almost unbelievable ineptness in making the Christian identifications. In an angry exchange, we have this:

VAL: God, I—! Lady, you!

MYRA (*laughing a little*): God you an' lady me, huh. I think you are kind of exaggerating a little in both cases.

And later this:

MYRA (*smiling and shaking her head*): We both got a little bit upset but that's over.

VAL: God, I. . . .

MYRA: God you and lady me? (*She laughs.*) . . .

These passages are omitted from *Orpheus Descending*, where Myra's name simply becomes "Lady" throughout.

Jabe Torrance, dying of cancer and hate, is Pluto, god of the underworld. He is scarcely a character, but rather a figure of melodrama or a conventional symbol of death. In neither version will the music of Orpheus move him to surrender Eurydice. His marriage to Myra was one of convenience, not love; but even the convenience seems to have turned to hate. He seems to share the attitudes of his townsmen, for all we can tell to the contrary; indeed, they become intensified in him: "In (Williams') plays, too, time is the real villain. . . . For the largest group of characters, it has dimmed sexual power and sexual appeal. . . . But the men and a few women whom time has disappointed are inclined to turn vicious. . . . the envious old men of *Orpheus Descending* and *Sweet Bird of Youth* employ race prejudice, murder and castration as their ways of taking revenge on the world." [17] In the revised version Torrance will have a bit more reality, if only because we see him on his return from the hospital and sense his malevolence as the leader of the antagonists. But Williams cannot, or will not, humanize Death beyond personifying him as a stage villain.

In the process of inflating his characters with symbolic values, Williams deprives them of human values by forcing them to do and say things, as in Myra's dying speech or in the dialogue just quoted, that would not otherwise occur to them. As a viewer remarked after seeing *The Fugitive Kind,* the film version of *Orpheus Descending,* "It would have been a more honest picture without all the fuss about mythology." Cassandra Whiteside is a case in point. As a realistic character, a Southern girl, she has vitality, a sharp outline, and an interesting contradiction in her character: she is driven by self-destructive impulses to heed the "good advice" of the dead people in the graveyard: "Just one word—live!" As a mythological character, she is self-conscious:

The first (Cassandra) was a little Greek girl who slept in the shrine of Apollo. Her ears were snake-bitten, like mine, so that she could understand the secret language of the birds. You know what they told her, Snakeskin? They contradicted everything that she'd been told before. They said it was all stuff and nonsense, a pack of lies. . . .

Later she pours libations of rum on her great-aunt's grave. The playwright seems to feel called upon to explain her literary speech:

DOLLY: . . . She's got two degrees or something in *lit-era-chure.*

BEULAH: Six degrees of fever if you ask me!

In Act II cockcrows punctuate the "betrayal" scene between Myra and David, and serve as transition to the scene between Val and Vee Talbott in which Vee brings to the store her painting of the Church of the Resurrection. Vee's name is short for Veronica, and the picture of Christ she will paint, that turns out to look like Val Xavier, will correspond to Veronica's veil.

Val himself has obvious attributes that link him to Adonis and Dionysus: "surpassing beauty and grace and strong physical appeal"; he even has eyes that glow in the dark. His writing is a

[17] Popkin, "The Plays of Tennessee Williams," pp. 54-55.

colorless device for representing him as a poet. For all that Williams insists upon fitting Val to a pattern of Christ's passion and death, one looks in vain for his Christlike attributes. He commits adultery with a woman, then tries to persuade her to shorten her husband's life. He scorns "decent" conduct as prompted solely by fear and cowardice and would substitute for it "love." But "love," it turns out, must not require commitment nor should it hold the lover responsible for the consequences of his own actions. Nonetheless, and strange as it may seem, Val Xavier and subsequent Williams heroes and heroines are in the playwright's eyes "martyrs of love" and are, because of their sufferings, to be held innocent of sin or crime. "If they suffer," says Henry Popkin, "they suffer unjustly, and Williams elaborately establishes their fundamental innocence. They suffer for us in a sense, so that love may be free." [18]

If the attributes are not there, are the actions? The more the playwright tries to accommodate symbolically the elements of Christ's passion to the character of Val Xavier, the more one becomes aware that this ingenuity, instead of completing the parallel, only makes the basic discrepancies more glaring. Christ foretold his death as a necessary sacrifice, and willed it; Val does neither. His ignorance of the forces converging on him only underscores his human limitations—and his self-centeredness. Christ insisted on his divinity and acted in obedience to his Father; Val has nothing beyond himself, and hence he can act only for the sake of self-assertion. Christ preached a moral law that he came to fulfill and sought disciples; Val seeks only his own freedom and holds no doctrine except the pre-eminence of sexual love and of the art that celebrates it. One has the odd feeling that Williams knows Lawrence's story far better than he knows the gospels. After studying the play, it is hard to recall an action of Val's that is entirely free of self-interest and that genuinely deserves to be called Christlike.

It is surely not a case of a convinced Christian who sincerely turns to Christian symbols to draw a reverent comparison. Williams has described his religious feeling, a feeling that he finds necessary to life: "It isn't associated with any particular church.

[18] *Ibid.*, p. 51. He lists, besides Val Xavier, Chance (*Sweet Bird of Youth*), Brick (*Cat on a Hot Tin Roof*), Kilroy (*Camino Real*), and Blanche DuBois (*A Streetcar Named Desire*).

It's just a general feeling of one's dependence upon some superior being of a mystic nature." [19] Christianity is only a beautiful allegory to Williams—literary raw material available (however inaptly) for appropriation.[20] It is a case, rather, of a Nietzschean transvaluation of values.

In this wholly spurious attribution of Christlike qualities to Val we have, in fact, one of the earliest instances in Williams' plays of a programmatic intention that in time is to become plainly tendentious: to exonerate from guilt, and indeed to exalt as heroic, the rebel and the wanderer. Datum: society is evil. That being so, whatever constraints society imposes are, of course, evil too. What Williams exalts in the teeth of society is "dionysian nomadism," to use a term coined by Denis de Rougemont. "Sensual love is a powerful symbol of the body's freedom and the spirit's," says George Painter; "but so also is the ability to wander." [21] The character of Val and his love for Myra combine both of these symbols. Williams has insisted upon his close personal identification with Val's attitudes and values, and he has stated that he found among bohemians, drifters, and the dispossessed "a kind of freedom I had always needed. And the shock of it against the Puritanism of my nature has given me a subject, a theme, which I have never ceased exploiting." [22] It could be Gide speaking.

In the Veronica theme, Williams pointedly combines sexuality with Christian mysticism at a crucial stage in the action. The incident of Vee's portrait of Christ has an important plot function. Yet the combination backfires badly, and the incident fails to fulfill its function. It is important to see why it failed, and how the playwright sought to remedy it in the revised version. For the sake of convenience, I will compare the treatment in both plays before turning to a general consideration of *Orpheus Descending*.

The description of Vee in the stage directions is interesting, indicating the playwright's intention: "*She is a heavy, middle-aged woman, about forty, whose personality, frustrated in its contact with externals, has turned deeply inward. She has found*

[19] See Wager, *The Playwrights Speak*, p. 228.
[20] See Tischler, *Tennessee Williams*, p. 239; also footnote 24 below.
[21] George D. Painter, *André Gide: A Critical and Biographical Study* (New York: Roy, 1951), p. 51.
[22] See Tischler, *Tennessee Williams*, p. 239.

refuge in religion and primitive art and has become known as an eccentric. Although a religious fanatic, a mystic, she should not be made ridiculous. Her portrayal will contain certain incidents of humor, but not be devoid of all dignity or pathos. She wanders slowly about with a vague dreamy smile on her face. Her expression is often bewildered."[23] Vee tries to help, and to convert, the prisoners in her husband's lock-up. Dolly says, and it's probably true: "She hasn't lived as a natural wife for ten years or more . . . so her husband has got to pick up with some bright-skinned nigger." She is puritanical and censorious, but she is not hypocritical like the other women. Her sincerity, as well as her genuine interest in art, place her with Val in the line-up of opposed forces.

The women give a leering interpretation to her charity toward vagrants and to her painting them as figures in "The Last Supper," a work that she has been unable to complete because she has never seen the face of Jesus. When she brings Val to the store, therefore, they assume—as does the audience—that she is as sexually attracted to him as they are. Yet this appears to be a mistake on their part—and ours, despite the fact that the steeple in her painting of the Church of the Resurrection is patently, even blatantly, a phallic symbol; and despite the fact that she becomes increasingly upset when Val touches her feet, then grasps her thighs to keep her from falling. After all, what is there except lack of active malice to distinguish her from the sex-starved maenads? This confusion seems to me fatal; for her purpose in the action is to convince the audience absolutely that Val will be killed by the mob, that he will be killed on a tree like Christ, and that—also like Christ—he came as a savior, the incarnation of love and freedom, but that his message was rejected and he was crucified. Now, for this to succeed—for the audience, that is, to feel the sense of inevitability and to see in Val a symbolic value beyond himself—it must believe in her vision as genuine. They must accept it as supernatural and prophetic. Hence the stress on her painter's vision that sees things as they are to the heart and not just as they appear to the eye, and on her physical blindness that contrasts with her inward vision.

In Act III of *Battle of Angels*, after references to Dr. Hector's

[23] Williams, *Battle of Angels*, pp. 130-31.

having just preached the Seven Last Words from the Cross, Vee makes her entrance. She is at once caught in a crossfire of shopping, gossip, a quarrel between Jabe and Myra upstairs, failure of the telephone service, and Blanch's underhanded attempt to get money back for merchandise she never paid for. Vee even contributes to this planned confusion with a long childhood reminiscence.

Vee has at last seen the vision of Jesus, face to face, and has painted the picture. The vision occurred at sunrise, before the Passion began, when Vee was by the cottonwood tree on the way to church. Since then, her spirit has been at peace: "I been tormented. He took all the torment off me. . . . Evil thoughts. Those men in the lockup, they write nasty words on the walls. At night I can see them. They keep coming up in my mind. He took that cross off me when he touched me." When she sees Val, she is overcome with shock and cries, "No, no! . . . Le' me go! Leave me be! . . . Naw, I can't stay, le' me go!" She struggles with the women, her eyes following Val as he crosses to the confectionery: "Where's he going *to*?"

Remember that the women—and the audience—do not yet know what the picture contains, nor why Vee was so shocked to see Val; and now she wants to take it back without displaying it: "It's not to be touched by you, you foul-minded thing!" (Why hadn't she recognized Val in the painting earlier?) Then Beulah snatches the painting, looks, gasps, and shrieks with laughter. The haloed head of Christ is "a wonderful likeness" of Val Xavier. When the women tell him of Vee's vision, she protests: "No! You're all of you cooking up something without no excuse!" Then Dolly and Beulah round on her, to pay her back for her censorious gossip: "She's got to have her eyes opened, now, once an' for all. A vision of Jesus? No, but of Val Xavier, the shoe clerk who sold 'er them shoes." And Dolly drives the charge home by pointing out that the site of her vision, where Jesus touched her on the bosom, is the local lovers' rendezvous: "(*She thrusts her hand against VEE's bosom. VEE cries aloud as though the hand were a knife thrust into her, and, turning awkwardly, runs out of the store.*)"

It is not merely a case of a playwright trying to do too much, and going the wrong way about it by letting too much else happen, so that focus is lost. What else is an audience to think but that Dolly and Beulah, although cruel and venomous, have told the truth about Vee; and that Vee's repressed sexual desires have returned disguised as religious fantasies? Every clue about Vee, save the author's description, points to just that; and this critical incident occurs in an atmosphere which, like the whole play, seethes with sexuality evoked by the priapic catalyst Val. And it doesn't change our minds to hear later that Vee went mad.

In *Orpheus Descending* Williams controls the two important scenes involving Vee Talbott and Val by isolating them and treating them as separate episodes. In Act II, Scene 2, Val is alone in the store when she brings her painting of the church. He studies it very seriously, and there develops between them a dialogue without sexual overtones that demonstrates the importance of art in the life of both. "I have to wait for—visions," says Vee; "no, I—I can't paint without—visions. . . . I couldn't *live* without visions!" There is a new touch; Vee was born with a caul: "It's a sign that you're going to have visions, and I did, I had them!" Since she began painting, her whole outlook is different: existence now makes sense, where before it did not. Val draws from her a horrified admission of all the awful things she's seen in Two Rivers County: beatings, lynchings, runaway convicts torn to pieces by hounds. They have both been witnesses to such horrors. "We seen these things from seats down front at the show," says Val. "And so you begun to paint your visions. Without no plan, no training, you started to paint as if God touched your fingers. (*He lifts her hands slowly, gently from her lap.*) You made some beauty out of this dark country with these two, soft, woman hands. . . ." He lifts them to his mouth, and Vee gasps. At that moment Talbott appears and ominously puts an end to the scene: "Jabe Torrance told me to take a good look at you. . . . Well, now, I've taken that look."

The crucial scene of the vision (Act III, Scene 2) occurs earlier in *Orpheus Descending*, and just before the incident in which the men of the town threaten Val. Its earlier placement improves it as a foreshadowing device. Again it begins as a twosome between Val and Vee, but this time without the painting. It is sunset of Holy Saturday—the emphasis is now upon resurrection, not crucifixion—and Vee staggers in, blinded, having just this moment seen the vision. She has seen "the two huge blazing eyes of Jesus Christ risen!—Not crucified but Risen!" She relives the vision as she recalls it to mind: "And then a great—. . . . His hand!—*Invisible*! I didn't *see* his hand!—But it *touched* me —here! (*She seizes VAL's hand and presses it to her great heaving bosom.*)" As before, her husband appears, and as she comes back to the present, she realizes that it was Val's eyes she saw: "You! . . . You! . . . The Ey-es!"

(*She collapses, forward, falls to her knees, her arms thrown about VAL. He seizes her to lift her. Two or three man are peering in at the store window.*)

TALBOTT (*pushing VAL away*): Let go of her, don't put your hands on my wife! (*He seizes her roughly and hauls her to the door. VAL moves up to help VEE.*) Don't move. (*At the door, to VAL*): I'm coming back.

VAL: I'm not goin' nowhere.

Both scenes have served to arouse the sheriff's suspicions—but without arousing ours—that Val is "messin' with his wife." Williams still takes the risk of combining sexuality and mysticism where Vee is concerned, but I think this time more successfully. Whether the audience believes the vision is something that may vary; but that it understands the meaning of the vision is far more likely than it was before. The two scenes now contribute logically enough to the climactic scene of Val's lynching. Moreover, Vee is clearly no longer one of the maenads; she is told off by Beulah as early as Act I. Thereafter, she appears only with Val and her husband, so that she has no further associations with the other women to confuse us. Her sincerity and her pathos are greater when we can concentrate on her more fully in isolation. Finally, her scene with Val is made to serve thematically by linking her painting with the image of the forces of darkness and light—the Battle of Angels: "Along the road as I walked, thinking about the mysteries of Easter, veils! . . . seemed to drop off my eyes. Light, oh, light! I never have seen such brilliance! It *pricked* my eyeballs like *needles*! . . . Yes, yes, light. *You* know, you know we live in light and shadow, that's, that's what we *live* in, a world of—*light* and—*shadow*. . . . A world of light and shadow is what we live in, and—it's—confusing. . . ."

III. *Orpheus Descending*

When we turn to *Orpheus Descending* as the long-meditated

statement of a mature playwright, the first change we notice is that the action, besides being more episodic, is happening now, not in a flashback. There is no epilogue. The prologue supplies exposition, more of it being needed now, and establishes the non-realistic style of the play by the use of direct address to the audience, arbitrary lighting, and unmotivated music. The towns-women's function as a chorus of maenads is formalized rather than disguised. Williams quickly establishes the theatrical conventions he will use. While making freer use of these elements, however, he has reduced the number of "big" effects—the storm, flood, and power failure have been eliminated, along with the fate-figure of the woman from Waco—and integrated the action better by strengthening motivation of character.

The revelation of the past centers on Lady, daughter of an Italian immigrant organ-grinder, Papa Romano, who took up bootlegging in Twin Rivers, planted an orchard, and opened a wine garden that became a lovers' rendezvous. When Romano sold liquor to Negroes, the local vigilantes, known as the Mystic Crew, set fire to the orchard and wine garden, and he died trying to put out the flames. At the time of the fire, Lady and David Cutrere were lovers. After that he jilted her to marry wealth and position. Lady then married Jabe Torrance, without knowing that he had been "leader of the Mystic Crew the night they burned up her father in his winegarden on Moon Lake." Lady and Jabe do not live as man and wife; Beulah believes that Lady now counts the days until his death, that she wants to make as much money as she can with the confectionery and then begin a new life.

The story of Papa Romano, the lovers' orchard, and Jabe's part in their destruction gives Lady much stronger motivation and also prepares for Val's death by fire. In *Battle of Angels* the fore-shadowing had been inept: Val had quit a job when the place next door burned down, because "I don't like fire. I dreamed about it three nights straight so I quit. I was burnt as a kid and ever since then it's been something I can't forget."

David is the brother of Carol Cutrere—the prophetic Cassandra of the earlier play. One of Carol's violent brushes with the law brings him to the store to help her. His confrontation with Lady is now a major scene (Act II, Scene 1), and it is effectively juxtaposed with a scene between Carol and Val in which she tries to warn him: "You're in danger here, Snakeskin. You've taken off the jacket that said 'I'm wild, I'm alone!' and put on the nice blue uniform of a convict! . . . The message I came here to give you was a warning of danger! I hoped you'd hear me and let me take you away before it's too late." The play adheres to the myth of Cassandra but with much less self-consciousness. Val says later, "His sister said she'd come here to give me a warning. I wonder what of?"

Lady cannot hold to her resolution to avoid David: "I have something to tell you I never told before. . . . I carried your child in my body the summer you quit me but I had it cut out of my body, and they cut my heart out with it! . . . I wanted death after that, but death don't come when you *want* it, it comes when you don't want it! I wanted death, then, but I took the next best thing. *You* sold *yourself. I* sold *myself. You* was bought. *I* was bought. You made whores of us both!" She thinks David doesn't even remember their love; on the contrary, he remembers nothing else, and he agrees with her that back in "those wine-drinking nights . . . you had something better than anything you've had since!"

This scene in the Ibsenian manner does several things. We now know that Lady has suffered three losses—her father, David, and her child; and this prepares us for the frenzied battle she wages at the last to hold Val when he tries to leave her. It helps to create a more vivid death-in-life for her, a realistic equivalent of Eurydice's stay in hell, that does not have to rely on dialogue like this to make its point: "Oh, oh, oh, I wish I was dead—dead—dead." Also, the disclosure that Lady conceived David's child prepares us for the disclosure of her pregnancy at the end of Act II, without having to introduce a pregnant Beulah from time to time to keep the subject in mind. In each case, repetition or parallelism and organic complication have been the strengthening devices.

The disclosure of Lady's second pregnancy is withheld from Val until the last possible moment. It comes only after Lady has done her best to keep Val with her or to make him take her with him; and it comes from an unsympathetic and disapproving character, Nurse Porter, whose competence we are not likely to question: "The moment I looked at you when I was called on this case last Friday morning I knew you were pregnant. . . . I also knew the moment I looked at your husband it wasn't by him." Lady says: "Thank you for telling me what I hoped for is true." The confirmation suffuses her with wonder and joy, and her sense of fulfillment prompts her to release Val: "You gotta go now—it's dangerous for you to stay here. . . . You've done what you came here to do. . . . You've given me life, you can go!" In her exaltation she calls out to Jabe:"I've won, I've won, Mr. Death, I'm going to bear!" There is a rush of movement in which Jabe kills Lady and tries to kill Val. When he fails, he says, "I'll have you burned! I burned her father and I'll have you burned!" Then he rushes into the street, shouting: "The clerk is robbing the store, he shot my wife . . . !" The posse captures the fleeing Val. Then Carol, with the Conjure Man, is left to pronounce the epitaph: "Oh yes, his snakeskin jacket. I'll give you a gold ring for it. . . . — Wild things leave skins behind them, they leave clean skins and teeth and white bones behind them, and these are tokens passed from one to another, so that the fugitive kind can always follow their kind. . . ."

Lady emerges as a character of more substance, sharper outline, and more vehement emotions. Her Italian background, her non-Southern manner, help to set her off from the people of Twin Rivers, even though she has adopted many of their attitudes and values. In Act III, Scene 1, it is Jabe himself who tells Lady what the audience has known all along: "We burned him out, house and orchard and vines, and 'The Wop' was burned up trying to fight the fire." She now has a strong motive for revenge, for trying to persuade the nurse to "shorten his suffering" with an overdose of morphine, and for her redoubled determination to open the confectionery as a second wine garden before Jabe dies: "I want that man to see the wine garden open again when he's dying." Her frenzied refusal to go down to defeat provides emotional storm enough without a stage cloudburst.

With the dramatic focus shifted to Lady, Val's character dwindles a bit in importance. He is in many respects the same, but the playwright has found ways to make him more sympathetic, so that his few actions may prove more acceptable, less nakedly selfish. Williams has had to soft-pedal his rebelliousness, to trim his dramaturgic sails. Val's chief fault is still that he is intended to *be*, rather than to *do*, to affect others by what he *is*, rather than what he *does*. Character in drama best defines it-self by action, not by attribution.

This Val Xavier appears on cue, as if summoned by the Con-jure Man's wild Choctaw cry. He is not a writer but a guitarist and folksinger. He, like Carol (who lies about her age), is older, —"about thirty"—but with the same symbolic snakeskin jacket, the "wild beauty," the suggestive "slew-foot" walk, and sexual prepotency as before. Indeed, the revision heightens his excep-tional powers. His eyes do not now glow in the dark like a dog's, but his "temperature's always a couple degrees above normal the same as a dog's, that's the truth." In his "job interview" with Lady, he boasts that he can "sleep or not sleep as long or short as I want to," that he can hold his breath three minutes without blacking out, can go a whole day without passing water; and, as supreme example of self-control: "Well, they say that a woman can burn a man down. But I can burn down a woman. . . . I'm saying I could. I'm not saying I would." Williams' efforts to cre-ate in Val the essence of sexuality, a combination of Priapus and Dionysus (and now Apollo), strike me as ridiculously overdone; all the more so when his hero resorts to the tradition of The Vaunt. But it is worth noting that Williams has turned the sexual boast to good account, since the vernacular phrase subtly links the love of Val and Lady with the fire that will kill him.

Val's aphrodisiac effect on the women of the community is assumed, rather than shown at length, action now being concen-trated in fewer characters. His sexuality and allure are illustrated principally in connection with Lady and Carol Cutrere.

At first sight of Carol, Val is startled. They have met before, in New Orleans night spots, but Val is evasive. Later in Act II, Scene 1, she accuses him of having stolen her cousin's watch, and this time, admitting the connection, he tries to return it through her: "When I stole that I known it was time for me to get off the party, so take it back, now, to Bertie. . . ." Just as we learn that Val has been on "a Goddam party" for fifteen years and has now quit, so we learn that Carol has set herself actively against the county and all it stands for, because it defeated her in the days when she was "a Christ-bitten reformer" and devoted her whole life and fortune to the cause of social reform. The citi-zens had thrown her out of town on a charge of "lewd vagrancy."

Wherever she appears, as now, the townswomen at once begin to gossip and to accuse her of being "corrupt."

Corruption has to do with why Val has decided to change his life. He evades Carol's sexual advances, explaining: "I don't go that route. Heavy drinking and smoking the weed and shacking with strangers is okay for kids in their twenties but this is my thirtieth birthday and I'm all through with that route. . . . I'm not young anymore." This is a curious speech for a man who will boast of his prepotent virility. What has age to do with it? Later, he tells Lady: "I'm done with all that. . . . I'm not tired. I'm disgusted." What disgusts him is that, except for a few who have never been "branded," people are either bought or buyers, as if human beings were "carcasses of hogs." Despite the life he has led, despite his disgust, he asserts his innocence: "Lady, I'm thirty today and I'm through with the life that I've been leading. . . . I lived in corruption but I'm not corrupted. Here is why. (*Picks up his guitar.*) My life's companion! It washes me clean like water when anything unclean has touched me. . . ." Later (Act II, Scene 1) he will contradict himself when he recalls his life at fifteen: "I learned that I had something to sell besides my snakeskins. . . . I was corrupted! That's the answer. . . ." Was he or wasn't he? Is he or isn't he? Shall we take his word for it that art is sacred, that it has the power of absolution against any corruption, that it may even be the sole proof of integrity? We seem to be dealing here with Williams' curious attitude toward the guilt or innocence of his characters, and we recall that the playwright uses martyrdom to establish their "fundamental innocence." Yet the insistence on innocence actually serves to raise suspicions of guilt and corruption.

In *Battle of Angels* we had the strange, unconvincing relation of Val with the woman from Waco. Confessing the incident to Myra, Val had said: "This woman from Waco come to my room that night. Well, I was drunk. What happened was accidental. Afterwards, I was disgusted with her and with me. I said to her, 'Listen, I don't want nothing like this; I'm getting away!' " When she turns up in Twin Rivers, we expect him to be concerned for his freedom, not his guilt; but his emotion is strangely in excess of what the situation seems to call for: "Oh, God, Myra, I've washed myself in melted snow on mountains trying to get the touch of her off my body. It's no good. . . . You can't understand what it is to be hounded by somebody's hate. . . . I'm sick. [I feel] Like something was crawling on me. Something that crawled up out of the basement of my brain." Williams' younger hero feels forever soiled by a sexual encounter that was, he says, "accidental" and for which he was not responsible. His older hero talks out of both sides of his mouth, saying "I was corrupted!" but also "I lived in corruption but I'm not corrupted." Whatever the truth is, we expect some proof through action. Val has announced that he's "through with all that route." So the dramatic question has been raised, and the action of the play must abide by it. Does Val mean it when he says he has given up the old life? Will he so act in his new circumstances as to be neither buyer nor bought? And how can he stay free, one of the few who have never been "branded," yet prove that his rehabilitation or regeneration is genuine?

For all that Carol's warning to Val was true prophecy, the only alternative she offered was to join her in the old, self-destructive life of flouting society and jooking. He does not understand her message or heed it because he is already partly tempted by Lady's offer of quarters in the store—an unspoken invitation to become her lover. He resists Lady's offer because he suspects her of trying to buy and use him. In the ensuing quarrel, he upbraids her as "a not so young and not so satisfied woman, that hired a man off the highway to do double duty without paying overtime for it. . . . I mean a store clerk days and a stud nights, and—." When he decides to leave, she is reduced to pleading: "No, no, don't go. . . . I need you! To live . . . to go on living!" The *"true passion of her outcry touches him then,"* and he stays and becomes her lover. Thus, at the end of Act II, he has performed the critical action that leads to the climax, and it is a fatal action.

Similarly, at the climax itself, where Val's regeneration must be confirmed without question, we have a repetition or parallel action, but with stronger motivation for Val to leave and, a little later, to stay. First, he has been menaced by Sheriff Talbott and the men and told to leave the county before sunrise. When he resists Lady's pleas to stay, it is a contest of love and sheer self-preservation; and, as such, a clear and understandable conflict, compared to the selfish Val of *Battle of Angels*, the artist so much concerned with his freedom and his book that he seemed barely concerned about the woman he got with child and that his avowals of love sounded hollow indeed. Now that the physical danger to Val has been visibly increased, and since the debate between Val and Lady is finished without his having learned that she is pregnant, the way is clear for Val, the instant he does learn, to make a definite decision and achieve a sharp reversal of intention. "Why didn't you tell me before?" says Val, and now there is simply no question of his leaving; the decision is instinctive, and it places him unequivocally on the side of life—at the risk of his freedom, his art, his own skin.

Val has made a tragic choice with tragic consequences, not a selfish choice that a tendentious playwright tries to foist upon the audience. It is his action, not his art, that cleanses him of whatever guilt he bears.

In giving the play this ending, Williams has altered the myth. Orpheus loses his own life for love of Eurydice, thereby exhibiting the most Christlike action he performs in the play. The meaning of his choice, and therefore of his death, transcends the conflict between the desire of wild things for freedom and the hostility of a society that, because it has surrendered its freedom in the buying and selling of its members, now lives in a hell of hate and malice. It transcends also the preoccupation of both plays with the pre-eminence of art. In the mature play even as it is shown to have a power akin to resurrection, art is finally subordinated in importance to moral action. For Williams, art still comes only from the free spirit who is an individualist and a rebel—even Vee Talbott with her puritanism must pursue her vision in the face of the town's derision and antagonism. It is still important that the spirit of wild things live on; and in this play it does so, but less through the inspiration of art itself than through the example of moral action, "so that the fugitive kind can always follow their kind. . . ."

Orpheus Descending represents a considerable technical improvement over its earlier version. It also represents the beginning of a shift in Williams away from the confused and sentimental anarchy which the earlier play preaches.[24] Love, which in

24 "It is the frightening final power of death in Williams' dramatic equation that produced two different responses: the rage for sexual satisfaction in the early plays; and the religious quest in the later ones," says Dan Isaac, who sees Williams as a poet of death and a religious mystic. He calls "the proliferation of Christ figures" in the plays following *Cat on a Hot Tin Roof*

Battle of Angels was shown first and last to be a lure and a distraction from the true course of freedom, is again scrutinized suspiciously: "Love? That's the make-believe answer," Val tells Lady. "It's fooled many a fool besides you an' me, that's the God's truth, Lady, and you had better believe it." But Val's subsequent actions, which are intended to show the genuineness of his rehabilitation, illustrate a change of heart that repudiates this sentiment. There is, after all, such a thing as decency, it seems; and it acts not out of fear but out of love. That much Williams can show us, and he does. What he cannot yet show us about Val—with or without myth, with or without realism or theatricalism—is whether, in losing his freedom, he found it.

---

a continuing but unsuccessful "attempt to bestow upon suffering and death a meaning that would transcend the limits of human accomplishment," adding that this includes the character of Chris Flanders in the revised version of *The Milk Train Doesn't Stop Here Anymore,* which he regards as Williams' "most complex and obscure" play. "It is also Williams' most concentrated attempt to formulate and expound a metaphysic that will answer the questions that terrify, indeed traumatize, his major dramatic figures: the meaning of life under the aspect of death in a godless universe." Dan Isaac, "A Streetcar Named Desire—or Death?" (*New York Times,* 18 February 1968).

Although Isaac detects Buddhist tendencies of passive acceptance in *The Night of the Iguana* and *The Milk Train,* Esther Jackson finds "a growing unity and a more coherent rationale" that point to Christian faith in all the plays from *Orpheus Descending* to *Iguana.* These later plays, she says, "reflect an increasingly sure moral position," with Williams coming to "define the condition of man in terms very much like those of orthodox Christianity and to pose, therefore, for human redemption and reconciliation, the forgiveness of God. This 'Christian' cycle of sin-suffering-expiation-redemption is perhaps most clearly defined in *The Night of the Iguana,* a play in which the protagonist seems to pass through all the stages of this progression in his time of life on the stage." Esther Merle Jackson, *The Broken World of Tennessee Williams* (Madison: University of Wisconsin Press, 1965), p. 158.

Tennessee Williams was received into the Catholic Church in January, 1969.

CHAPTER XI

EUGENE IONESCO:
The Existential Oedipus

Even I cannot say whether I am a Christian or not, religious or not, a believer or not, a mystic or not; I can only say that my upbringing was Christian. The title of the play *Hunger and Thirst* is, in fact, biblical. We all hunger, we all thirst. Our hungers and thirsts are various: for the fruits of the earth, for water, for whisky, for bread; we hunger for love, for the absolute. The bread and wine and meat for which the hero Jean thirsts are only substitutes for what could have gratified a hunger and thirst for the absolute.[1]

I.

The comic-tragic world of Eugene Ionesco is thoroughly, devastatingly, modern—the last place we should look for myths. It is filled with clutter and debris, yet it appears to bear no relation to a living past. It is an enclave in time, cut off from the past and also leading to no future other than an indefinite extension of its dreary, and sometimes horrifying, self. The characters who people it may each have had a past, yet they seem to come from nowhere and to be going nowhere, although they are of course going to die. They are prisoners of the present, so much so that

---

[1] Eugene Ionesco, quoted in Simone Bemussa, *Eugène Ionesco* (Paris: Éditions Seghers, 1966), pp. 8-9 (my translation).

   I have borrowed for this chapter the title of the chapter on *Oedipus Rex* in Richmond Y. Hathorn's excellent study, *Tragedy, Myth, and Mystery* (Bloomington: Indiana University Press, 1962).

it dominates their lives, even to the point that they may come to wish for no more than its indefinite continuance. Such a world is uncongenial to myths because myths give the present meaning by explaining the past and the future. Yet Ionesco's plays might serve as illustrations of what Antonin Artaud sought for the "theatre of cruelty": a way to extract from classical myths the powerful forces still struggling within them, while discarding their "defunct images."

From his earliest plays Ionesco has seemed intent on devising his own myths—myths based on his own experience of life—for his highly confessional theatre. The last thing one would expect him to do would be to dramatize classical myth. Take *Amédée; or, How to Get Rid of It*. It creates an original image to express marital guilt over the death of love, or to express "the ever greater and greater encroachment of death on our lives" [2]—that of a corpse in the bedroom that grows and grows until it shatters the door and fills the flat, while husband and wife accept its presence and try to carry on life from day to day. A playwright of such originality could well dispense with tales, however perdurable, handed down from distant times and places. He cannot, because he thinks mythically, entirely avoid resemblances to them. *Rhinoceros* evokes the myth of Ulysses resisting the spell of Circe while his men are transformed into swine. But Ionesco was writing from personal experience of fascism, and the evocation is incidental. *Exit the King* may remind us of *Everyman*, but only to make us aware of the distance separating medieval and modern man and their respective theatres. Again Ionesco's source was personal: "I wrote that work that I might learn to die." [3] Having contemplated the unthinkableness of death for insatiable man, he recreates the Faust legend in *Hunger and Thirst* and lets man satisfy his infinite longings—only to confront him with the same horror, now in the guise of eternity, that he faced when it was called extinction.

Writing directly from experience and his own responses to life, he developed a symmetry in his works that became more and more apparent as he systematically explored the dialectic of

---

[2] George E. Wellwarth, *The Theater of Protest and Paradox* (New York: New York University Press, 1964), p. 63.
[3] Eugène Ionesco, *Journal en miettes* (Paris: Mercure de France, 1967), p. 167.

man's absurd condition. There is no solution; but there is an answer, and it is the same in both cases: "One can do nothing. One can do nothing. One can do nothing. One can do nothing." [4] If *The Pedestrian in Air* seems to rework the myth of Icarus almost by inadvertence, it leaves it broken, truncated, without the clean shape of the catastrophe in which the young overreacher, having soared too near the sun, plummets to his death. His Icarus, Berenger, takes a flight of the imagination only and returns "safely" to earth; but what he has seen of the infinite waste spaces of the universe leaves him a broken man within, one who can only return to the unutterable mystery of mundane existence. Given the paradox of existence that is Ionesco's beginning and ending, it seems unavoidable that any classic myth in his hands would break off, remain incomplete. However, the fourth play he wrote, *Victims of Duty* (1953), consciously borrows one of the most famous of all classic myths, that of King Oedipus, to embody the existential dilemma of modern man and also to exemplify the kind of theatre that Ionesco believes must supplant the theatre of the past.

Choubert, the anti-hero of *Victims of Duty*, voices Ionesco's critique of that theatre: "All the plays that have ever been written, from Ancient Greece to the present day, have never really been anything but thrillers. Drama's always been realistic and there's always been a detective about. Every play's an investigation brought to a successful conclusion. There's a riddle, and it's solved in the final scene. Sometimes earlier. You seek, and then you find. . . . The police arrive, there's an investigation and the criminal is unmasked. It's a thriller. A naturalistic drama, fit for the theatre of Antoine." [5] And the classics? "Refined detective drama. Just like naturalism." It is no accident that we think at once of Sophocles' tragedy, *Oedipus Rex*, that splendid thriller with its distinguished detective, its successful investigation, its solved riddle, and its unmasking; we are meant to do so. So far as the tragedy itself is concerned, it is easy to dispose of Ionesco's disparaging polemic. It is, as Richmond Hathorn points out, "only externally a crime-and-punishment play; internally it is a

[4] *Ibid.*, p. 39.
[5] This and subsequent quotations from *Victims of Duty* are from *Three Plays by Eugène Ionesco: Amédée, The New Tenant, Victims of Duty*, trans. Donald Watson (New York: Grove Press, 1958), pp. 117-66.

moral drama of self-recognition." [6] We can also exonerate it from any charge of being blood-and-thunder melodrama. Sophocles, in keeping with the law of decorum, relegates all violent deeds to the antecedent action or to the wings; whereas Ionesco, availing himself of the freedom of later theatre, which he also condemns, climaxes his play with an almost gratuitous murder committed on stage. What are the playwright's real objections, and what kind of drama would he have take its place?

His objections have to do with an Aristotelian emphasis upon plot, and a certain kind of plot, at that, and with style or method, which he labels "refined naturalism," by which he appears to mean pointless imitation of physical or external reality. He exaggerates grossly for polemical purposes: the theatre of Sophocles depended upon nonillusionistic conventions of playwriting and staging to an even greater degree than Ionesco's. What he does not state explicitly here is his objection to the Greek use of distinct genres, comedy and tragedy, and their strict maintenance. It is based upon his desire to realize in theatrical terms his personal view of life, which is that "the comic is tragic, and that the tragedy of man is pure derision." [7] He has explained this elsewhere: "In *Victims of Duty* I tried to sink comedy in tragedy: in *The Chairs*, tragedy in comedy or, if you like, to confront comedy and tragedy in order to link them in a new dramatic synthesis. But it is not a true synthesis, for these two elements do not coalesce, they coexist: one constantly repels the other, they show each other up, criticize and deny one another and, thanks to their opposition, thus succeed in maintaining a balance and creating tension. The two plays that best satisfy this condition are, I believe: *Victims of Duty* and *The New Tenant*." [8]

There lies behind these esthetic objections a different metaphysic, a different view of man and existence. In Ionesco's "tragic farces" there is no place for the traditional hero or a heroic view of life. Greek tragedy pushed the exceptional man to the limits of his nature, simultaneously exalting the godlike in him and warning him of the dangers of self-intoxication, by centering his being in the active will. Just as Ionesco will not adopt alterna-

[6] Hathorn, *Tragedy, Myth, and Mystery*, p. 90.
[7] Eugène Ionesco, "Experience of the Theatre," trans. Donald Watson, in Robert W. Corrigan and James L. Rosenberg, eds., *The Context and Craft of Drama* (San Francisco: Chandler, 1964), p. 286.
[8] *Ibid.*, p. 286-87.

tively two ways of looking at man in drama, tragedy and comedy, but insists on juxtaposing them in permanent clash, so he will not permit the magnification of man, or accept a belief in supernatural powers that influence or control his destiny; thus he gives us man suffering, rather than man active.

There is a further objection, especially pertinent to *Victims of Duty*. Even as it placed the tragic hero in high relief, Greek drama bound him to the community; for the ongoing life of the group, its spiritual and physical health, were its basic concern: that was what it existed to celebrate. If the tragic hero was his people's redeemer, it was by becoming a sacrificial victim offered to restore health to man and the earth. Ionesco has no such faith to sustain him. Man's suffering and sacrifice can only appear meaningless to him. The Sphinx propounded the riddle of life to Oedipus. Ionesco's anti-hero will face the same riddle. His answer will be the same: man. For Ionesco, what else is there? But with what a difference! For he must also add: "One can do nothing." It is the anti-thesis of Gide or Sartre.

II.

Victims of Duty is a five-character play that lists a sixth character in its *dramatis personae*—"MALLOT *with a t.*" This is a clue to the objective of the play's action, which is *to find Mallot*. The parallel with *Oedipus Rex* is close: "To find the slayer of Laius and lift the plague from the city of Thebes." The dramatic question the action raises is thus: Who is Mallot—what is his crime, and where shall we find him? Although a murder occurs later on in the play, no identifiable crime, plain or hidden, appears to be involved at the outset. We might expect the quest to be pointless, but it will not be: there *is* a Mallot. What seems pointless, yet is as unavoidable as it is inexplicable, is the fact of his guilt.

In proceeding in this fashion to examine *Victims of Duty*, I am making certain assumptions about drama and proposing to hold Ionesco's theory of drama to them. Theatre is the most human, and the closest to life, of all the arts. "It is based upon a pretense and its very nature calls out a multiplication of pretenses," says Thornton Wilder; hence, it invites the audience to use to the full its imagination, its powers of make-believe; and because of its very closeness to life, it not only permits but encourages an extreme degree of distortion on the playwright's part. It achieves all this through the frank employment of conventional, rather than naturalistic, devices.[9]

Ionesco seems to have been born knowing this, or to have learned it early and well as a child, watching the deliberate distortion of life through fantasy that he found in Punch and Judy shows, with their maximum demands upon the spectator's imaginative acceptance. (Behind every Ionesco play, whether or not it explicitly involves domestic squabbles as does the archetypal booth-show, is a Punch and Judy scenario.) Regardless of what else we encounter in Ionesco's theatre, we shall not be limited by realism; and *Victims of Duty* is an outstanding example of the dramatist's innate ability to break out of the bounds of time, place, and verisimilitude, and yet to do so within the standard box-set of tables and chairs with only, but appropriately enough, the addition of a toy stage.

Now, by all means let the playwright have as much freedom as he needs, and let him depart as far from realism as he wishes, in order to capture the particular sense of reality that it is his to give. But the one thing without exception that he must be held to is that his work constitute an action—and yes, that the imitation of that action consist of a beginning, a middle, and an end. The playwright may develop his plot on thematic principles or otherwise disregard strict logical coherence to achieve his particular aim. He may prefer an entirely internal drama or one as full of external tussle as he wishes. His play may, by design, be far more "theatrical" than it is "dramatic," [10] or its action may be merely flaccid or attenuated because he could do no better; but a plot of some kind it must have. Regardless of how disdainful of it Ionesco may claim to be, this much resemblance between traditional drama and his own plays he must allow.[11] A play

[9] Thornton Wilder, "Some Thoughts on Playwriting," in Corrigan and Rosenberg, *Context and Craft of Drama*, pp. 231-41.

[10] This distinction, a very useful one in dealing with existentialist drama and the "theatre of the absurd," is made by Eric Bentley in his review of *Waiting for Godot*, the *locus classicus* of the "theatrical" play, because its frame of action consists of waiting, which by definition suspends the will and kills time.

To me "theatrical" is anything which achieves its desired effect through performance; "dramatic" involves consequential action, that is, significant change directed to some aim or end. See Eric Bentley, *What Is Theatre?* (Boston: Beacon Press, 1956).

[11] Kenneth Thorpe Rowe proceeds on the same assumption in *A Theatre in*

that cannot be defined by its action is either a poor play or not a play at all. This goes for Ionesco as for anyone else. In assuming that *Victims of Duty* can be so defined, I have looked for it to pose a dramatic question (formulated above), and further assumed that it will answer it by providing the action with a crisis or turning-point that leads consequentially to a relevant climax.[12]

Ionesco believes that the surest way to achieve the universal is to concentrate to an extreme degree on the individual. We may therefore expect him to be highly subjective in his treatment of the Oedipus myth, and we shall waste our time if we insist on point-to-point correspondence. Despite his polemic approach, we should not expect him to satirize Sophocles by direct parody. With these allowances in mind, we may ask: how much of the myth will he reconstitute in his own work, how well will it serve his view of life, and will that work contain the esssentials of drama?

At rise, we are in another of those *petit bourgeois* interiors, with the middle-aged Choubert reading the newspaper and his middle-aged wife Madeleine darning socks, just as Mr. and Mrs. Smith were doing at the opening of *The Bald Soprano*. But such placid domesticity in an apparently realistic style is disarming, a booby-trap for the unwary. Ionesco will shatter the placidity and the realistic illusion as soon as possible. We begin with a leap from the cosmic to the cloacal: "Nothing ever happens," says Choubert. "A few comets and a cosmic disturbance somewhere in the universe. Nothing to speak of. The neighbors have been fined for letting their dogs make a mess on the pavement. . . ." Very soon, and without quite knowing how, the unoffending Choubert is trying to help a shy young man (the Detective) locate a former tenant—by name Mallot, but whether with a "d" or "t," both Choubert and the Detective are uncertain. The whole action hinges on this apparently trivial question. Mallot has evi-

---

Your Head (New York: Funk & Wagnalls, 1960). He demonstrates that Ionesco's *The Chairs* affirms "plot structure as the foundation of drama," despite Ionesco's assertion: "I detest the reasoning play, constructed like a syllogism, of which the last scenes constitute the logical conclusion of the introductory scenes, considered as premises." Rowe says of *The Chairs:* "Never has a play moved with more relentless syllogistic logic from scene to scene . . ." (p. 109).

[12] Crisis and climax complete the "plot structure ·as the foundation of drama."

dently become a criminal, but the detective begins to treat Choubert as if *he* were the guilty party.

The Detective's questioning of Choubert turns to bullying, then to brainwashing. Madeleine treacherously aids and abets the young man in this. Was it Mallot with a "d" or a "t"? From the outset, Choubert cannot remember. His attempt to do so turns into an effort to recapture the past, and this in turn plunges him into his own depths. The trail of memory that he follows under the Detective's interrogation becomes the way into his unconscious, his hidden emotional life. Time dissolves into an eternal present (there is no past or future for the unconscious, only *now*), where all that Choubert has known and felt is stored up to be relived as keenly as if it were happening for the first time. (Choubert at one point even travels ahead in time, foreseeing his own old age and Madeleine's.)

The descent into the past and to the center of the self reveals terrible quarrels that took place between his parents while Choubert as a child looked on helplessly. His mother threatens suicide by poison; his father first tries to prevent her, then forces the poison on her. Madeleine appears as Choubert's mother in the flashbacks; in her own person she alternately joins the Detective in forcing Choubert to go down deeper and hesitates to go on with the interrogation, fearing that when he does so, she may lose him. Similarly, the Detective becomes Choubert's father in the flashbacks, while in his own person he keeps hammering at the helpless man: "You must never stop." At the same time, both Madeleine and the Detective are curiously detached, even calloused, observers of Choubert's agonized inward journey —a point which is explicitly acted out later in the play when they take seats as spectators while Choubert exposes his sufferings on the tiny stage.

Dying, his mother speaks to Choubert of his father: *"You must learn to forgive, my child, that's the hardest of all. . . . The time for tears will come, the time for repentance and remorse.* You must be good, you'll suffer for it if you're not and you never learn to forgive. When you see him, obey him, kiss him and forgive him." [13] We have already witnessed the tears she predicted.

[13] Here and below I have taken the liberty of underscoring those parts of the quoted passages of the play that stress the theme of guilt and forgiveness.

Now the theme of repentance, remorse, and forgiveness invests Choubert's quest with a wearisome burden of guilt that must be lifted: "*Who will have mercy on me?*" he cries. "*I could never forgive myself.*" For what? For his hatred of his father, for his hatred of his father's selfishness and violence; for his own pitilessness towards his father's frailties; most of all, for his own contempt: "You used to hit me, but I was stronger than you. My contempt hit you much harder. *That was what killed you, wasn't it?*" He defends himself: "Listen . . . I had to avenge my mother . . . I *had* to . . . What *was* my duty? . . . Did I really *have* to?" He has already asked his father to "forgive us as we forgave you." But his father has not answered: father cannot hear son, as son in turn cannot hear father; and he cries out again: "*Who will have mercy on me, I who have been unmerciful! Even if you did forgive me, I could never forgive myself!*"

Then, in an ironically counterpointed *tirade*, we hear the father's lament for all he felt, but never said to his son—the son who would be his murderer: "I lived in a perpetual state of rage. . . . The good I did turned into evil, but the evil done to me never turned into good. . . . I had a horror of mankind. . . . You were born, my son, just when I was about to blow our planet up. It was only your arrival that saved it. At least, it was you who stopped me from killing mankind in my heart. *You reconciled me to the human race and bound me irrevocably to the history, the crimes and hopes, despairs and disasters of all men. I trembled for their fate . . . and for yours.*" The speech foreshadows the crisis of the play—that moment when Choubert elects to stay on earth and live his life in society. There is further irony in that the thing which his father had wished to communicate but could not was the very thing that proved crucial in his son's life. (Unheeded, Choubert had told his father: "If you would look at me, you'd see how alike we are.")

The father, like Laius of old, had tried to kill his child: "My head," he says, "was spinning with unspeakable remorse to think I'd not wanted a family and had tried to stop you coming into the world. *You might never have been, never have been!*" This last idea is fundamental to Ionesco's thought. In a journal entry, meditating his own death, he says of his life: "Yet this will have existed. No one can prevent this from having existed." [14] Two

[14] Eugène Ionesco, "Selections from the Journal," trans. Rosette C. Lamont,

men meet and come to blows: the father who had rage in his heart until his son's birth "justified and redeemed all the disasters of history," and the son whom he once tried to kill. They meet and come to blows—not once and fatally as strangers on a roadway, but often as strangers in the same house where the son felt the father's presence to be a barrier on his own road to life.

Where is Jocasta in all this? Richard Coe says *Victims of Duty* may be interpreted as "a dramatic illustration of Freud on dreams, or a satire on the Oedipus-complex." [15] If so, we have to do not only with the Oedipus myth and the Oedipus tragedy, but also with the Oedipus-complex! In which latter case, the figure of Jocasta becomes even more important. Wallace Fowlie, speaking of *Victims of Duty*, ascribes to dream and mythology the figure of "the son in the dual role of slayer of his father and of redeemer" and stresses the influence of the mother: "Under the power of the maternal force in this household, both father and son attempt to justify their existences." [16] Dramatically speaking, Ionesco is nowhere explicit; if incest and oedipal conflict are there, they are so obliquely and by inference. Theatrically, however, the answer to the question is plain: Jocasta is there before our eyes, embodied in the actress playing both *wife* and *mother*.

In the first episode of Choubert's journey backward in time and downward into himself, Madeleine changes markedly from the humdrum housewife to the seductive woman she once was and uses her allurements to beckon him onward: "Hold tight the handrail . . . Down . . . go on down . . . if it's me you want!" In middle-age she is bossily maternal but never affectionate: she shows no love for her husband. In both stages of her husband's quest—the descent into the unconscious and the ascent into the empyrean—she is like Jocasta in first urging him forward to find Mallot, then trying to stop him when she thinks she may lose him; similarly Jocasta sought to dissuade Oedipus when she saw that what the oracle foretold had come true.

Her alliance with the Detective is evident from the outset. It is she who invites him to enter their flat and she who induces

in *Yale French Studies*, No. 29 ("The New French Dramatists"), n.d., p. 4.
[15] Richard N. Coe, *Ionesco* (New York: Grove Press, 1961), p. 108.
[16] Wallace Fowlie, *Dionysus in Paris: A Guide to Contemporary Theater* (New York: Meridian Books, 1960), p. 234.

her husband to help him find Mallot. The Detective represents law and authority, which in the play are totalitarian. Madeleine subscribes to the government's propaganda about practicing renunciation and detachment, which are euphemisms for individual irresponsibility in letting the government take over and invade the citizen's private life. In any situation involving her husband and authority, Madeleine sides with the latter. It is interesting to consider the role of Madeleine-Jocasta in the light of Erich Fromm's interpretation of the myth, where the myth is seen as having as its central theme "one of the fundamental aspects of interpersonal relationships, the attitude toward authority"; [17] for this theme is central to *Victims of Duty* also.

The myth, says Fromm, symbolizes "the rebellion of the son against the authority of the father in the matriarchal family"; and the roots of the struggle go far back into the ancient fight between the patriarchal and the matriarchal systems of society. The matriarchal system with woman as lawgiver in both family and society emphasized sexual promiscuity, ties of blood and of soil, and passive acceptance of all natural phenomena. It held that all men are equal, that the happiness of man is the aim of life, and that human life and existence represent the supreme value. By contrast, the patriarchal system invested in the father the final authority in the home as well as the dominant role in a hierarchically organized society that gave predominance to rational thought, undertook to change or control natural phenomena, and stressed respect for man-made law. In fact, it made obedience to authority the main virtue of life. Jocasta, says Fromm, in consenting to the killing of Oedipus, performed an act that, although legitimate from the patriarchal view, constituted the unforgivable crime from the standpoint of matriarchal ethics. She was betraying the role of woman as wife and mother, the life-giver and life-nourisher. And since human life and happiness are the aim of matriarchal society, it follows that capitulation to the hard, abstract reign of force imposed by the patriarchal system was treachery to the child and to woman's own nature.

Madeleine's turning against her husband is unconsciously done because it is habitual. She treats his sufferings with annoyance

[17] Erich Fromm, *The Forgotten Language* (New York: Rinehart, 1951), pp. 195-96, 202 *et seq.*

and nagging or, worse, with calloused detachment that would be impossible if she loved him. Richard Coe, recalling "the horrifying sadistic glee of Madeleine as she watches her husband tortured" in the brainwashing episode at the center of the action, remarks: "In this deliberate destruction and betrayal of the inner life, for fear 'of what the neighbors say,' woman, in Ionesco's world, is guiltier far than man. Adam is betrayed by Eve. Choubert is betrayed by Madeleine . . . and betrayed in the most cruel and sordid manner, to the police." [18]

Who is the Detective? What does his menacing figure represent? Since Ionesco is nothing if not a metaphysical writer, we might expect him to make the Detective the equivalent of Tiresias, with more than human power. But he does not. Theatrically, the role, like Madeleine's, provides a double image not merely in that the Detective is shy and polite at first, then cruel and brutal, but also in that he is young enough to be Choubert's son, and therefore in the scenes of father-son conflict, the ages of the actors are reversed. An entry in Ionesco's journal may ultimately help us identify this representative of the police. Ionesco, describing therein an erotic dream he had, tells how he tried to interpret it to his friend Z. He had wished to make love to an unknown woman, but everything conspired to foil him. Police shadowed him. He had to catch a train. He lost his luggage. People blocked the corridors. And so on. "The police are my conscience, of course," said Ionesco. "I wanted to leave, but my luggage prevented me. I wanted to take my luggage with me." "*No*," replied Z., "*in reality you did not wish to be free. Your luggage was an excuse, a pretext. It is precisely your luggage you would have to give up if you truly wished to be free.*" [19]

Shall we see the Detective as conscience, that is, as Choubert's own moral sense, originating with him? Or shall we take him to be a kind of Freudian super-ego, the representative of public opinion, the censure of The Others? If the latter, then we have a standard of custom imposed upon the person from without but regarded by the unquestioning citizens as an absolute standard of right and wrong. And does such a standard reflect a metaphysical order of good and evil? It will not do so in Ionesco's play. So it raises a question as to whether the guilt Choubert feels has a rational basis, or whether it is irrational only.

[18] Coe, *Ionesco*, p. 58.
[19] Ionesco, *Journal en miettes*, pp. 107-8 (my translation, emphasis added).

In Sophocles' play, the king's unseen antagonist is Apollo, and it is the victory of the god that is signalized in the catastrophe. (Tiresias, his representative, warned Oedipus away from undertaking the quest and so did just the opposite of the relentless Detective.) But there is no God in Choubert's world, or in Ionesco's either; and the playwright cannot make the Detective stand for anything more than human. Unlike Apollo, the antagonist is there before our eyes throughout. But he is not alone. Madeleine and, later, Nicolas d'Eu and the Lady are antagonists also, because they are his allies. He represents the state, an abstraction that stands for society, for The Others, without whose consent he could not do what he does. But Choubert is also his own antagonist, for there is something in him—Ionesco cannot name it or explain it—that makes him a party to the crime of the Many against the One, even when he is that one; hence, he is a sharer in the universal guilt by which the state and The Others impose their will.

Choubert appears on the toy stage, groping his way like a blind Oedipus to find out who he is. Madeleine and the Detective sit to watch him, like unsympathetic playgoers. As he journeys toward the center of himself, Choubert sees in the distance a magical city, "fountains and flowers of fire in the night . . . a palace of icy flames, glowing statues and incandescent seas, continents blazing in the night, in oceans of snow!" Conflicting emotions that both rend and heal overwhelm him: " I feel strong. I feel weak, I feel ill, I feel well, *but I feel, above all, I feel myself, still, I feel myself.*"

But at the very center, the magical world of light vanishes and night surrounds him, "only one butterfly of light painfully rising. . . ." The curtains of the toy stage close and Choubert vanishes, to reappear only after he has begun to surface. At the supreme moment of self-assertion, he drew back from the brink of death: extinction. This is the crisis of the play, or rather its first main crisis. *Victims of Duty* may be structurally unique in requiring two crises, each the equal of the other metaphysically and hence as indispensable as the other in depicting the dialectic of human absurdity. At the second and final crisis, the same fate will confront him: death, extinction. And again he will have to choose.

In inducing Choubert to retreat and try a new tack, the Detective makes a significant appeal:

You must realize Mallot's got to be found again. *It's a question of life and death. It's your duty. The fate of all mankind depends on you.* . . . Remember and then everything will come clear again. . . . [*To MADELEINE*]: He'd gone down too far. He's got to come up again . . . A little . . . in our estimation.

One might expect that Choubert, having recovered his essential self, would break free of the Detective's domination when he comes back to the surface, but he does not. Instead, influenced by that appeal to duty, he continues to turn over his memories, trying to share them with Madeleine. He remembers Mallot's nickname: Montbéliard. "Why yes, good Lord, yes," he exclaims. "It's true . . . it's funny, it's true." And with this, the direction changes: Choubert goes off in search of him above ground, across oceans, forests, the mountains of Europe. He begins a mystic ascent, a painful, exhausting climb up sheer walls of rock. "He mustn't rise too high above us," says Madeleine, beginning to vacillate at the danger of this new course. But the Detective, adamant, drives him on: "You must be a man to the bitter end. . . . Come on now, one last effort." When Choubert reaches the mountain peak and can see right through the sky, however, there's no sign of Montbéliard. Here again, at the opposite pole, are freedom and affirmation: "I'm alone. . . . I can run without walking! . . . I'm not dizzy. . . . *I'm not afraid to die anymore.*"

Now the Detective realizes that Madeleine was right: "I've driven him too far. Now he's getting away from us. . . . My dear old chap, we've both got on the wrong track." They redouble their appeals to Choubert. Madeleine plays on his sympathy: "It's not good to be alone. You can't leave us. . . ." She pretends to be an old woman starving for bread: "Have pity, pity!" They solicit Choubert with "all the advantages of everyday life in society": sensual pleasures, wealth, position, security, patriotism, revenge, fame, power, a second chance at life. "If you like," says the Detective, "you can start life afresh, learn to walk again . . . fulfill your ambitions." And always there is the appeal to duty.

But Choubert appears unheeding. He is transformed, bodiless. He can fly. "I'm bathing in the light. . . . The light is seeping through me. *I'm so surprised to be, surprised to be, surprised to be.*" But suddenly, mysteriously, distress overcomes him. He feels ill. He cannot bear it—and he jumps. This is the second and final crisis.

"The act of climbing or ascending," says Mircea Eliade, "symbolizes *the way towards the absolute reality*; and to the profane consciousness, the approach towards that reality arouses an ambivalent feeling, of fear and of joy, of attraction and repulsion. . . ." [20] Choubert had been ecstatic. "I no longer fear death!" he had cried. But when it seemed that the moment of deliverance was at hand, he could not, or would not, break free; instead, he jumped.

Choubert awakes, presumably "himself" again. "Where am I?" He finds it strange that Monsieur Chief Inspector is still there, even stranger that the Detective found his way into his memories. "*A new character, a LADY, who takes no notice at all of what is going on,*" has appeared and sits to one side. The Detective resumes his bullying and takes all credit for having rescued Choubert, while insisting that the search continue. Madeleine, too, resumes her badgering. From here on, Choubert regresses outwardly, becoming more and more babyish.

Again the moment has passed when we feel that Choubert might have asserted himself. But the reversal does not take place. On the downward journey, he had found himself; in the empyrean, he had lost his fear of death; but the fall to earth returns him to the bondage of the waking world and to life in society. A change of sorts occurs, nonetheless: there enters a preposterous but formidable figure, a writer named Nicolas d'Eu. At once the Detective finds himself on the defensive, even contemplates flight. But he is reassured when Nicolas says: "Carry on, carry on, don't let me interrupt you!" Madeleine, meanwhile, returns to her original character, and at the Detective's barked request races back and forth from kitchen to living room, bringing cups of coffee until all the surfaces are covered with them.

The Detective continues his hypnotic domination of Choubert: "I'll give you back your strength. You can't find Mallot, because you've got gaps in your memory. We're going to plug those gaps!" He forces bread on Choubert, who begins to stuff himself like a reluctant child. The Detective tries to win over Nicolas d'Eu, who asks him his attitude toward renunciation and detach-

[20] Mircea Eliade, *Images and Symbols: Studies in Religious Symbolism*, trans. Philip Mairet (New York: Sheed & Ward, 1961), p. 51.

ment. "My duty, you know, my dear Sir," says the Detective, "is simply to apply the system." Nicolas also chats incongruously (if anything is incongruous in this chaotic world) about theatre, and we come back to the idea proposed earlier: "I've thought a great deal about the chances of reforming the theatre. Can there be anything new in the theatre?"

Nicolas wants a theatre that reflects the tone of the age, utilizes a new kind of psychology, a different logic, based on contradictions: "We'll get rid of the principle of identity and unity of character and let movement and dynamic psychology take its place. . . . We are not ourselves. . . . Personality doesn't exist." As I see it, Nicolas here plays the devil's advocate and is not straightforward spokesman for the dramatist, even though he asserts: "We've got Ionesco and Ionesco, that's enough!" There is ambiguity in the statement: "We'll get rid of identity and unity of character." It sounds like faded Pirandellism or a totalitarian slogan. Choubert's twofold quest, surrealist and oneirical as it may have been, affirmed the existence of self at opposite extremes. That self persists beneath all the distortions and confusions that society creates in a person's consciousness. Its essential awareness is that of surprise: "I'm so surprised to be, surprised to be, surprised to be. . . ."

The tension increases as Nicolas challenges the Detective and the latter defends himself while continuing to force bread into the babyish Choubert: "Why Monsieur Nicolas d'Eu, I'm only doing my duty! I didn't come here just to pester him! I've really got to find out where he's hiding, Mallot with a t at the end. There's no other way I can do it. I've no choice. As for your friend (Choubert)—and I hope one day he'll be mine. . . . I respect him, sincerely I do!" Duty, regardless of what action it may require, becomes a categorical imperative. Everything one does can be justified by appeal to authority. Conscience has abdicated. Renunciation and detachment have won. The state is supreme. Nicolas' manner becomes more dangerous as the Detective weeps and protests: "I didn't want to upset your friend! . . . I swear I didn't! . . . It's he who forced *me* to come into this flat. . . . *I* didn't want to, I was in a hurry. . . . They insisted, both of them. . . . I'm only a pawn, Monsieur, a soldier tied to his orders. . . ."Suddenly, Nicolas brandishes a knife and thrice stabs the Detective, who dies crying: "I am . . . a victim . . . of duty!" Madeleine, impervious to the violent death except as a nuisance, takes out her annoyance on Nicolas: "It's such a pity it had to happen in our flat! . . . Who's going to help us find Mallot now? . . . We've got to find Mallot! His sacrifice [*indicating the DETECTIVE*] shall not have been in vain! Poor victim of duty!" Echoing her, Nicolas now assumes the Detective's role and badgers Choubert: "Come on, eat, eat, to plug the gaps in your memory!" Choubert protests: "I'm a victim of duty, too!" And Madeleine: "We're all victims of duty! . . . Swallow! Chew!" Now they are all at it, including the Lady, who up to now had simply looked on. "[*While all the characters are ordering one another to chew and swallow, the curtain falls.*]"

A beginning, a middle—and an end of sorts, although the process may be assumed to continue indefinitely in this surrealist nightmare of man in society. Because Ionesco wishes to show Choubert as victim to the end, he introduces Nicolas to provide a climax by killing his antagonist, only to become his persecutor in turn. But then, as Madeleine says, "We are all victims of duty." Or as Sartre, Ionesco's *bête-noire*, might say: "Hell is the others." The conclusion seems to be that each of us is Choubert, *but also one of The Others*. Conceivably, Ionesco could rewrite his play with Madeleine as the central figure, or the Detective, or Nicolas, or even the Lady, and repeat the essential action with variations to suit the particular person. It is merely a matter of point of view. For this is another parable about Everyman and the inescapable experience of man's existence among his fellows. The dialectic of downward and upward, of the subjective and the objective, of the self and others, carries throughout. The action ends, as it must, in an impasse of paradox and surprise, because this is Ionesco's existential or metaphysical view. And the form and tone of the play extend its dialectic, with the comic and tragic, the frightening and the funny, seen as coexistent and coextensive. Life is not an alternation of the tragic and the ridiculous; it is both things at once, or the same thing viewed simultaneously in its two aspects.

As Ionesco's theatre has developed, its unity and consistency have become clearer. Each play tends to throw light on the others, so that beyond the shock of their bizarre theatricality, we can see how they are related. In this respect, two plays seem to me especially useful as coordinates in placing *Victims of Duty: Amédée*, produced the same year, and the later *Rhinoceros*. In *Amédée* the protagonist escapes from his intolerable situation simply by flying away with his burden of guilt while protesting to his wife and the neighbors he leaves behind: "I didn't want to run away from my responsibilities. It's the wind, *I* didn't do anything! . . . It's not on purpose! . . . Not of my own free will! . . . Forgive me, Ladies and Gentlemen, I'm terribly sorry! Forgive me!" This is escape drama in both senses of the term: a vivid fantasy, and an evasion on the playwright's part, as if he could not think how else to end his play. In taking the easy way out, he negates the essence of human nature as he showed it in *Victims of Duty*, and as it will appear in *Rhinoceros*. Amédée's resort to flight repudiates his humanity. This transcendence may free him from earth, but it also leaves him alone, cut off from his fellows. Honor Matthews has examined *Amédée* in connection with the theme of Cain and Abel in the theatre: "The weight of responsibility which will inevitably involve men with the weight of failure and of guilt, appears to be essential for the life which we recognize as human, and, if this pattern were ever to be broken, life as we know it would end." [21]

Her further comment brings us to *Rhinoceros*, which in its situation is the obverse of *Victims of Duty*, and to a different solution: "So long as man desires his brother's keeping he must be his brother's keeper." [22] Like so many of his plays, *Rhinoceros* has its source in Ionesco's own life. As an adolescent in Rumania during the rise of fascism there, he saw people all around him joining the Iron Guard: "Everyone except me. Somehow, I didn't espouse the reigning ideology. To this day I still don't know how it happened. All I know is that I was quite alone." [23] Berenger, the frightened "hero in spite of himself," as Ionesco calls him, feels that something must be done to save the world where every-

[21] Honor Matthews, *The Primal Curse: The Myth of Cain and Abel in the Theatre* (London: Chatto & Windus, 1967), p. 214. She calls *Amédée* "a fantasy of the integrated self" in which Amédée accepts the fact of his deed (the murder of love) and, by taking its consequences upon himself, transcends the limitations of his human condition, but at the cost of his nature.

[22] *Ibid.*

[23] Quoted in Walter Wager, ed., *The Playwrights Speak* (New York: Delacorte Press, 1967), p. 158.

one is going mad and turning into a rhinoceros; he even feels
that he alone can do it (though he knows that is not true), but
also that others ought not to leave him to do it by himself. So
there he sits, half of him wishing he had joined the others in
their trumpeting, the other half of him resisting. At the close, he
is not even sure that he *can* hold out. But something inside him
—a sense of duty—tells him he must try. Ionesco's dialectic of
the absurd reduces itself to two propositions: His duty to humanity is the same as his duty to his own nature; for to betray
himself is somehow to betray the others, and to betray the others
is somehow to betray himself. Keeping faith (and it is a faith,
for he does not know *why* it is so, only that it *is* so), he will not
be able to say, "I am free." He will probably not be able to say,
"I no longer fear death." But by his constancy he will have
affirmed something without which neither statement would have
any meaning or worth.

Ionesco presents an action that is an ironic inversion of ancient
symbols and a picture of life that is at once funny and demonic.
What we see in *Victims of Duty* is a mocking parody of the individual's initiation into society, into a new state of being, but
without the supernatural meaning that initiation symbolized in
older societies: "'Initiation' means, as we know, the symbolic
death and resurrection of the neophyte, or in other contexts, the
descent into Hell followed by ascension into Heaven. Death—
whether initiatory or not—is the supreme case of the rupture of
the planes [of reality]," says Mircea Eliade.[24] The initiate, having undergone death and rebirth, is by definition *one who knows*.
As Ionesco presents him in Choubert, he is one who, through
suffering that is communally inflicted, experiences the most intense life as he approaches absolute reality, both at the center
of himself and at the center of the world, but who, afterward
as well as before, *cannot remember*. This ritual of initiation is
a ritual of alienation. He returns from his intense inner life
to what is, by contrast, a zombie existence, a living death.
Choubert's "death" cannot, like Oedipus' exile, lift the plague
from society. Society *is* the plague. All its members are, like
Choubert, mutilated. This is not the tragedy of an exceptional
man who suffered a peculiarly horrible fate; it is the laughable

[24] Eliade, *Images and Symbols*, p. 49. See also p. 132 above, note 28.

tragedy of the ordinary man whose fate is irrational, gratuitous, and without meaning, all the more so for being unavoidable.

In the nonreligious world depicted in Ionesco's play, Choubert's quest for the ineffable in himself or in the transcendent world must end in failure, for it is not to be found in the profane life of the modern, desacralized *petit bourgeois* interior. "All that we dream is capable of realization," Ionesco has said. Artistically, perhaps; existentially, by no means. That is his burden in play after play. He dreams of the absolute, but cannot achieve it; he speaks of God, but cannot believe in him.

There is further irony in the means whereby Choubert is driven to search for Mallot with a t. What appears to be a brutal police interrogation also resembles psychoanalysis, a technique of remembering that is, however incidentally painful, ultimately intended to heal by bringing the patient to a new state of knowledge. But psychoanalysis itself reflects, on the plane of philosophic naturalism, the initiatory pattern of the ancient religious ordeals; and, as with them, there hangs over the crises in Choubert's unconscious a religious or mystical aura to which Ionesco can give no name.[25]

Once you have grasped the extent of evil, of cruelty and meaninglessness, in this waking world to which the initiate returns, you find it amazing that the playwright can hold to his conviction that man's plight is ridiculous, and that he can exemplify it in plays that are both horrible and funny. Ionesco does not mince words: "If you have been everywhere a foreigner and a stranger, as I have, you find that cruelty and hatred are the dominant factors in human affairs. That's a discovery I've never got over—that people are out to kill one another; if not directly, then indirectly."[26] The guilt in *Victims of Duty* is only partly irrational—that is, arbitrarily imposed from without. It also springs from a desire to kill one's brother (whatever the actual relationship may be); and that desire, even without the deed, constitutes a grave crime and produces real guilt. What to Ionesco is absurd is that he does not know why this should be so; it simply is so. And if he does not resign himself to it, neither does he deny it.

[25] Mircea Eliade, *The Sacred and the Profane: The Nature of Religion*, trans. Willard R. Trask (New York: Harper & Row, 1961), pp. 208, 210.
[26] Quoted by Vera and John Russell, "Ionesco on Death," *Chicago Sun-Times*, 15 September 1963.

We cannot, therefore, regard the individual man (Choubert or another) as good, and the group as evil. Ionesco does not subscribe to the old maxim: "The senate is a beast, the senators are good men." Nor will he subscribe to Rousseau's sentimental variant of it: "Men are good by nature and made bad by society." Yet he cannot subscribe to the older view: "Man is a fallen creature with a natural bias to do evil." [27] He cannot, although the play is suffused with a nostalgia for something precious that has been lost. His is a darker view: "As soon as an idea, a conscious intent, wish to to be realized in historical terms, they are disfigured, become the opposite of what they were, turn monstrous. Social conditions may be based on the opposition which exists between conscious thought and the obscure tendencies which work against a concrete realization of the idea. . . . Does man always claim to do the opposite of what he deeply wishes?" [28] It is as if there were a demonic reversal operating at the heart of things. A conscious wish to do good at once releases an unconscious wish to do evil. The process is apparently not reversible: there is no indication that a conscious wish to do evil creates an unconscious wish to do good. That is why it is truly demonic. Choubert's father had cried out in his grief: "The good I did turned into evil, but the evil done to me never turned into good. . . ."

And where does art stand in this equation—art that is for Ionesco a sovereign good, a "secular prayer," solace in an absurd world, but that has its source in that same unconscious?

For man's struggle to find his own center, of which Schlegel had spoken so urgently, Ionesco substitutes a vision of "racial introversion" reduced to a single motive: murderous hate. We see it as much in the persecution of Choubert as in the slaying of the Detective. It is through hate, not love, says Ionesco, that we are members one of another. We are bound by its invisible web, and there is no escaping it, except at the cost of our humanity or our life—and these turn out to be one and the same.

In view of this, one might think that Ionesco would end by

[27] The latter two quotes are by W. H. Auden, "Criticism in a Mass Society," in Geoffrey Grigson, ed., *The Mint*, No. 2 (London: Routledge & Kegan Paul, 1948), p. 7.
[28] Ionesco, "Selections from the Journal," p. 6. Here he is very close to Sartre, who ascribes our insincerity and bad faith to that part of ourselves which we refuse to acknowledge.

echoing the sentiment of that Greek tragedian who concluded his masterpiece of "distinguished naturalism" with: "Never to have been born is best." But the modern playwright remains paradoxical. "I'm surprised to be," says Choubert; and the astonishment of consciousness, despite all its anguish, seems to Ionesco well worth it. That Ionesco should emerge as a playwright of affirmation is the most astonishing thing of all, but it is a fact which *Victims of Duty* demonstrates, and which his subsequent plays make even more apparent. It is why Ionesco can write in his journal: "A dream I will no longer remember will be that of universal existence, the dream of my actual self. 'What did I dream?' I ask myself often as I wake up with a hazy remembrance of captivating things which have disappeared in the night of eternal forgetfulness. The only thing I am left with is the regret of being unable to remember. I will die, torn abruptly from the dream of reality. . . . I will not remember, nor will there be an 'I' to do the remembering. *Yet this will have existed. No one can prevent this from having existed.*" [29]

Not even God.

[29] *Ibid.*, p. 4.

CHAPTER XII

CONCLUSION:
Myth and Mystery

The uses of classical myth that we have examined in studying more than a score of plays by ten dramatists who wrote during the first 60 years of the century have required for their success a theatre that transcends the restrictions of realism and naturalism. They have also, without exception, served to express the dramatists' concern with ethics and metaphysics: man's nature, his relation to his fellows, his place in the universe, and the forces in that universe that surround him and affect his destiny.

André Gide regarded classical myth as subject matter that has been stripped by the perspectives of time and distance of all but its universality and beauty. It was not that myth contained endless meanings; rather, the poet could, through his interpretations, attribute endless meanings to it. He gave myth a psychological, rather than a philosophical, emphasis: myth as a clue to the unconscious self. Other playwrights followed suit, even those not primarily concerned with depicting psychology of character.

But Gide eventually, through his preoccupation, approached the philosophical. He used the heroes of myth as exemplary symbols in the construction of a new ethic derived from a "new orientation," that of instinctual man versus society and its restraints. His heroes exemplify titanism, that is, the possibilities of exceptional man, who realizes his true self in his conflict with society and the gods. Their deeds are the archetypal justifications for Gide's revolt against bourgeois civilization and its values. Hence, they are a way of repudiating the guilt accumulated from the puritanical world of his childhood, substituting new moral and ethical conventions, and illustrating them in action.

The key to Gide's theatre of myth is the exaltation and celebration of exceptional man; its aim is self-transcendence. It necessitates the rejection of the past—its beliefs and institutions —as dead and stultifying; all the past, that is, except the world of art which he exempts from his indictment. Gide's estheticism subordinates ethics to art—an inversion of bourgeois values that completes the revolutionary overthrow of the past.

Thus the revolt against the past is justified by invoking a still earlier past, pre-Christian as well as anti-bourgeois. Through recourse to myth, the playwright is at one stroke delivered from the necessity of imitating or recreating faithfully the dreary bourgeois world, and yet enabled to bring it into high relief by reducing aspects of the myth to the deliberately banal, as in the intellectual vaudeville of *Oedipe*. The contrast produces a shock among the philistines. In sum, Gide uses myth to undermine recent tradition by invoking a remote tradition that still has vitality; he turns the authority of myth, which he equates with the culture of classic Greece, against the invested authority of the recent past to break the grip of its dead hand upon the present and the future.

Cocteau turned to myth as to an objective correlative or concrete universal that would obviate the need for implied or verbal symbolism and hence would help to achieve "a beauty which can come to life only on the stage." The narrative outline of myth is, he found, well adapted to a concrete, visual drama. Transposed in time, its elements of the magical and marvelous can be hidden under simple objects of everyday life to serve as traps for theatre poetry. The incidents of myth discourage the literal plausibility which realism demands and respond instead to heraldic, rather than detailed, psychological treatment of character. Yet (as Gide showed) they also invite new psychological interpretations. And so they suit theatricalism, a style of drama and presentation that seeks freshness by creating a magic of illusion that is not the illusion of reality, in order to realize the possibilities of the theatre as a poetic medium. Theatricalism can, for example, take full advantage of instantaneous transformations of character in myth as poetry of the theatre.

Here Cocteau came upon one of his most fruitful ideas. The element of the arbitrary which myth introduces into both action and character can be extended to the sense of time. Drama is, to begin with, a profound foreshortening or telescoping of the action it imitates. In the world of myth that foreshortening can be made still more acute. Time can be speeded or slowed by showing existence moving at different rates on different planes. This acceleration of time as in a sudden transformation of character, or its deceleration as in the immobility of a spell, can eliminate all the intermediate steps or stages of the normal pattern of life. The effect is to create a sense of the supernatural, of mystery. Also, by dramatizing the simultaneity of time, the playwright can permit the spectator, already godlike in his omniscience, to see a mythic action as it might appear to the gods in timeless contemplation: an action which, because everything is known already and predetermined, has no before or after. Giraudoux borrowed from Cocteau the idea of the pattern of pin-pricks in the folds of time, using the acceleration of time as a synonym for destiny made manifest.

For Cocteau myth can be exploited for its gratuitous beauty and made to effect inexplicable emotional responses. Myth is a means of short-circuiting the reasoning faculty so as to appeal directly to man's instinctive or sub-rational emotions. It can plunge the spectator at once into a world where his dulled responses are stimulated by having no rational elements to cling to. Thus myth aids in applying the poetic vision to everyday life, so that a "modern mythology" becomes visible to the jaded eye. Myth is the poet's domain, the exaltation of poetry his object.

Robinson Jeffers turned to myth as offering the poet usable sources of emotion to produce impassioned speech in a sophisticated civilization, when war has lost its epic dimensions and religion no longer provides soil for poetry to fix its roots in and to flourish. Jeffers regards the family as a source both of the highest poetry and of the lowest comedy. One has only to involve his characters in its emotion-producing events to obtain the passionate utterance that will move reader or spectator. In this he echoes Aristotle's statement that the most beautiful tragedies were composed about a few great families that suffered or did things of a dreadful nature.

Jeffers reanimates myth in his plays by stressing the barbarity of the action and by using depth-psychology in creating motivations for his characters. In placing his emphasis on the family as such, rather than on the marvelous, he was the first playwright studied here to add the element of incest to the myth of Orestes and Electra. O'Neill, Giraudoux, and Sartre did the same after him. Gide, also writing after Jeffers in this case, enlarged the element of incest in the Oedipus myth, both literally and symbolically, as Jeffers had done and as did Cocteau and Ionesco.

Jeffers' dramatization of the Orestes story is openly didactic. It expounds his view of man as caught in the trap of his own racial introversion, and it offers as an example to him Orestes, cured of his madness through mystical communion with the God of nature. Man should uncenter the mind from himself and, turning away from humanity, embrace pantheism.

Jeffers' God is wholly undramatizable and his philosophy of Inhumanism largely so. Therefore, his use of the supernatural and personification of forces of nature are purely theatrical conventions. Later, he tends to adapt Greek tragedy instead of re-creating myth in original, independent works. The violence of the myths permits him to stress the characteristics of independence, courage, pitilessness, and endurance that are needed for an existence where nature shows neither charity, nor chastity, nor pity. For him, the contemporary significance of myth seems to lie in its implied warning to modern man that, despite his vast scientific control of nature, nature is also within him, and himself he has not learned to control.

Jeffers' is a poetic theatre, traditional in its emphasis on language. It uses variations on the formal devices of Greek tragedy instead of a radically different theatrical style.

For Eugene O'Neill, God is a great belief man once held but lost, and the loss has made him inconsolable. When he undertook to dramatize the Orestes myth, therefore, he had to leave out all trace of the supernatural. Yet he wished to inject into his modern psychological drama a sense of ineluctable fate. His basic view might be called scientific determinism, but its poetic expression in *Mourning Becomes Electra* is a curious combination of defeated idealism and demonic self-punishment. His equivalent for the ancient curse is the puritan taint, but the mechanism of the characters' doom is their conflicting and incestuous desires of love and hate. O'Neill saw the myth as story, and for much of his trilogy carefully worked out correspondences between his plot and the action of the Greek original. He succeeded in so transmuting the myth that it creates its effect without relying on thematic parallels or allusive imagery. He centered his tragedy in a "drama of family love and hate," using only psychological motivation as the common ground between him and his audiences. He reconciled myth with realism, modifying the latter only to the extent of emphasizing the formal design of repetition and reversal and seeking in his total conception to express simultaneously "unrealistic truth—lying reality." O'Neill called the subconscious "the mother of all gods and heroes"; but in his trilogy it is rather the mother of demons.

The plays of Giraudoux use myth principally to show man's proper place in the universe and to bring into relief man's most humanly admirable qualities by pitting him against the gods. The latter are, to Giraudoux, convenient symbols of fate or destiny. At the same time they can serve as man's conception of the forces, more than human, that surround him with which, out of dissatisfaction with his own humanity, he may attempt to ally himself in order to achieve self-transcendence. He does so at his peril, Giraudoux thinks. It comes of ignoring or neglecting his right relations to cosmic life, and to his duty, which is to become his most human self. Because he sees theatre as a temple for the celebration of man, Giraudoux uses it to present through myth idealized portraits of characters that serve to show what man could become if he cultivated his own humanity.

In dramatizing myth, Giraudoux, like Cocteau, disregards realism and creates a poetic theatre which permits him to retell myths in novel ways. He uses the supernatural prodigally and often fancifully for whimsical or ironic effect. He gives characters naturalistic motives, at the same time making them self-consciously aware of the role they have been assigned in and by the myth. This is a deleterious effect of his sometimes undisciplined theatricalism. But he succeeds in the main in creating from myth moving drama, extremely attractive characters, and a poetry of the theatre.

The least direct use of myth, disappointingly enough, is found in the plays of T. S. Eliot. He sometimes retains thematic re-semblances to his sources, but so displaces the plot and charac-ters of myth that any vestiges of it are no longer forcefully and dramatically recognizable. Myth—or rather, a Greek play—serves him only as a point of departure; and he moves further and further from the myth, not only softening its harsh or brutal incidents, but also internalizing its overt action and isolating his characters from one another.

Eliot would regard the timeless theatricalism of Cocteau and Giraudoux, along with fantasy and historical drama, as an eva-sion of the "immediate task," which is, as he sees it, primarily the creation of a new verse form that can be applied to a style of modified, but contemporary, realism. In practice he attempts to work beneath and behind realism to create a symbol of the unseen, because he is reluctant to break the realistic mold which his own use of verse has already partially invalidated.

It is regrettable that the foremost poet of his generation, and the only dramatist of the group dedicated to a specifically Chris-tian view of life, was so hesitant and theatrically unadventurous in his plays, and so bound by self-imposed restrictions. In so far as classical myth is concerned, Eliot's dramas prove nothing about its viability for a Christian theatre.

Sartre's *The Flies* dramatizes the first principles of his existen-tial humanism. It is his only original venture into classical myth, and one necessitated as much by the restrictions of the Nazi censorship in occupied Paris as by his search for a classic prece-dent to make acceptable his hero's slaying of his mother.

Sartre found the myth of Orestes congenial to his theatre of situation, where contemporary issues are dramatized without concern for realism or psychological interest in character. His play, however, borrows strong situations from the Greek drama-tists and then weakens them in order to make existentialist points in debate. In the light of his philosophy, the high points of the play are Orestes' discovery that man is free and his subsequent defiance of Zeus, both of which are additions to the myth; but the violent turns of plot work against Sartre's placing the em-phasis elsewhere. Since Zeus, also an addition, is a generalized antagonist who represents man's religious beliefs and society and all its institutions, his confrontation with Orestes becomes a de-bate, with the myth providing most of the drama. Sartre, in short, uses myth as the basis of an agit-prop drama designed to convert the spectator to the doctrine of existentialism.

Anouilh, although he dramatizes three of the best-known stories in classical mythology, changes some critical element in each to make all three express his obsessive themes of Innocence and Experience, the assertion of one's "purity" in an absurd and corrupting world.

The playwright repeatedly reminds us of the existence of the myth so that, for example, his play about Orpheus and Eurydice takes place simultaneously in the timeless world of myth and in the grubby reality of a French city today. The principals are both the great lovers of myth and an ordinary couple, both transfigured and burdened by a great love that life prevents them from realizing.

His play about Antigone utilizes Sophocles' framework, with additions, and relies upon the authority of both myth and tragedy to make acceptable an action that is grounded in a view of life as absurd. Until the climax, we see a modernized Antigone who is a recognizable copy of Sophocles' heroine. But Anouilh shows that Sophocles' heroine would have capitulated if her religious faith had been undermined as, in this play, it is. Anouilh's heroine, however, goes beyond the destruction of her religious motive and rebels against a life where sordid acceptance perpetuates what is not worth living. Realistic dialogue is contained within an action that employs the formal devices of chorus, prologue, and epilogue; neutrality of scene and dress throws the focus upon the debate between Antigone and Creon. Even more so than in Sartre, this gives the myth a strongly generalized and abstract quality.

In the Medea story motivation and ending are changed to make the heroine's action less a revenge than a realization of her true self through evil, a fact which requires her to take her own life along with that of her sons. Again, as in the other plays, the characters are conscious of their fated roles in the myth. But the theatricalism of the writing is designed to involve the spectator rather than render him detached. Myth serves Anouilh as parable, to express his pessimistic view of life and to add the weight of its authority to the claim of inevitability for actions that are grounded in the gratuitous.

Tennessee Williams has long sought to use theatrically the full resources of drama and the theatre. In midcareer he revised a youthful play, *Battle of Angels*, as *Orpheus Descending*. Together they constitute his one sustained effort to adapt a classical myth, that of Orpheus and Eurydice, to modern characters in a modern milieu. Both times he wrote for a basically realistic theatre. His efforts to transcend it consist largely of making characters and milieu serve a symbolic purpose by constant allusion to both pagan and Christian symbols. He attempts to invest his hero with larger-than-life, even godlike, attributes by making him an artist with powerful sexual allure, whose message of freedom through sexual love and poetry is ignored by the populace, but whose disturbing presence stirs them to a frenzy of repressed sexuality that explodes in violence. In the catastrophe Orpheus is lynched and the Eurydice he brought back from the dead by giving her a child is murdered. What Williams' dramatized myth demonstrates is that to name is not to create. His passive hero, who originally refused to admit his obligations to Eurydice, is forced in the revision to make a tragic choice that negates, out of love, the doctrine of sexual and artistic freedom by which he tried to live. The improvements of *Orpheus Descending* over its original are in the direction of simpler conduct of the action and of stronger character motivation. On the evidence, Williams has not found classical myth an accommodating vehicle for his obsessive themes and has returned to modern stories, while continuing to exploit theatrical elements in order to avoid realism, even though that is the style that seems most directly related to his talents as a playwright.

Eugene Ionesco stands in the forefront of the French dramatists who, after World War II, created what has come to be called "the theatre of the absurd." Historically, his affinity is with the subjective theatre of German expressionism, to which he adds the element of black humor and the oneirical preoccupations of French surrealism. Philosophically, he stands with the existentialists, looking at life as absurd, because inexplicable, but tending more and more to celebrate in his plays the wonder of existence and its unique value.

As an extremely confessional and lyrical playwright, he rejects the European theatre of the past *in toto*, advancing in its place a dramaturgy that discards external action as much as possible and that instinctively flouts the realistic theatre. He has no diffi-

culty in imposing an imaginative theatre that will express the
paradox of man as a creature whose plight is both tragic and
ridiculous. He draws his fables from experience, however, even
though they may seem to resemble themes from Greek myth.

But in *Victims of Duty* he uses the myth of Oedipus to attack
conventional theatre and to recreate the guilt of modern man
that links him to his fellows and makes him their victim. Their
collective guilt is shown as the basis for a totalitarian state, the
ultimate social expression of an absurd existence. Ionesco inverts
the idea of the tragic hero, the sacrifice of the one for the life
of the community, the ritual of initiation that admits a man to
a new state of being in society, and the triumph of divine order
—all elements that are found in Sophocles' *Oedipus Rex*. He
presents instead a modern, demonic society where man's inner
life bears no relation, except that of guilt, to the external world,
and where social forces combine to mutilate that inner life. Yet
the play paradoxically affirms the value of existence, despite its
inability to explain the basis of its own affirmation.

These uses of myth form the bases for dramas which, without
exception, make serious statements about contemporary man by
expressing through language and the other arts of the theatre
the inward significances rather than the outward appearances of
his nature, actions, and destiny. The playwrights, to the extent
that they create out of myth, vision, and artistry a sense of
wonder and awe, give expression to the awareness of mystery
that myths have always existed to embody.

But, with few exceptions, they offer us a diminished image
of man.

BIBLIOGRAPHY

Aeschylus. *The Oresteian Trilogy,* trans. Philip Vellacott. London: Penguin Books, 1956.

Albérès, René-Marill. *Esthétique et morale chez Jean Giraudoux.* Paris: Librairie Nizet, 1957.

Alberts, Sydney Seymour. *A Bibliography of the Works of Robinson Jeffers.* New York: Random House, 1933; reissued, Rye, N.Y.: Cultural History Research, Inc., 1966.

Ames, Van Meter. *André Gide.* Norfolk, Conn.: New Directions, 1947.

Anouilh, Jean. *Five Plays.* New York: Hill & Wang, 1958.

————. *Medea,* trans. Luce and Arthur Klein. In Eric Bentley, ed., *The Modern Theatre,* No. 5. Garden City, N.Y.: Doubleday Anchor Books, 1957; also in Jean Anouilh, *Plays,* Vol. III. New York: Hill & Wang, 1967.

Auden, W. H. "Criticism in a Mass Society." In Geoffrey Grigson, ed., *The Mint,* No. 2. London: Routledge & Kegan Paul, 1948.

Bemussa, Simone. *Eugène Ionesco.* Paris: Éditions Seghers, 1966.

Bentley, Eric. *A Century of Hero-Worship.* Philadelphia: Lippincott, 1944.

————. "Comedy and the Comic Spirit in America." In Alan S. Downer, ed., *The American Theater Today.* New York: Basic Books, 1967.

————. *The Dramatic Event: An American Chronicle.* New York: Horizon Press, 1954.

————, ed. *From the Modern Repertoire,* Series One. Denver: University of Denver Press, 1949.

————. *In Search of Theatre.* New York: Vintage Books, 1954.

————. "The Making of a Dramatist," *Tulane Drama Review,* V, no. 1 (September, 1960).

————, ed. *The Modern Theatre.* Vols. I, V, and VI. Garden City, N.Y.: Doubleday Anchor Books, 1955, 1957, and 1960, respectively.

————, ed. *The Play: A Critical Anthology.* New York: Prentice-Hall, 1951.

————. *The Playwright as Thinker.* New York: Noonday Press, 1955.

————. *What Is Theatre?* Boston: Beacon Press, 1956.

Bieber, Margarete. *History of the Greek and Roman Theater.* Princeton, N.J.: Princeton University Press, 1961.

Bodkin, Maud. *Archetypal Patterns in Poetry: Psychological Studies of Imagination.* New York: Vintage Books, 1958.

Boorsch, Jean. "The Use of Myths in Cocteau's Theatre," *Yale French Studies,* III, no. 1 (Fall, 1949).

Bowen, Croswell. *The Curse of the Misbegotten.* New York: McGraw-Hill, 1959.

Brustein, Robert. "Sweet Bird of Success," *Encounter,* XII, no. 6 (June, 1959).

Carpenter, Frederic I. *Robinson Jeffers.* Twayne's U.S. Authors Series, Vol. 22. New York: Twayne Publishers, 1962.

Chiari, Joseph. *The Contemporary French Theatre: The Flight from Naturalism.* London: Rockliff, 1958.

Clancy, James H. "The American Antigone," *Educational Theatre Journal,* VI, no. 3 (October, 1954).

Clark, Barrett, ed. *European Theories of the Drama: With a Supplement on the American Drama.* Rev. ed. New York: Crown, 1947.

Clurman, Harold. *Lies Like Truth: Theatre Reviews and Essays.* New York: Macmillan, 1958.

Cocteau, Jean. *A Call to Order.* London: Faber & Gwyer, 1926.

————. *Cocteau on the Film: A Conversation Recorded by André Fraigneau.* New York: Roy, 1954.

————. *La Difficulté d'être.* Paris: Morihien, 1947. Trans. Elizabeth Sprigge as *The Difficulty of Being.* London: Owen, 1966.

————. *The Hand of a Stranger (Journal d'un inconnu),* trans. Alec Brown. London: Elek, 1956; New York: Horizon Press, 1959.

————. *The Infernal Machine: A Play in Four Acts,* trans. Carl Wildman. London: Oxford University Press, 1936.

————. *Maalesh: A Theatrical Tour in the Middle-East,* trans. Mary C. Hoeck. London: Peter Owen, 1956.

————. *Oeuvres complètes de Jean Cocteau.* Vol. V. Geneva: Éditions Marguerat, 1948.

————. *Orphée: A Tragedy in One Act and an Interval,* trans. Carl Wildman. London: Oxford University Press, 1933.

————. *Orphée.* Film. Paris: Éditions André Bonne, 1950.

————. *Round the World Again in Eighty Days*, trans. Stuart Gilbert. London: Routledge, 1937.

————. *Théâtre*. Vols. I and II. Paris: Gallimard, 1948.

————. *The Typewriter*, trans. Ronald Duncan. London: Dennis Dobson, 1947.

————, and Jacques Maritain. *Art and Faith: Letters Between Jacques Maritain and Jean Cocteau*. New York: Philosophical Library, 1948.

————, and André Maurois. *Discours de Receptions de M. Jean Cocteau*. Paris: Gallimard, 1955.

Coe, Richard N. *Ionesco*. New York: Grove Press, 1961.

Cole, Toby, ed. *Playwrights on Playwriting*. New York: Hill & Wang Dramabooks, 1960.

Coulanges, Fustel, de. *The Ancient City: A Study of the Religion, Laws, and Institutions of Greece and Rome*, trans. Willard Small. Boston: Lee & Shephard, 1874.

Crosland, Margaret. *Jean Cocteau*. London: Peter Nevill, 1955.

Desan, Wilfrid. *The Tragic Finale: An Essay on the Philosophy of Jean-Paul Sartre*. Cambridge: Harvard University Press, 1954.

Donahue, Francis. *The Dramatic World of Tennessee Williams*. New York: Frederick Ungar, 1964.

Eliade, Mircea. *Cosmos and History*. New York: Harper, 1959.

————. *Images and Symbols: Studies in Religious Symbolism*, trans. Philip Mairet. New York: Sheed & Ward, 1961.

————. *Myths, Dreams, and Mysteries*, trans. Philip Mairet. New York: Harper & Row, 1967.

————. *The Sacred and the Profane: The Nature of Religion*, trans. Willard R. Trask. New York: Harper & Row, 1961.

Eliot, T. S. *The Complete Poems and Plays*. New York: Harcourt, Brace, 1950.

————. *The Confidential Clerk*. New York: Harcourt, Brace, 1954.

————. "A Dialogue on Poetic Drama," with John Dryden's *Of Dramatick Poesie*. London: Etchells & MacDonald, 1928.

————. *Selected Essays*. New York: Harcourt, Brace, 1950.

————. "Tradition and the Individual Talent." In *The Sacred Wood*. London: Methuen, 1920.

Else, Gerald F. *The Origin and Early Form of Greek Tragedy*. Cambridge: Harvard University Press, 1965.

Falk, Doris V. *Eugene O'Neill and the Tragic Tension*. New Brunswick, N.J.: Rutgers University Press, 1958.

Falk, Eugene H. "Theme and Motif in *La Guerre de Troie n'aura pas lieu*," *Tulane Drama Review*, III, no. 4 (May, 1959).

Fergusson, Francis. "Eugene O'Neill." In Morton D. Zabel, ed., *Literary Opinion in America*. Rev. ed. New York: Harpers, 1951.

————. *The Idea of a Theater*. Garden City, N.Y.: Doubleday Anchor Books, 1953.

————. Introduction, *Aristotle's Poetics*, trans. S. H. Butcher. New York: Hill & Wang, 1961.

Fiedler, Leslie A. *No! in Thunder: Essays on Myth and Literature*. Boston: Beacon Press, 1960.

Fitts, Dudley, and Robert Fitzgerald, trans. *The Oedipus Rex of Sophocles*. New York: Harcourt, Brace, & World, 1949.

Fowlie, Wallace. *Dionysus in Paris: A Guide to Contemporary Theater*. New York: Meridian Books, 1960.

Frazer, Sir James G. *The New Golden Bough*, ed. with Foreword by Theodor H. Gaster. New York: Criterion Books, 1959.

————, ed. and trans. *Pausanius's Description of Greece*. 6 vols. London: Macmillan, 1913.

Fromm, Erich. *The Forgotten Language*. New York: Rinehart, 1951.

Frye, Northrop. *Anatomy of Criticism: Four Essays*. Princeton, N.J.: Princeton University Press, 1957.

Frye, Prosser Hall. *Romance and Tragedy*. Boston: Marshall Jones, 1922.

Gassner, John. "At War with Electra," *Tulane Drama Review*, III, no. 4 (May, 1959).

————, ed. *Best American Plays*, Third Series, 1945-1951. New York: Crown, 1952.

————. "Tennessee Williams: Dramatist of Frustration," *College English*, X, no. 1 (October, 1948).

Gide, André. *The Journals of André Gide*, trans. Justin O'Brien. 4 vols. New York: Knopf, 1947-51.

————. "Lettre à Angèle," *Nouvelle Revue Française*, September, 1899.

————. *My Theatre: Five Plays and an Essay*, trans. Jackson Mathews. New York: Knopf, 1952.

————. *Pretexts: Reflections on Literature and Morality*, ed. with Introduction by Justin O'Brien. New York: Meridian Books, 1959.

————. *So Be It; or, The Chips Are Down*, trans. with Introduction by Justin O'Brien. New York: Knopf, 1959.

————. *Two Legends: Oedipus and Theseus*, trans. John Russell. New York: Vintage Books, 1958.

Giraudoux, Jean. *Amphitryon 38*, trans. and adapted by S. N. Behrman. New York: Random House, 1938; also in Giraudoux, *Three Plays*, Vol. 2, trans. Phyllis LaFarge and Peter Hurd, New York: Hill & Wang, 1964.

————. *Electra*, trans. Winifred Smith. In Eric Bentley, ed., *The Modern Theatre*, Vol. I. Garden City, N.Y.: Doubleday Anchor

Books, 1955; also in Giraudoux, *Three Plays*, Vol. 2. New York: Hill & Wang, 1964.

————. *La Guerre de Troie n'aura pas lieu*, trans. as *Tiger at the Gates*, by Christopher Fry. New York: Oxford University Press, 1955.

Grant, Michael. *Myths of the Greeks and Romans*. Cleveland: World, 1962.

Graves, Robert. *The Greek Myths*. 2 vols. Baltimore: Penguin Books, 1955.

Greenwood, Ormerod. *The Playwright: A Study of Form, Method and Tradition in the Theatre*. London: Pitman, 1950.

Grene, David, and Richmond Lattimore, eds. *The Complete Greek Tragedies*, trans. by various hands. 4 vols. Chicago: University of Chicago Press, 1959.

Grossvogel, David I. *The Self-conscious Stage in Modern French Drama*. New York: Columbia University Press, 1958.

Guicharnaud, Jacques, and June Beckelman. *Modern French Theatre from Giraudoux to Beckett*. Yale Romanic Studies, Second Series, 7. New Haven: Yale University Press, 1961.

Hall, Donald. "The Art of Poetry: T. S. Eliot," *The Paris Review*, XXI (Spring-Summer, 1959).

Hathorn, Richmond Y. *Tragedy, Myth, and Mystery*. Bloomington: Indiana University Press, 1962.

Hemmings, F. W. J. *Émile Zola*. Oxford: Clarendon Press, 1953.

Henn, Thomas Rice. *The Harvest of Tragedy*. New York: Barnes & Noble, 1966.

Herbart, Pierre. "A Key to André Gide." In Cecil Hemley and Dwight Webb, eds., *Noonday 2*. New York: Noonday Press, 1959.

Hethmon, Robert. "The Foul Rag-and-Bone Shop of the Heart," *Drama Critique*, VIII, no. 3 (Fall, 1965).

Highet, Gilbert. *The Classical Tradition: Greek and Roman Influences on Western Literature*. New York: Oxford University Press, 1949; reissued as paperback in 1957.

Hobson, Harold. *The French Theatre of To-day*. London: George C. Harrap, 1953.

Hungerford, Edward B. *Shores of Darkness*. New York: Columbia University Press, 1941.

Inskip, Donald. *Jean Giraudoux: The Making of a Dramatist*. London: Oxford University Press, 1958.

Ionesco, Eugène. "Experience of the Theatre," trans. Donald Watson. In Robert W. Corrigan and James L. Rosenberg, eds., *The Context and Craft of Drama*. San Francisco: Chandler, 1964.

————. *Journal en miettes*. Paris: Mercure de France, 1967.

————. "Selections from the Journal," trans. Rosette C. Lamont. In

Yale French Studies, No. 29 ("The New French Dramatists"), n.d.

————. *Three Plays by Eugène Ionesco: Amédée, The New Tenant, Victims of Duty*, trans. Donald Watson. New York: Grove Press, 1958.

Isaac, Dan. "A Streetcar Named Desire—or Death?" *New York Times*, 18 February 1968.

Jackson, Esther Merle. *The Broken World of Tennessee Williams*. Madison: University of Wisconsin Press, 1965.

Jeffers, Robinson. *The Double Ax and Other Poems*. New York: Random House, 1948.

————. *Hungerfield and Other Poems*. New York: Random House, 1954.

————. *Medea*. New York: Random House, 1947.

————. *The Selected Poetry of Robinson Jeffers*. New York: Random House, 1937.

————. *Such Counsels You Gave to Me and Other Poems*. New York: Random House, 1937.

————. *Themes in My Poems*. San Francisco: Book Club of California, 1956.

Jones, David H. *The Plays of T. S. Eliot*. Toronto: University of Toronto Press, 1960.

Juhasz, Leslie A. *The Major Works of Sartre*. New York: Monarch Press, 1965.

Kaufmann, Walter. *Nietzsche: Philosopher, Psychologist, Antichrist*. New York: Meridian Books, 1956.

Kenner, Hugh. *The Invisible Poet: T. S. Eliot*. London: W. H. Allen, 1960.

Kerenyi, C. *The Heroes of the Greeks*. London: Thames & Hudson, 1959.

Khim, Jean-Jacques. *Jean Cocteau*. La Bibliothèque idéale. Paris: Gallimard, 1960.

Kitchin, Laurence. *Mid-Century Drama*. London: Faber & Faber, 1960.

Kitto, H. D. F. *Form and Meaning in Drama: A Study of Six Greek Plays and "Hamlet."* London: Methuen, 1956; New York: Barnes & Noble, 1957.

————. *Greek Tragedy: A Literary Study*. Garden City, N.Y.: Doubleday Anchor Books, 1955.

————. "Greek Tragedy and Dionysus." In John Gassner and Ralph G. Allen, eds., *Theatre and Drama in the Making*. Boston: Houghton Mifflin, 1964.

Knox, Bernard. "Sophocles' Oedipus." In Cleanth Brooks, ed., *Tragic*

Themes in Western Literature. New Haven: Yale University Press, 1955.

Kracauer, Siegfried. *Orpheus in Paris: Offenbach and the Paris of His Time*, trans. Gwenda David and Eric Mosbacher. New York: Knopf, 1938.

Langer, Susanne K. *Feeling and Form*. New York: Charles Scribner's Sons, 1953.

Lea, F. A. *The Tragic Philosopher: A Study of Friedrich Nietzsche*. London: Methuen, 1957.

LeSage, Laurent. *Jean Giraudoux: His Life and Works*. University Park: Pennsylvania State University Press, 1959.

Long, Chester C. "Cocteau's *Orphée*: From Myth to Drama and Film," *Quarterly Journal of Speech*, LI, no. 3 (October, 1965).

Lumley, Frederick. *Trends in Twentieth Century Drama*. London: Rockliff, 1956.

Manthey-Zorn, Otto. *Dionysus: The Tragedy of Nietzsche*. Amherst, Mass.: Amherst College Press, 1956.

Marcel, Gabriel. *L'Heure théâtrale*. Paris: Librairie Plon, 1959.

Marsh, Edward Owen. *Jean Anouilh: Poet of Pierrot and Pantaloon*. London: W. H. Allen, 1953.

Matthews, Honor. *The Primal Curse: The Myth of Cain and Abel in the Theatre*. London: Chatto & Windus, 1967.

Mauriac, Claude. *Jean Cocteau: ou, La Verité du mensonge*. Paris: Odette Lieutier, 1945.

Mauriac, François. *Second Thoughts: Reflections on Literature and Life*. Cleveland: World, 1961.

McCollom, William G. *Tragedy*. New York: Macmillan, 1957.

Miller, James E., Jr., ed. *Myth and Method: Modern Theories of Fiction*. Lincoln: University of Nebraska Press, 1960.

Millet, Fred B., and Gerald E. Bentley. *The Art of the Drama*. New York: Appleton-Century, 1935.

Morgan, George Allen. *What Nietzsche Means*. New York: Harper & Row, 1965.

Murray, Gilbert. *The Classical Tradition in Poetry*. Cambridge: Harvard University Press, 1927.

————. "Excursus on the Ritual Forms Preserved in Greek Tragedy." In Jane Ellen Harrison, *Themis: A Study of the Social Origins of Greek Religions*. London: Merlin Press, 1963.

Neubauer, Peter B. "The Century of the Child," *The Atlantic Monthly*, CCVIII, no. 1 (July, 1961).

Nietzsche, Friedrich. *The Birth of Tragedy* and *The Genealogy of Morals*, trans. Francis Golffing. Garden City, N.Y.: Doubleday Anchor Books, 1956.

O'Brien, Justin. *Portrait of André Gide: A Critical Biography.* New York: Knopf, 1953.

O'Connor, Frank. *The Art of the Theatre.* Dublin: Maurice Fridburg, 1947.

——. *The Mirror in the Roadway: A Study of the Modern Novel.* New York: Knopf, 1956.

O'Neill, Eugene. *The Plays of Eugene O'Neill.* Wilderness Edition, 12 vols. New York: Charles Scribner's Sons, 1934.

Oxenhandler, Neal. *Scandal and Parade: The Theatre of Jean Cocteau.* New Brunswick, N.J.: Rutgers University Press, 1957.

Painter, George D. *André Gide: A Critical and Biographical Study.* New York: Roy, 1951.

Peacock, Ronald. "Public and Private Problems in Modern Drama," *Tulane Drama Review*, III, no. 3 (March, 1959).

Pitoëff, Georges. *Notre Théâtre.* Paris: Messages, 1949.

Popkin, Henry. "The Plays of Tennessee Williams," *Tulane Drama Review*, IV, no. 3 (March, 1960).

Potter, Stephen. *Some Notes on Lifemanship.* New York: Henry Holt, 1951.

Praz, Mario. *The Romantic Agony*, trans. Angus Davidson. 2nd ed. London: Oxford University Press, 1951.

Pronko, Leonard Cabell. *The World of Jean Anouilh.* Perspectives in Criticism Series, 7. Berkeley: University of California Press, 1961.

Pucciani, Oreste, ed. *The French Theatre Since 1930.* New York: Ginn, 1954.

Rieff, Philip. "A Modern Mythmaker." In Henry A. Murray, ed., *Myth and Mythmaking.* New York: George Braziller, 1960.

Rowe, Kenneth Thorpe. *A Theatre in Your Head.* New York: Funk & Wagnalls, 1960.

Russell, Vera and John. "Ionesco on Death," *Chicago Sun-Times*, 15 September 1963.

Sartre, Jean-Paul. *Existentialism*, trans. Bernard Frechtman. New York: Philosophical Library, 1947.

——. *The Flies*, trans. Stuart Gilbert. In John Gassner, ed., *A Treasury of the Theatre.* Rev. ed. Vol. II. New York: Simon & Schuster, 1956.

——. "Forgers of Myth." In Toby Cole, ed., *Playwrights on Playwriting.* New York: Hill & Wang Dramabooks, 1960.

Schlegel, Friedrich. *Gespräch über die Poesie*, in his *Kritische Schriften.* Munich: Carl Hanser, 1956.

Senior, John. *The Way Down and Out.* Ithaca, N.Y.: Cornell University Press, 1959.

Skinner, Richard D. *Eugene O'Neill: A Poet's Quest.* New York: Longmans, Green, 1935.

Sokel, Walter H., ed. *Anthology of German Expressionist Drama: A Prelude to the Absurd.* Garden City, N.Y.: Doubleday Anchor Books, 1963.

Speaight, Robert. *Christian Theatre.* New York: Hawthorn Books, 1960.

Squires, Radcliffe. *The Loyalties of Robinson Jeffers.* Ann Arbor: University of Michigan Press, 1956.

Steiner, George. *The Death of Tragedy.* New York: Knopf, 1961.

Styan, J. L. *The Elements of Drama.* Cambridge: Cambridge University Press, 1960.

Thody, Philip. *Jean-Paul Sartre: A Literary and Political Study.* London: Hamish Hamilton, 1960.

Thomson, J. A. K. *The Art of the Logos.* London: George Allen & Unwin, 1935.

Tischler, Nancy Marie. *Tennessee Williams: Rebellious Puritan.* New York: Citadel Press, 1961.

Tynan, Kenneth. *Curtains.* New York: Atheneum, 1961.

Van Doren, Mark, ed. *The New Invitation to Learning.* New York: Random House, 1942.

Wager, Walter, ed. *The Playwrights Speak.* New York: Delacorte Press, 1967.

Wellwarth, George E. *The Theater of Protest and Paradox.* New York: New York University Press, 1964.

Wilder, Thornton. *The Ides of March.* New York: Harper, 1948.

————. "Some Thoughts on Playwriting." In Robert W. Corrigan and James L. Rosenberg, eds., *The Context and Craft of Drama.* San Francisco: Chandler, 1964.

Williams, Tennessee. *The Glass Menagerie.* New York: Random House, 1945.

————. *Orpheus Descending* with *Battle of Angels.* New York: New Directions, 1958.

Wilson, Edmund. *The Wound and the Bow.* Boston: Houghton Mifflin, 1941.

Young, Stark. *Immortal Shadows: A Book of Dramatic Criticism.* New York: Charles Scribner's Sons, 1948.

Zola, Émile. Preface, *Thérèse Raquin,* trans. Kathleen Boutall. In Eric Bentley, ed., *From the Modern Repertoire,* Series Three. Bloomington: Indiana University Press, 1956.

INDEX

Schlegel, Friedrich: *Conversation on Poetry* summarized, 4-6; call for man-centered mythology, 5-6; anticipates modern views of myth, 6-7
Schorer, Mark, 236
Scientism, 13, 27
Shelley, Percy B., 7
Siegfried (Giraudoux), 184
Skinner, Richard Dana, 172-73
Sodom and Gomorrah (Giraudoux), 206
Sophocles: appreciation by Gide, 60; source of Anouilh's *Antigone*, 266; use of decorum, 313; mentioned, 150, 266, 316
Speaight, Robert, 145
Steiner, George, 180n
Strange Interlude (O'Neill), 176, 177
Straw, The (O'Neill), 176
Streetcar Named Desire, A (Williams), 281
Styan, J. L., 258
Summer and Smoke (Williams), 281
Swinburne, Algernon, 22, 23
Symbolism, 78, 79-81

"Theatre of cruelty," 123, 124
Theatricalism: rise of, 3; Cocteau's theory and practice, 72-76; devices in Cocteau, 105, 204, 205, 215; in Giraudoux, 203, 204-5, 215; in Eliot, 212; in Williams, 280, 302
"Thoughts on Greek Mythology" (Gide), 34-36
Thus Spake Zarathustra (Nietzsche), 22
Time: in Cocteau's *Antigone*, 78; relativity in *Orphée*, 83-84
Titanism, 33, 277
Tower Beyond Tragedy, The (Jeffers). *See* Jeffers, Robinson
"Tradition and the Individual Talent" (Eliot), 210
Trojan War Will Not Take Place,

The (Giraudoux). *See* Giraudoux, Jean
Tynan, Kenneth, 271

Ulysses (Joyce), 207

Vanbrugh, Sir John, 33
Vatican Swindle, The (Gide), 59
Victims of Duty (Ionesco). *See* Ionesco, Eugène
Voltaire, François Marie Arouet, 35, 67

Waiting for Godot (Beckett), 315n
Waltz of the Toreadors, The (Anouilh), 273
Wilder, Thornton, 314-15
Wildman, Carl, 76
Williams, Tennessee: moral basis of human dignity, 278; *Orpheus Descending*, 278-79; *Camino Real*, 279; preference for theatricalism, 280; *The Glass Menagerie*, 280, 281; *Cat on a Hot Tin Roof*, 281, 308; *The Rose Tattoo*, 281; *A Streetcar Named Desire*, 281; *Summer and Smoke*, 281; incest theme, 282; Adonis-Aphrodite pattern, 282, 283; mythic elements in, 282; recourse to myth, 291; death theme, 308-9n; religious development, 308-9n; *The Milk Train Doesn't Stop Here Any More*, 309; *The Night of the Iguana*, 309; summary, 338-39; mentioned, 1
—*Battle of Angels*: Christian elements, 280; stage history, 281; synopsis, 283-91; Gassner on revisions, 291; four-fold interpretation, 291-93; Christian symbology, 293; Veronica theme, 297-300; mentioned, 339
—*Orpheus Descending*: Christian elements in, 280; theme, 281;